Happy Birthday —
Mum · April

Paul.

D0742556

The Inland Empire

THE INLAND EMPIRE

Unfolding Years,

1879–1929

John Fahey

UNIVERSITY OF WASHINGTON PRESS

Seattle and London

This book was published with the assistance of grants from the Andrew W. Mellon Foundation; and from the Washington Commission for the Humanities, a nonprofit organization supported by the National Endowment for the Humanities and by private contributors.

Copyright © 1986 by the University of Washington Press
Manufactured in the United States of America

All rights reserved. No portion of this publication may be reproduced or transmitted in any form or by any means, electronic or mechanical, including photocopy, recording, or any information storage or retrieval system, without permission in writing from the publisher.

Library of Congress Cataloging in Publication Data

Fahey, John.
  The inland empire, unfolding years, 1879–1929.

  Bibliography: p.
  Includes index.
  1. Washington (State)—Economic conditions.
2. Washington (State)—Social conditions. 3. Idaho—
Economic conditions. 4. Idaho—Social conditions.
5. Spokane (Wash.)—Economic conditions. 6. Spokane
(Wash.)—Social conditions. I. Title.
HC107.W2F34   1986   330.9797'303   86-11167
ISBN 0-295-96406-5

TO PATRICK J. GLEESING

Contents

Illustrations

Preface

Not many writers treat the Inland Empire as a social and economic unit, although they usually think of it as one. This book attempts to provide a cohesive narrative of the major social and economic themes in the emergence of the Inland Empire as an integrated region, although its regional unity is slipping away now, and emphasizes eastern Washington and Spokane as central.

With an outstanding exception, geographer Donald W. Meinig's *The Great Columbia Plain*, historical accounts of the Inland Empire in the past fifty years confine themselves to single topics or districts. And Meinig deliberately stops at 1910, leaving the later years for someone else. I can't claim that this book takes up where Meinig left off, because our viewpoints are different, but this book does cover nineteen more years of the twentieth century.

The origin of the term Inland Empire seems lost. It appeared in pioneer newspapers and in railroad promotional booklets before its preemption by Spokane newspapers and chamber of commerce as a phrase with a nice ring, suitable for claiming the inland Northwest from the Cascades to the Rockies, south to the Wallowas, and north into the geographic triangle of British Columbia continuous from the U.S. Okanogan.

The Inland Empire is a state of mind as well as a place; it expands and contracts, depending on who is defining it. Sometimes other inland cities find it convenient to be part of the Inland Empire and sometimes not. In this book, the Inland Empire is the counties of Washington east of the Cascade range and those of northern Idaho linked by lumbering and mining to Spokane.

I have necessarily passed over areas and topics in order to concentrate on primary ones, and I justify these omissions by the evident need for a compact account of larger themes. Two respected surveys, Earl Pomeroy's *The Pacific Slope* and Dorothy O. Johansen and Charles M. Gates's *Empire of the Columbia,* demonstrate this need by their kiss-and-run attention to the Inland Empire.

With few exceptions, western historians tend to regard the Inland Empire as hinterland, that is, a place tributary to wherever they happen to be writing about. To California historians the Northwest is the Oregon country, to the Oregonian the Inland Empire is the interior, and to Seattle it is that somewhat maverick, artless colony east of the Cascades that produces wheat, fruits, electrical energy, and hick legislators. The mining labor wars, lieu land controversies of the Northern Pacific, May Arkwright Hutton, and Grand Coulee Dam stand as the historical monuments of the Inland Empire even in recent accounts.

My bibliography is not intended as a comprehensive list of information about the Inland Empire. Other accounts appear in county historical society periodicals, regional magazines, and similar publications. For a critical summary of Pacific Northwest historiography, see Kent D. Richards's "In Search of the Pacific Northwest: The Historiography of Oregon and Washington," in the *Pacific Historical Review,* 50, number 4 (November 1981): 415–43.

Obviously the fifty-year period from 1879 to 1929, described in this book, was conditioned by what happened before it. For earlier history, read Meinig's *The Great Columbia Plain* and the redoubtable thirty-first volume of H. H. Bancroft's *Works,* entitled *History of Washington, Oregon, and Montana, 1845–1889,* which, although it bears Bancroft's name, was written by Frances Fuller Victor.

The period 1879 to 1929 begins with intensive development of the Inland Empire by design—that is, railroad promotion to attract large settlement for specific objectives—and closes with the waning of private development without comprehensive federal participation. In 1879 the territorial legislature petitioned Congress for a representative for eastern Washington to recognize its growing population, and in 1929 the stock market crashed, ending an era. These events can serve as milestones.

I receive a lot of help in gathering information for a book. The notes acknowledge contributions except those of archivists and librarians, and I especially thank them here. The major contribution is that of my wife, Peggy, who sustains both author and work.

John Fahey

The Inland Empire

CHAPTER *I*

An Influx of Strangers

When claim jumpers invaded eighty farms near Dayton, vigilantes dug ominous open graves—ugly oblong shadowed holes—as a warning. The jumpers moved on. Waiting graves said "Don't tread on me" dead straight, as straight as a green flag bearing a golden snake one hundred years earlier. Men who piled their wives, their children, their parents, and all of their goods on wagons to move a thousand miles came to win, not lose, came to find ground of their own. They put up with cold, and hunger, and dust, and sunburn to reach eastern Washington and they did not intend to put up with trespassers. They banded together, secretly as often as not, to drive out and punish interlopers and meddlers. And they admired heroes with land and money, because power rested with men who had land and money.

The immigrants of 1879 had read the pamphlets and newspaper puffery tempting them to move to "the best poor man's country in the world," where work was "plentiful at $20 a month with board" and those seeking "prairie for grain" would "by a very little effort" find what they wanted. But the immigrants discovered that not a tillable 160-acre tract of public land remained open near Walla Walla, and the nearby mountains had been stripped of sawing timber. They pushed northward into the bunchgrass dunes of the Palouse country, wagon after wagon, day after day: a train of thirteen wagons from Wisconsin, Arkansas Baptists who wintered in Colorado and rolled north on the western skirt of the Rocky Mountains, trains that had bumped along the prairie ruts from Michigan, and hordes sailing up the Columbia River on steamers from Portland. "An influx of strangers," the *Walla Walla Union* called them, converging on "the Mecca of immigrants, the Palouse." [1]

They found only one large town in this interior country, Walla Walla, and two smaller, Dayton and Colfax, with settlers' outposts at Spokane Falls, Cheney, Yakima, Ellensburg, and Pomeroy. Walla Walla—tidy, level, watered by streams gurgling beneath its board sidewalks, could be reached by stage lines of Utah, Idaho, and Oregon that converged on Kelton, Utah, 535 miles distant. Tall Lombardy poplars swayed beside whitewashed church steeples, and saplings and frame houses lined curving streets. But it was "badly sewered" and gave off "abominable odors," a lady complained. Its back alleys bristled with household trash, and its stately spires were shams, sighed the rector of St. Paul's, for "Walla Wallans . . . are wholly bent on making money. . . . I cannot say that they are opposed to religion. . . . They tolerate it as a good institution for preserving the peace and for keeping their wives from prying into their business." [2]

Immigrants were not surprised to discover that everything was not the way the advertising said it would be. They had been disillusioned by corruption in Ulysses S. Grant's administration, public disclosures of venal business practices, and politicians who tried to steal the presidency from Rutherford B. Hayes. They looked on authorized promises with cynicism. And the country was primitive: only three years had passed since George Custer died on his surrounded hillock; Chief Joseph led his Nez Perce this way in retreat before a one-armed general only two years earlier; in 1878, rampaging Bannocks and Piutes had alarmed the whole Northwest; Chief Moses agreed in the spring of 1879 to go to the reservation; and Indian bands still crossed eastern Washington on their way to buffalo hunts along the Judith.

But for a man alert to bird songs of a dawning country, portents abounded. In 1879, John Wesley Powell, completing his survey of western lands, told the federal government that its land laws were "antiquated and incongruous"; the Northern Pacific, pressed by a deadline on its land grant, completed its final resurvey of a route through the interior—a fact not lost on settlers; Spokane County separated from Stevens; and the territorial legislature asked Congress to recognize the growing population of eastern Washington by granting another territorial representative. The legislature also passed an indecisive herd law for eastern Washington, signifying the end of its free-ranging cattle business.

These signs meant that settlers would have problems with their land titles, that the railroad would impose the pattern of commerce, and that immigrants (shielded by those incongruous land laws) would shoulder aside those who had arrived earlier, the Indians, and then the cattlemen. Vacant land lay on both sides of the road to Colfax north of the Snake River while Colfax yawned and stretched itself awake, with two hotels, about fifty shingled, unweathered buildings, a boardwalk along one side of Main Street, and a sprinkler cart laying summer dust. But choice land along the streams around Colfax was spoken for, too, and immigrants pushed out from town.

James A. Perkins had reached Colfax in 1870, built a sawmill, and claimed land. He would become a banker and merchant. George Comegys, a college-trained lawyer, came in 1878 to practice law, raise stock, and mine. Four years later he would be speaker of the territorial house, and then a respected banker at a new town, Rosalia. In 1879 a Tennessee father of ten arrived, J. P. T. McCroskey, who founded a dynasty. His sons would be prominent farmers, a lawyer, a judge, and a politician. Perkins, Comegys, and McCroskey were leaders and boosters; they rallied their towns. And they were exemplars of a frontier class—the pioneers who built because prosperity for the town meant prosperity for them. In their way they mirrored the nation's capitalists who sought achievement through competition, self-expression, and control of their environment. Such men became resident capitalists along with the scions of wealthy Oregon families sent "to find a town to grow with," bent from the first on wealth and position. Newspapers called them "progressive" men, and every town that would amount to anything had them.[3]

When they claimed land or bought from an earlier settler at $10 an acre, nearly all the onrushing immigrants planted wheat. By 1880 a network of roads for hauling wheat striped the countryside from Colfax to Snake shipping points—Penawawa, Almota, and Wawawai, each with warehouses, dock, saloon, and jerry-built frame hotel and houses. The network reached to new settlements: Rosalia, Palouse City, Farmington, and the hamlets on Union Flat. Farther west and north, it reached to Spangle, "a flourishing town with a live preacher as a wheel horse," and Spokane Falls, grown in one year from twenty houses to eighty-one "good, durable wooden structures," reported the *Union*. The people of Spokane, it said, "are a better class than are usual to a new frontier town. They have sentiment and good cooks. . . . They have a future and faith in it."[4]

Thomas Burke, the Seattle lawyer who would promote Wenatchee, had a sharper eye for towns than most. "Three or four cities . . . seem to absorb everything," he wrote a friend. "There will probably be one or two large towns in eastern Washington. One of these, I think, will be Spokane Falls. . . . [Others] will contend for second place;—and which will capture the prize it is hard to tell."[5]

Settlers claimed public lands under a variety of federal laws: pre-emption, allowing 160 acres at $1.25 an acre to anyone who built a dwelling and lived on the acreage; homestead, 160 acres to the head of a family who improved and lived on his tract; timber culture, 160 acres with trees on proof that the applicant kept 40 in good condition; desert land, 640 acres at 25 cents an acre on proof that some was irrigated within three years; timber and stone, unfit for farming, sold at negotiated prices; or soldier's bounty. The regulations for land claims forced a settler "to lie to obtain title," quipped an editor, and proofs required "witnesses with extraordinary memories."[6]

Fibbing to secure title, outwitting a clumsy bureaucracy, seemed to settlers merely part of the land game. They told themselves that the regulations, written by easterners, did not take into account the real conditions in the West (in fact, many rules were modified as time passed). For many, 160 acres were too few for a paying wheat farm; they got additional land by filing under a different law or by deceit. Undoubtedly some claimants speculated in land, and the sale of relinquished claims to later migrants became common. Although much of the agricultural land of the Palouse belonged as land grant to the Northern Pacific, and would be sold to settlers by the railroad, the government opened a land office at Colfax in 1878 to serve the increasing migrant flow. The registers (the federal agents in land offices) clung to wordy, legalistic old application forms because they received 22.5 cents for each hundred words.[7]

Two hundred miles to the west, where fingers of migration poked into the Yakima country, the *Yakima Record* complained of "homesteads on which there are no homes; preemption claims upon which there is no sign of residence or culture; and timber culture claims upon which there has never been any plowing, fencing, or planting." The land office shortened the time between final proof and payment for land under the Timber and Stone Act to stop settlers, as they did in the hills of southeastern Washington, from filing to reserve wooded land, cutting the trees, and leaving without paying. Land officers learned to recognize frauds. On the other hand, for some time the officers refused to admit that cottonwood, Lombardy poplar, aspen, and similar sturdy trees preferred by settlers could be called "timber trees" for timber culture claims. In Washington, D.C., the under-staffed General Land Office struggled through a backlog of paper that delayed final titles to eastern Washington land two, five, or even ten years. If government processes were slow, settlers' practices were often shady. Thus each abused the other. Land Commissioner William Sparks in 1885 alleged that three-quarters of the final preemption entries in Washington had been frauds. Too harsh a view, no doubt, but tuned to the spirit of the new country.[8]

These strangers invading the Palouse meant to stay, to civilize the rolling meadows with crops, build towns, scrape roadways along the easy grades of streams, and eventually grace it with schools, churches, theaters, and the other amenities of a stable society. Indians had merely crossed the area—camping seasonally, returning to favored haunts to fish or trade, and then moving on. The cattlemen used it as a free range, sometimes putting up a shanty and barn as a home ranch in bottomland along one of its creeks, and sometimes abandoning their herds in winter to lounge in hospitable Portland until a spring roundup. By laws and sales methods, however, the government and the railroads insisted that the country be broken up into many small farms.

As settlement spread, the cattlemen retreated to the drier districts, the uplands of northeastern Washington and the bare foothills of the Cascades. Some did not go meekly. Near Creston they pulled up homesteaders' stakes. Elsewhere they drove their animals through planted fields to trample crops. But this was bravado. They were already beaten by falling prices for beef and, in 1880–81, a punishing winter that decimated herds. The cattlemen trailed survivors to Wyoming for sale. Their two-season overland drives from Walla Walla to Chicago were virtually over. (A second devastating winter, 1889–90, destroyed half the cattle around Yakima and nine of ten animals on the frigid tablelands of the Big Bend—central Washington.) The cattlemen had lost the pivotal contest for water because settlers headed first for a stream or a waterhole, fenced it, built house and shed, and closed it to cattle. And as farmers furrowed the range, sheep crowded cattle off the remaining grasslands. Wool could be stored until sold, or even shipped long distances, and local buyers took mutton. As cattle herds shrank or backed away, sheep flocks advanced; they crossed the countryside in spring to the mountain meadows of eastern Washington and northern Idaho and in winter foraged on wheat stubble as they banded homeward. When the Northern Pacific barred sheep from railroad lands to prevent overgrazing, sheepmen bought or rented large areas from the railroad, and in the next decade such herders as the Harder brothers, the McGregor family, and the four Coffin brothers (Yakima merchants) became landowners, packers, farmers, and investors, as well as sheepmen.[9]

Playing the land game and sharing the hardships of pioneering fostered mutual dependence among settlers. Faced with land jumpers or thieves, they often joined for justice on their terms. A coterie drove a man out of Oakesdale after he was reported to have refused to support his wife in Oregon. About fifty masked men tarred and feathered a young white man who brought his black wife to a Walla Walla band concert. Nearly every town harbored secret societies of men whose views coincided, and they dealt with misfits. "Various secret societies are said to be in flourishing condition," remarked the *Walla Walla Union*, meaning lodges and protective rings. At Pomeroy, Masons and Odd Fellows formed earlier than churches, but law-and-order leagues were common, too, among Christian sects.[10]

A vigilance committee dealt "a superior quality of justice" to land jumpers near Colfax. Close to Fairfield, a citizen's posse, hunting a suspected rustler, lynched his brother because they considered both men the wrong kind. Farmers who caught a rustler's accomplice hanged him by a rope, threatening to leave him "until his tongue lopped out" if he did not reveal the names of horse thieves. Stockmen in a Whitman County protective association chipped in to pay a sheriff's deputy of their choice, and the local newspaper predicted they would "fill the cells of the county jail." A jumper who pitched his tent in a grain field, to be bought off, was dumped in a road by indignant neighbors and given minutes "to make himself scarce."[11]

This protective instinct lingered, even after public committees and legislative petitions became the style. Masked men hanged alleged murderers from a courtroom window at Colfax while a grand jury, convened to indict the killers, reported that it could not fix guilt but gratuitously recommended ridding the courthouse loft of pigeons.[12]

Men carrying guns attracted no particular attention, although neither farmers nor town businessmen habitually wore sidearms. But a man heading cross-country or into timber where he might encounter wild animals took along a firearm. With violence barely below the surface of daily life, territorial law banned toy pistols. In Dayton, a land jumper accosted in the street set off a gunfight that cost one man his leg. Prudent people blinked at secret pacts to run riffraff out of town, just as they looked past prostitutes—painted ladies plainly visible on streets and in stores—as long as the women kept to their class. But let a frolicking, or perhaps drunken, young man from a good family fall in with a prostitute, and a citizen's committee would be there to accuse the woman of "leading him on" and counsel her departure. In hard new country, settlers were not tolerant of misfits or people who did not know their place. A boob deserved to be bilked; a troublemaker, to be run off.[13]

Some early immigrants who brought paper money—greenbacks—

into the Palouse learned that merchants discounted it. They trusted gold, and, politically, called for silver coinage, too. A new settler without savings worked for someone else until his farm started to pay; many rented their teams and drove as teamsters, or hired out seasonally as bricklayers, carpenters, or railroad or harvest hands. Later some would work in Idaho mines during their off-seasons. A good workhorse cost $50, a wagon $150, and a simple iron plow $40. As they could, these settlers broke sod for planting and put up family shelters on their own land. Lumber was dear. Families lived in sheds, tents, sod houses, or even roofed pits until they could build a house, and then it was likely to be a boxy frame costing about $300, perhaps 16 by 24 feet with two or three rooms in a row and later a connected kitchen lean-to with a water pump outside the back door. Eventually the family erected a springhouse to store water. One settler thought farmhouses resembled upturned piano boxes; another remembered such a house, 12 by 14 feet, with wind fanning through cracks as the green boards shrank. Few homes contained more than a table and homemade benches or chairs, bedsteads, a stove, and coal-oil lamps. In summer, dust sifted through cracks, and in winter, snow. When snow fell, the men and boys often went to the hills for trees to skid home behind horses for lumber and firewood. Some shelter had to be put up for animals, for without his horses, the farmer could not break the tough Palouse sod. Until it was all turned under, however, the bunchgrass provided hay without cultivation.[14]

Turning the Palouse ground was slow—perhaps ten or fifteen acres a year, gradually enlarging the tilled area by struggling days driving an iron-tipped plow into the turf as horses strained to pull it. The settlers burned off the bunchgrass, turned the root-tangled sod with their walking plows ("footburners"), pulverized the soil with peg-tooth drag harrows, and seeded. In drier counties, settlers sometimes dragged timbers behind horses to uproot sagebrush and then disked the soil. A few simply dug out the sage with hoes, and burned the brush as fuel. A settler seeded by hand until he sold a crop to buy or rent a mechanical seeder drawn by four horses abreast. Once his seed was in, he hoped for rain, hoped against too much heat, against winds that lifted his seeds out of the shallow soil, against squirrels or crickets, and against a drop in wheat prices. In winter he repaired tools, readied seed, sharpened fence posts, hauled firewood, fixed house and shed, spread manure, cared for stock, and toiled at the dozens of other tasks neglected during his long days in the field in planting and harvest seasons.[15]

Women worked as hard as the men, sometimes in the fields beside them. Little wonder that most farm men and women looked gaunt, drawn, and burned. From dawn to dusk, the farm woman made or fixed clothes, cooked meals, cleaned, tended her kitchen garden, and preserved vegetables and fruits, perhaps in jars made from discarded bottles. Potatoes, apples, and root vegetables went into a root cellar. Farm families of eastern Washington, however, bought a surprising amount of their clothing and food from town stores, or bartered with neighbors. Milk could be delivered, poured into a bucket left by the door—not sanitary but cheap. Occasionally a man spent two or three days a month on a trip into town for provisions, buying on credit until he sold his crop, and returning with manufactured cloth, coffee beans, flour, sugar, coal oil, factory-made nails, and so on. The Whitman County assessor by 1892 counted 1,581 sewing and knitting machines in farm homes. The farmer's bib overalls, his hat, his boots, and his tobacco came from stores; his wife probably owned a store-bought dress, shoes, and bonnet.[16]

For everyday wear the farmer might put on homemade clothes and dress his children in hand-me-downs, but if he wished to make a "respectable appearance" in Spokane, declared the *Spokane Falls Globe*, he would spend forty-five dollars for suit and overcoat, five dollars for underclothes, five for boots, two for gloves, two for a hat, and two dollars for a shirt. The *Globe* estimated that this wardrobe equaled a load of oats at forty cents a bushel, a load of corn at forty cents, one steer at eighteen dollars, a cow at sixteen, two loads of hay at eight, two cords of wood at eight, forty bushels of potatoes at six, and a load of straw at one dollar and twenty-five cents.[17]

Harnesses, saddles, tools, ammunition—nearly all were factory made. And if a farmer could afford them, he could order barbed wire and farm machines, but he contrived his own barbed-wire gate, the unpredictable "Palouse gate" with prickly strands that always seemed to tangle when the gate was opened. At first farmers used barbed wire reluctantly, thinking it a cruel wire, but it was cheaper than twisted strands or rails. On the other hand, many could not afford fences of any kind. Graham B. Dennis, who manufactured fencing in Spokane for a while, could not sell it and eventually traded his stock for two town lots. Some farmers dug double ditches to keep livestock out of gardens.[18]

Travelers expected hospitality at any farm home. The farm wife kept fruitcake, crocks of brown beans, and spareribs or pork in aspic to feed itinerants, and the family gave up their beds, sleeping on the floor. In return, a guest passed along gossip of the countryside, political talk, news, and rumors.[19]

In the earliest years, settlers' entertainment was as spartan as their lives: potluck parties in larger homes, picnics, and quilting bees that the whole family attended. Newlyweds often suffered the noise of banging tin pans and shouts until the bridegroom gave the merrymakers money for refreshments. In town, debates among businessmen (resolved: "Civilization has done man no good"), educational or political speeches, touring singers, amateur theatricals, and later even phonograph concerts passed as amusements with such pastimes as walks, taffy pulls, and sewing or reading clubs. Ladies fed a midnight supper at whist or pit card parties. Country schools staged spelling bees, fiddlers' contests, and occasional dances. A young woman visiting town remembered playing croquet followed by a stroll to the cemetery to visit a child's grave, not knowing that a few yards away friends were burying another child.[20]

County fairs and holidays, especially the Fourth of July, marked major community social events. Counties organized fairs to advertise their products, showing their finest, often with a rented carnival performing lustily on a dirt midway. Races, sack-sewing, baking, muscular strength and other contests crowned local champions.[21]

Churches lagged behind settlement by ten years or more for practical reasons. A church required a cluster of believers willing to contribute money for a pastor and perhaps a structure, and not many settlers could spare money. For some years, rural congregations met with circuit-riding pastors—carrying Bible, songbook, and rifle, observed a worshiper—for prayer and instruction at someone's home. In the early eighties, for example, the Methodist Episcopal denomination supported one circuit rider north of the Snake River. Catholics might see priests who had come mainly to convert Indians.[22]

As the rector at Walla Walla lamented, women seemed more interested in churches than men. Perhaps men felt that some harsh actions they thought necessary to survival could not easily be explained as Christian deeds, or perhaps they felt that churches, like congressmen, were out of touch with the real conditions of settlers' lives. Yet even in more genteel times, a newspaper editor would conclude that only one-third of his readers belonged to a church and, of those, 76 percent were women. Rural pastors may not have seemed practical to men who asked their advice on debts, drunkenness, or business ethics. Farmers who grew watermelon were not likely to cotton to a preacher who claimed that melons, as the original forbidden fruit of Eden, caused summer ailments. Socially pastors ranked with teachers—both low paid, both likely to move. Pastors rarely led their communities. Lawyers, who often quoted the Bible in court, stood as acknowledged intellectual leaders.[23]

A good many rural congregations could neither find nor pay a pastor; they federated with other small groups into a community church, smoothing over any doctrinal differences, which seemed to suggest that one sect was pretty much like another. As towns enlarged, crossroads churches disbanded and farm families drove to town for services. Country churches changed only slightly in moral strictures while young people, chafing, drifted away. A number of rural pastors, inadequately trained for raw hard work, left the pastorate, feeling unappreciated.

Yet by the turn of the century, church membership in eleven of the fifteen eastern Washington counties was higher than the 26.9 percent average for the state. Surprisingly, 73 percent of the scattered 486 residents of arid Franklin County claimed church membership—more than half, Methodist Episcopalian. Only Columbia, Ferry, Okanogan, and Stevens counties fell below the state average, perhaps because of scattered populations. As might be expected, the urbanizing counties—Spokane, Walla Walla, and Yakima—claimed the highest proportions of church affiliation. In town, churches were easier to get to, membership carried social benefits and sometimes was useful in business. The largest denomination in these three counties was Roman Catholic, but that affiliation was generally less useful for advancing in society or business than Congregational or Episcopal membership. Out in the country, the churches rooted only slowly. Many years later, when eastern Washington was relatively stable and civilized, one in four country pulpits would be empty. But in this, Washington was no different from other sections of the West.[24]

If, in the minds of immigrants, the Walla Walla country was full and the Palouse filling, large sections of eastern Washington lay open. Settlers pushed gingerly beyond the Palouse into drier districts—the Big Bend, treeless plateaus gradually rising from 370 feet above sea level at the junction of the Snake and Columbia rivers to 2,700 feet in Lincoln and Douglas counties. Here and there, the Big Bend erupted in rocky outcrops and occasionally bloomed with a verdant creekbed or waterhole. Basalt-walled canyons—coulees—marked ancient riverbeds. Settlers wore crossings in places where the walls had broken. (One crossing became Coulee City.) Except on its edges, at Reardan and Sprague in Lincoln County and Ritzville in Adams, the Big Bend sustained no towns of note, but men soon saw that with water this dry soil flowered. An army surveyor, plotting a road from Ritzville to Camp Chelan, remarked that the country would produce wheat.[25]

The Northern Pacific main line ran southwest from Spokane through Sprague to Pasco station by 1881 and immigrants, buoyed by rails, filtered from the Palouse into the dry counties. The railroad offered immigrant fares to lure more settlers, $44.60 from Chicago, compared with $74.35 first class. A minor rush gobbled land in Lincoln County between 1880 and 1884, and by 1887 a flour mill had opened at Sprague with farmers' pledges to deliver it 50,000 bushels of wheat. In this dry country, farmers learned quickly that they could not crop the same ground every year; they let half their tilled land lie fallow, gathering moisture, while they planted the other half, alternating.[26]

Chary patrols ventured even farther into the dry districts. In Grant County, the first recorded deed described ground south of a monster basalt landmark, Steamboat Rock, in 1885. For the adventurous who went too far into the sagebrush desert, the dare proved calamitous. A railroad engineer, Edward J. Roberts, laying track for the Central Washington Railroad in August 1888, saw pillars of dust moving toward him and as they neared discovered that the dust followed settlers abandoning farms. Families knocked down houses, piled furniture and goods on one wall, hitched the wall to oxen or horses, and dragged out of the Big Bend, defeated. Before machinery plowed and planted deeper, heavy dust storms sometimes blew seed out of the ground. But not everyone retreated. By 1890, Lincoln County held 8,917 people, Douglas 2,800, and Adams 2,099.[27]

Some settlers pushing inland along the Columbia from Portland had turned northward at The Dalles to cross desert to Yakima or ride twenty miles farther to the Kittitas Valley where one, John A. Shoudy, named a townsite for his wife: Ellen's burg. At Yakima huddled a few frame houses and three general stores, one run by Charles and Joseph Schanno, who claimed the flat where the town would grow. Their Schanno ditch, scraped with hand tools, had shown that with irrigation Yakima's arid earth blossomed. On the hills above the town, on mountain slopes, and on the plateaus along the Columbia, Charles Splawn, A. J. Splawn, Ben E. Snipes, and others ran large cattle herds. Snipes was said to own 125,000 animals. A. J. Splawn, it was said, rode with gold in his saddlebags; he dickered for cattle without dismounting his horse, and if the price was not right, rode away. Although the government opened a land office at Yakima in 1880, only a trickle of migrants straggled into these precincts. Most settlers had their eyes on the Palouse. In 1879 the assessor counted only 318 families in Yakima County but 22,665 cattle.[28]

To the north, where the Wenatchee River flowed into the Columbia, a few white men and Chinese sluiced gold from sandy river bars and Samuel C. Miller ran a general store. He sold a few plows to Indians determined to cultivate the land rather than give it up. Columbia River steamboats delivered mail and an occasional passenger. Most of Wenatchee's early settlers moved over from Ellensburg, intrigued by riverside orchards.

At likely points along the Yakima and the Columbia, settlers built cabins and scratched ditches. Almost from the beginning of migration, men recognized that irrigation held the key to farming here. Between 1879 and 1882 a cabin or two appeared at Kennewick, Richland, and Prosser—specks on an open country still largely devoted to herding. To a man used to unbroken space, however, the district seemed to be filling, and cattlemen complained that settlers were breaking up eternal range.[29]

Most settlers reached Yakima over Satus Pass between Yakima and Goldendale, on a road scraped by ten men, using a team of horses and picks and shovels to shorten a winding government route from The Dalles to Yakima. By Satus, stagecoaches jounced between The Dalles and Yakima in five days. A settler might wheedle a ride with a four-mule team hauling wool to The Dalles, or going home, over a road where one traveler saw nothing but "horn toads, lizards, and gravel beds."[30]

The Northern Pacific puffed Yakima, as it had other towns, although the residents of Yakima City had to move their buildings on rollers to relocate in North Yakima, the railroad's town. But by the mid-eighties, this steep, rolling country with benches overlooking river canyons had roused; its irrigation ditches lengthened (one, the Union, also powered a flour mill); and land sold briskly. The first Northern Pacific train reached North Yakima on Christmas Eve 1884. Four years later when its Cascade tunnel opened, the railroad sold townsite land worth $10,147 in seventeen days. That year (1888) settlers filed on 207,000 acres of government land and 50,000 more of public desert in the Yakima area. And if they could not find a stream bank to claim, perhaps newcomers could drill for water. A land company imported boring machines said to drill an eight-inch hole 2,400 feet deep. (In fact, for some years after, promoters asserted that wells would furnish water for widespread irrigation.)[31]

Most of the newly tilled ground produced fruits, vegetables, alfalfa, and experimental crops of tobacco, watermelon, peanuts, broom corn, and sorghum. Insect damage to western Washington hop fields encouraged Yakima farmers to plant hops, despite low prices.[32]

Living conditions could be as harsh as in the dry counties. New arrivals sometimes lived through winters in tents, sitting by outdoor fires holding their sleeping children on the coldest nights. A summer visitor, after noting the "size and perfection" of Yakima's hops, went on: "The moment we left the watered streets of the town the dust-clouds . . . became gigantic and overwhelming . . . chocolate-colored powder of the roadways . . . about six inches deep. . . . The fresh morning breeze whirled it aloft."[33]

By contrast to settlers struggling to scratch out farms, the Moxee farm, six miles from North Yakima, stood as the showplace—6,400 acres of range and experimental crops. Owned by Gardiner G. Hubbard, founder of the National Geographic Society, and his son-in-law, Alexander Graham Bell, inventor of the telephone, Moxee produced alfalfa, hops, and fruit, and its resident Scots manager also experimented with tobacco, cotton, sorghum, broom corn, and sugar beets. After the Smithsonian Institution (of which Hubbard was a regent) pronounced a soil sample ideal for tobacco, the Moxee company tried Havana, Sumatra, and Virginia varieties and sold cigars (the Moxee Belle and Fleur de Yakima) for several years until frost destroyed its plants.[34]

Hubbard and Bell rarely saw the place before giving it up in the panic of 1893 (and any revival died with Hubbard's death in 1897), but it was more than simply an extravagance. In its way, Moxee symbolized eastern Washington's search for distinctive crops and the inclination of absentee rich men to bet a little money on new country, as they did on every emerging section of the West. For one, Marshall Field, the Chicago merchant, bought 15,000 acres in Whitman and Spokane counties, sending an agent to sell some and manage the rest. His ground would introduce seed production in the Inland Empire. Near Harrington, the California Land Company operated a corporate farm on fifty sections for stockholders who earned 233 percent on their investment. Opie Read, the humorist of the "Arkansas Traveler," Richard F. Outcault, creator of the Yellow Kid and Buster Brown cartoons, and Charles Crewdson, Chicago author, hoped to form a summer colony near Bridgeport for prominent Chicago friends, but turned their land into orchard tracts for general sale.[35]

The unforgettable year 1893 sank more than Moxee farm. It ruined hundreds of farmers and businessmen; it scarred everyone who lived through it, leaving a covetous spirit among many who resolved never to be destitute again. (For a few, of course, the panic of 1893 was a bonanza, with land and goods selling at desperate bargains on every hand.) Signs of incipient panic had been evident for several years. "That there is a depression in agriculture needs no demonstration," declared the *Colfax Commoner* in 1890. "All farm products are reduced to such a low price that after a year's hard labor, they [farmers] have scarcely anything left but a meager living." Merchants pressed farmers to pay their accounts, but the newspaper's editor advised them to "go slow," lest crowded farmers sell their wheat "at ruinous prices."[36]

The 1890 Palouse harvest had been so bountiful that railroads could not move it for months. Country editors called rail delays a "wheat blockade," smacking of collusion between railroads and elevator companies, and the *Spokane Falls Review* noted "voices from the Palouse . . . growing more ominous every day. The farmer cannot sell his wheat at any price. The elevator companies cannot store it and the railroads cannot haul it away." Well into the winter, wheat piles lined railroad tracks. It was a tragedy for the moment, but a foretaste of years to come.[37]

Then in mid-1891 wheat prices bounded on the Chicago exchange. Only later did growers learn that the rise was not due to improved demand but partly to a brazen attempt to corner the market by James G. Fair, the Comstock mining millionaire, whose warehouses bulged with grain that he would dump on the market for the next three years. Washington's mortgaged indebtedness per capita was the highest in the United States at the time; one in four farms was mortgaged at interest rates up to 36 percent. (Lenders often computed interest monthly to disguise the annual rate.) And taxes seemed unusually burdensome. "Men of property and financial standing," fretted the *Yakima Herald*, "are compelled to let their taxes become delinquent, owing to the closeness of the money market." Men lost jobs. The Northern Pacific fired its white workmen on the Spokane and Palouse branch to replace them with Chinese at lower wages.[38]

A declining federal gold reserve and stock market crash threw the country into panic as approaching summer warmed the days in 1893. Wheat prices fell back. Dealers still held unsold grain from 1891 and 1892. Democratic and Populist newspapers blamed the tariff and the government's single-metal monetary policy; they called it the "Cleveland panic." Hard times were hardest in the West and South. Panic toppled banks like scythed wheat. Seven of ten failed in Spokane, dragging down affiliated country banks with them. "No one can borrow money as there is none to be had," warned the *Dayton Chronicle*.

"Should the mortgage companies foreclose, taking all the farmer possesses, the merchants and mechanics will be left entirely." A Walla Walla banker, convicted of accepting deposits in his insolvent bank, fled the country; he would be pardoned by the governor in 1911 after paying off all living creditors.[39]

Farmers called mass meetings. One at Pullman issued a resolution declaring that creditors who forced payment "would bring disaster and ruin"; another at Palouse City resolved, "Whereas . . . the products of our year's toil are either decaying in unthreshed stacks, [or] moulding in granaries . . . we deem it unwise and uncharitable to exact or demand from these debtors money payments at this time and season." The governor visited eastern Washington to assess the disaster for himself. In towns, men formed into companies for Coxey's army to demand federal public works—road construction to employ them. Foreclosures threw most of the major buildings in Spokane into the hands of lenders. In the country, when a loan company foreclosed, it received letters, "Take warning and foreclose no more mortgages," signed with skull and crossbones. A sheriff selling a crop for a creditor found sixty farmers on hand to confuse the bidding. A loan company demanding a crop mortgage as security sent four men to guard against its harvest, but a mob drove them off at night and the debtor quickly cut his fields while a court deliberated. Judges stopped receivers from taking foreclosed land prematurely. Farmers survived by barter, extended credit, and frugality; they parched wheat as a coffee substitute and ate sparsely, opening preserved fruits and vegetables only for company; some went to the Coast to work in logging camps. Stores reduced their stocks to staples and a few dry goods.[40]

Merchants closed. Those who held on posted signs, "Selling for cash only." Stores held "calamity sales." Farmers paid harvest hands in wheat. The *Colfax Commoner* chided farmers for "confining themselves to mere wheat raising" instead of branching into hogs, butter, gardens, and other produce—advice that was to be repeated for decades in eastern Washington. Falling prices for wool and mutton halted sheep drives to market. Such eminent companies as Ben Snipes, cattleman turned banker, and Allan C. Mason, the Tacoma financier who lent thousands to Yakima-area farmers, went down in the panic—Mason, they said, because he tried to carry his debtors through the hard times.[41]

Yet Yakima's crops flourished (three thousand acres of hops alone), and the *Yakima Herald* ventured its opinion that Yakima had escaped the worst of the panic. "We read of total loss of crops and starvation prices," the editor wrote. "Here in Yakima, though prices have been poor . . . the farmers . . . have at least come out with the balance on the right side." Not many districts could feel so optimistic. County warrants were discounted 50 percent throughout the state; counties cut back their buying and, with business and farming, seemed to stand still in late 1893 and early 1894. But the 1894 crops proved fair and a few more immigrants filtered into eastern Washington. The Spokane land office handled five hundred new filings. Yakima's population doubled in eighteen months. Spokane, Colfax, and other towns, piqued that no immigrant trains ran west of Helena, formed an immigration bureau to entice more settlers. By 1895 the worst seemed to be over. The *Colfax Commoner*, to cheer its readers, pointed out that in February 1895 fewer farmers needed crop mortgages and more paid their debts. Farmers no longer handed lavish meals to harvest hands. Now threshing crews dragged along their own chuck wagons.[42]

By 1896 the price of wheat was rising again, aided by another rumored scheme to corner the market. It hit one dollar a bushel on the Chicago board on August 21, 1897, the highest in six years. Wheat shortages in Argentina, Russia, India, and Australia held Liverpool prices high. In eastern Washington, "evidences of renewed hopefulness are seen on every hand. . . . The improvements do not show the expenditure of much money, but more careful attention" to buildings, fences, and machines, remarked an editor. Wheat rose twenty-one cents a bushel in one month at Yakima. The panic was over.[43]

As a consequence of panic, many farm and city properties had changed hands through foreclosure and sale. Banks and merchants had gone out of business. Prominent men had toppled, their social ranks evaporating with their fortunes. New faces appeared in counting houses, stores, and on farms, but towns did not rally to an evident spirit of community renewal. Farmers did not diversify crops rather than rely on wheat. Rural political unity proved a myth when good times returned. Panic had not instilled a fear of debt. The Dutch Hypotheekbank of Spokane lent millions to farmers. Some farmers, having outlived the panic, paid up and moved away. Their neighbors eagerly went into debt to buy their land. (In this manner, Kelso brothers bought six thousand acres in the Horse Heaven district and then farmed it with a steam thresher.) Tales of privation, distress, and luck circulated for years, but few people changed the way they lived or the way they farmed.

On the other hand, the editor of the *Colfax Commoner* detected more social life after the panic. "Now every ambitious school district has its literary society. . . . Entertainments, lectures, exhibitions, socials, parties, and dances are much more numerous," he observed. Like other towns, Colfax sent a delegation to the Klondike for gold to make everyone rich. More than three hundred persons joined in chasing a captive bear on Steptoe Butte until their dogs tired. Then they shot the bear. Perhaps simply surviving the panic made everyone a little giddy. In 1899, Whitman County recorded one divorce for every six weddings.[44]

As the towns grew and the countryside settled up, entertainments waxed more elaborate: well-known speakers and singing groups appeared in the auditorium above a store (inevitably called the "opera house" by townspeople), authors read from their books, magicians and acrobats amazed. The chautauqua, a week of lectures and performances, would linger until World War I. But by then, airplane flights turned eyes skyward and roaring automobiles raced around dusty tracks at country fairs.

Prosperity burnished the wheat fields like a rising sun, brightening the country. Many farmers paid all their debts with a single harvest. Wheat sold for seventy-five cents a bushel or more—it flirted with one dollar from time to time—and Palouse land that brought ten dollars an acre in 1893 rose to forty or fifty. Three mortgage companies that once held 75 percent of Whitman County's farmland quit business in the Palouse, asserted the Seattle *Post-Intelligencer,* because nobody needed loans. (The newspaper's figure seems an exaggeration.) The wheat districts advanced "from poverty to affluence, from depression to prosperity, from general despondency to universal hope, elation, and contentment," opined the *Spokesman-Review.*[45]

As the nation recovered from panic, immigrants started westward again, arriving in eastern Washington by dozens, then hundreds. The Northern Pacific reported that it sold half a million acres in the year ending June 30, 1898—more than it sold in all the previous six years. The Burke syndicate's promotion of Wenatchee, now one-fourth owned by James J. Hill of the Great Northern and on his main line, drew several hundred seeking irrigated tracts. Wenatchee, too, had moved to get on its railway. In one five-day period, the Wenatchee Development Company claimed that it sold $100,000 worth of lots in its new Wenatchee. Burke gave Chelan County four lots for a courthouse to pin down the county seat. Helped by loans from the railroad, Jacob and Harry Shotwell (and four other Shotwells) scraped dirt irrigation ditches from the Wenatchee River—a fourteen-mile Shotwell and a twenty-two-mile North canal. Other canals fingered from creeks and rivers of the Wenatchee area.[46]

An abundant 1897 wheat crop, and rainfall above normal, tempted settlers to risk the Big Bend again. They pushed into Adams, Franklin, and Douglas counties, and Lincoln and Adams soon produced more wheat each year than Walla Walla. Sometimes Lincoln challenged Whitman County. The 1897 yield had been more than twenty million bushels; it would double in eastern Washington before 1910. Most of the settlers in these dry counties claimed their land between 1897 and 1902 and many would hand it down to sons. Because the soil was light and moisture precious, they needed large farms to let half lie fallow. Nearly everyone kept a few milk cows, hogs, and chickens, and gradually Big Bend farmers added sheep. Sheep fit into the fallow cycle; they ate the weeds in fallow fields and fence rows.[47]

The familiar calls for settlers sounded again. Some eastern editors scolded that publicity for Washington amounted to "seduction of capital and population . . . gross and fraudulent exaggerations." (Easterners did not fathom the enthusiasm of the West.) Some ambitious towns had sent agents to show their products at the Columbian Exposition of 1893 in Chicago; now, they renewed their campaigns for immigrants. Railroad handbills, farm-paper ads, and testimonial booklets urged farmers to leave midwestern areas pinched by drought and grasshoppers—to come to the enchanted, healthful West. Louis C. Frey, a publicist for Pasco, passed out thousands of paper slips bearing the words "Keep your eye on Pasco." When he sold $120,000 worth of land in the sandy town, he spent it for more advertising. The vice-president of a Spokane bank, Orris Dorman, boarded immigrant trains to distribute dodgers about his Big Bend lands for sale. E. F. Benson, cattleman and politican, toured the Northwest promoting Yakima and its state fair. Typical boomers they were, among hundreds who confidently touted the future fecundity of their sections. Each hamlet clamored to be a metropolis. "May we ask in the name of common sense, how can every little postoffice . . . expect to be a county seat?" inquired the Pomeroy *East Washingtonian*.[48]

But not only pamphleteering moved families west. The talk, the constant conversation about the West, and letters from old friends who had migrated—these were perhaps more compelling. And settlers came: French from Minnesota, Dunkards, and Spanish-American War veterans formed colonies for Yakima. Dutch in Michigan towns, awed by stereopticon slides of Yakima orchards, came to see for themselves. At any hour the trains reaching eastern Washington disgorged newcomers, the land offices crowded with men poring over maps and plats. Russian-Germans and Germans colonized farms in Lincoln and

Adams counties, sowing them with German names that remained on rural mailboxes into third and fourth generations.[49]

To men in business, the panic appeared to have demonstrated a simple economic truth: business was good when settlers came. They believed that immigration meant prosperity, not seeming to reflect that good times fostered immigration more than immigration fostered prosperity. At every hand, land companies sprang up to publicize their acres and chambers of commerce opened immigration bureaus to trumpet their districts. Farmer testimonials, photograph booklets of lush orchards and fields, letters to old hometown newspapers, to friends, and to foreign-language newspapers—the propaganda bombarded farmers in eastern and midwestern states. The wonders of Washington glittered in millions of words. The people who had come to eastern Washington in the past twenty years had been sold on this new country by just such devices, and now they proposed to sell someone else.

CHAPTER 2

The Railroads: Beneficent, Malignant, Fickle

When he saw that the Northern Pacific Railroad would resume construction in 1879 to avoid forfeiting its federal charter and its land grants, the new president of the Oregon Steam Navigation Company, Henry Villard, moved to forestall this threat to his dominance of the inland trade. He consolidated his routes by forming the Oregon Railway and Navigation Company—the river fleet, the coastal vessels of the Oregon Steamship Company, and the Columbia River and Walla Walla Railroad.

Villard and his Walla Walla railroad were singular: The forty-four-year-old Villard, square jawed with ramrod spine, a newspaperman by calling who ran away from his parents' home in Bavaria at sixteen to emigrate to the United States, had reported the Lincoln-Douglas debates and the Civil War for New York and Chicago newspapers. After the war, taking up the movement for civil service reforms, he studied corporate and public finance so thoroughly that when he returned to Germany for his health in 1873, the European bondholders of the Oregon and California Railroad sent Villard to Oregon as their representative to rescue the faltering company. He also acted for Boston owners of the Oregon and Transcontinental Company who turned over to him the management of the Oregon Steam Navigation and their companies purchased from Simeon G. Reed and his associates. Among the Reed companies, Villard acquired the Columbia River and Walla Walla.

The Walla Walla railroad had been planned, financed, built, and managed virtually by one man, the physician-businessman Dorsey S. Baker, a paradigm of the resident capitalist who by enriching himself built up his town. Baker's railroad was the first to penetrate any section of eastern Washington. He built it with the cheapest materials, spending not more than $10,300 a mile on construction when railroads customarily cost two to three times that, and opened it between Walla Walla and the river in October 1874. (The Oregon Railway and Navigation Company spent more than $31,000 a mile extending its main line from Wallula to the river in 1881.)

The *Walla Walla Union* declared that, by Baker's railroad, "the farmer has been given a cash market for every pound of surplus produce he can raise; . . . trade has been quickened; new industries and manufacturers have been established in the Walla Walla country." The *Union* estimated that Baker profited by half a million dollars but no one else made money from his railroad.[1]

Leaving Walla Walla, this odd railway coasted by gravity for five miles to Whitman station before attaching to a locomotive for the rest of the trip to the river. It ran no trains in darkness, to avoid hitting cows and horses on the roadbed. The Oregon Steam Navigation Company bought the line in 1877, improved the grade, and replaced the narrow with standard-gauge track. Baker turned to banking; he and his brother-in-law, John F. Boyer, organized the first commercial bank in eastern Washington. As a pioneer line, Baker's one-man railroad was the antithesis of the emerging railway era, a time of long hauls by lengthening trains using Andrew Carnegie's tough steel rails, more powerful locomotives, stronger construction, and larger freight cars.[2]

With the Northern Pacific resuming construction and Villard trying to head it off, railroads entered Washington Territory in spirited competition; they would be inextricably linked with populating and developing the region. For half a century they would acquire land and sell it, promote settlement, finance irrigation, choose townsites, connect the farms and towns to markets, deliver merchandise and haul away crops, impose rate structures, enhance the tax base, exert political influence, and make possible the exploitation of the region's fields, forests, and mines. Railroads affected almost every aspect of life in eastern Washington, the most significant commercial force in the area's development. Towns coveted railroad service. Dayton, for one, promised to ship $100,000 worth of grains, fruit, wool, flour, soap, and beer if someone would build a railroad to it.[3]

The citizens of eastern Washington regarded railroad companies as solid and constant, warranting gratitude or contempt—sometimes both at the same time—as the seasons changed. But in fact the railroads were tangles of alliances, reorganizations, stock issues, and political and legal disputation, although successive Northern Pacific directorates maintained a reasonably steady record of paying dividends on capital stock and of selling the railroad's granted lands.

The citizen was likely to encounter a railroad first through its advertising. Villard publicized the inland country vigorously beginning in 1879 to increase its population and monopolize the resultant carrying trade. Soon after, the Northern Pacific revitalized its immigration department, spreading two and a half million pamphlets in a single year throughout the midwestern and eastern states and 955 immigration and land sales offices in the United Kingdom and Europe, and placing ads in 167 U.S. newspapers.[4]

Both Villard and the Northern Pacific focused their foreign promotion on Germany, The Netherlands, and the Scandinavian countries, where they showed traveling exhibits of Washington and Oregon farm products at markets and fairs. But emphasis on foreign immigrants soon diminished in favor of moving Americans. "I would rather have one settler from Illinois or Wisconsin, who had opened a farm there, than half a dozen emigrants from England or any other European country," R. M. Newport, immigration agent, wrote a Northern Pacific vice-president. "I see no good reason why we should pay large bonuses to secure foreign emigration when we can, by a judicious outlay, largely increase the emigration from other states in the Union."[5]

Declaring themselves a board of immigration, officers of the Northern Pacific subsidized Eugene V. Smalley's slick illustrated magazine, *The North West,* which endured for two decades. Portland, Walla Walla, and eventually other towns circulated elaborate booklets about their environs; Oregon and Washington organized state (territorial) agencies to promote themselves, although by 1886 Oregon had altered its appeal to attract investors rather than homeseekers. Many of these publications emphasized healthful living. The Northern Pacific's *Settler's Guide* of 1883 extolled eastern Washington as "without exception or drawback one of the most healthful and exhilarating climates on the globe," where "the poor man . . . can earn a living easier than in the East, as labor is in demand, wages are good, and provisions are cheap."[6]

Few poor men migrated, in fact. Those with money could afford to move and invest in new country. The poor could not, unless they drifted across the land taking odd jobs. If they reached Washington, they usually could neither buy land nor pay their living expenses while waiting to grow and sell a crop.

Families in eastern states or Europe might deliberate for months, even years, before migrating; for them, moving to Washington meant cutting roots, perhaps forever. Families in American states and territories often sent one of their men to scout the country. When his impressions were favorable, they moved. Many were moving for the second, third, or fourth time, seeking the one ideal place for the farm, orchard, or business that would make them independent. Towns like Walla Walla teemed with these itinerants, eager to find good land, rush to rumored gold mines, or start shoestring businesses. When migrants came from Europe, they often huddled in enclaves that clung to old-world languages, religions, and customs.

A settler's second encounter with a railroad was likely to be in the purchase of land, even if he claimed a tract from the federal government at $2.50 an acre. The Northern Pacific offered credit: four dollars an acre with a down payment and four subsequent payments at 7 percent, reasonable (perhaps enlightened) in a time when moneylenders often demanded 1 percent a month. A man could buy 160 railroad acres for cash at $2.60 an acre, a total of $416, or on time for $724. The railroad's $2.60 represented the government price plus ten cents an acre for its costs of surveying, bookkeeping, and administering the land. As time passed, these prices changed. Railroads tried to adjust prices according to the quality and potential use of the lands.

But when a settler bought government or railroad land, title to his acres might be uncertain for years, even decades, because of claims to granted lands by the Northern Pacific. In confrontations over titles to land, the settlers learned to fear and then to oppose the railroad. They regarded attempts to classify and reprice lands, when the Northern Pacific offered Whitman County tracts at eight to ten dollars an acre, as repudiating the railroad's pledge to sell cheaply.[7]

The main difficulty with conferring clear title lay in the routes selected by the Northern Pacific. In its original charter of 1864, the company received the odd sections of land on both sides of its track as a congressional subsidy for the northern transcontinental route, the notion prevailing that the railroad could pay off its construction bonds by selling the land, and that settlers would fill in the even-numbered sections under the homestead, preemption, and similar federal programs. In giving the subsidy, Congress stipulated that title could not pass to the railway until the land was surveyed. Surveying predictably lagged, for the federal government had millions of uncharted acres in western territories, and the Northern Pacific, required to pay for surveying, was bankrupt from 1873 to 1879. While Congress nagged the company to move with dispatch, the Northern Pacific struggled to attract settlers to buy the land so the company could pay for surveying it. And railroad engineers changed the route, not once but several times—in 1870, 1872, 1880, and 1882. The 1872 route map showed nothing more than a straight line across Washington Territory. (The track, when constructed, substantially followed the 1882 route.)[8]

The railroad's charter also provided that if land within its grant was already claimed by someone else for homestead or mine, the company could select other lands within forty miles of its track in lieu of those taken—"lieu lands." As the Northern Pacific surveyed through Montana, finding thousands of acres occupied, it selected lieu lands in Washington to replace them. New railroad selection lists were published for eastern Washington in 1882, 1883, and 1884. As the railroad issued its newest list, the federal General Land Office dutifully mailed local land offices revised colored maps showing the area the railroad claimed. A settler might find his acreage outside the railroad claim on one map and inside it on another. The register—the administrator who ran a local land office—would not convey title if the map showed a tract inside the railroad's claim. The withdrawals technically relied on practices of the Department of the Interior rather than statutes, and the General Land Office charged that the Northern Pacific "compelled settlers to purchase waivers . . . to which the company might never have any color of legal right."[9]

Scores of settlers sued the railroad. To avoid trying all of these cases, the General Land Office chose the ones its agents felt would offer the best tests of settlers' rights. One was the suit by a farmer, Guilford Miller, whose homestead entry had been accepted in 1884 on 160 acres near Almota. Miller had worked the land since 1878, but the land office took six years to complete the paperwork on his entry. The Northern Pacific claimed Miller's farm as an indemnity tract (lieu land). Miller protested and the land commissioner, W. A. J. Sparks, who suspected lively frauds in western land titles, favored Miller. To reassure themselves, citizens interested in this test case carried it forward to the secretary of the interior, but he was so slow that President Grover Cleveland eventually wrote him a scolding letter—"such a condition of public lands should no longer continue"—that moved the secretary to confirm Sparks's decision. Miller kept his land.[10]

In another test, Charles Cole and eighty other settlers who had occupied their lands since 1878 challenged the railroad when the local land office and General Land Office refused to process their entry papers. Cole appealed to the secretary of the interior, who, in 1893, ruled for him. In Cole's case, his title—and the titles of his neighbors and hundreds of other settlers in a similar fix—was in doubt for fifteen years. He could have built a home, raised a family, and reaped fourteen harvests without being sure his land would ever belong to him.[11]

Of course, neither Cole nor Miller actually handled their cases; they were farmers unschooled in law. Attorneys, often hired by groups of farmers to test railroad claims, carried the cases from office to office until they forced decisions.

Although the government, the settlers, and the railroad hoped test cases would solve title contests, disputes over titles did not subside until 1898, when Congress passed, as a rider by Senator John L. Wilson of Washington to the Sundry Civil Appropriations Act, a provision validating settlers' titles to ground they occupied. Four years later, the U.S. Supreme Court denied Northern Pacific claims against valid homesteads.[12]

Despite confrontations that lasted more than two decades (and flared occasionally after that), hundreds of immigrant families bought land from the Northern Pacific without difficulty. The railroad never tried to oust settlers, and after 1894, when the government allowed settlers to pay for their surveys, many obtained clear titles in a short time. In 1899 Congress removed a requirement that public lands be surveyed in sequence, and the Northern Pacific rapidly accelerated surveys on desirable lands.[13]

The railroad often sold tracts before they were surveyed, issuing the buyer a "cash certificate," and delivering a deed when the government approved its surveyed grant. Much of eastern Washington was sold through the Northwestern Improvement Company, a Northern Pacific subsidiary formed to manage coal deposits, sell land, and promote townsites. Between 1880 and 1890 more than seven million dollars worth of Palouse farmland went, mostly on credit. A peak sales year, 1888, pushed land sales up 68 percent, partly because of settlers' discouragement with other areas—the Dakotas, for one, where crops failed widely in 1886. Although land sales fell in the panic years, 1893 through 1895, they reached new highs in 1898, and the bulk of the Northern Pacific's salable land in Washington was taken by 1902.[14]

At the height of land selling, the *Spokane Falls Chronicle* estimated that twenty-eight hundred immigrants a month arrived by way of the Columbia, while roads thronged with families moving from Kansas, Nebraska, Iowa, and Minnesota. Spokane Falls, then a village incorporated less than a year by a townsite company busily selling town lots, built a barn as an "immigrant house" where moving families could bed until they found land to buy. A booklet, *The Pacific North-*

west, published by Villard's companies, advised settlers to bring at least five hundred dollars to build a house, buy livestock, seeds, farm tools, and provisions.[15]

Such speculative buyers as Levi Ankeny, the Oregon banker's son who would become a United States senator, bought large areas; he took 1,314 acres at an average price of $2.80 between 1882 and 1885. Orris Dorman, a Spokane land broker, purchased 9,500 acres in 1901 for about 48 cents an acre, and met trains to sell them to immigrants. Benjamin Snipes, the Yakima stockman, acquired 1,059 acres at $2.66 an acre between 1886 and 1888. But the spectacular buy was that of the Coffin brothers, Yakima; they acquired 32,000 for an average of 48 cents an acre between 1895 and 1900.[16]

Villard's Oregon Improvement Company, a land-selling and town-site firm, brought a crusty retired army general, Thomas R. Tannatt, from its New York immigration office to peddle 150,000 acres of the Palouse that Villard got for $2.60 an acre from the Northern Pacific. Tannatt resold it for five to ten dollars an acre through offices in New York, Portland, and Colfax, then resigned to raise fruit and serve twice as mayor of Walla Walla.

By disposition, settlers were contentious. They fought about land among themselves, with the government, and with the railroads. They believed fervently that their security lay in owning a little ground.

For decades the Northern Pacific grant itself remained in dispute. Many a politician forged his career attacking this unconscionable giveaway of public lands; many a country editor enlived an otherwise dull edition with an editorial damning the grant and the railroad. John C. Lawrence, who would be a member of Washington's first railroad regulatory commission, alleged that the Northern Pacific selected lieu lands "far in excess" of its due.[17]

But the Northern Pacific had not received all the lands it was entitled to, and to keep its grant after bankruptcy in 1893 enacted a transcontinental charade. The directors authorized a bond issue to finance repurchase of the granted lands and in 1896 sent a new president, Edwin W. Winter, to buy back the land for a reorganized railroad company. With the master in bankruptcy as auctioneer, Winter visited every hardscrabble county seat along the railroad line, and, as the master quickly read a list of county railroad lands to be auctioned, Winter bid on them from a duplicate list. In plaid surtout and brown derby, the slender, goateed, bookish Winter stood a little apart from spectators, bidding quietly as the master knocked down large blocks in a few minutes. Occasionally a local citizen bid. Winter shut him off with an overwhelming bid. In Missoula, when a local offered perhaps two hundred dollars for 160 acres, Winter countered with $15,000. Most tracts sold to the railroad for one hundred dollars. In Washington, Winter thus bought, for a new Northern Pacific, lands foreclosed for $1,210,000, paying in second mortgage bonds.[18]

Rebuying the land did not still controversy over the grant. Charles L. Van Doren, a law examiner in the General Land Office, recalled that in 1921, for one of the massive federal hearings, the railroad produced "about a carload" of documents that took two years to sift. Claims for alternative routes, overlaps for the main line and the Kalama-Tacoma route, and nine forest preserve withdrawals between 1898 and 1924 involving at least 193,000 railroad acres, complicated the issue. The validity of railroad claims was ostensibly determined in 1939 when a master in chancery, the Spokane attorney Frank Graves, opined that in Washington the Northern Pacific received 430,524 acres fewer than warranted. Coincidentally the final order for this decision was signed by Federal Judge Lewis B. Schwellenbach, soon to be secretary of labor.[19]

Railroad land sales and the concomitant rapid occupation of public lands under the homestead, timber culture, and other federal programs led to a general impression by 1890 that the best eastern Washington land had been taken. Much of eastern Washington was marginal by farmers' standards. The Big Bend of the Columbia River, the dry flatlands and hills of the Yakima River and its tributaries, and rocky northeastern Washington lacked rainfall, easy conversion to farming, and transportation. These areas could not be sold merely by opening a sales office.

Villard's initial objective had been to protect his interior commerce and Portland's position as the center of Northwest trade, and, failing that, to capture the most profitable inland districts for his railroads, or perhaps to seize the Northern Pacific itself. He achieved his first purpose by building a line from the Snake to Portland along the south bank of the Columbia and, in agreements among railroads on territories and routes, offering the Northern Pacific access to Portland over his line. From there the Northern Pacific built its line through Kalama in southwestern Washington into Tacoma. Villard's expansion of his system and his promotional efforts beginning in 1879 partly carried out his second purpose, and for a fleeting three and one-half years, beginning in 1881, Villard controlled the Northern Pacific, raising funds to purchase his stock through a noted "blind pool"—a pooling of investors' monies for a purpose Villard did not at first reveal to them. Wealthy men invested simply on their faith in Villard's business judgment.

Through a holding company, the Oregon and Transcontinental, Villard ran the Oregon Railway and Navigation Company and the Northern Pacific in harmony and wrapped into the holding company the alliance (forged by Elijah Smith and Boston associates) that ensured the Union Pacific entry to Portland and delivered Portland a second transcontinental rail service. Under Villard, the Oregon and Transcontinental planned a network of railroads that anticipated nearly all the strategic water and rail routes of the Pacific Northwest.[20]

Ironically Villard elevated Puget Sound to a strong competitive position by pushing completion of the Northern Pacific track, building from east and west simultaneously. From a temporary town on the Columbia, Ainsworth, the railroad built eastward through the dusty, empty coulees, using Irish powdermen and Chinese laborers, touching but one village, Spokane Falls, and founding others, Sprague and Cheney, where the houses "are all bran new, . . . and shine like lumber from the mill."[21]

At Sprague, the railroad erected roundhouse and shops, and the townspeople danced on the shop floor illuminated by locomotive headlights and red-and-green lanterns, for Sprague felt that the railroad shops ensured its future prominence. When the roundhouse burned in 1896, Sprague residents earnestly believed a rumor that the railroad company set the fire to justify moving its shops to Yardley, east of Spokane.

The construction crews from east and west met near Garrison, Montana, to drive a gilded spike—not golden—signifying completion of the single track on September 8, 1883. (They tore up six hundred yards of track to relay as a showpiece for the railroad's guests.) Learning that General Ulysses S. Grant was among the personages Villard brought to those bleak Montana hills for this ceremony, a number of former soldiers in the crowd wanted to shake the general's hand. They were hustled away by a fussy, bespectacled German, Paul Schultze, western land agent for Villard, when Villard growled, "General Grant will hold no reception here today." Although the continent at last was stitched by rails through its northern states and territories, the celebration was desultory. Most of the guests could hardly wait to leave the place.[22]

The Kalama-to-Puget Sound track opened the same day without fanfare. Four months later, in January 1884, Villard lost his grip on the Northern Pacific in a stockholders' revolt. The Oregon Railway and Navigation Company and the Northern Pacific competed strenuously although they shared tracks.

From time to time thereafter the railroads agreed to divide the interior into regions of influence—compacts that proved monotonously brief but showed the railroads' imperial disregard for the farmers and merchants they served. Lasting railroad truces were impractical because their subsidiary roads met and crossed, roads such as the 123-mile line built in 1887 and 1888 by George W. Hunt with the financial backing of Charles B. Wright, a controlling stockholder in the Northern Pacific. Hunt's line, from Wallula Junction (or near it) to Walla Walla and Eureka Flats, invaded the older counties of eastern Washington that Villard regarded as belonging to his Oregon system.[23]

Contracts, public or secret, to divide territories broke up regularly in disagreements among railroad stockholders and Portland's furious objections to being bartered like an Oriental bride. And Oregon businessmen and river towns, through their congressmen, bullied the federal government into removing navigational barriers in the Columbia in a series of annual river improvement projects, just in the way that Seattle pushed its Lake Washington canal.

A catalog of railroads, stock transfers, and agreements would show the complexity of relationships among the railroads with which farmers and settlers dealt, but it would be more illustrative than useful, for railroads changed often. Their track seemed permanent; their management was not.

The Northern Pacific planned a Cascade mountain route through Stampede Pass with a terminus at Tacoma. For three years, however, its western terminus was Wallula Junction, where it met the Oregon Railway and Navigation line. After Villard lost control, the Northern Pacific built an elaborate switchback to cross the Cascades until it could complete a Stampede Pass tunnel on a suitable grade. Using the tunnel, the Northern Pacific entered Tacoma July 2, 1887.

From its main line the Northern Pacific sponsored feeder lines. The most important in eastern Washington were its Spokane and Palouse, meandering southward from Marshall through Palouse wheat-shipping towns, and its Spokane and Idaho, which left the main line at Hauser Junction, Idaho, and ran to Coeur d'Alene Lake to connect by steamboats with the Coeur d'Alene Railway and Navigation Company route to Wallace, Idaho, tapping the principal mines of the region.

The Spokane and Palouse (originally the Eastern Washington Railway Company) was ostensibly directed by Anthony M. Cannon, Spo-

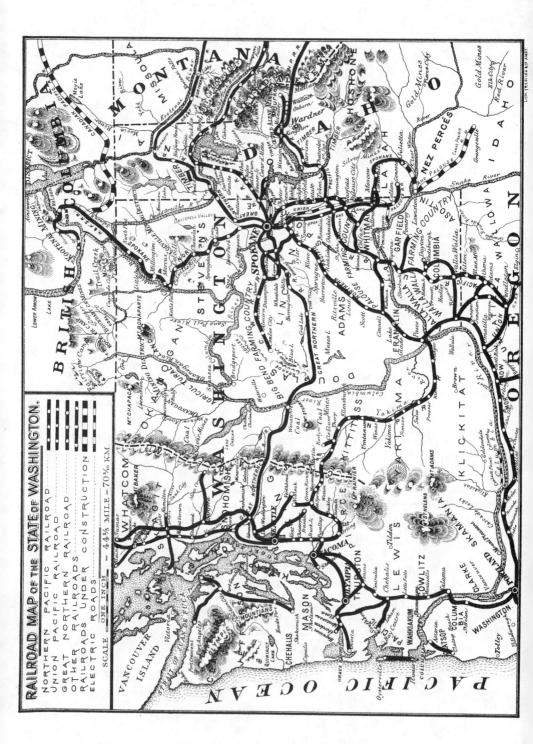

32 *The Railroads: Beneficent, Malignant, Fickle*

kane banker, mill owner, councilman, and investor, and constructed between 1886 and 1888 despite a court suit by the Oregon and Transcontinental intended to stop work both on the Spokane and Palouse and the Cascade switchback. The Spokane and Palouse opened the rich commerce of the Palouse country to Spokane and the Northern Pacific; it ran through Spangle, Rosalia, Oakesdale, Belmont, Garfield, Pullman, Colton, Moscow, and Genesee, and carried the mails after 1888. In 1899 the Northern Pacific, which held all its stock, formally bought the road.

The lines to the Coeur d'Alene mines were built by Daniel C. Corbin under contracts with the Northern Pacific and passed to the Northern Pacific in 1888, although the railroad was in court until 1909 settling contractors' claims against the Corbin roads and had to reconstruct the roadbed to Wallace almost immediately after taking it over. Nevertheless the jerry-built lines allowed the Northern Pacific to monopolize the mining traffic for a decade and share strongly in it after that, until construction of the Bunker Hill smelter in 1917 shifted the heaviest mine traffic to the Oregon-Washington Railroad and Navigation Company, a Union Pacific subsidiary.

After he sold his Coeur d'Alene lines to the Northern Pacific, Corbin built the Spokane Falls and Northern through the northern valleys of eastern Washington along the Columbia and, by branches, reached the mining districts of southeastern British Columbia. Thus Corbin opened northeastern Washington to Spokane and the Northern Pacific (although his railroad eventually sold, to Corbin's ire, to the Great Northern).

As opportunities for traffic appeared, the Northern Pacific built or underwrote other feeders: the North Yakima and Valley to Naches, Moxee, Spitzenberg, Farrow, and Parker, fruit-shipping stations; the Connell Northern, sixty-one miles to Adco and Shrag, shipping points for Palouse wheat; and the disputed Washington and Columbia River from Dayton to Pendleton, which used Northern Pacific main-line tracks to reach Pasco and, like the Hunt line, trespassed into the domain of the Oregon Railway and Navigation Company.

The map on the facing page was printed in color in the Northwestern and Pacific Hypotheekbank report for 1893. It depicts eastern Washington railroad routes fairly accurately, but suggests extensive mining surrounding Spokane, and shows extensions of the Nelson & Fort Sheppard and Spokane & Palouse railroads never built. A few minor misspellings appear, e.g., Washtucia for Washtucna. (Reproduced by the Eastern Washington University cartographic laboratory.)

And there was the Hunt road, not a Northern Pacific suzerainty, perhaps, but assisted by Wright, who then controlled the Northern Pacific. Wright's connection was hidden, for in 1888 Hunt signed contracts with prospective shippers along his intended route to contribute cash or wheat to the railroad's costs and deposited these contracts with the Walla Walla Board of Trade to be returned to Hunt when he finished the line. Hunt promised freight rates as low as those of the Oregon Railway and Navigation. Construction of his road was turned over to the Oregon and Washington Territory Company, in which Hunt held the majority stock, because a corporation could take right-of-way by eminent domain. Rather than being grateful when Hunt's line started operations, however, some shippers sued to back out of their contracts, arguing that Hunt had started his tracks a mile or two from the point originally proposed and had not personally built the road. The state supreme court directed them to pay up.[24]

As if interlocking companies were not confusing enough, bankruptcies, reorganizations, and changing policies mystified the farmer and merchant. They could not be sure who really owned the Northern Pacific or the Union Pacific, a confederation of stockholders in various roads. For years, interior shippers sought to discover whom they might influence to change routes, schedules, and rates; they were continually baffled by learning that the men they thought owned the railroad did not. Country editors railed. The Oregon Railway and Navigation, said one, "more closely resembles a bold and wealthy gambler than the wise and honorable business corporation it purports to be . . . a high-handed system of bluffs and bragadocia."[25]

If editors oversimplified, legislators and railroad commissions complicated their reports with legal language, tables of mileage, rate structures, citations of state regulations, and justifications of their methods of computing rates and taxes. For the farmer and the merchant, the rate discrimination and erratic scheduling seemed to emanate from a nebulous hierarchy of railroad managers who, they suspected, answered ultimately to eastern investors with power to blunt the best efforts of government to regulate them.

As if to sustain this wry view, the Union Pacific was indeed related to the Chicago, Milwaukee and St. Paul (which built across eastern Washington shortly before World War I) through the New York banking house of Kuhn, Loeb and Company. And when the Union Pacific went into receivership, ostensibly losing its Oregon Short Line and the Oregon Railway and Navigation Company, it nevertheless maintained control of both by interlocking stock ownerships.

The Oregon Short Line (leased to the Union Pacific in 1887) met the Oregon Railway and Navigation at Huntington in northeastern Oregon, and through the Oregon Railway and Navigation held the securities of the Columbia and Palouse, the Walla Walla and Columbia River, and other feeders serving grain shippers in Washington south of the Snake and such Palouse towns as Colfax and LaCrosse. The Columbia and Palouse ran from Connell, on the Northern Pacific, 117 miles to Moscow, Idaho, and branched from Colfax to Farmington, where it met the Washington and Idaho, which branched two ways, into the Coeur d'Alene mines and into Spokane. The Washington and Idaho opened in 1888 with driving of a gilded spike at Oakesdale. The company spotted the countryside with its cramped frame station houses costing up to $450 each and paid for its grading and tracks with money advanced by the Oregon Railway and Navigation, which held its mortgage bonds. The Oregon Railway and Navigation also operated ocean vessels to San Francisco and steamers along 117 miles of the Columbia and seventy-eight miles of the Snake, upriver from Portland to Lewiston. In Spokane, it owned a union depot and real estate not used for railroading.

To combat railroad discrimination in rates and services, independent investors, farmer associations, and alliances of towns organized their own railroad companies. Scores incorporated, published prospectuses, sold stock, and collapsed. For a time every locality seemed to be planning its own. Walla Walla would build to Puget Sound, Spokane to Missoula via Post Falls, Goldendale to the upper Columbia to meet the Canadian Pacific—there were the Starbuck and Pomeroy, the Spokane and Big Bend, and so on, chimeral and spiteful. A few of these small lines, built, were quickly gobbled by the big railroads through stock transfer or purchase.

Perhaps the most notorious regional railroads were the Seattle, Lake Shore and Eastern Railway and the Central Washington Railroad. Conceived by Seattle investors as a cross-state line to Walla Walla with a branch to Spokane Falls, the Seattle, Lake Shore and Eastern began construction in 1887 from Spokane Falls westward and from Seattle eastward. The Northern Pacific, working day and night, built a parallel track within sight of Seattle, Lake Shore and Eastern crews, and of the Seattle's $5.6 million in bonds, the Northern Pacific bought all but $5,000 worth; of the Seattle's capital stock of $4.1 million, the Northern Pacific bought $3.1 million. Therefore, when the Seattle, Lake Shore and Eastern defaulted interest payments, the Northern Pacific foreclosed, acquiring a line from Spokane into Lincoln County that it subsequently operated as a branch. The area then was desolate flatland broken by basalt outcroppings.

The Central Washington, using funds advanced by the Northern Pacific but masquerading as independent, built its line from Cheney to Coulee City between 1890 and 1893 (extended to Adrian in 1903 by the Northern Pacific); it was operated by a receiver for twenty-six months, then leased to the Northern Pacific by exchanging stock.

In this fevered climate of railroad construction, the advent of James J. Hill seemed to promise deliverance from imperious railroads. Hill, with a fortune in coal and railroads in Minnesota and Manitoba, confident that he could profit by cheaper rates and efficient management, proposed to extend his St. Paul, Minneapolis and Manitoba Railway without a federal subsidy to Everett, Washington, crossing Washington State on a relatively direct route. Renamed the Great Northern, Hill's railroad passed through Spokane and picked new townsites—Wenatchee, for one, which would grow from 451 residents in 1900 to more than 4,000 by 1910 with irrigation and vigorous promotion by Hill lieutenants.

The stumpy Hill himself—bearded and bald, hands on hips, Prince Albert coat spreading across his paunch, carnation in buttonhole—addressed town and farm audiences crowding auditoriums, town halls, and street platforms. His gospel: Jim Hill would give them better service at lower rates. To pay him his due, Hill was genuinely interested in the construction and operation of railways. Improved efficiency on the Northern Pacific in 1897 launched rumors that Hill had taken control. On his Great Northern, Hill increased tonnage on an average cross-country train from 179 tons in 1890 to 281 by 1897 by enlarging freight cars and bettering the roadbed.[26] He realized that Everett could not compete as terminal with Puget Sound and extended the Great Northern to Seattle (with inducements from Seattle promoters), forcing the Northern Pacific to Seattle, too. He threatened to bypass Spokane unless the town provided free right-of-way, and of course got what he asked.

The farmers and merchants of the interior counties believed Hill's gospel until they discovered that the Great Northern made rates much like other railroads. Then they named a pernicious weed Jim Hill mustard. They did not comprehend, however, that by the close of the nineteenth century, Hill, with cooperation from the banking house of J. P. Morgan, had taken advantage of the Northern Pacific's weak financial structure to grasp control of that road too. With Morgan, Hill worked to neutralize the Oregon Railroad and Navigation Company in Washington. He and Morgan did not get along well, particularly after Morgan named the insufferable Charles S. Mellen president of the Northern Pacific.[27]

As he crossed the northern West, Hill's stratagem was to build branch lines into the country on either side of his main route. Smaller companies often sold their tracks to him rather than meet his competition, and major lines granted Hill concessions for his promise to stay out of their territory. In eastern Washington, Hill had won concessions from the Northern Pacific by agreeing not to build into the Palouse and, again through Morgan, acquired Corbin's Spokane Falls and Northern. Mellen urged territorial splits and branches that Hill did not want, and as soon as he could persuade Morgan, Hill dumped Mellen.[28]

The dilemma of the populace was that the principal crops of eastern Washington, grains and soft fruits, had to be exported. Farmers desperately needed railroads, and cities needed railroads simply to be cities. The network of commerce relied on railroads, which rapidly superseded the horse and wagon. Merchandise moved on rails to cities for distribution by rail throughout rural districts. Farmers who ventured to town, and moneylenders who traveled into the country, rode on railroads.

Abused and patronized, the region needed its railroads, and the railroads acted like gods—beneficent, malignant, fickle. They gave here and they took there. Their oracles dwelled in boardrooms in New York, Boston, Philadelphia, London, or Berlin, but the aftershocks of their rituals and decrees jolted the countryside. The railroads freed eastern Washington's people from their rivers but shackled them instead to steel tracks—until the automobile came.

But if railroads used their power in finance and politics, the people also worked every mean advantage available to them. County commissioners in Yakima, for one, licensed forty-nine saloons and gambling houses where the Northern Pacific camped four thousand men building its Cascade tunnel. The men who represented railroads were perhaps no less reasonable than the ones they served, but they were perpetually cast as antagonists. Citizens demanded more service, more taxes, and more benefits than railroads could afford. As a result, railroads against the people evolved into a hierarchical contest: the farmer against the railroad, the town against the railroad, the county against the railroad, and the state against the railroad.[29]

The end of the panic of 1893 set off strong new publicity campaigns by railroads to settle the open, unproductive regions through which

their lines passed—those bleak, homeless districts yielding no revenue. Both the Northern Pacific and Oregon Railway and Navigation
companies had been in receivership; both reorganized, changing their
names—the Oregon from railway to railroad, the Northern Pacific
from railroad to railway.

The Northern Pacific now advertised most heavily in country newspapers of midwestern states. It sold more than 389,000 acres (not all
in Washington) in 1896, a million in 1899, and two million in 1901
and again in 1902. The railroad's campaigns would continue, trying
to outshout California, until 1935.[30]

The postdepression campaign to fill up the countryside benefited
from a fortuitous turn in the climate—four years of above-average
rainfall from 1893 to 1897. The stony flats of the Big Bend could
produce grain with such rainfall. A disaster for uncut Palouse crops in
1893, the rains convinced many a settler that with a little luck he
could grow crops in the dry lands, and he bought acreage from the
railroad. The panic had depressed grain prices below the costs of
planting and harvesting, but as hard times passed, grain prices rose.
In 1897, wheat opened the selling season at 63 cents a bushel, floating
upward to 85 cents, a bonanza. To the newcomer, prosperity seemed
to permeate the inland counties.

Untilled land offered at 90 cents an acre in the spring of 1897 with
ten years to pay could not be sold; by midsummer its price doubled
and then tripled. Not only the railroads but the towns promoted the
lure of rising crop prices and available ground. The leading towns of
eastern Washington, including Spokane and Colfax, had joined in
1894 to support an Eastern Washington and Northern Idaho Bureau
of Immigration with a central office in Chicago to distribute their literature throughout midwestern states. The states extolled their unsettled lands, the cities called for immigrants, and the railroads touted
eastern Washington. The Northern Pacific ran new colonist sleepers,
each family section fitted with a bed, table, and curtains. Travelers
might buy (and keep) complete bedding for three dollars. One end of
each car was fitted as a kitchen. Families began arriving by trainloads,
to be met by salesmen handing out dodgers for land opportunities.

With advertising, the Pacific Northwest entered its longest period of
population growth before World War II. The immigrant rush lasted
until 1910, when the transcontinental railroads virtually completed
their main-line construction. The settler in eastern Washington, regardless of occupation, felt the intense competition between Portland
and Puget Sound for commercial preeminence. And no matter how

fast eastern Washington filled with new residents, western Washington grew faster—growth that foretold the coming century, when western Washington would dominate the state's commerce, politics, and state offices.

Nevertheless the effects of railroad-induced expansion were spectacular in eastern Washington. Towns sprang up along the tracks or at crossroads leading to them. Older settled counties like Whitman grew in population from 19,109 in 1890 to 33,280 by 1910; Walla Walla County grew from 12,224 to 31,931. The number of farms increased rapidly in those districts not already crowded: Adams County farms increased from 783 to 1,263 between 1900 and 1910, Benton from almost none to 1,239, Douglas from 854 to 1,730, Franklin from 61 to 620, and Lincoln from 1,911 to 2,139. These five were dry counties devoted to grains and livestock range where farms covered hundreds of acres tilled and harvested by machine. In the same ten years, 1900 to 1910, the aggregate values of farm machines in those five counties tripled to nearly four million dollars, an average of $572 per farm. By 1910 the highest grain yields were from Whitman and Lincoln counties—the ones with the largest investments in machines—with Adams rising fast.[31]

Access to markets by railroads made possible this expansion. The older grain-growing counties—Asotin, Columbia, Garfield, Walla Walla, and Whitman—started to invest in machines before the others, but their spending did not quite double in the same decade. Here and there puffed a gasoline tractor, but most machines moved with horses and mules.

Washington's irrigated regions also grew, likewise dependent on the railroads for their markets. These districts sold their produce first to Puget Sound, then broadly through the Pacific Northwest states, and eventually sent fine fruits across the northern United States. Chelan County's population rose from 3,391 in 1900 to more than 15,100 by 1910; Franklin, growing wheat in its flatlands, also filled its stream banks with irrigators, rising from 696 to 5,153 in ten years; federal irrigation helped increase Okanogan from 1,467 to 12,887, although the county's highlands remained cattle country and Indian reservation. And Yakima, preeminent among Washington's irrigated areas, increased in a decade from 4,429 to 41,709.

Naturally, new settlement and new machines pushed upward the investment needed to buy and till the land. In 1890, shortly before the panic of 1893, one in every four farms in eastern Washington had been mortgaged; in the prospering years after the panic, as hundreds paid off their debts, the proportion of mortgaged farms fell to one in five;

but then the costs of machines, buying additional land, shipping, and the few amenities of rural homemaking required farmers to take loans more often, and by 1910 one in every three farms carried a mortgage. Machines, crops, animals, and, above all, the land were pledged against short-term and long-term debts.

As farm districts filled, the cities of eastern Washington expanded. Unlike midwestern states where farm settlement attracted railroads and cities sprouted at distribution points, in eastern Washington the railroads opened unsettled areas and started towns. Jim Hill might snort that "the State of Washington is . . . the worst example [of building roads without towns]" brought about by "the Villard policy of building and buying railroads running from paper towns to a wagon track," but in fact when towns sprang up, the railroad was already there.

With the persuasion of railroad pitchmen, irrigation developers, land speculators, real estate agents, loan companies, and others, Spokane County had swelled to nearly 140,000 persons by 1910. Its businessmen started a civic publicity committee called the 150,000 Club to spur immigration. In 1900 Spokane issued 675 city building permits valued at $1.2 million; in 1910, it wrote 2,184 permits worth $5.4 million—the biggest building year until 1943. Nearly ten thousand homes built in this period would still be there seventy years later.[32]

Spokane, luckily if foolishly, had erected an elaborate downtown district of massive granite and brick buildings in 1890 and 1891 on the ashes of the city that burned in 1889. Nearly all the largest structures, including the Auditorium with the nation's largest theatrical stage, had been foreclosed in the panic of 1893. But as these buildings passed from receivers back to private owners after the panic, Spokane stood as a sturdy, inspiring metropolis when migrants poured into eastern Washington. The major urban place between Minneapolis and Puget Sound, Spokane—with its tall buildings and waterfall—awed travelers who had seen nothing from train windows for days but dusty

Hatched areas show annexations to Spokane between 1881 and 1930. Spurred by rapid growth during its immigrant rush, 1896 to 1910, Spokane annexed many districts that lay nearly vacant until after World War II. The unannexed peninsula, upper right, is Great Northern property, left out of the city because the railroad threatened to shut down its shops there if required to pay city taxes. (Based on maps by the Spokane city plan commission. Drawn by Julie Ross, Eastern Washington University cartographic laboratory.)

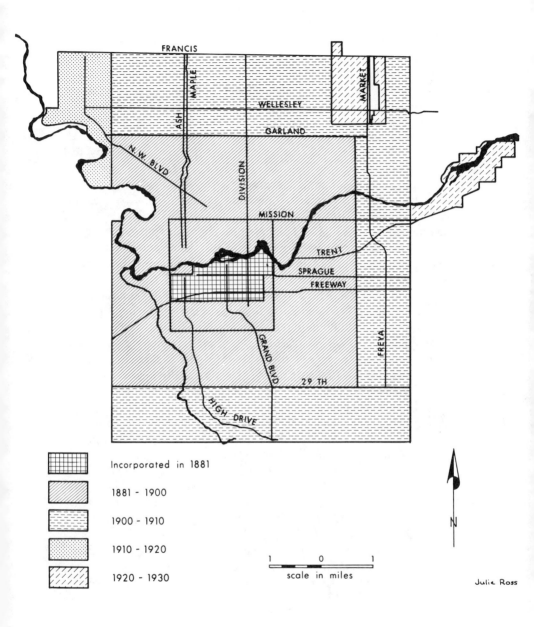

FRANCIS

ASH

MAPLE

WELLESLEY

MARKET

GARLAND

N.W. BLVD

DIVISION

MISSION

TRENT

SPRAGUE

FREEWAY

FREYA

GRAND BLVD

29 TH

HIGH DRIVE

	Incorporated in 1881
	1881 - 1900
	1900 - 1910
	1910 - 1920
	1920 - 1930

1   0   1
scale in miles

N

Julie Ross

The Railroads: Beneficent, Malignant, Fickle 41

one-street, false-fronted frame hamlets, unpainted, sunbaked, and inert. Between 1900 and 1910, the city continued to build impressive downtown blocks—the Empire State, Hutton, Paulsen, Palace, and Old National Bank—and it offered theaters, restaurants, stores, attorneys (250 in 1900 and 372 by 1910), physicians (112 in 1900 and 269 in 1910), and dentists for patronage by residents of the surrounding country. In 1907 Spokane virtually doubled its land area from 20.25 square miles to 37.25 by annexing five large tracts platted by real estate promoters.[33]

In Spokane County three-fourths of the population lived in towns—more than half in Spokane—but even in bucolic areas, urban centralizing was evident. In Yakima County, one in three lived in the city of Yakima; in Walla Walla, the pioneer farming area, 60 percent lived in town. Smaller towns (less than 2,500 residents) doubled between 1900 and 1910—before automobiles inexorably phased them out by lengthening a day's travel to more than a horse-and-wagon round-trip from farm to town. The apogee of rural population expansion was passed in eastern Washington by 1910. Except for the remotest areas, rural populations stabilized or declined after that while towns grew.

As symbols and defenders of their presumed singularity, the important towns had newspapers. It is almost possible to trace railroad expansion by the locations of newspapers, especially because railroad managers sometimes hired editors to start newspapers at likely townsites, hoping to entice settlers and merchants—to build a town, in effect, around the newspaper. Along the Northern Pacific route, one could read the *Yakima Republic,* the *Yakima Record,* and the *Spokan Times,* founded in 1879; the *Cheney Sentinel* and *Pasco Pilot,* 1881; *Sprague Herald,* 1882; Ritzville *Adams County Record,* 1885, and *Times,* 1887; and the Lind *Adams County Leader,* 1900. The formal incorporation of these towns often followed founding of a newspaper by two to five years, when editor, residents, and railroad agreed that a town, in fact, existed.[34]

At the height of migration to eastern Washington, a fourth transcontinental railroad, the Chicago, Milwaukee and St. Paul, surveyed its ill-conceived western extension to the Pacific Coast, passing through parts of the state not directly served by the Northern Pacific, Great Northern, and Union Pacific (recently extended to Yakima by a system called the North Coast, intended to be a major line). In central Whitman County, the Milwaukee chose Malden as headquarters for its division between Idaho and the Cascades. Malden came into being when farmers donated land for a townsite laid out by the Milwaukee Land Company, the railroad's subsidiary. The donors regarded the

Milwaukee as guarantor of their prosperity, and Malden, with round-house, offices, and railroad employees' houses, was a rousing town of a thousand for perhaps three decades, until the railroad moved away. Malden boasted five hotels (one, rooms with baths, was said to cost $90,000), two lumberyards, a telephone system, and two banks.[35]

Towns more experienced than Malden had turned less hospitable to railroads. For one, Spokane declared the Milwaukee would not be franchised to enter the city until it pledged terminal rates, but backed down when the railroad shrugged that it would pass by Spokane. The Milwaukee's principal shipping points in eastern Washington remained small while better sites on earlier railroads grew. The Milwaukee Land Company auctioned lots in the new towns in 1908, Malden, Marengo, Palisade, Kenova, Seabury, and Kittitas. By the mid-twenties the long trains no longer stopped at small stations and automobiles were taking over shorter hauls.

Spokane's attempt to blackmail the Milwaukee into terminal rates showed a hardening of citizens' attitudes toward railroads, evident as well in continuous attempts to regulate them. Farmers' associations and city merchants had advocated regulation for years, but Washington's first positive step was passage of an act in 1890 by the first state legislature to fix ceilings on freight rates for wheat and other important agricultural commodities, tying rates to those in effect on December 31, 1890. But railroads that evaded the law were guilty only of a misdemeanor. The law was tightened in 1891 over the governor's veto, and again in 1893.[36]

Legislators from eastern Washington regularly demanded a state regulatory agency, often with a governor's support. Populist Governor John R. Rogers asserted that "the people have for years been entitled to relief from excessive charges. . . . The wind raised by the passage through these [legislative] halls by railroad attorneys has toppled over legislature after legislature."[37]

Bills for a railroad commission failed in each session between 1893 and 1905, although the legislators from rural counties passed a measure in 1893 requiring railroads to fence their tracks to protect livestock, but in 1905 the legislature approved a three-man commission (salaries: $4,000 a year) with powers to inspect and evaluate railroad company accounts and order reasonable rates upon hearing a complaint. One of the members of this first commission, former Whatcom County prosecutor and legislator H. A. Fairchild, wrote the bill. Another member, J. C. Lawrence, had been state superintendent of public instruction, land office employee at Waterville, and warehouse owner and banker at Garfield; he cut an important figure in farming towns of eastern Washington, often proposed for public office.

The commission proceeded conscientiously. Its members visited other states, held town meetings to hear opinions in farm areas, and asked for annual reports from the railroads. Its valuation study published in 1909—despite strenuous efforts to gather information, and based in part on estimates of future traffic—revealed serious inadequacies. The Northern Pacific and the Oregon Railroad and Navigation Company advised the commission that incomplete records prevented them from supplying data on their original investments in construction, tracklaying, and equipment.[38]

The report offered the first comprehensive review of railroad operations for citizens of the state, but it told them what they already knew: railroads were expensive to build and operate, their interlocking ownerships a maze, and their construction financed almost entirely from bonds.

The report disclosed that more than 40 percent of the Northern Pacific and Great Northern freight consisted of lumber (mainly from western Washington); 18 to 20 percent grains; and very small percentages of fresh fruits, mostly consigned out of state. The Oregon Railroad and Navigation Company hauled approximately 30 percent grain, nearly all to Portland, 15 percent lumber, and 3 percent logs. These figures delineated the differences in commerce going to Portland and to Puget Sound.[39]

The commission complained that the Great Northern failed to maintain its trackage between 1900 and 1906, causing numerous accidents; in the next two years the railroad spent $10 million in repairs. A section of the report written by Fairchild observed that the Northern Pacific in Washington enjoyed "more than a reasonable return" on its investment.

While the commission's findings furnished farmers and merchants their ammunition for some years in seeking better schedules and lower rates, the report also confirmed the precedence of western over eastern Washington, for lumber from the western slopes of the Cascades accounted for nearly half the revenues of the Northern Pacific and Great Northern. In attempts to regulate railroads, eastern critically needed the support of western Washington. Westside businessmen and legislators felt no reciprocal need; they were confident of enough power to proceed on their own.

Until the commission attempted to regulate railroads, the bulk of railroad litigation in the state's courts had been farmer and merchant associations suing for alleged rate discrimination and the land-title cases. (Had there been no railroads and no moneylenders, the legal paraphernalia of the state could have been considerably reduced.) With a railroad commission, however, the impetus of litigation reversed. Now railroads were plaintiffs, suing to enjoin commission orders, and soon for relief from tax assessments.

The commission, in an attempt to relate grain rates to the costs of service, ordered the railroads to coordinate wheat shipments between lines and charge a single rate, the Joint Wheat Order. The Northern Pacific, Great Northern, and Oregon Railroad and Navigation contested the order in different courts, delaying enforcement until March 1909, when the state supreme court upheld the commission. (Under the law, the burden lay with the railroads to demonstrate the order unreasonable.)[40]

By this time the pace of railroad construction was slowing, rolling stock needed replacing, engines and cars were aging, and freight cars were often too few. Railroads across the United States, in general, needed repairs to roadbeds and renovation of their equipment. In Spokane hundreds of railroad workers were laid off after 1910. The construction era was over.

Opening of the Panama Canal in 1914 brought lower water-freight rates and faster sea shipments from west to east coast. Chicago, Minneapolis, and other large midwestern railroad centers, fearful that their industries might move to coastal cities, supported railroad company petitions to the federal Interstate Commerce Commission for lower rates to meet water competitors. The railroads did not reduce their rates to Spokane or other intermountain cities. Forgetting their railroad parentage, inland cities sued in the courts, petitioned the commission, and badgered their congressmen for rate relief. The railroads contended that cities such as Spokane usually got the best of it in these suits. On its own initiative, the Interstate Commerce Commission launched a grain-rate study that produced fifty-three thousand pages of transcript and twenty-three commission orders, but continued the so-called Columbia Basin differential, imposing a 10 percent higher rate to Seattle on shippers in eastern Washington south of the Snake.[41] Some commission orders afforded relief, but it was mixed, for the commission faced the fact that railroads somehow had to compete with seaships.

If terminal rate disputes ever were resolved, they were settled in a time when railroads were entering a decline, although none was yet apparent in their traffic or political influence. The railroads' hopes for new traffic now depended on developing the areas along their tracks rather than building into new territories or cutting rates. In answer to calls for better service, Jim Hill declared that if all the rails needed could be laid, they would require two-thirds of the nation's annual steel production, and the "labor . . . for such ordinary extensions and improvements as are now being made is not to be had in sufficient quantity on any terms." At the same time, an assistant general superintendent of the Northern Pacific observed that the company had reached its limit of service as a one-track line. And motor trucks were taking some business from the railroads; by 1921 the legislature would act to regulate them.[42]

In many eastern Washington counties, railroads continued to be the single largest businesses and property owners. Continually strapped for revenues and limited by the state's reliance on property taxes, counties often levied heavy assessments against railroads. The railroad's proportion of the tax burden varied wildly from county to county. Statewide, the state, county, and municipal governments collected from 8.8 to 10 percent of their annual revenues from railroads between 1922 and 1929, but such counties as Franklin, Adams, and Grant demanded 44 to 52 percent of their tax money from railroad companies. Franklin in 1929 assessed railroad property at $272,670 and all other real property in the county at $179,463. Established grain counties such as Whitman, Lincoln, and Walla Walla generally expected 16 to 20 percent of their incomes from railroad taxes, and Yakima, 9 percent.[43]

In 1925 the Northern Pacific filed suit in Thurston County against the state and twenty-three counties, paying only part of its taxes under protest, but did not pursue the case. With the Milwaukee and the Spokane, Portland and Seattle, the Northern Pacific also filed nine suits against alleged inequable taxation in federal district court, asking relief from assessments of 1924 and following years. The Great Northern paid its taxes under protest; the Oregon Railroad and Navigation Company neither protested nor paid. Consolidated, the cases dragged through 1932, when the courts refused the railroads the relief they asked. The litigation embarrassed taxing districts that could not raise revenues sufficient to pay their operating costs.[44]

By this time it was clear that the glory days of railroading were past. The Great Northern had begun abandoning feeder lines as early as 1917. From the 1930s onward, railroads would not pioneer new districts but would struggle to maintain a decaying network of rails and compete with highway and air carriers. Gone were messianic railroad potentates such as Villard and Hill, and in their place was corporate bureaucracy. Before long, railroad officers would not ponder what they might do next to exploit the land but rather what they must do to stay in business.[45]

CHAPTER 3

The Grain Trade

On its stationery, the LaCrosse office of the Pacific Coast Elevator Company advertised the wheat country in red and black: "The land of never failing crops, of high wages, of happy and contented people." A patchwork of grain and fallow soil, Washington's wheatlands seemed endless, deep-rooted, changeless. But the solid hardworking people were servants rather than masters of the land they had come deliberately to tame.

From its earliest settlement, the inland region had to export its wheat (except for the most disastrous crop years, the United States always produced a surplus of wheat), and selling their wheat tangled farmers in a web spun by exporters and millers and caught them in the competition for commercial ascendancy between Portland and Puget Sound. Railroads fed the contest. The Northern Pacific at first intended to ship eastern Washington wheat to the great milling centers of the Middle West, an intention disparaged by John Muir, the railroad's superintendent of traffic at Portland, as "more for effect and to show a spirit of liberality than anything else," but the Oregon Railway and Navigation Company's rates to Portland soon forced the Northern Pacific to turn to Portland, too. "This change, while satisfactory to the merchants of Portland (because it protects their business) will create more or less dissatisfaction east of the mountains," Muir observed. Dissatisfaction was hardly the word for the feelings of farmers; for half a century, Washington wheat growers trod as near to revolt as they dared.[1]

Markets, transportation, wheat diseases, weather, and the costs of machinery—the Washington wheat farmer wrestled them all. Sometimes his frustrations led him to think of throwing it all aside. In such a mood, one farmer offered to trade two sections—1,280 acres—for a new Rambler bicycle. Yet in the good years, the wheat farmer prospered. Wheat, the pioneer crop for much of the West, was comparatively easy to grow; the country's soil, moisture, and temperatures were suited to wheat; and wheat was competitive.[2]

To sell his wheat, the eastern Washington grower had to find his place in a well-established world grain trade. As the *Seattle Times* put it, "When the Chinaman eats wheat, the farmer will wear diamonds." In earliest territorial days, a few intrepid men in the Walla Walla country—Philip Ritz, Samuel Wait, and Dorsey Baker among them—sold personally to New York or Liverpool buyers; they were substantial men in an elemental commercial period. Few dryland farmers of eastern Washington, working with seven or eight hundred acres, could afford such risks or even find their way through the tiers of buyers, exporters, carriers, and manufacturers rapidly forming as national combines by consolidation and merger. How could the individual grower penetrate a market in which a twenty-nine-year-old with a million dollars could attempt a corner and, when confronted by the packing magnate Philip D. Armour, in a single hour of selling drop the Chicago price from $1.85 to 20 cents a bushel? It was whispered that only intervention by bankers into Joseph Leiter's raid on grain futures staved off a world wheat panic.[3]

The Columbia River grain fleet—ugly, flat-bottomed hulls like wagon beds—increased from five to eighty-one vessels, floating wheat downriver to Portland while the railroads opened millions of acres too far from the rivers to ship by water. For nearly twenty years, farmers planted an average of 100,000 new acres each year to wheat in eastern Washington. The state's annual harvest rose from about nine million bushels in 1890 to nearly 26 million by 1900, and by 1910 to nearly 37 million, seven-eighths of it reaped in eight counties: Lincoln, Whitman, Adams, Walla Walla, Douglas, Grant, Franklin, and Spokane.[4]

Portland merchants had participated in the grain trade for thirty years, dealing chiefly with San Francisco, New York, and Liverpool, and they perceived the flood of grain from eastern Washington as their opportunity to displace San Francisco as the principal grain port of the Pacific Coast, especially because California growers plowed under wheat for vegetable and fruit crops. The wheat traffic through Portland warranted formation of large handling and processing companies that grew bigger as the flow increased.

A step or two behind Portland, the grain business of Puget Sound also enlarged—often handled by branches of Portland companies—

while nascent combines of millers and commercial bakers extended the possibilities for big sales. To ensure their supply and enlarge milling capacity, the coastal exporting and milling companies opened or bought eastern Washington warehouses and mills until the wheat districts smothered in subsidiaries chained to Portland and Puget Sound. Except for a lonely few, the rural mills that once ground for hometown patrons and nearby farmers closed or were swallowed.

The first truly international exporter to locate in Portland was the Scot shipper and trader, Balfour, Guthrie and Company, which sent W. J. Burns to Oregon in 1877 to open a one-man office, doubtless attracted by Portland's commerce with Liverpool and the impending resumption of Northern Pacific construction. Burns, with his special knowledge of the Pacific Northwest, would be president of the company from 1911 to 1925. Balfour, Guthrie had been established in San Francisco for nearly a decade, and by 1881 was also exporting from Puget Sound. Through its Interior Warehouse Company, the trader placed warehouses along railroad lines in eastern Washington, and in 1901 bought the string of sixteen warehouses in Whitman and Latah (Idaho) counties operated by the Palouse merchant, investor, and moneylender Aaron Kuhn. Ten years later Balfour, Guthrie opened Crown Mills at Portland, adding the refurbished Lamar mill near Walla Walla the next year, enabling the company to deal in wheat or flour.[5]

Balfour, Guthrie would remain strong in the export trade until about 1938, when it shifted to a domestic business. It pioneered the marketing pattern that others adopted: buying offices in the larger inland towns, agents in the countryside to dicker for wheat directly with farmers, delivery to its own warehouses, exporting, and grinding wheat into flour for domestic and foreign sales. Balfour, Guthrie also wrote mortgages for farmers secured by future crops.

In the eleven years after Balfour, Guthrie reached Portland, two Oregon companies emerged as major factors in the grain market: the Portland Flouring Mills, founded in 1884, and Kerr, Gifford and Company. The Portland Flouring Mills, organized by the pioneer Oregon banking firm of Ladd and Tilton, absorbed bankrupt mills at Portland, Oregon City, and Salem. The bank assigned an employee, Theodore B. Wilcox, to manage its mills. Directed by Wilcox for thirty years, Portland Flouring Mills became one of the largest private grain-handling companies in the Pacific Northwest. Through subsidiaries—the Seattle Flour Mills, Puget Sound Flour Mills, Puget Sound Warehouse Company, Pacific Coast Elevator Company, and others—the Portland Flouring Mills bought or built more than two hundred country warehouses and opened buying offices. To increase its milling capacity, it acquired Tacoma, Seattle, and Spokane mills and nine modern country mills (including those at Walla Walla, Prescott, Lind, and Odessa). The company's storage and milling plants at Portland occupied 19 acres with 900 feet of waterfront above Swan Island.[6]

Kerr, Gifford and Company, formed in 1888 by Peter Kerr and associates, also opened buying agencies in Spokane and country towns and bought country mills to produce flour and feed. Eventually Kerr, Gifford expanded nationwide, keeping its headquarters in Portland, with offices in the major cities of the Pacific Coast, in New York, Kansas City, and Winnipeg.[7]

Shortly after the organization of Kerr, Gifford, a well-established midwestern firm, F. H. Peavey and Company, constructed a one-million-bushel grain elevator at Albina, a port area soon incorporated into Portland, and, as the Pacific Coast Elevator Company (sold after ten years to Portland Flouring Mills), rapidly built a network of twenty-nine country elevators along the routes of the Oregon Railway and Navigation Company, at Dayton, Walla Walla, Farmington, Colfax, Waitsburg, Garfield, Pomeroy, Guy, Diamond, Truax, Endicott, Elberton, Tekoa, and Oakesdale—storage points ranging in capacity from 25,000 to 75,000 bushels. Although Peavey entered milling in midwestern and eastern states in 1928, its Pacific Coast business remained grain handling.[8]

A Portland wholesale grocery run by three brothers, with feed mill, oatmeal, graham, and rye plants, enlarged after 1902 into Albers Brothers, whose reputation would rest mainly on manufacturing cereals and pancake flours. Albers Brothers Milling Company expanded to San Francisco and Los Angeles by mergers, and to Seattle, Tacoma, and Bellingham by purchases. Its capital stock paid a 100 percent dividend in 1919. Ten years later, Carnation Milk Products Company acquired Albers.[9]

With the extension of the Northern Pacific to Puget Sound and completion of the Great Northern, inland grain in quantity reached Puget Sound mills. Balfour, Guthrie is said to have shipped the first full cargo of wheat from Puget Sound (Tacoma) in 1881, and although lumber remained the Sound's major cargo, flour milling grew during the nineties. One of Seattle's large early companies, Centennial Mills, had been started in Spokane in 1889 by Moritz Thomsen, a former Danish sea captain financed in milling by Dutch investors. Thomsen diligently expanded his business and in 1894 moved to Seattle. He remained at the head of Centennial for forty-three years, making his company powerful in western bakery and Asian grain trades. To expand milling capacity, Thomsen bought control of the Tacoma Grain Company and mills at Portland, Wenatchee, Vancouver, Sprague, Ritzville, Creston, and Reardan in the Northwest and at Kobe, Japan. Tacoma Grain operated forty inland warehouses for Centennial, and in partnership with Seattle Grain (acquired in 1920 from Portland Flouring Mills) and the Pacific Coast Biscuit Company, Centennial also controlled the Northern Grain and Warehouse Company, which leased more than one hundred wheat-country warehouses with a combined capacity of five million bushels.[10]

Centennial made and sold some of the best-known household flours in the West: Big Loaf, Gold Drop, and a line of breakfast cereals that included Wheat Manna and Uncle Sam's Rolled Oats. Many a farmer who sold his wheat to a Centennial agent bought it back for his kitchen and his breakfast table.

In time, Seattle rose to first place in the Northwest in exporting flour, and Portland dominated the trade in wheat. The Pacific Northwest produced about 10 percent of the wheat but accounted for 20 percent or more of the nation's grain exports. Perhaps large investments in Puget Sound mills, and arbitrary railroad rates, bound Seattle to emphasize flour in its international commerce; its flours went principally to California, the Orient, and eventually to Central and South America.[11]

Although Portland was connected by rail to California before 1890, less than 20 percent of the Pacific Northwest wheat crop moved outside the Northwest by rail—considerably less in many years—except in wartime, when coastal shipping seemed precarious. When the grain trade of the region was well established, more than 80 percent of the wheat exported from Washington and Oregon loaded at Columbia River ports (Longview and Astoria accounted for perhaps 3 percent, and Portland the rest) while more than 64 percent of the flour went from Seattle.[12]

Although the California-based Sperry Milling Company, the largest flouring firm on the Pacific Coast, did not enter the Northwest under its own name until it bought the Creston mill in 1916 and built a large Spokane mill in 1918, Sperry merged in 1904 with the Tacoma Warehouse and Elevator Company, which dealt throughout the wheat country. Sperry, too, produced well-known brands: Drifted Snow household flour and Wheat Hearts cereal.[13]

Seattle also supported smaller companies: a hay trader and mill reorganized as Charles H. Lilly, flour miller, in 1905, the Seattle Flouring Mills, successor to the pioneer Hammond Milling Company, and others.[14]

The company that would dominate Seattle's flouring industry was founded in 1911 by Oliver W. Fisher, a miller from the age of twelve, who moved to Seattle from Montana. Fisher's family dynasty, Fisher Flouring Mills Company, blended hard Montana with soft Washington wheats by a silk-sifting process to make Fisher's Blend, a famed all-purpose flour, as well as feeds and cereals. The company maintained warehouses and resident buyers in three states. By the midtwenties, it was buying $7.5 million worth of grains a year and its Seattle elevators and mills occupied five acres with loading docks at Harbor Island, a man-made island at the estuary of the Duwamish River.

With the approaching completion of the Panama Canal in 1914, Seattle voters in 1911 approved forming a port district and a commission to develop a public harbor, and the following year voted $15 million in bonds for port construction. Between 1913 and 1924, the commission directed a massive port project, including the Hanford Street elevator, completed in 1915 to hold 500,000 bushels of wheat (and enlarged within ten years for 1,500,000) with adjacent wharf space for 300,000 more bushels in sacks. Oddly enough, until the district built a belt railway, the public docks were virtually without rail service. The Northern Pacific and Great Northern went to Fisher and Lilly but not to public docks. Perhaps 60 percent of Seattle's export business continued to pass through private wharves, but the district strengthened Seattle's role as a Pacific port, especially significant in Asian trade.[15]

Portland also enlarged its public harbor. In 1910 its voters approved creation of a tripartite dock commission (port, state, and city) and $2.5 million in bonds, augmented by $3 million more in 1917 and $5 million in 1918, for an extensive municipal terminal on 153 acres at the lower end of Portland's frontage on the Willamette. After World War I, Portland rebuilt its Willamette waterfront to handle cross-river automobile traffic, create railway grade separations, and eliminate aged wooden docks.[16]

The large coastal mills and buyers wove the Washington wheat farmer into the fabric of their trade. The individual farmer rarely grasped the intricacy of brokering and milling; he had little appreciation for the money reserves necessary to buy and store grains, meshing charter-ship schedules with delivery contracts, changes in world wheat supply (although newspapers often reported them), and the other practical aspects of the grain trade. The farmer knew well, however, that he was spending more money to raise wheat and getting less for it, and as he distrusted the railroads he also distrusted exporting and milling combines, partly because they were large. He believed they fixed prices, limited his sales outlets, overestimated the dirt and smut in his grain for grading, and generally lorded over him. The country mills outside the combines were neither numerous nor large enough to offer an alternative market. By 1922, more than 40 percent of the Pacific Northwest's milling was sited in Seattle, Portland, and Spokane, and much of the rest was the production of inland mills owned by coastal firms.[17]

Independent mills survived, such as F. M. Martin and Company, a middle-sized plant established in 1908 at Cheney by a former implement dealer, which sold Martin's Best flour in Spokane and the surrounding area. To compete with white blended flours, Martin bleached his—and for years battled whispers that bleaching poisoned his flour. And other local brands were popular: Colville's Top Notch and Yakima Flour's Miller's Best. But these were exceptions. When Washington State's Bureau of Statistics and Immigration surveyed the business needs of eastern Washington towns, thirty-nine wanted flour mills.[18]

Millers and exporters, for their part, were tied to the varieties of wheat suited to the region, and eastern Washington's farmers continually changed, trying to find the best-selling, hardiest strains—and soon those resistant to disease as well. At times, seventy different kinds of wheat were grown simultaneously, more than 60 percent of them soft varieties with low gluten content, unsatisfactory by themselves for commercial breadmaking. Wheat falls into two general classes: the hard, suited for breads and breakfast cereals, and the soft, for cake and pastry flours. Washington's major mills customarily used harder wheats from western and central Montana to blend with softer Washington varieties, and exporters sold abroad those varieties least suited for American trade.

When pioneer wheatgrowers spread across the Palouse into the Big Bend, they first raised a variety known as Little Club in the Palouse, one called Bluestem in the Big Bend (adaptable to dry counties), and Red Chaff in the transition zone between. Some seeded Turkey, Russian, and other strains that had produced well in the states they emigrated from. These were primarily spring wheats, one harvest a year, and when farmers tried them as winter wheat for increased annual yields, more than half their plantings froze out, requiring them to reseed. The dryland farmer typically planted only half his land, letting the other lie fallow. Only in the thirties would the practice change in the Palouse, when studies showed that the ground held moisture without fallowing and that unseeded land was more susceptible to wind and water erosion.[19]

Despite frequent switching, no standard strain prevailed, but beginning in 1894, W. J. Spillman, next Claude Lawrence, and then a succession of other scientists at the agricultural experiment station in Pullman, experimented with grain genetics, producing hybrids with desirable characteristics. As one of these men, E. F. Gaines (for whom a wheat would be named), observed, "Building new wheats is a continuous process," because growing conditions change: a strain falls to disease, tractors plow deeper, chemical fertilizers increase yields, and so on. Improved strains, distributed to farmers, would be popular for a decade or more before a new one appeared. For example, Hybrid 128 accounted for perhaps 20 percent of Washington's wheat production between 1918 and 1925.[20]

Early in the twentieth century, a wheat disease known as "stinking smut" blackened Washington fields. Infected wheats produced clusters of black spores in grain heads. Scattered in threshing, spores blew miles in a wind, sprouted in warm, moist ground, and contaminated new fields. Farmers treated seed to control smut. Buyers penalized farmers for smut in grain, and by 1912 smut was a chief concern at meetings among growers, shippers, and millers. The agricultural experiment station, over eleven years, developed hard Ridit, which proved to be smut-free, hardy, with a plump kernel, and eventually was adopted by many Washington farmers and distributed to growers in other nations. The station shortly after released Albit, a soft strain resistant to smut, which replaced Hybrid 128 "with all the desirable characteristics that Spillman sought in the old days," declared Gaines, "winter hardiness, stiff straw, non-shatterability, and good yield."[21]

For farmers and brokers, continuous changes in wheat varieties posed selling problems: crops varied in quality from year to year and softer grains brought lower prices. Exporters resisted unfamiliar strains. A Dakota farm editor estimated that before World War I, Pacific Coast prices had approximated 88 percent of those paid midwestern growers, but after the war, with improved strains and marketing, western prices sometimes exceeded all others.[22]

Indicative of the evolving practices of wheat growing, a 1939 survey would count thirty-seven varieties in use in eastern Washington, twenty-one of them new since 1918, and find that the proportions of winter to spring wheat changed almost every year.[23]

While farmers tested wheat varieties, exporters and millers elevated Washington to a place of importance in world grain trading—a fluctuating marketplace, fiercely competitive. Exports of wheat from Pacific Coast ports, escalating in 1907, remained vigorous (if not steadily enlarging) until World War I, and wheat production increased nearly every year between 1907 and 1919. From 1911 to 1919, Washington harvested more than 40 million bushels a year. From 1895 to 1910, production had averaged only a little more than 26 million.[24]

During harvest, workers slept on straw and sacks in the fields; one man in the crew drove to town daily for repairs, parts, food, and supplies; and crews often changed overnight, "new men constantly being hired as not many cared to work long in the harvest fields." As one farmer recalled, one of the "longest and most unpleasant jobs was delivering the wheat. . . . It took from August to November to get the grain into the warehouse. The road had many steep grades and was full of chuckholes. We could haul only twenty-five sacks on a wagon pulled by four horses and it took a full day to make the round trip."[25]

When the farmer delivered his wheat, he often did not sell outright but took warehouses receipts for it. The receipts were treated as negotiable, like money, and could serve as collateral for loans.[26]

Although Washington was emerging as a wheat supplier, some of its methods surprisingly lagged behind those of other wheat-producing areas. Until the twenties, virtually all of Washington's wheat was sacked for delivery, even as bulk elevators at Astoria echoed empty; in bountiful years, warehouses overflowed and wheat sacks lined railroad tracks for miles. Undoubtedly their large investment in warehouses induced buyers to specify delivery in sacks. But farmers found bulk grain tanks dangerous to maneuver on hillsides, and they rarely could afford trucks for bulk shipment. Roads were bad. Wagonloads of sacked wheat bumped from farm to warehouse; truckloads tore up roads, broke axles and wheels, and mired in mud. Railroads pleaded chronic shortages of tank cars. Sometimes they shipped on flatcars with tarpaulins tied over loose grain.

Moreover, most of the wheat consigned to domestic and foreign markets moved by ocean vessel, and until World War I, sailing ships dominated coastal fleets. Shipmasters refused to load bulk wheat for fear it would shift in rough waters and capsize their vessels; they could mix cargoes of flour in barrels and wheat in sacks.

All of these conditions, and habitude, persuaded farmers to sack their wheat, but sacks were expensive, sometimes almost impossible to buy. Several state administrations tried to increase sack and twine supplies by making them at the penitentiary. With 550 convicts so employed, the penitentiary profited. But the farmers accused the warden of setting bag prices, and finally, when it became a political liability, bag manufacture was dropped. A warehousemen's war was a bonus—a war such as the one at Garfield where the price of a sack fell briefly from 8.5 half cents to a penny. Usually sacks were dear. Wheat in sacks was customarily graded, cleaned, and bulked—if graded and bulked at all—at seaports where buyers penalized farmers for dirty or low-quality grain. Until he received a report of the grade, the farmer could only guess his return, and if penalized for dirt or paid less than expected, he believed himself cheated.[27]

During the war, when grain sacks cost 25 cents each in lots of one million ("probably the best argument yet for bulk handling," said a newspaper), large crops and good prices allowed farmers to overlook sack prices and supplies. But after the war, bulk shipping spread rapidly, advocated by farmer's wheat-marketing cooperatives. These new organizations owned few warehouses to amortize; they asserted that bulk shipments returned higher profit to the farmer, and that by pooling grain they could stabilize prices.[28]

Associations of farmers were hardly a new idea. Farmers had banded together in every section of inland Washington against railroads, against taxes, for education and fraternity, and so on. United Palouse farmers persuaded Jim Hill, Charles Mellen, and A. H. Mohler of the Oregon Railway and Navigation Company to come to Colfax together to talk about railway rates. They heard many promises but got little action.[29]

And farmers tried pooling. When one near Sprague won first prize for his wheat at the St. Louis fair, his neighbors, relying on his notoriety, pooled their 1904 harvest to sell 300,000 bushels at three cents above market quotations. But they did it only once. A Farmers Grain and Supply Company based in Spokane proposed a pooled Puget Sound elevator. It was never built. In 1909 to promote membership the Farmers Union leased forty warehouses and bought sacks and twine in carload lots. Union warehouses operated in almost every county of eastern Washington, nearly all of them stock companies that converted to cooperatives under federal or state laws, with notable exceptions such as the Union Elevator and Warehouse Company of Lind, founded by stockholders in 1906 and conducted as an independent for more than three-quarters of a century. And from 1911 to 1921 the Pacific Northwest Tri-State Company, stockholder owned, acted as a grain-selling agency in Seattle for a score of eastside local associations, but expired with formation of the Washington Wheat Growers Association.[30]

The Cheney Union Warehouse Company, which included men from the Farmers Grain and Supply, erected a 15,000-bushel bulk elevator at Cheney, thinking it the first cooperative bulk storage in the Pacific Northwest. By 1920 Washington State counted fifty-five cooperative grain elevators and warehouses.[31] Two years later, despite frequent complaints about warehouse practices, the State Department of Public Works virtually had abandoned its attempts to regulate warehouse accounts or practices. Too complex. Too variable.[32]

After the war, export brokers also replaced sack warehouses with bulk storage at seaports, and chartered steam vessels for economic bulk hauling by the Panama Canal to Atlantic and European customers.

The Washington Wheat Growers Association, and its parent, the Northwest Wheat Growers Association, formed immediately after the war with a promotional campaign led by Aaron Sapiro, a San Francisco attorney who had shepherded California citrus growers into a powerful marketing organization. Invited by the Washington Farmers Union, Sapiro spoke in union and town halls during 1919 and 1920, explaining the advantages of unified marketing. He closed each meeting by reading a four-page contract and urging farmers to sign before leaving. As the Colfax Gazette recognized, "reliable men" stood on both sides, some supporting and some opposing wheat pools. At a meeting in Colfax, about two hundred attended, but only thirty-five signed contracts; at Pullman, forty-four signed.[33]

The Washington association intended to ally with growers in Idaho, Oregon, and other states to form a subsidiary warehouse company, expecting that warehouse receipts would provide collateral for loans to the association, allowing it to pay growers part of their money before wheat had sold. With sales offices in Portland, Seattle, and Ogden, the association entered the market in 1920. By the end of the next year, its manager, George C. Jewett (not the Jewett of Potlatch Lumber), reported the pool had sold 15 million bushels of the 1920 crop but explained that "considerable wheat was lost [to the association] because of chattel mortgages and demands that the grain be marketed immediately so that the spot market price could be secured for application on debts." In other words, farmers needed quick cash to meet their debts and, regardless of the theoretical advantages of pooling, could not afford to wait for orderly selling.[34]

In addition to farmers' debts, the association faced other troubles. Prices fell so fast in 1920 that Jewett had to ask some farmers to pay back some of the money they had already received. Fearing continued price collapses, farmers preferred to sell quickly for themselves, and a number refused to deliver their crops to the association, arguing that they had signed membership applications rather than contracts. The association, near disintegration, was forced to sue four Whitman County growers as a test case of alleged failure to deliver 1922 crops, and, when the association won, its show of enforcing contracts made farmers even less willing to sign contracts that bound them for seven years. Farmers who stayed in the association got prices 14 percent higher than they probably would have received selling outside the pool, and the association handled increasing volumes of wheat (one million bushels in 1920 rose to 12 million in 1922) but increased its volume by extending eastward, selling Montana grain in 1921 and Dakota in 1922. Although its plan from the start had been to expand into other states, with the goal of a national pool, the association's Washington, Idaho, and Oregon members concluded that by selling Montana and Dakota wheat their association competed against them. Idaho's association disbanded early in 1924, and by the end of that year, Oregon's and Washington's had also broken up.[35]

Meanwhile, in 1921 a central wheat sales agency formed at Kansas City, Missouri—later named the United States Grain Growers, Inc.—with approval of the American Farm Bureau Federation, and Jewett was elected one of its vice-presidents. Almost immediately, disputes flared over compulsory pooling (after all, the pool had sued its members in Washington), and many large growers' groups dropped away. The farm bureau called for the agency's reorganization, but by 1924 the central pool expired. Wheat pools would continue regionally active through the twenties in the Dakotas, Minnesota, Indiana, Nebraska, Oklahoma, Kansas, and Texas until federally sponsored marketing cooperatives replaced them. But other than small, local, temporary pools (the Whitman County farm bureau bought sacks as a pool in 1928), the pools were dead in Washington, where the system had started.[36]

Compulsory pooling, however necessary for cooperative selling, seemed to violate farmer customs. Growers especially resisted holding grain for orderly selling. Washington farmers traditionally sold soon after harvest. Waiting was not their nature. But there were other factors that broke up the pool movement. Farms were bigger and investments in machines substantial, and whether prices went up or down, the individual farmer felt compelled to use his machines for greater production to make headway against his debts. During the war years (1917–19), Washington farmers produced an average of 32 million bushels a year; from 1920 through 1929, they averaged 41 million bushels (fewer than 25 million in 1924 but more than 50 million in 1923 and 1927).

Wheat growing had become an uncertain business; the lower the price, the more the farmer felt he had to produce. Farmers became pessimistic. If this year was good, next would surely be bad. And a subtler, perhaps unrecognized element affected the wheat business: the automobile, the telephone, and the radio allowed farmers to learn quickly the extent of disasters in the market. No longer could one failure be regarded as an individual tragedy. Many growers quit. And with machines that could cover larger areas, their neighbors bought their land.

Field machines appeared in Washington's wheat areas almost from the first; reapers, harvesters, binders, and other machines were in general use in California, and in the Walla Walla and Palouse sections of Washington, before the emergence of Washington's dryland wheat growing. Before machines, threshing had been earthily primitive. "About 25 or 30 wild horses were run over the grain for three or four hours and then the grain was put in a pile until the wind blew the chaff away," one farmer recalled. Another: "A threshing ground was prepared by removing some dirt from a tract of ground, making it slope toward the center. This threshing ground was tamped down until it was quite hard, then wheat piled on it, and the boys and girls of the family rode horses over it until the grain was threshed."[37]

But by the mid-eighties, combined reapers and threshers, pulled by horses or mules, had become familiar in Walla Walla and Snake river wheat areas. Knapp, Burrell and Company, the Portland dealers, established a large branch house at Walla Walla for farmers "supplying themselves with the latest and most economical machines and implements." Farm machinery, manufactured by midwestern and California companies—McCormick, Deering, Holt, Deere, and others—was heavily promoted. "Former methods of advertising, such as catalogs, testimonials, and lists of available prospects were broadened," said Cyrus McCormick. "Propaganda which depended on innuendo and inference as much as upon direct statement was introduced."[38]

For the first thirty years of the twentieth century, the principal machines for wheat cultivation were tractors, seed drills, twine binders, combined reaper-threshers ("combines"), and improved plows, harrows, and other tilling implements made with hard steel rather than iron. Field demonstrations showed farmers what these new machines would do, as salesmen pushed their lines in a picnic atmosphere.

Developed in California, the combines were familiar in Washington in the nineties—huge, ungainly contraptions of chains and levers, some with cutting bars forty feet long, that required as many as forty-four horses. Adjustments for hillside reaping, cumbersome and unreliable, discouraged growers in hillier districts from using them. Some top-heavy machines tipped over on slopes. Farmers traveled miles in 1893 to see the Holt Link Belt Side Hill harvester (thirty-two horses) at work near Endicott on the farm of Lillis Smith, wheat king of the Palouse.[39] At least one of the giant combines appeared in the Pullman area in 1900, and another by 1902. A state college professor observed in 1906 that the combined harvester was displacing older machines in the Palouse, but so slowly that unthreshed wheat still rotted in shocks. He found farmers cautious about heavy investments in threshers; yet, with larger farms, machines were becoming necessary. And the buyer had to be his own machinist. One farmer wrote in his diary: "The 101 chain broke several times, the elevator broke about four times, the chain ran off the big 66 sprocket which bolts to the 88 chain sprocket . . . and finally broke the 66. . . . I worked until 11 o'clock that night but did not get near all the troublesome things repaired."[40] Chain-driven harvesters had to be greased and oiled in the morning and again at noon, and sometimes took an hour to start. Between 1900 and 1914, thresher capacity doubled and automatic twine cutters, feeders, weighers, and blowers were added, making the machines more complicated than ever.[41]

Seeing that specialized machines would sell to a growing market, a number of local manufacturers (most short-lived) entered the field. The Spokane Harvester Works survived for more than a decade, and while it prospered, the Spokane chamber of commerce considered, but dropped, the notion of raising $175,000 to underwrite factories to enlarge the city's farm-machine business. There were the Blewett Harvester, established in Spokane and moved to Pendleton; the Idaho National Harvester and Rhodes Harvester companies, Moscow; the Inland Automatic Thresher, Post Falls; the Colfax Harvester, which built the McRae combine, named for Alexander McRae, who founded Spokane Harvester; Bateman Harvester, Wallace; the Dunning-Erich Harvester Company, Harrington, which by 1918 was also producing track-laying tractors; Gilbert Hunt Manufacturing Company, Walla Walla, builder of the "Pride of Washington" harvester; and others. Perhaps the best known of these local machines was the compact "Little Idaho," relatively easy to maneuver on hills and comparatively cheap; between 1910 and 1916 the maker, Idaho National Harvester, sold them throughout the western states, but, as combines converted from use of horses to gasoline power, the company liquidated.[42]

For a time, wheat growers hitched tractors to combines, harvesters, and other machines built to be drawn by horses, but the stronger pull and speed of the tractors broke them. Ungainly, noisy, swallowing boiler water and fuel (wood or straw) in gulps, steam tractors turned forty acres of virgin soil in one day near Quincy for the Walla Walla stockman, B. F. Babcock, and harvested fifty acres a day near Walla Walla. Soon manufacturers, and occasionally a mechanically inclined blacksmith or farmer, mounted engines on threshers and combines to turn the mechanism while horses pulled the contraptions. Next manufacturers introduced self-propelled steam combines, and—although the self-propelled machine might not achieve general use in eastern Washington until after World War II—one appeared in Whitman County in 1901; five years later thirteen puffed through fields within sight of Oakesdale.[43]

Almost at the same time that the steam-propelled farm machine was spreading across eastern Washington it was displaced by gasoline engines (farmers often substituted kerosene)—engines with concentrated power, endurance, requiring small space and needing no care when idle, all advantages over horses. No wheat man slowed his work out of compassion for a tired tractor. By 1906, eleven companies manufactured gas tractors; ten years later, 170.[44] The early sales of gas tractors were impressive, and so were breakdowns. Hundreds of farmers ran tractors all night rather than restarting them in the morning, hiring boys to pour in gas. Such treatment snapped parts. Manufacturers had not foreseen this; they had no network for spare parts.

Drumming advertising by manufacturers escalated "the farmer's bill for new equipment beyond all reason," reflected Cyrus McCormick, who patented the famous pioneer reaper and joined in formation of International Harvester in 1902. Machines that might last ten years were declared obsolete in five; newer units thrust on dealers forced them to use high-pressure sales tactics at nearly "ruinous" prices. In a secret Spokane session, the 140 members of the Inland Empire Hardware and Implement Dealers Association pledged to maintain price levels; they heard a report that the average dealer's margin in eastern Washington was 12 percent, although costs of selling and handling amounted to 18 to 19 percent. Many dealers lost ten to thirty-five dollars on each machine they sold. To penalize those who cut prices nevertheless, the association urged manufacturers to withhold deliveries.[45]

The Idaho National Harvester's ads sold not only combines but stock in the company. Under the headline "Are You a Sucker?" (you were if you didn't buy stock in the company) the firm boasted of efficiency and low price. It planted items in country newspapers describing "this wonderful machine accomplishing what no other . . . had done—it threshed grain without cracking it."[46]

And with a barrage of advertising, farmers bought: Walla Walla dealers in 1902 sold their entire stock of eighty-eight combines; Spokane, with five threshing-machine and seven harvester dealers, ordered 750 carloads of implements during 1903; J. I. Case, John Deere Plow, and Mitchell, Lewis and Staver (Portland subsidiary of a Wisconsin firm) established large branches in the city in 1909 and 1910. Holt and Best, a Walla Walla dealer, claimed 500 combine sales in thirty days of 1907; for the 1910 harvest, Walla Walla houses ordered 125 threshers and 250 combines. Everywhere the machines rolled across Washington's wheat fields.[47]

Farmers slowly sold off their horses. Hunt's "Pride of Washington," with a gas engine under the feeder box to run gears and cogs, required fewer horses to pull; the Holt self-propelled combine, made in Stockton, California, and introduced in Washington in 1913, replaced thirty-two horses and cut forty to forty-five acres a day; and Holt's and Houser and Haines's "baby" combines, propelled by a thirty-gallon gas engine, required only three men and tracked through fields at two miles an hour, cutting twenty-five acres a day. The Holt cost $3,000. A great many of these machines were bought with chattel mortgages to harvester manufacturers, to dealers, moneylenders, or banks. In each county, wealthy men lent money, often after dealers or banks turned down a farmer's application.[48]

As World War I approached, more and more eastern Washington wheat growers bought engines—farmers like E. A. Densome of Adams County, who bought a 75-horsepower gas engine to plow 2,000 acres and auctioned his thirty-two horses. Twenty-five hundred farmers turned out in one day to see twenty tractors perform at a power-farming demonstration by the state college. As war engulfed Europe, traveling French army officers would buy all the surplus horses they could find in Washington.[49]

Machines were not novelties, although there was some pride and curiosity involved, but economies. Machines clearly covered more ground than horses, and a survey showed that harvesting with a binder and threshing machine cost Palouse farmers an average of $5.00 an acre; with header and stationery thresher, about $4.00; but with a large combine using thirty-two horses and five men, only $2.50 an acre; and with the "Little Idaho," using six or eight horses and two men, $1.00.[50] Over a year, gas cost less than feed.

Enterprising farmers with big machines custom harvested for their neighbors for a price of every tenth bushel; families of brothers, working adjoining farms, often bought one combine among them.

As machines took over much of the cultivating and harvesting, farmers hired seasonal help—"bindle stiffs"—from the floating bands that migrated from job to job. Harvest employment led to one of those aberrant times of high emotion akin to colonial witch-hunts. When fires and explosions damaged their machines, farmers excitedly deduced that irate job-seekers set the fires, and they fastened on the emerging union, the Industrial Workers of the World (Wobblies), as instigator.

Wobblies tried to persuade farm workers to strike for three dollars a day near Garfield in 1910. At Uniontown, a citizens' posse ran off seven "agitators"; and a federal judge in Spokane, admitting new citizens, asked bluntly if applicants were "reds."[51] But a rash of thresher and combine fires (more than forty machines had burned between 1900 and 1913) in the Palouse kindled farmers' fury. They charged that Wobblies placed matches in fields. When sixty machines burned in 1914 in Whitman County alone, a Colfax banker offered a $1,000 reward for catching anyone putting inflammable materials in harvesting machines. Farmers hired detectives, formed secret councils, and set their town marshals to arresting suspected men. One unfortunate field hand, suspected of igniting a harvester, was dragged through stubble with a rope around his neck. He was about to be hanged when the sheriff intervened.[52]

The impetus for IWW organization in the Pacific Northwest had been filthy, brutish logging camps. The union would accomplish little in agriculture, even though a surplus of workers before the war encouraged farmers to offer lower wages for harder work. But the Wobbly office in Spokane fanned emotions with bellicose pronouncements: the union would organize all harvest hands in the Palouse and Big Bend and move from there into the fruit and hop fields. Hearing that, farmers set up protective associations; they would not be coerced by vagrants; they would not be burned out of their fields. Perhaps some fires were arson, but a five-man investigating team from the state college blamed the fires on explosive smut in dry grain and machine sparks in grain dust. Manufacturers already were adding spark arrestors and shielding to prevent fires, and for nearly ten years the *Colfax Gazette* would distribute kits to drain static electricity from wire separators to prevent smut explosions.[53]

The Industrial Workers of the World lingered in harvest crews through the twenties, but juries soon rarely convicted anyone of the charge commonly leveled against them, criminal syndicalism, the crime of advocating overthrow of the capitalist system, and the union waned under federal attack. Brief strikes for higher wages by harvest hands in 1923 were throttled by strikebreakers from Spokane. But the emotion had drained. The union had not changed working conditions in wheat areas, and the farmers had begun to see the Wobblies for what most were: rootless, unschooled men looking for a better life.

During the war, wheat prices had risen faster than those of other farm products, and thinking that high prices would continue, farmers in 1920 planted for a large crop. They plowed their wartime profits into machines and more land. The average price per bushel had been 82 cents in 1915; in the next year, with Europe at war, wheat rose above $1.25 and kept rising (with a federal price guarantee); in 1919 it peaked at $2.06, highest in the memory of Washington farmers (the highest between pioneer days and 1947), and stayed at wartime levels into early 1920. But by the middle of 1920 the price had slipped; the 1921 crop fell from $1.96 to 92 cents a bushel. "Wheat production in Washington . . . is the largest in six years; the value the lowest in six years," fretted a grain newsletter from the Spokane and Eastern Trust Company, Spokane. Farmers rushed to sell before prices fell lower. "Many are compelled to sell to meet obligations contracted when everything was high," observed the *Colfax Gazette*. Dealers shipped as rapidly as possible—but the volume of wheat moving, amid steadily falling prices, filled elevators and warehouses and piled along railroad tracks.[54]

"The past year will be remembered by the present generation as a time of tumbling prices of all products and materials, cancelled contracts, and unprecedented losses in all lines of business and industry," reported the state supervisor of banking in his review of 1921. "Liquidation of debts was disappointing to both debtor and creditor."[55]

An early casualty of the grain debacle was the "boy wonder," Max Houser, a one-time Pomeroy grain buyer whose meteoric rise had made him something of a marvel in the marketplace, in 1913 "the largest grain exporter in America." He had served with Theodore Wilcox in the regional federal food administration in the war (Secretary of Commerce Hoover's agency) and had simultaneously operated his private business through the Pacific Grain Company. When Wilcox died in 1918, Houser's company bought the Portland Flouring Mills and its subsidiaries, including 145 warehouses, eleven mills, and Portland docks. But as he moved fast, Houser wakened whispers that his accounts had been manipulated before prices collapsed, catching him, and nearly every other broker, with unsold wheat stocks. His bankers stepped in and shortly sold the Portland Flouring Mills to Sperry, which operated the old mill for only a year and held the company for four before dissolving it.[56]

With its acquisition, however, Sperry took the warehouses and elevators in Pacific Northwest states operated by the Portland Flouring subsidiary, Pacific Coast Elevator Company. Sperry already operated six Washington mills, including those in Tacoma and Spokane, and its purchase of parts of the Houser empire catapulted Sperry into leadership in the Northwest wheat trade. Like Houser, others were shaken by the careening market: the New York exporter Strauss and Company took over the faltering Northern Grain and Warehouse Company, Strauss's entry into Pacific Northwest trading, and Centennial was forced to reorganize.[57]

Flour mills had expanded between 1917 and 1921 to meet wartime and immediate postwar demands. Now they produced more flour than they could sell. Older mills (such as Centennial's at Reardan and Sprague) closed, and newer ran below capacity. For two decades millers would complain that they had overbuilt by 35 to 50 percent—claims largely for political impact, for the excess was nearer 15 percent. The surplus capacity stimulated mergers among mills in midwestern states beginning in 1922 and climaxing in formation in 1928–29 of General Mills, Inc., the industry's giant.[58] These mergers, of course, affected Northwest millers. Consolidations of commercial bakers took place at the same time, so that by the late twenties, large suppliers were selling to giant users. In every cranny of the grain trade, the war and its artificial stimulus for the wheat and flour trade, leading to the market collapse of 1921, significantly changed the conditions of growing and selling.

For Washington's growers, the twenties were frustrating and disappointing. Short crops did not, as before, ensure higher prices for the next harvest. Australian and Canadian wheat, the revival of European production, reluctance among deficit nations to buy grain, and relatively high prices for American wheat all wobbled the world market. And Americans were turning away from the pies, hotbreads, and other pastries that consumed soft wheat. Many dieted to lose weight. Women wanted a pencil-slim look. People counted calories and practiced Fletcherism: chewing each mouthful slowly. Even fashion seemed to have turned against the American wheat farmer, and, like Atlas, he balanced the world on his shoulders.

Attempts before the war to unify had failed largely because Washington's farmers distrusted collective marketing. Without political strength, simply cooperating did not seem to change the farmer's lot. Now wheat farmers throughout the United States called for federal relief. The farmers of Washington were encouraged by the success of their unpretentious lobby to modify federal wheat-grading regulations, combining two white classes into one—a move farmers thought might save them from two to six cents a bushel.[59] An overwhelming wheat crop everywhere in the nation in 1923 quickened the campaign for federal relief. George Jewett, formerly of the Northwest Wheat Growers Association, lobbied for relief. A traveling *New York Times* writer said farmers felt that "if the government could set an artificial price for silver during the war to stimulate production . . . why cannot the government now set an artificial price for wheat?"[60] Idaho Senator Frank A. Gooding introduced a price-fixing bill. Senator Charles McNary of Oregon and Gilbert N. Haugen of Iowa sponsored a measure to establish a federal corporation for agricultural exporting.

The McNary-Haugen idea, that the government buy farm surpluses to store or sell abroad until U.S. prices rose, defeated once in Congress and vetoed twice by President Calvin Coolidge, nonetheless provided a national platform for debating the condition of American wheat farming; it defined and fused the farmers' stake in federal succor. With the Portland chamber of commerce leading the Pacific Northwest, wheat growers solicited businessmen for funds to send representatives to the national capital. As usual, not every farmer agreed. Idaho farmers of the Palouse would have none of it: "The injection of artificial influence would bring about worse conditions in the wheat situation than already exist"—their view in an editor's words. Lobbyist Harry E. Goldsworthy, Rosalia, wangled an audience with Coolidge himself, but confessed that "at the end of the conference, he was unable to determine just how the president stood" on farm relief.[61]

Old Professor Spillman, who thirty years earlier had conducted the beginning experiments for hardier varieties, warned growers, "No hope can be held out for increased prices for wheat for the next ten years," and counseled them to adopt the implement makers' method of sustaining prices by production controls.[62] Farmers always argued that weather, insects, and plant diseases took control out of their hands. As if to prove their point, a prolonged dry spell shriveled Washington. In 1923 Washington was fourth among wheat-producing states; but in one year it fell to twelfth, its fields crumbling dust.

The dry years reduced yields in the Palouse and Walla Walla regions, and they devastated dryland farmers of the Big Bend. (The state's average yield of 25.3 bushels an acre in 1923 fell to 14.1 in 1924.) Many farmers could not forage enough grain to seed another crop. Near Waterville, farmers harvested if they could estimate a yield of four bushels an acre.[63] The legislature appropriated $250,000 from the reclamation revolving fund to buy seed for wheat farmers; 388 farmers applied, mostly in Douglas, Grant, and Adams counties, and a few from Franklin, Okanogan, Benton, and Chelan. Even Lincoln County had been partly burned out by the relentless sun; some farmers there replanted fields they had not tried to harvest.[64]

The drought went on, driving families away, searing the furrowed deserts of the Big Bend, where the situation became worse. "I have exceeded the authority granted me by the legislature," admitted the commissioner of public lands, "as to the length of time which I may permit tenants to remain on the land who are unable to pay their rental" in Grant and Douglas counties. Governor Roland Hartley vetoed a second appropriation for seed wheat, maintaining that public funds should not support private business.[65] No one missed the irony of the state denying farmers what they wanted from the federal government: succor with public monies.

The farmer was trapped not only by weather but by the machine, which forced him to balance the size of his farm against the capacity of his machines. The 1930 census would show a progressive decline in the number of farms in dryland wheat areas of Washington, owing to consolidation of farms, increased machine use, and abandoning of some marginal sections planted when prices were high. By 1929 Big Bend farms averaged a thousand acres; those of the Palouse, 600. Since 1910, when combines were becoming commonplace, the number of farms of more than one thousand acres had doubled: 89 percent of these thousand-acre places lay in fourteen eastern Washington counties; 52 percent were in the five principal wheat counties—Lincoln, Douglas, Adams, Walla Walla, and Whitman. In all of these but Walla Walla, with its city growth and irrigated orchards, population declined through the twenties. By 1930 more than half the farmers in Whitman, Lincoln, and Adams counties were tenants, not owners. (Half of Washington's farms were mortgaged.) The six largest wheat-producing counties, 17 percent of the state's farms, owned approximately 44 percent of the implements and machines. (By contrast, there remained an average of five horses or mules per farm in these six counties.) The statistics showed what was happening: As farmers bought machines, they enlarged their acreages by purchase or rental (often from neighbors who failed or quit to move to town), and fewer and fewer growers were becoming bigger and bigger. These were not newcomers; an impressive number had farmed in the same places for ten or fifteen years or more.[66]

Warning transient workers away from harvests, the *Colfax Commoner* summarized the wheat farmers' experience: "Great grain farms and large individual farmers now have their combines—huge machines that carry out all the operations of threshing with a minimum of human help. With these machines increasing in number so rapidly, it is obvious that many who go to the wheat belt for summer jobs will be disappointed."[67]

In less than half a century, Washington's wheat farmers had evolved as an integral part of world grain trade; they could not command it, only respond. In order to pay their debts, they had to continue to produce. All their efforts for half a century had been to build up production. Now there was too much wheat. The secretary of agriculture scolded them for "engaging in destructive competition, each, by surplus production, beating down the price . . . for all." A Palouse editor found that small comfort for the farmer praying for relief from Congress while prices fell.[68]

Delegates from eleven wheat-producing countries met in London to consider a world engulfed in grain where farmers sold wheat "at figures much below the cost of production," a world "with so much bread in it that bread has become a problem."[69] On every hand, oracles solemnly urged farmers to do what they could not afford to do—cut production. Washington's farmers had struggled to win this land. Now that it was theirs, they felt their substance slipping from them.

CHAPTER *4*

Barefoot Schoolboys

He was a skinny, heavy-browed, earnest man with a Buffalo Bill mustache and goatee—a restless, traveling man who left his native Maine to wander as an itinerant editor of radical agrarian newspapers. He was a storekeeper, farmer, and politician, and when at the age of fifty-nine after seven years in Washington, this man of the people, John Rankin Rogers, was sworn in as governor, the farmer seemed at last to have bred adversity to political virtue. Like farmers, Rogers believed the common people to be oppressed by government, railroads, capital, and politicians; his program called for better schools, tax reform, low railway rates fixed by law, and fewer government agencies. "The great plain people . . . are to unite against organized aggression of the privileged few," he preached in his inaugural address.

Rogers's election seemed a watershed of artless rural righteousness in politics. But like so much in politics, that was a myth. He had been elected by an urban majority in western Washington, and his 1896 slate—the fusion of Populist, Silver Republican, and Democratic tickets—included two of eastern Washington's most ingenious politicians: George Turner, a veteran of intrigue on whom Rogers relied, and Patrick Henry Winston, a witty, outrageous platform speaker who had stumped the state for the Republicans in the previous campaign. Winston joshed publicly about his skips from one party to another.[1] In retrospect, Rogers's victory was less one of the people than a temporary diffusion of traditional party allegiances, his backers less a constituency than a coalition of politicians, driven momentarily from regular parties, and citizens discounted, if not abused, by regulars.[2]

Politics inevitably mirror social and economic conditions. The farmer suffered from soggy weather, low prices for his crops, rising production costs, inadequate credit, almost no money—farmers rarely saw money—and isolation. Farm conditions did not improve with Rogers's administration. The governor's signal contribution to rural life was the barefoot schoolboy law, which he had introduced and managed as a Populist member of the 1895 legislature, providing state support for public schools to help those impoverished rural districts unable to pay for decent schooling. State politics did not really change under Rogers. Henry McBride, the Republican lieutenant governor for Rogers's second term, found "the railroad lobby so powerful that measures had to be approved by it before they could be brought to the legislature."[3]

Rogers's election suggested to farmers, however, that their efforts to organize for political strength had borne fruit. When he died a few months into his second term—the lone Populist still in the government—Rogers left farmers a meager heritage: horticultural and road commissions and an increase from six to eight dollars a pupil in state funding for common schools. His supposed Populist base in the legislature vanished in his first term. Once in Olympia, legislators voted with their old parties. Rogers could persuade them to enact little of his program. In the general disappointment at his performance, his attorney general, Winston, classed Rogers among "frauds and asses" he had voted for.[4] As lieutenant governor, the Republican McBride became governor, already at odds with his party for his determination to establish a railroad commission.

His ineptness in the statehouse aside, Rogers left the barefoot schoolboy law. Urban legislators had opposed Rogers's measure, men like Joseph Gandy and Frank Tull of Spokane, and Moses Bull of rich Whitman County, who saw it as "taxing larger counties . . . for the sparsely settled," and the Spokane school board protested that it would force shortening the city's school year.[5]

Rogers intended to help those desolate, dusty, one-room crossroad shacks with separate privies out back for girls and boys, where frightened young teachers in their first jobs boarded with a family in the neighborhood until they fled at the end of one year, to be replaced by another. As Washington entered statehood, women had begun to outnumber men as elementary teachers, although paid less: women at $38.59 a month and men at $44.16 in Lincoln, one of eastern Washington's prosperous counties.[6] A new teacher, arriving at Lind, hesitated to get off her train when she saw the "dirty, bearded men and dusty streets," but she endured a year there, harassed by the Ku Klux

Klan, who painted signs on her house and burned crosses on hills because she was Catholic.[7]

Before Rogers's barefoot schoolboy law, perhaps one in three farm children went to school. For the other two, distances were too great, their work was needed on the farm, their fathers saw no benefit in schooling, or they lacked clothes—indeed, were barefoot. Farm families with enough money who valued education sent their children to live with families in towns during the school year, and some towns charged them tuition. In the ungraded country schools, pupils huddled on hard wooden benches, with "buildings and furniture of the poorest description," using books (if any) selected by farmers on the school board, struggling to write, read, and do simple computations.[8] Country schools ran perhaps three months, usually in summer when roads were passable, and few of their pupils stayed four years.

Rogers's stratagem was the allocation of state funds based on attendance, not on a census of children in a school district as before, forcing the schools to act against truants. He could not dispel their isolation, but more money might help these crossroads schools. Even a well-to-do town like Spangle occasionally canceled a school term for lack of money, and two eastern Washington counties, poor dryland wheat areas, operated no schools. Five counties had only one apiece.[9] When the legislature raised state support to ten dollars a pupil, counties organized new schools on short notice for the money, using shacks fitted with boards for desks and benches, and thrust farm children into them.[10]

Washington's school superintendents had been overwhelmed by expansion since statehood. Yakima County built twenty-five new schools between 1890 and 1895, trying to keep up with settlers; Spokane put up eight new schools in 1899—and in 1900 reported them overflowing.[11] Towns used churches and houses for temporary schoolrooms, as enrollment in eastern Washington's elementary schools rocketed from roughly thirty-six thousand in 1895 to more than eighty-six thousand by 1910 and continued to rise.[12]

Schools in towns improved measurably after 1900, with new buildings and terms of six months or more. (Washtucna, a wheat-shipping point, spent $10,000 for a concrete five-room schoolhouse.) Some, like Kennewick, operated free buses for country pupils. Half a hundred town schools added manual, household, and agricultural training to their curriculums. Of nine thousand teachers in Washington, 7,200 were women; their salaries now $64 against men's $77 a month. Spokane voted $400,000 for new school construction in 1909 (and used the buildings until 1980). But for many rural districts, improvements in town schools simply showed more starkly the gap between town and country. Conditions were not uniform in eastern Washington: a survey of 1,187 graduates of Whitman County rural schools in 1916 showed an unusual 67 percent continuing to high school, forty-two children working as farmhands, sixty-eight boys and eighty-five girls helping at home, and ten working as domestic servants.[13]

When Mrs. Josephine Corliss Preston took office as state superintendent in 1913, she counted 1,743 one-room schools and twenty districts with no schools at all. In wheat-growing counties, where farmers bought out their neighbors in good years, some schools had shrunk to one or two children. As late as 1922, in fact, 144 Washington school districts enrolled fewer than four. Half of these tiny districts were in five eastern Washington counties: eighteen in Grant, seventeen in Douglas, eight in Adams, and seven each in Whitman and Lincoln, forlorn, insular cloisters for teachers and children who rarely saw anyone but the families within a few miles.[14]

A matronly forty, Mrs. Preston understood town and country schools from her nine years as Walla Walla County superintendent; she knew how hard some rural school boards strained to provide their children with a meager education. She set about making the schools better. She imposed systematic, modern office procedures on the superintendent's office, adopted simplified spelling ("thru" and "stopt") in her bulletins, and in her brisk, emphatic manner, lifted rural education out of dust and neglect. For her imperious ways, her office staff called her the Duchess behind her back, but teachers and farmers on school boards hailed her; she would speak at the dedication of the meanest country high school and write letters to every pupil who finished the eighth grade, more than twenty-one thousand when her reign ended in 1928 with defeat in a Republican primary election.[15]

In her sixteen years as superintendent, Preston insisted on better rural schools, better teachers, and better teacher housing. After Governor Hay, in his 1913 message, recommended that schoolhouses be used for adult education, lectures, and shows, she pushed schools as community centers, perhaps hoping that some farm fathers would be less hostile to schooling if they visited the schools. By 1928, more than 310 districts were operating community centers. Into centers, Preston intended to cram the farmers' education and social life; and only by diligent lobbying could E. O. Holland, president of the state college, wrest 4-H club work from her.[16] She promoted "standardization"—a report card for schools (developed by the Washington Education Association) on their structures, equipment, and teachers' accommodations. Ramshackle buildings began to disappear (the typical improved country school would be a rectangular whitewashed frame building with two windows on each side), although for some districts, physical progress was too costly, and when she left office, most eastern Washington rural schools still used outdoor toilets and fewer than one in five had fenced or leveled schoolyards. Except for the poorest, however, conditions were better. More than half reported adequate ventilation and lighting, most had a water supply, and three out of four possessed books, pens, and other essential supplies.[17]

As superintendent, Preston declared that three "paramount problems" shackled rural education: taxes, teachers' living conditions, and teacher training. Despite increased state monies (she often applauded Rogers's barefoot schoolboy law), funds remained slim in rural areas. To distribute money better, she campaigned to consolidate districts and by 1922 had raised the number consolidated to eighty-two, located in every eastern Washington county but Ferry and Benton. (The superintendents of both protested that winter roads made uniting impractical.) By 1928, there were 396. Farm families did not wholeheartedly approve consolidating rural with city schools, fearing "the moral and other conditions of these towns" would seduce their children. When Seattle built Roosevelt High School for one million dollars, the *Grange News* commented on its cost, "while hundreds of country districts assessing themselves to the limit are yet unable to provide five months' school in the crudest school buildings." To educate their children, the paper added, farmers must send them away, "with all the cost in money and character" that separation exacted.[18]

Preston harangued counties to dissolve their poor, small districts (she even urged a law to close such schools) and required superintendents to report why they did not. Douglas County answered, "All too poor. Farmers won't come back." And Whitman: "The children would have no school activities." Teachers went willingly to consolidated districts, Preston argued, rather than "lonely one-room schools," but to encourage teachers to take rural schools she cajoled the counties to build teachers' cottages (an idea then spreading across the United States). "Boarding around," she sniffed, infuriated farm wives who toiled while schoolmarms sat, and invaded the privacy of rural homes. Two-thirds of the state's teachers' cottages rose in eastern Washington counties: Walla Walla built twenty-seven, Adams and Whitman each twenty-six, and Garfield twenty-four for their isolated schools, ranging from new two-room cabins to remodeled six-room houses.[19]

As a result, a few teachers stayed more than one year, but too many, as farm districts complained, learned to teach in the country in order to apply for jobs in towns. Chelan, one of the progressive educational counties, kept 60 percent of its teachers for two years or longer by the end of the twenties—perhaps the best record of rural areas. Rapidly urbanizing Yakima kept 90 percent, the highest retention in Washington. In Adams, Franklin, and Klickitat, with windswept plateaus between farms, only one in four teachers stayed for a second year, and some cottages stood empty.[20]

Preston's superintendency spanned the years in which many farm families, some with the slimmest bank accounts, bought automobiles to chug over sandy trails, penetrating their isolation. During her tenure, state enrollments grew one-third (from about 224,000 in 1913 to more than 339,000 in 1928), the high schools increased ten times, and costs of education tripled. Her ceaseless battles for school funds angered Governor Roland Hartley, hell-bent for economy in state government, who plotted to pack the State Board of Education "to break down Mrs. Preston's organization" with "men who would stand up against our Big Bertha." Then he turned her party, and many of her rural constituents, against her by labeling her a "tool of the power trust," the private utilities. Farmers by and large supported the concept of public power; they were dismayed by testimony before the Federal Trade Commission that their duchess had edited, as one of a series on state industries, a monograph for classroom use that was biased in favor of private power companies.[21]

Preston fought, too, to improve teaching. Before the war, most elementary teachers spent two years in a normal school, but could enter it out of the eighth grade; in the teachers' colleges they went by the unflattering name "sub-normals." By her last year as superintendent, two years of normal school after high school was standard. Certification remained variable, but teachers were prepared better, paid better ($1,050 a year for elementary and $1,500 for high school teachers in Yakima), and encouraged to continue teaching by a retirement system started in 1923. Children read from free textbooks, sat in equipped, ventilated, and lighted rooms for the most part, and nearly one in four went to high school. Mrs. Preston's successor, Noah D. Showalter, former principal of the Cheney Normal School, who believed that children learned best at an individual pace, reformed the elementary curriculum in 1930 just before depression froze the system for a decade. Three years later, voters approved a 40-mill tax limit (teachers had publicly opposed such a limit in 1924), which, in effect, weakened the fiscal positions of the poorest districts.[22]

But, to turn back, the farmer liked to think that he and his kind had united to elect Governor Rogers, for the farmer was a joiner: he and his wife joined organizations for social, educational, economic, and political reasons. Through unity he might find power. Nearly all these organizations staged elaborate social events and—through traveling programs, schools, and partisan newspapers—tried to educate their members. Many pioneer farmers' groups had been informal, but organizations now were formal with rules and rituals.

Of them, the Patrons of Husbandry—the Grange—would be most enduring. California organizers carried the Grange into Washington Territory in 1871 and 1872 and linked it with Oregon's. The Oregon Grange's chief aims were cooperative sales and purchasing, lower freight rates, and patronizing home tradesmen.[23] While Portland remained the center of inland trade and transport, these purposes coincided with those of eastern Washington (Walla Walla County once petitioned to be joined to Oregon). But the panic in 1873 separated Washington's fifty locals from Oregon, and the influx of settlers beginning in 1879 splintered the locals until the newcomers forged common interests with older settlers. The Washington Grange began to attract members again after 1881, and the farmers' concern for the provisions of a state constitution, as Washington approached statehood in 1889, revitalized the Grange as a forum for rural interests. Nonetheless the Grange in Washington grew slowly; by 1903 it had only 724 members.[24]

The Grange opposed the new state constitution as creating an office-seeking class, "the most worthless class that can exist," with too many positions at high salaries, encouraging machine politics, allowing secret sessions, and permitting foreigners to own Washington lands and businesses.[25] The constitution passed without correcting these alleged deficiencies.

The Grange's influence had been weakened by a rival, a "labor union" for farmers, the Farmers Alliance, introduced into the territory in 1880 by the Chicago editor of an Alliance paper, the *Western Rural*, but the Alliance was in turn enervated by national factions competing for the locals' allegiance.[26] Farmers' demands for responsive government pushed the Alliance into politics. With an organizer from Missouri, Ahira Manring, the Washington Alliance grew to 246 locals in seventeen counties. Almost wholly controlled by eastern Washington men, the Alliance declined a formal tie with the Spokane Trades Council but cooperated otherwise with organized labor; it advanced a program of government loans on real estate, equal taxation, and legislative action "to compel railroads to fulfill their obligations . . . as common carriers."[27]

The Alliance drew farmers to it by massive picnics, cooperative stores (four in Whitman County alone), mutual buying, and management of farmer-owned warehouses. Alliance members led in forming a stock company for a railroad from the Palouse to Puget Sound, which was never built, and claimed credit for an 1891 law requiring private warehouse operators to store grain until authorized to sell or move it, allowing farmers to hold stored wheat for favorable prices. But political activism and economic depression turned many farmers away from organizations, and by 1894 the Alliance had "waned in numbers and influence, and gradually died out."[28]

If the Alliance failed to last as a political and social force, it nonetheless etched distinctly the divisions in political objectives between farmers and organized labor (although farm groups seem not to have understood this lesson for another twenty years). The Grange was also withering as the Alliance dried up, torn between idealism and practical politics, a dilemma summed up in the state master's plea to "throw off the party whip—vote for men who serve the interests of agriculture."[29]

As the Grange gathered strength, Carey B. Kegley was master from 1906 to 1917. A farmer from Guy (and onetime socialist candidate for the legislature), Kegley cooperated with organized labor and reform groups to pass the direct primary ballot in Washington, woman suffrage, local option prohibition, and the eight-hour workday. Kegley's Grange counted 2,813 members in nine counties; his "direct and vigorous methods" (which made some enemies) spread the Patrons across Washington and caught the eye of the national Grange, where Kegley became prominent in conservation and suffrage movements. But his formal alliance with organized labor drove away some members, and after he died in 1917, the divisive tenure of William Bouck disheartened others, while the farm bureau emerged, ascendant with the "farm bloc" in Congress.[30]

The Grange's rival during Kegley's years was the Farmers Educational and Cooperative Union, a stepchild of the shattered Alliance. Using the name "union," but not affiliated, farmers had opened cooperative stores and warehouses before the union reached Washington. (One of these, the Union Elevator and Warehouse Company, formed by five farmer-stockholders at Lind in 1906, would become the largest private grain marketing company in the Pacific Northwest by midcentury.) The national Union's president chartered the original Washington chapter at Waitsburg in 1907, said to be the first one west of the Rocky Mountains, and the Union, "a purely business organization," flourished in Adams, Douglas, Lincoln, Walla Walla, and Whitman counties, precisely the ones least represented in the Grange.

The Union also used rituals and social activities—picnics for two thousand or more—and fostered cooperative grain warehouses and elevators, most later dissolved as stock companies and reformed as cooperative corporations. The Union's long-term aims coincided with the Grange's: tax relief, parcel post (which the Grange claimed as its own), and improved roads. Their problems also were the same as the Grange's: fluctuating membership and political differences. The Union's peak years, 1919 to 1922, slipped away in postwar depression and federal assistance to cooperatives.[31]

But the Grange endured. Once bitten by the Grange bug, some farmers put much of their spare time into it. Grange insignia for men was a sash with a tan apron trimmed in red; for women, white sash and apron. And even more enticing than community and ritual, to the practical farmer, were the Grange's cooperative stores.

Albert A. Goss, educated in city schools in Spokane and Portland, onetime country store and dairy operator, in 1920 assumed management of the state Grange cooperative warehouse system, with its sixty-one low-profit affiliated stores. Finding "unsound business practices"—only three stores with good credit ratings—he centralized accounting and recapitalized the cooperative with a stock issue. The warehouses handled foods, clothing, equipment (some their own brands), and eventually petroleum products.

As manager, Goss was quickly tangled in a cleavage between the state and national Granges. Washington was among the maverick Granges that lobbied in the national capital. The quarrel ended with dismissal of William Bouck, state master, who formed the competing Western Progressive Grange. He had been a controversial leader—a socialist and firebrand. His 1918 state convention had been locked out in Walla Walla by provoked (and perhaps subverted) citizens resisting the Grange's political coloring under Bouck. After a court ordered him to drop the word "grange," Bouck's new organization became the Western Progressive Farmers, weak and little noted.[32]

The Bouck controversy crippled the Washington Grange, and when, following an interim master, Goss became state master in 1922, eastern Washington counties had dropped away, slow to return. For years the Grange's smallest memberships were in Lincoln, Spokane, Adams,

Douglas, Kittitas, Walla Walla, and Okanogan counties. Eastern Washington farmers, however, favored the Grange's stand for cooperatives, publicly owned power, tax revision, and prohibition. In enlarging state membership to perhaps twenty thousand (one in each four Washington farmers) and lobbying for farmers' interests, Goss—a slender, rather short, intense man noted for lengthy reports—advanced himself to the executive committee of the national Grange, the post of farm land bank commissioner in 1933, and national master in 1940.[33]

The Grange—ritualistic, social, and educational—attracted farmers with meeting halls functioning as neighborhood centers. Occasionally someone resigned, protesting the Grange was too social, and it gradually abandoned secret rituals. It established insurance, cooperative buying, boys' and girls' clubs (juvenile Granges), and sponsored instructive demonstrations and lectures. But the Grange, stubbornly nonpartisan, had lost its power to bring about political changes by itself. As the farmers' voice, it continuously confronted rivals: the farmers' union in the early 1900s and the farm bureaus after the war.

Farm bureaus grew from groups of farmers who raised money, largely through dues, to support the demonstration and consulting work of county agents. The county units coalesced as state federations to coordinate their work and naturally served as farmers' forums. In a national convention a few weeks after the end of the war, county agents planned national and state federations to represent farm interests and in 1919 launched an organizing campaign that made the American Farm Bureau Federation, for a time, the largest farmers' organization in the United States. Delegates from county bureaus in Washington, Oregon, and Idaho met at Yakima in August 1919 "to attain concerted action on farm questions," and those from Washington and Idaho formed five-man organizing boards.[34]

Local bureaus told each member to find another member, thus pyramiding membership. They enrolled farmers who already belonged to other organizations, and Washington's bureau grew quickly—an estimated seven hundred farmers joined in Whitman County in eighteen months—and the national federation seemed to speak with a strong voice in Congress. But farm bureaus ran into familiar problems: waning participation during depression and internal struggles over political issues. The Washington Farm Bureau Federation, in debt, virtually disintegrated in the mid-twenties, to be resurrected by a handful of county units that paid off its obligations. It would not again be as large as the Grange, and the national federation failed, in large measure, to lobby its program through Congress.[35]

For all his proclivity to join, the eastern Washington farmer lacked legislative power. Statewide farmer organizations (after the war, Washington was among those states with the most) split farmers into competing factions. Legislators could accuse Albert Goss of sitting in the galleries to tally their votes after warning them to "vote right" on farm bills, and the *Grange News* could plead for farmer ballots; but, in truth, sectionalism was stronger at the polls, and urban King and Pierce counties steered the legislature with their city votes.[36]

Although the farmer's organizations did not deliver political power, they offered him recreation and instruction. It is a truism that nobody farms as well as he knows how, and nearly everyone wanted to tell the farmer how: colleges, railroads, chambers of commerce, and business associations bounded into the field with missionary zeal, leading the master of the Washington Grange to comment wryly, "The farmer should be more prosperous with so much . . . free advice."[37]

Most of the farmers' knowledge stemmed from experience; farm journals often passed off theory as fact (bands around trees would kill coddling moths in orchards, for instance), and the federal Hatch Act of 1887, authorizing agricultural experiments and research in each state and territory, was intended to bring scientific methods to farming. The Smith-Lever Act of 1914, establishing agricultural extension, was meant to carry this scientific information to the farmer. By its funding, the act attached the extension service to each state's land-grant college—in Washington, the State Agricultural College, Experiment Station, and School of Science opened in January 1892 in Pullman. (In 1905 its name was shortened to State College of Washington.) Even before the Smith-Lever Act, county agents were working in eight counties with legislative and county support.[38]

The college, after a first term marked by internal bickering, had to be reorganized as the panic of 1893 enveloped the nation, and reopened September 13, 1893 "in the little, old, red, wooden building known as college hall with a faculty of 10, a student attendence of 23 . . . in the midst of a pouring rain which meant the destruction of the Inland Empire wheat crop."[39]

The college launched farmer institutes in its first year, and one of the teachers on a traveling team, John O. Scobey, called for farmers to switch to dairying from wheat, "the lazy man's crop." At Colton, farmers and faculty debated whether a dose of red pepper would kill a horse. (It wouldn't.) Another college teacher advised farmers to plant sugar beets.

Much of the college's early testing aimed at identifying the crops best suited to Washington soils and climates, and, after 1898, genetic breeding of wheat varieties. Between 1893 and 1907 the college published eighty-five bulletins, mailed to six thousand farmers, and in 1908 issued its first "popular" bulletin, "to give in brief, concise form the best information which it is possible to obtain by experiment or observation," or as a newspaper editor remarked, "short, easy discussions for the busy farmer who doesn't want experimental data."[40]

Railroads also distributed information (often information from the college) through the mid-twenties. The Oregon Railway and Navigation Company one year handed out free seeds to promote crop diversity and arranged cattle auctions for improved breeding, and another year carried college teachers through Whitman, Garfield, Columbia, and Walla Walla counties to advocate peas as a crop to rotate with wheat. Railroads and college joined to sponsor boys' and girls' corn-growing contests (a youngster near Prescott raised 122 bushels an acre). The Great Northern and Northern Pacific similarly ran farm demonstration trains with college lecturers aboard. "Our train of several cars was well equipped with grains, forage plants, tillage implements, and illustrated materials," reported agronomist Leonard Hegnauer, whose first assignment at Washington State College was to prepare exhibits for train tours. "Machinery was carried on open flat cars to be easily seen and studied. Most of our discussions took place in the open."[41]

And farmers visited the college, grown in a few years to a three-story brick building with a long hitching rack in back. When automobiles became common, the college's vice-president, O. L. Waller, tore out the racks while President E. A. Bryan, a horseman, was away.[42] In time, the college planted demonstration plots at Pullman, opened winter schools for farmers, and convened field demonstrations. During the 1909–11 biennium, it conducted 117 institutes attended by more than twenty-three thousand, and operated ten trains and a riverboat to instruct more than fifty-eight thousand at 223 stops, covering western as well as eastern Washington.[43]

After the U.S. Department of Agriculture contributed $1,440 and the Wahkiakum County Pomona Grange $760 to hire an agricultural specialist for the county, the Washington legislature (in 1913) created a bureau of farm development to assist counties to employ "agriculturists," although not all counties could raise the money. By the time of the Smith-Lever Act, consequently, Adams, Benton, Douglas, Okanogan, Spokane, and Walla Walla counties were employing trained men. Before the war, the college opened specialized experiment stations—at Lind for dryland farming and at Prosser (on eighty acres donated by the Northern Pacific) for irrigation.⁴⁴ Crowds of twenty-five hundred were common at field demonstrations of hill-climbing tractors.

Washington had opened its agricultural college well after most other states. In fact, the Association of Land-Grant Colleges was formed two years before Washington became a state. Although this association's main purposes were trading information and elevating teaching and research, it necessarily homogenized the fields of interest—extension, home economics, and engineering—among the states. The association was proud of its part, and that of the colleges and extension service, in politicizing farmers through farm bureaus. A speaker at the association's 1920 convention declared (and no one demurred) that "extension divisions should consider it both a great privilege and an unprecedented opportunity to give every possible assistance" to the bureaus' political efforts.⁴⁵

Farm experiments in Washington, as in other states, tended to be practical, to solve under farm conditions the problems of crop type and yield, disease, storage, seed quality, and so on. The extension specialists often pointed to successful farmers as models, and in their early work their advice reflected the rudimentary state of farm science. Not all of the counsel was useful, and some perhaps was inaccurate. Hegnauer, on one occasion, protested the yield data from tiny grain test plots, trampled by horses and flooded by wastewater, as "unreliable, if not misinformation."⁴⁶ But most of the advice was better than farmers got from other sources, and they trusted it.

Through their association, colleges often competed for prestige and recognition. All colleges were raising their standards of scholarship, and the Grange chided them for it, declaring that the University of Washington "breeds contempt for working people," and Washington State College "unduly stressed" academic studies.⁴⁷ Delegates to annual association meetings conceded that they knew little about the farmer and his family as people, and a new field, rural sociology, emerged (partly in response to the American Country Life Association, of which Josephine Preston was Washington state chairman). Parallel studies started in several states, including Washington—inquiries into the farmer's health, his wife's duties, what he thought, and his standard of living. With the rise of sociology after the war, the farmer was both beneficiary and subject of research. The federal Purnell Act of 1925 expanded experiment and study. In 1929, Washington State College specialists held 6,810 meetings in one year for an estimated 152,700 farmers and their families, and sponsored boys' and girls' clubs enrolling nearly eight thousand.[48] Educating the farmer had become a major element of rural life in Washington.

Fairs, one of the oldest means of educating the farmer—and making money and publicizing a town—appeared early in Washington. Walla Walla held one of the first in 1866, and in 1880 the *Walla Walla Union* remarked, "All admit that properly conducted agricultural fairs . . . are very conducive to the prosperity and well-being of the community." Dust hid the races at Spokane's first fair in 1886, and then rain dampened speeches and muddied visitors camped in tents by the track. Not all fairs profited. Spokane's nearly always lost money, and Whitman County's, started in 1887, closed for several years after.[49] Fairs showed off local products, lured spending visitors, and functioned as a rite of passage. Revelry was as much a part of early fairs as exhibits, contests, and midways. Lectures, demonstrations, and exhibits offered farmers information as well as recreation.

Because of their locations, the largest fairs were Spokane's (an industrial exhibition in 1890, turned into a fruit fair in 1894, and merged in 1901 with an interstate fair) and Yakima's state fair, sanctioned by the legislature in 1893 on condition that Yakima provide a 120-acre site. Despite hard times that year, Fred Parker drove a buckboard through the valley to collect money, and thirty-one Yakima merchants gave their notes to finance the land and building—a 40-by-150-foot auditorium beside a grandstand for races.[50] On a "glorious day" in September 1894 the Dayton town band (twenty-six pieces) led an opening parade. Perhaps the most conspicuous exhibit was a quilt sewn round-robin by chapters of the Women's Christian Temperance Union across the state; the *Herald* called it "eccentric."[51] The state fair showed farm produce and animals, wagons, and harness; the state college (very new) passed out leaflets on tree scale; an oculist fitted eyeglasses; and, of course, there were speeches.

Fairs were widespread enough by 1903 that an association was formed to avoid date conflicts: Yakima, September 28–October 2; Spokane, October 5–13; Walla Walla, October 19–24; and Lewiston, October 26–31. As county fairs flourished, the 1917 legislature limited county government expenditures for fairs on the basis of population. The state fair, in decline, revived despite Governor Louis Hart's attempt to save the state $50,000 a year by closing it, and Yakima built a 12,000-seat auditorium for lectures, moving pictures, and demonstrations, and a campground for families who came by car.[52]

As automobiles swelled attendance and forced fair promoters to compete, fairs turned progressively more commercial. A number became notorious for shoddy carnivals, gambling, and sensational acts (airplane stunts, once balloons had become commonplace), and the *Grange News,* among others, warned its readers of fairs "turning into wild west shows."[53]

Between fairs, traveling lecturers and performers appeared in small-town "opera houses," often for advertising purposes—movies by Ford to show automobile models, or a quartet that walked offstage in mid-song to reveal that their music came from that marvel, the phonograph. The chautauqua, sometimes lasting a full week with its series of evening lectures and pseudoscience, lingered well into the twenties.

As educational ventures, the Spokane chamber of commerce mounted two ambitious projects: the Holden and the Spillman tours, lecture junkets to advocate diversified farming. The idea of diversity was not new: Washington State College people had talked diversity from the beginning, although Enoch Bryan, in his practical way, pointed out that the eastern Washington farmer's investment in horses, land, and machines for wheat made switching crops impractical. Bryan suggested that towns provide capital and guarantee markets for new crops. None did, and the farmer stayed with wheat.[54]

Spokane hired a platform lecturer with a national reputation, Perry G. Holden, agricultural extension specialist for the International Harvester Company, to tour 140 Pacific Northwest towns in the fall of 1913 evangelizing alfalfa as an alternate crop, accompanied by speakers on livestock and dairying—a brassy crusade for diversified farming like those Holden conducted in other parts of the United States. At Colfax, Holden—bald, suited, hat in hand, standing on a platform of planks and sawhorses—introduced by the mayor after the town band played, shouted "Wheat farmers will have to give up," as wheat farmers, wearing suits, ties, and hats—their go-to-meeting clothes—stood in the street listening respectfully. That was a typical scene on the tour. Holden declared that schools should devote half their instruction to farming.[55]

With 125 Holden campaign leaders in towns of Oregon, Idaho, and Washington to publicize his tour, and "alfalfa weeks" and "corn weeks" in the schools, Holden's proselytizing ran into early 1914. Spokane businessmen distributed seed corn (two pounds for twenty-five cents) to farmers willing to try it, and in the fall the *Spokesman-Review* claimed that 100,000 acres had been turned to forage crops and corn. The Holden tour did not change farming, but it afforded farmers a day in town, food for thought, a celebration of their importance (rare enough), and perhaps a picnic or banquet. And it demon-

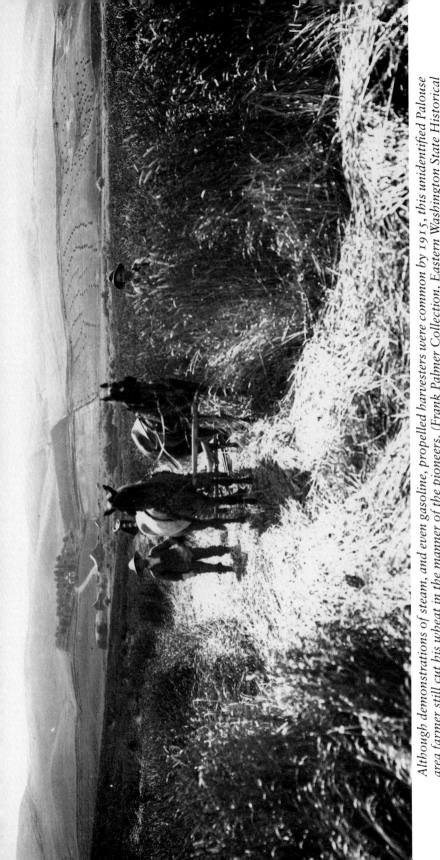

Although demonstrations of steam, and even gasoline, propelled harvesters were common by 1915, this unidentified Palouse area farmer still cut his wheat in the manner of the pioneers. (Frank Palmer Collection, Eastern Washington State Historical Society)

Harvesting machines which both reaped and threshed—"combines"—were in general use during the nineties although they were often ungainly and dangerous for hillside use. Some required as many as forty-four horses. By the time of this photograph, 1912, self-propelled steam combines were becoming common in the Inland Empire. (Washington State Historical Society, Asahel Curtis Collection 25660)

The family turned out to shock oats on this Spokane valley farm about 1909. The river valley, east of Spokane, came into its own under irrigation, primarily as producer of fruits and vegetables. (Frank Palmer Collection, Eastern Washington State Historical Society)

The William Shafstall homestead near Othello, in the Big Bend, about 1909. Note the sagebrush in the background, and the sand piled against the end of the clapboard, windowless house, extreme right. Intrepid pioneers who tried to farm this dry country in periods of above-average rainfall often were driven out by later periods of drought. (Washington State University: Manuscripts, Archives, and Special Collections 78-940)

A prosperous Big Bend farm, the Bill Schoryman place near Quincy, 1913. Quincy was promoted as an irrigation project and, although the large-scale development fell through, the windmill demonstrates that this family had water for household use and perhaps irrigation. (Washington State University: Manuscripts, Archives, and Special Collections 70-364)

An unpainted crossroads country school at Narcisse in Stevens County, about thirteen miles east of Colville. The school was ventilated and lighted by two windows on either side, and heated by a wood stove. (Note woodpile in lean-to, right.) Two of the boys wear baseball mitts but this school, like most rural schools, had no playground. (Philpott album)

Spartan whitewashed homes rose where settlers converted desert rangeland to farms and orchards with irrigation. The major irrigation projects relied on river diversion and reservoirs but smaller projects, such as this one near Moses Lake, depended on water pumped from wells. (Washington State Historical Society, Asahel Curtis Collection 21840)

Apple harvesting was never like this. A posed publicity picture for Skookum Packers, Inc., about 1920 shows the canvas bags pickers wore to avoid bruising fruit. Behind the ladder, a brace holds up a heavily laden tree branch. (Skookum)

"The Same Old Taste"

Remember the good old days—when you used to go out in the orchard and pick the finest, reddest, juiciest apple on the end of the limb? Didn't it taste good? Skookum Apples have that "same old taste."

They are the "pick" of the best apples from the best orchards in the world. Every one is as nearly a perfect apple as nature and man can produce.

Northwestern Fruit Exchange
World's largest distributors of boxed apples.
SEATTLE, WASH.

Dealers: Get name of local wholesaler from our representative in your city.

Skookum Apples

© 1916 N.F.E.

A colored magazine advertisement placed in the Literary Digest *and other magazines by the Northwestern Fruit Exchange, marketer for the Skookum Packers Assocation, in the early twenties. Heavily advertised, Washington apples dominated the luxury trade. (Skookum)*

Until Wenatchee-Okanogan and Yakima developed fruit marketing methods, the growers in flatlands along the Snake River flourished, sending their produce downstream to Portland. Growers are loading the steamer Almota at Wawawai landing in 1896, and evidently the vessel will also carry passengers. (Washington State University, June Crithfield Collection: Manuscripts, Archives, and Special Collections 78-227)

Percival and Andrus private bank, Cheney, about 1887, with the familiar false front of frame commercial buildings. The Walters harness store, however, built of hand-made brick, is fronted with terra cotta and iron pillars. Like most towns, Cheney had streets of packed dirt, dusty in summer and muddy in winter, and its few sidewalks of boards. (Eastern Washington University)

Observation car on the Washington Water Power Company electric line to Medical Lake and Cheney. For a brief era before the automobile, electric trains offered quick, frequent service to rural riders bound for Spokane. The WWP abandoned its line in 1922. (WWP)

This farmer near Cheney shows off his steam tractor with wood wagon trailing. Noisy, heavy, and clumsy, steam tractors pulled apart harvesting equipment built to be drawn by horses and were soon superseded by gasoline. (Geography Department Collection, Eastern Washington University)

Automobile tourists, 1920, lined up in front of the Spokane & Inland Empire electric railway terminal at Main and Lincoln in Spokane. The automobile already had diminished the electric line's passenger traffic, and auto trucks were taking its freight customers. (Eastern Washington State Historical Society)

Automobiles dispelled the farmer's isolation. The pioneer autoist often forded shallow streams in a roadless countryside and followed telephone wires toward the nearest town. The state's earliest automobile highway system was intended to provide farmers routes to their markets. (Washington State Historical Society, Asahel Curtis Collection 37649)

Main Street in Colfax, about 1922, ample evidence that farmers bought automobiles and used them to by-pass country stores for shopping in larger towns. (Washington State University: Manuscripts, Archives, and Special Collections 78-124)

strated Spokane's paternal concern for its rustic cousins. It was good publicity. As a Spokane businessman put it, "We've got to make those people back East know we're doing things out here."[56]

Ten years later the Spokane Chamber of Commerce and agricultural colleges sponsored Dr. W. J. Spillman in an automobile tour of northern Idaho and eastern Washington. As the first geneticist at Washington State College, now a consultant to the Bureau of Economics, U.S. Department of Agriculture, Spillman was widely known in eastern Washington. Spokane civic leaders—R. L. Rutter, J. W. Bradley, J. K. McCornack, Connor Malott, all bankers, Robbert Insinger of the Hypotheekbank, Frank Guilbert of the Good Roads Association, and others—drove the cars. Spillman, slender, ramrod erect, perhaps a little flustered by adulation, also advised diversified farming, holding out his parents' modest farm in Missouri as an example: "We did without most of the things that required money—but all the while we were living like royalty. We produced the family living on the farm."[57]

Spillman called his plan "balanced farming," warning that one-crop farming "is hazardous, depletes the soil, and is doomed to ultimate failure. . . . Sons and daughters inherit a worn-out farm." He urged wheat farmers to fortify themselves against price fluctuations by adding livestock, forage crops, poultry, orchards, and gardens.[58]

Doubtless a good many farm families took Spillman's advice (five years later 90 percent of Washington farms raised some poultry), but, as Hegnauer, who went with the caravan, summed it up, "The Spillman tour resulted in no sweeping revision. . . . It did, however, contribute . . . to the overall improvement program . . . to stabilize the agriculture of the region." Hard to tell precisely what Spillman accomplished: in the next few years, beef cattle and sheep numbers increased on grain farms, but not poultry because chickens required constant care, and hog-raising declined. Country stores sold "eastern" lard. The *Yakima Morning Herald*'s view was pessimistic: "In the movement for diversification many farmers added dairying and the outcome has been that we now have overproduction and prices are extremely low." The *Grange News* commented, "The average wheat farmer will not milk cows." Bryan had put his finger on the central problem twenty-five years earlier: involved in world export markets and heavily in debt for equipment and land, the dryland wheat farmer could not risk substantial change.[59]

Despite the farmers' respect for Spillman, his image of contentment in farm life may have struck some of his listeners as old-fashioned— nostalgia for a remembered plainer past—as farming evolved into specialized big business, and cars, telephones, and radios burned away the farmers' isolation like sunshine on a morning fog. The state college radio station began broadcasting in 1921; Spokane was on the air by 1925. Wenatchee apple blossom queen Rosella posed with a National Broadcasting Company microphone. The world war closed out old times. Military service thrust farm boys into a callous world that showed them new places, taught them to rely on machines, and challenged their homely values. When they marched home, they found the farm changing: there were gas engines in place of horses, an automobile in the barn, trucks rutting country roads, a new catechism of material progress and science, and country sweethearts gone to work in the city.

CHAPTER *5*

Irrigation

Walter N. Granger bent close to the earth to pour canteen water into a furrow, watching to see if the ground held moisture. Satisfied that it did, the sturdy, bearded man stood to look again at the barren flats and slopes of the Yakima River country. For days, Granger had ridden horseback over these hills, from creekbeds to the summit of Snipes Mountain for a bird's-eye view, seeing in his imagination the layout of a canal network to irrigate this brown ground.

Only weeks earlier, the president of the Northern Pacific, Thomas F. Oakes, had summoned Granger to St. Paul to offer a proposition: Granger could option 90,000 acres of railroad land at $1.25 an acre if he would build an irrigation system. Before he accepted, Granger rode out to inspect this arid country wrinkled by streams rising in forested mountains to its west.[1]

The railroad owned so much land here that a system the size Oakes wanted would be one of the largest in America, and he called Granger because Granger had built four irrigation systems in Montana—near Bozeman, in Strawberry Valley, and in Sun River Valley. Oakes knew that before Granger moved West for his health, he had been a persuasive traveling salesman earning $15,000 a year. A man who could build and sell, he was precisely the man Oakes needed.

Now forty-four and ready for something new, Granger finished his investigation and accepted Oakes's offer. Together they formed the Northern Pacific, Yakima and Kittitas Irrigation Company and appropriated 1,000 cubic feet per second of Yakima River flow. As the principal stockholder, the Northern Pacific furnished construction funds through a bond issue and Granger built, scraping canals in the gravelly earth with horse-drawn scoops, his men living in movable tent towns. On March 26, 1892, he smashed a bottle of champagne on the headgate of his diversion outlet on the Yakima to open the first twenty-five miles of canal while a town band played lively airs. The *Yakima Herald* called this "the beginning of the most important system of canals in America."[2]

The *Herald*'s boast was more than local pride, for Granger's projects in the Yakima were the most ambitious private systems of dozens attempted in Washington. A number of ditch builders verged on heroism, scratching crude but workable canals with primitive tools and insufficient capital, but private irrigation could provide neither the comprehensive system nor the financing to bring the entire valley under ditch. The low values of the land and lack of markets ruled out expensive construction.

One stark fact impelled the builders: the only way to convert this land to farm production was with water. Otherwise it might remain perpetual range. The builders tapped the Yakima, the Naches, and their tributary streams with weirs and dams to divert stream flow into their canals, letting the water ripple by gravity to tilled fields. But stream flows were seasonal. To irrigate the land adequately required storage reservoirs to save water and pumps to lift it to fertile flats that gravity would not reach. The builders' challenge was to repair nature—a challenge glittering with the tinseled dream of reclaiming unused land for settlement by the landless of America. Reclaiming land was Congress's idea, at any rate, and as a result, much of the West's and Washington's struggle to irrigate took place in political arenas.

In the work of repairing nature, a spirit like that of a medieval crusade betrayed the innocent, for nearly everyone who promoted and used irrigation was astoundingly innocent. They knew next to nothing of hydrology, climate, soil chemistry, or perculation; they demanded more water than they needed and fought to get it, and experimented, sometimes disastrously, with financing irrigation.

Walter Granger's system diverted flowing water from the Yakima into a projected sixty-mile canal with planned laterals and branches of 550 miles covering 40,000 acres. He platted two townsites, one aptly named Sunnyside on a treeless slope above the river and the other Zillah, named for Oakes's daughter. The railroad trumpeted Sunnyside as if it were already in bloom; it passed out booklets at the Chicago world's fair of 1893, hoping to beguile prospective settlers at $45 to $65 an acre, 5 percent down and a second installment in two years. The settlers' purchase contracts guaranteed them water forever.

Most who came planted alfalfa for sale to stockmen and set out fruit trees for themselves.

Spartan whitewashed homes were rising, Granger had opened a model irrigated farm, and his canals were lengthening when the panic of 1893 shattered his roseate prospects. The Northern Pacific declared bankruptcy, again. Settlers abandoned dry acreages. Granger, who had traded his option on railroad land for one-third of the irrigation company's stock, was offered and took the railroad's share of the company; he arranged with local merchants to accept his bank drafts at par and, despite depression, single-handedly kept the company afloat for eighteen months. Then his money ran out.

Unknown to Granger, the western land agent for the Northern Pacific, a high-living young German immigrant, Paul Schultze, had hypothecated stock in the irrigation company to raise money for his lavish Tacoma house, fashionable clothes, and women. The railroad had removed Schultze, who defaulted $100,000 due it, before a foreclosure suit against Schultze by the California Safe Deposit and Trust Company ruined the irrigation company as Granger labored to save it. The suit wiped out Granger as well as Schultze. The latter could not face dishonor; he shot himself. The receivers hired Granger to manage the company he had owned.[3]

As the nation recovered from panic, the reconstituted Northern Pacific tried to revive irrigation; in 1895–96 it rebuilt the crumbling Kennewick ditch, downriver from Sunnyside, and instructed its engineers to identify likely irrigation sites throughout Washington, withdrawing railroad lands from settlement wherever irrigation seemed feasible "to prevent the land getting into the hands of speculators and into so many different hands that it would be difficult" to develop units for irrigation.[4]

Members of the Christian Cooperative Movement (Dunkards) bought the Sunnyside townsite, settled three hundred families there in six years, and gave them deeds that banned gambling, liquor, and weeds.

Investors who had loaned the Northern Pacific, Yakima and Kittitas Irrigation Company funds for canal construction, headed by Roland H. Denny of Seattle, son of one of Seattle's founders, formed the Washington Irrigation Company to acquire the Sunnyside project in 1900, retaining Granger as manager. An important member of this new company was the attorney Elbert F. Blaine, who had handled old Arthur Denny's investments and property, had joined Denny's sons

Charles and Roland in real estate promotions in Seattle and Yakima, and would become a forceful spokesman for private irrigation in Washington.[5]

The new company circulated extravagant booklets in eastern and midwestern farm states, and settlers again came to Sunnyside; the company sold them land only when they also bought water rights at $30 to $60 an acre, explaining that bankers made loans only to farmers with water rights. By and large, settlers who bought from the Washington Irrigation Company were satisfied; their contracts were honored, they were allowed to pay in five annual installments at 6 percent interest, and a number paid for their land and water with income from crops, although O. L. Waller, irrigation engineer at the Washington experiment station, wrote Granger that the farmers used too much water—"they would have drowned themselves" if they had run the canals.[6] By 1905 the company operated more than seven hundred miles of canals and laterals covering 36,000 acres, and one of every five residents of the Yakima Valley lived on the Sunnyside project. Granger proclaimed it the fourth largest irrigation system in the United States.

The Kennewick and Sunnyside projects were heavily advertised. Nowhere in Washington was the bounty of watered land more shamelessly extolled. But settlers often faced high costs for water and land, especially if they bought from previous owners. As a general rule, nearly three-fourths of the original buyers of irrigated tracts sold their land within three years, partly because they tired of competing strenuously for water. While the state's major irrigation enclaves bristled with battles for water, the federal government in 1902 organized its Reclamation Service. Immediately petitions showered the service for federal help for western irrigation schemes. One petition, signed by 106 Washington citizens, demanded development of a Tieton-Cowiche project west of Yakima, where one of the promoters, the Yakima hardware merchant and lumberman George S. Rankin, had planned a private system. When the legislature refused to assist him in building a reservoir, Rankin asked his neighbors to sign a petition and Congressman Wesley L. Jones to interest the Reclamation Service.

Jones, a "plain, solid man . . . earnest," as the Seattle *Post-Intelligencer* saw him, was an Illinois native who moved to Yakima to practice law; elected to Congress in 1899 when he was thirty-four, he saw in federal irrigation for his adopted state his chance to advance his political career and perhaps unseat Levi Ankeny in the Senate. Jones, who relished sonorous platitudes, could speak unblinkingly then and later of "farms for the homeless, homes for the farmless," and this suited the congressional notion that irrigation would open new settlement areas for the landless. Washington's senators, Addison G. Foster, a Tacoma lumberman, and Ankeny also supported irrigation, although Ankeny, an owner of the Prosser Land and Irrigation Company, victimized by charges of venality, was branded by *Collier's* as a "political harlequin" without much influence. Noting that he often slept through hearings, Ankeny's congressional colleagues rarely listened to him.[7]

With his career possibly at stake, Jones prudently insisted that conflicts over water rights to the Yakima River be resolved as a prerequisite to federal participation. Then he pushed the service to look at Washington State. The Reclamation Service investigated nine Washington locations between 1903 and 1905: the Yakima, Okanogan (in which Ankeny expressed interest), Synarep, Methow, Colville, Chelan, Big Bend, Palouse, and Priest Rapids. They found the Synarep a mere fancy; its reservoir, a lake on the Colville Indian Reservation, drained in the opposite direction from intended project lands. The Methow, feasible, would require the Reclamation Service to assemble land from dispersed private owners and the state college. The Colville was "a scheme with small possibilities." Priest Rapids, also feasible, was set aside because federal funds ran out before the survey was completed. The Chelan was primarily a hydroelectric and secondarily an irrigation project where a farmer-owned company installed generating machinery in 1898; it was dropped as a federal project because the service then was restricted to falling water—no pumping, no generation.[8]

The Reclamation Service's studies were virtually secret, for, as F. H. Newell, the service's chief engineer, told Jones, "If . . . we let it be known that a certain project is in contemplation, instantly every man owning a water right . . . freshens these up and the project becomes impossible."[9]

Service field engineers confirmed that large storage reservoirs would be needed to extend the irrigating season. The Washington Irrigation Company had tried to establish a system of dams and reservoirs but had been blocked by residents of the upper Yakima who opposed giving all the water to the lower valley.[10]

Although Newell advised Jones that "it will not be expedient to irrigate the . . . Yakima area at present," the Yakima system outlined by the Reclamation Service was comprehensive, including even irrigable land on the Yakima Indian Reservation, and white settlers, sure that Indian objections would be silenced, bought Indian land and marked off townsites at Toppenish, Wapato, and Mabton. But a Virginian who had come to Yakima in 1903 to farm, Lucullus Virgil

McWhorter, outraged by indifference to Indian claims, advised Indian landowners to sign no papers; he would summarize a decade of tribal travail in a fifty-six-page pamphlet, *The Crime against the Yakimas*. McWhorter brought the Indian Rights Association into the controversy and at last persuaded the federal government to give up its plan to open much of the reservation for settlement and agree instead to deliver water for irrigated Indian farms.[11]

As field studies closed in Washington State, Newell testified before a joint congressional committee that the Big Bend (on which the service spent $8,491) would be "the greatest irrigation project in the world—but the cost would be staggering." It would cover 1.6 million acres and use water drawn from Coeur d'Alene Lake, flowing by gravity through tunnels and a hundred-mile canal to the Grand Coulee near Steamboat Rock. Theron A. Noble, a Seattle civil engineer hired by the Reclamation Service for hydrographic surveys (a cartoon showed him Roosevelt-style with pince-nez and close-cropped hair), estimated the cost of the Big Bend at $26 million, or $1,625 an acre.[12] Even before seeing Noble's figures, Newell had made up his mind that the Big Bend "must be left for a future generation."

While the Reclamation Service scouted the field, private irrigators published grandiose schemes for new projects, some doubtless intended to forestall federal entry. The service could not have been impressed by these chimeral contrivances, but nevertheless at the end of 1904 Newell declared the Yakima "well covered with irrigation systems," others impractical or too expensive, and therefore the service would build nothing in Washington. Wesley Jones could not abide the decision.

Plain and platitudinous he might be, Jones was also a practical politician. He understood that the Reclamation Service's decision was justified by its field studies, but he knew that it could be reversed by political influence. As a member of the committee on irrigation and reclamation of arid lands, Jones witnessed the manipulation of reclamation funding, and he knew the background of federal reclamation laws. Born of a combination of conservation advocacy and congressional intent to open new lands for settlement, reclamation passed Congress in 1902 at the insistence of President Theodore Roosevelt, who championed a bill (which Jones helped write) that incorporated the maverick notion of Nevada Congressman Francis G. Newlands that federal projects could be paid off with proceeds from the sale of western public lands. Newlands saw the federal service superseding private investors as the chief builder and operator of irrigation projects, and states entitled to projects in proportion to public land sales within them. (Newell regarded the reclamation act as "simply a western scheme which had been successfully lobbied through against the opposition of the leaders of both parties.")[13] With a straight face, Jones could argue that federal irrigation would cost taxpayers nothing, and he could condone unscreened settlement (settlement without asking settlers' qualifications) on the ground that "farms for the farmless" implied the single criterion of farmlessness.[14]

Jones recognized that while Washington State was alive with settlers, California's farm population was declining. California congressmen viewed federal irrigation as a way to revive immigration to their state. Their interests and those of Washington could both be served by getting together, and obviously some states would get more federal money than others. Parceling the money would be a political decision.

Yet Washington's first dalliance with federal irrigation had been a frustrating affair. The state set aside 55,000 acres in the Yakima Valley, public and railroad land, for watering under the Carey Act of 1894 to reclaim arid western lands. Washington's plan was, in fact, less a reclamation program than a bid for federal subsidy. Fifty-five private canals already flowed with Yakima water while their managers warred for water, filing claim on top of claim without legal or legislative continuity. For instance, the legislature in 1900 decreed that water be measured in cubic feet per second but failed to translate this to the traditional miner's inch or acknowledge that six different units were then called a miner's inch in Yakima. Viewing the confusion, Waller snorted that if all the claims could be honored, Yakima water would cover the United States seventeen feet deep. Washington built nothing under the Carey Act. Governor Albert Mead agreed to withdraw the state's plan, then turned about, and when citizens petitioned for Reclamation Service studies, heatedly accused them of "robbing" the state of $550,000—ten dollars an acre for Carey land.[15]

This was the political climate when, in January 1905, Congressman Jones talked at length with Newell and others in the Reclamation Service. They were used to politicians demanding special benefits; they worked under continuous pressure from congressmen who made threats. Any change in the service's position on Washington would, of course, have to be justified. To do so, Jones and the service used a 1904 report by Cornelius H. Bliss, a federal assistant engineer, who carefully measured stream flows in forty-six large canals and several smaller ones, classified lands, analyzed water claims, and reviewed Yakima topography. His report, sent along by Noble, concluded that three-fourths of the irrigable land in the Yakima remained to be brought under ditch. Shortly after reading Bliss's analysis, Newell announced that the Reclamation Service would reconsider a federal project for Yakima if the state of Washington enacted enabling legislation and resolved conflicts over water rights there.

Jones wrote home to Yakima, "The matter is now squarely up to us." Noble, William W. Robertson, publisher of the daily *Yakima Republic,* and State Senator A. J. Splawn vigorously supported a Yakima bill in the legislature, opposed by Spokane men who preferred a federal Palouse project. The Yakima measure passed, granting the United States eminent domain and title to reservoirs and irrigation works and authorizing formation of water users' associations (exempt from the state franchise tax) to contract for repayment with the federal government. Mead, who had met with valley representatives, meekly signed the bill as an emergency act on March 4, 1905, so it could take effect immediately.[16]

Resolving conflicts over water rights meant some farmers would have to compromise and others sell out. With the slogan, "It's up to the people," an eleven-man committee of the North Yakima Commercial Club canvassed the valley, persuading some farmers to sign agreements with the Reclamation Service and raising money to buy the water rights of farmers who would not sign. By early January 1906, the committee's task was done. The *Yakima Morning Herald* published an "extra" when large Benton County interests "yielded to citizen pressure to sign a government water contract," clearing the way for the service. Water users' associations formed at Tieton and Sunnyside (and Sunnyside farmers demanded drainage as well as irrigation). User demands, and absentee owners speculating in land to be irrigated, delayed the start of work, but the federal service was now committed to Washington.[17]

The Washington Irrigation Company sold its Sunnyside system (but neither its land nor water rights) to the government for $640,000, perhaps one-third above replacement costs, and the Northern Pacific sold reservoir sites it had reserved at Lakes Cle Elum, Kachees, and Keechelus. The Reclamation Service started working in October 1906, replacing diversion works in the Yakima River and rebuilding earth canals (in good condition due to regular repairs). Following the federal example, the railroad sold land to settlers in farm-size units. The service delivered water for the 1907 growing season, charging $52 an acre payable in ten annual installments, and maintenance and operating costs of 95 cents an acre, adjustable each year.

Based on these costs, an orchardist who bought the maximum forty acres, built a modest home, supported a small family, and paid his irrigation charges needed an initial investment of about $3,500. Until his crops matured, he received no income from his farm. Little wonder that many settlers worked seasonally as farmhands, loggers, or even miners. But by 1918 a settler could sell an established, irrigated farm for a thousand dollars an acre. Conceivably he could sell ten acres to pay his debts and continue to cultivate thirty. Many did just that, reducing the size of orchards and increasing the number of growers.

By World War I, Yakima's irrigated orchards would be among the foremost exporters of apples for world trade, although less than 20 percent of Sunnyside was used for orchards. More than 60 percent was grasses and 20 percent, field crops. By then the federal system consisted of six units: the Kittitas, Wapato, Benton, Sunnyside, Tieton, and Storage (reservoirs); it extended to Mabton by a 500-foot pipe under the Yakima River and to Prosser by another pipe on a bridge.

As the Reclamation Service moved upriver to Kittitas, spirited citizens demanded comprehensive irrigation regardless of cost and, at one point, threatened to choose canal routes themselves while the district engineer fumed that "each locality used every effort to have work done in its own neighborhood first." The bickering so delayed construction that in 1911, several years after it should have been completed (and a time when irrigation districts in many states defaulted bonds), the Kittitas found no buyers for its bonds until the federal government and the Northern Pacific and Milwaukee railroads took them.[18]

Chronologically the first Washington federal project was the small, hapless Okanogan, authorized December 2, 1905, ten days before the Sunnyside and Tieton, to which Congressman Jones had also persuaded the Reclamation Service. The government used the water rights and ditch route of a disbanded citizens' association, and sold raw land at $50 to $75 an acre, much of it, a project manager later complained, to settlers with no experience in irrigation (unscreened settlement). As settlers planted Jonathan and Winesap apple trees and the project opened a first unit in 1908 and a second in 1910, assessments shot upward, from a relatively high $62 an acre to $100 in 1912, when service engineers rewrote water contracts with steeper rates to pay for lining the leaky main canal. The Okanogan sent two private contractors into bankruptcy. By 1912 several of its units were delinquent—not unusual on federal projects—and seepage water so damaged Conconully basements that the government bought the town. Three-fourths of the orchards were heavily mortgaged. When they could entice buyers at $250 an acre, the original settlers fled. "Setting down . . . these few facts is a very simple matter but they do not tell any of the heartaches, worries, and grief through which the water users passed during the period 1910 to 1929," wrote the Okanogan banker, Harry Kerr. The Okanogan paid dearly for federal development—its costs underestimated, water supply overestimated, burdened by hundreds of untillable acres.[19]

Although the Reclamation Service came into Washington three years after its beginning, federal irrigation came late to the state. By the time the Okanogan project was authorized, the service had completed plans for irrigation works in thirteen other states and three territories and had begun building a dozen, some of them the largest engineering works attempted to that time in the United States. The service engineers quickly discovered that construction costs were going to be higher than forecast and the Newlands repayment plan (land sales) impractical. The service and western congressmen were flooded with letters protesting costs, demanding longer repayment periods, and so on. In the Reclamation Extension Act of 1914, Congress prohibited increases in construction charges once they were stated in a public notice, except with consent of a majority of persons holding water rights, and tied maintenance and operation fees to the amount of water delivered.[20]

In much the same way that the Northern Pacific launched irrigation of the Yakima as private enterprise, the Great Northern created Wenatchee. Under Thomas Burke's overseeing, the townsite was laid out and promoted by the Wenatchee Development Company and managed by Arthur Gunn for the railroad. With a $15,000 loan from Jim Hill, Gunn in 1896 organized the Wenatchee Power Company, bought Jacob Shotwell's pioneer irrigation ditches, and enlarged them with a bond issue purchased by the Great Northern. When Gunn's company overextended itself, the railroad completed his construction work and at the same time financed Shotwell and A. C. Jones in their Cashmere ditch. Gunn's system, however, watered only company land. Wenatchee residents, eager for comprehensive irrigation, in 1901 raised funds to resurvey an old plan for a highline ditch that would reach most of the arable land.

A Northern Pacific land agent, Laughlin McLean, persuaded the builder of the Selah-Moxee canal near Yakima, W. T. Clark, to construct Wenatchee's comprehensive system. (Much of the land was claimed as Northern Pacific land grant. At places, the Northern Pacific and Great Northern tracks lay only thirteen miles apart.) Clark brought two engineers, Charles C. Ward and Marvin Chase, the latter destined to frame Washington's irrigation code and be the state's first hydraulic engineer.

Clark's project was built with a $225,000 loan from Robert Livingstone, manager of the Oregon Mortgage Company at Portland, to be retired by the sale of water service at $50 to $60 an acre (a figure that seemed very high). At that price, most residents refused to sign water contracts. Clark then would not build. Wenatchee irrigation—for the moment—hung in the balance until citizens' delegations persuaded landowners to agree to take water. With enough signatures, Clark started construction in 1902. He would have delivered water for the 1903 growing season had not the Great Northern misdirected four carloads of wooden penstocks. As Clark began scooping his canal high in the hills, new settlers raced into Wenatchee, seeking land and housing. The town swelled, and land prices, once $25 an acre or less, bloated to $400.[21]

Clark quietly negotiated to buy land to the south and east, toward Malaga and the Columbia River, enlisting Burke—and even Hill himself—to raise money for a bridge to extend his pipeline across the Columbia. In his grand manner, Hill solicited his rich friends at lunch in Seattle's Rainier Club to contribute to the bridge. The Great Northern stipulated that the bridge must also carry trains. Completed in 1908 by subsidiary companies, with Clark's pipeline hanging from it, the bridge was the first auto-wagon span across the Columbia. Irrigation on the river's east bank precipitated a new land rush that brought six thousand settlers into Douglas County within months.[22]

Clark's projects built up the Wenatchee area but he did not prosper from them, for his maintenance rates of $1.50 a month proved too low and his water supply unreliable. While land speculators occasionally reaped quick profits, Clark went broke. Warned that Clark's company would abandon canal maintenance for lack of funds, water users in 1914 formed a reclamation district, sold $500,000 worth of bonds, and bought the system. By then the flatlands between the river and Wenatchee's humpy brown hills marched with ranks of fruit trees. Again, dreams had outrun reality: the typical Wenatchee grower needed at least $1,890 to bring a forty-acre orchard to maturity, while costs for irrigation, house, clothing, and food burdened him with more debts. Dozens lost their land before their orchards produced. Clark supported himself by operating the Everbest Nursery but gradually turned his interests to irrigation in California and moved there.

Although irrigation was demonstrably expensive and developers often ran short of money or water or both, the tenuous prospects seemed not to dismay men who promoted new projects. By the 1920s, every one of Washington's nineteen counties east of the Cascades contained irrigation systems, although the others combined did not match the quarter-million acres under federal ditch in Yakima and Benton counties. In Yakima County, 93 percent of the farms were irrigated; Kittitas, 79.4; Chelan, 81.3; and Benton, 85.2 percent. In irrigated counties, farms were considerably smaller than in dry counties, for while Yakima County contained the largest number of farms, Whitman and Lincoln tilled the largest areas, more than 1.2 million acres in each.[23]

A singular contribution of the Reclamation Service was financing large reservoirs. Of 205 reservoirs in the state containing 447,789 acre feet of water, the service controlled 440,000 feet in seven reservoirs. Private systems continued to rely chiefly on stream diversion.

In nearly every irrigation area, however, water rights had been controversial. Predictably, when courts did not settle disputes, farmers and irrigation companies sought political solutions. The state recognized both riparian and appropriated water rights (riparian: a property right to use nonnavigable water adjoining or running through one's land; appropriated: the right to take water for reasonable needs by posting public notices of appropriation). Washington's courts upheld both rights, sometimes apparently contravening one decision by the next. One hoary suit (and the first review by the state supreme court of legislation on riparian rights) was that of forty-five neighbors who opposed Philip A. Johncox's appropriation from Ahtanum Creek as conflicting with their riparian rights, a suit that dragged through the courts from the 1880s until 1925.[24]

Those who appropriated water held their rights in chronological order, the first claim entitling its owner to first rights, the second claim to second rights, and so on. Claimants sued to settle the dates of filings, hours of postings, transfers to new owners, finicking definitions of water courses. One suit even contested drinking water for domestic animals. Obviously the later settlers argued that water should be used for the benefit of the largest number, a stance that gained ground with the expansion of commercial irrigation. The greatest good of the greatest number was politically attractive—advocated in economic and philosophical writings of the time—and basic to comprehensive irrigation.

Washington's buffeted, orphan first state legislature, 1889–90, enacted an irrigation law modeled on California's Wright Act of 1887, then heralded as progressive despite legal challenges that lasted until 1896.[25] The legislature convened late because President Benjamin Harrison neglected to proclaim statehood, delaying Washington's authority to function as a state or elect U.S. senators. Many legislators fell ill in abominable weather, and those who struggled through storms to Olympia found the capitol too small to hold all 105 members at one time.[26]

The Washington irrigation act did not fare much better than its framers: it put the adjudication of disputes over water in the hands of three local commissioners appointed by each county's superior court—minions who in practice could not contend with the variety and ferocity of their neighbors' demands—and permitted landowners to form irrigation districts that could condemn right-of-way, issue bonds (giving water rights and property as security), and levy assessments.[27]

Torn by disputes, irrigation counties and their legislators agitated for a comprehensive state water code. But in the panic year 1893, bills by Yakima and Kittitas members did not even get out of committee, and in 1895 Kittitas's Benjamin F. Barge, whose chief service in the legislature was to persuade the state to pay insolvent contractors building the Ellensburg normal school (of which he was principal), managed to pass only technical amendments to the 1890 act. Faced with unexpected costs, early districts went bankrupt while legislators constantly proposed amendments intended to balance the rights of water users against those of creditors. The stocky Barge, a promoter of the Tieton project, attracted more attention with his attempt to strike the word "male" from the state's constitution, to enable women to vote, than with his irrigation bills. By 1896 he left the legislature to join an inept federal commission trying to negotiate land claims with Northwest Indian tribes.

Meanwhile, contention over water clogged the courts and occasionally flared outside them. The Prosser Land and Irrigation Company broke away parts of a diversion dam for the Yakima reservation to restore normal river flow to its land, and engineers of the Washington Irrigation Company (on advice of their attorneys) dynamited a storage dam of the Union Gap Irrigation Company at Lake Cle Elum to save withering Sunnyside crops. Seattle newspapers extravagantly reported an "irrigation war" with armed men patrolling canals.

Hoping to promote a water code, two governors, Henry McBride in 1904 and Marion Hay in 1909, appointed code commissions (there were about seven thousand water claimants in court), Hay's headed by one of the respected irrigation spokesmen in the state, O. L. Waller. Professor Waller was frank about the situation: "Under the present statute, the only limit to the quantity of water an appropriator may claim and file upon is the measure of his greed." But neither governor pushed a code through the legislature. When Hay failed a second time, a Yakima senator opined that lumber and utility interests, bent on holding the rivers for themselves, defeated the code bill.

One of Clark's engineers, Marvin Chase, refereeing contests over water rights to Ahtanum Creek in 1914, was appalled to find 275 claimants. He solved their contention by defining thirty user categories based on the order of filing and the most beneficial uses. The concept of beneficial use reflected state court decisions and a popular conservationist view, enunciated for the nation by Gifford Pinchot, among others. Chase became a strong advocate of a state code. The operating and maintenance officials of federal projects formed an association, the Washington Irrigation Institute, and they, too, lobbied for a code.[28]

Finally in 1917 the legislature adopted a surface water code, much of it written by Chase, and the governor named Chase the state hydraulic engineer to enforce the new law. (Ironically, Washington, one of the first states to adopt California's pioneering laws for irrigation, was one of the last to pass a comprehensive code.) The state had been moving, in legal decisions, toward a doctrine of beneficial use, and districts toward establishing their power to assess members to meet deficits in debt retirement. While the code could not stop disputes or lawsuits, it set out a method of assigning rights in deeds and purchase contracts, a long step toward peaceful resolution of water contests.[29]

Aside from the complex and intense battles for water, irrigated farming could succeed only if new crops and new markets could be found, for there was a widespread feeling that the country did not need new farms. Congress might assert a policy of land for the landless in one breath, and in the next agree that foodstuffs were plentiful in America. But whether new farms were needed or not, investors continued to build canals because buyers wanted irrigated land. Irrigation was supposed to produce crop after crop without failure.

And so irrigation projects spread. The erstwhile railroad builder Daniel C. Corbin constructed a system in the valley east of Spokane, enabling his company to sell, for $500 a acre, land bought for as little as $12.50. His success in watering the gravelly valley encouraged others. By 1910 more than twenty plats for irrigated tracts covered the valley (with redolent names: Greenacres, Opportunity, Orchard Avenue, and others) drawing water from lakes. Eventually Corbin had to take water from the Spokane River to ensure delivery, while owners of recreational lake property bitterly fought drawdowns by irrigators.[30]

On the Washington side of the Snake River overlooking Lewiston,

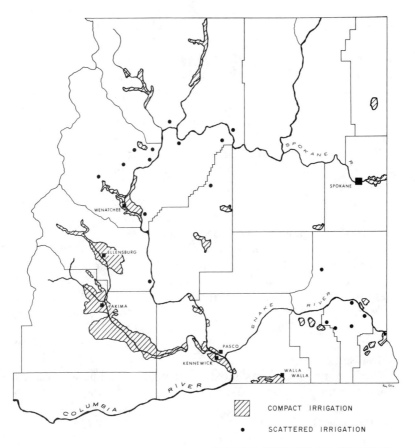

Irrigation in eastern Washington in 1930. Compact irrigation in the legend means substantial area development; scattered, small private canals, few of commercial significance. (Based on National Resources Planning Board, *Development of Resources and Economic Opportunity in the Pacific Northwest.* Map by Ray Ellis, Eastern Washington University cartographic laboratory.)

Idaho, an unemployed civil engineer, Cassius C. Van Arsdol, secured the backing of Boston investors including Charles Francis Adams, Jr., to build a canal system. His fourteen-mile ditch leaked, his flumes leaked, and water vanished into porous ground, but Van Arsdol called his place Vineland and sold tracts (later Clarkston). Worth pennies without water, the land irrigated sold for as much as $1,000 an acre.[31]

Wherever flatlands touched a stream, irrigation projects blossomed. The nine-mile Hawley ditch along the Touchet River; the Burbank, covering 12,000 acres with water from the Snake; the Gardena, carrying water twenty-one miles from the Walla Walla to 7,000 acres; the Moses Coulee Fruit Land Company, an oasis in Washington's desert; the Methow Canal Company, Larabee and Bolinger ditches to 15,000 acres along the Methow in Okanogan County. Land worth at best $60 with improvements soared to $350 an acre, inspiring older settlers to subdivide their alfalfa and stock ranches into irrigated tracts, sell, and move away.

The men who built these and other Washington irrigation systems had to be resourceful; their irrigation science consisted of surveying to be sure water would run by gravity to their land and judging porosity by pouring water into holes. That some succeeded was due to diligence and perhaps to luck; that others failed was not necessarily peculation or ignorance. Few men at first understood the costs of irrigation, the cycles or amounts of falling water, or the ins and outs of water laws. Some sincere men failed; some speculators succeeded. If the good guys did not always win, neither can settlers who bought heavily advertised tracts be written off as simply gullible. Irrigation patently freed farmers from relying on fickle rainfall, and seller and buyer both believed an abiding metaphor that helped build the West— winning independence by blissful labor on the fecund earth in healthful sunshine. Eden sounded no better.

To be sure, speculators lured unwary buyers while advocates of some feasible projects could not raise the money for them. Perhaps no one can count how many irrigation projects were talked about. Early settlers were leaving Quincy, a windblown railroad promotion irrigated by 250-foot wells, when the remaining residents formed a water users' association for a 500,000-acre project to be supplied from Lake Wenatchee. But the scheme burst when Washington's voters in 1914 rejected a $40 million bond issue for it. The Hanford Land and Irrigation Company, intending to use Priest Rapids, sank into receivership. The promoters of River Front Orchard Tracts, 266 acres along the Columbia, sold tracts to New Jersey, New York, and Pennsylvania residents, but collapsed after one new owner came to see his ground.

Denny and Blaine, builders of Yakima, touted a 250,000-acre development near Brewster, but it slipped from sight after a newspaper campaign.

The prominent Wenatchee citizen, once lieutenant governor, John A. Gellatly denounced "one outfit who operated out of Spokane, cheated the public to the tune of over two million dollars, and came near breaking one of the large banks of Europe." Perhaps he meant the Columbia River Orchard Company, whose promoters were convicted of issuing $4 million in fraudulent bonds on a 152-acre tract.[32] And there was to be a million-dollar electric generation and irrigating plant on the Methow. A man named J. W. O'Keefe invented a wonderful perpetual pump—guaranteed. And there was Arcadia.

With its evocative pastoral name, the Arcadia Orchards Company, organized in 1907 by a two-time Spokane mayor and insurance salesman, Floyd L. Daggett (with others), proposed to irrigate 18,000 acres twenty-two miles north of Spokane—"the largest commercial orchard tract in the world," an advertisement called it. Terraced scabland with scrubby pine, fir, and tamarack, the project drew on creeks and reservoirs that did not contain enough water for it. Daggett sold the company. Its new owners marketed lands and stock, cleared hundreds of acres, and built canals with loans from the Netherlands American Mortgage Bank that pyramided to $1.8 million between 1912 and 1920.

Illustrated with photographs of flourishing Wenatchee orchards, Arcadia's elegant prospectus contained contracts for customers to mail, agreeing to buy at $400 an acre, 5 percent down, $2.50 a month per acre for four years, and $5 a month for a fifth year. The company pledged to deliver a mature orchard when the buyer took possession—owing $3,620 on each ten acres which he would pay in three years, presumably from orchard income.

Arcadia sold tracts to hundreds who had never seen the place, some of them military men who intended to retire there. Most tracts were 10 acres, but one was 40 and another was 151. The company claimed that it planted a million trees. Some bore fruit, but for most the water gave out, frosts damaged buds, and buyers who came expecting to see blossoming slopes too often found instead weedy dry ditches. Dozens threw up their contracts; many sued. Arcadia's surviving tracts produced prize-winning Big A brand apples for perhaps a dozen years. In 1920 the Netherlands American Mortgage Bank formed a holding company to sell the rocky hills as best it could.[33]

Of all of Washington's largest irrigation proposals, perhaps the unbuilt Palouse created the most lasting animosity. Begun and scrapped three times between 1892 and 1898 by private investors to irrigate 53,000 acres of fine-grained sandy loam near the confluence of the Palouse and Snake rivers, the Palouse project seemed sure to be built in 1904 when the Reclamation Service reported it costly but feasible, recommending a larger project of 150,000 acres. Lands were withdrawn from settlement, routes of canals surveyed, and dam sites core-bored.[34]

But after two years of further review, a consulting engineer turned down the Palouse, ostensibly because the river flow could not supply the intended reservoir, Washtucna Coulee. Rumors circulated. The Reclamation Service dropped the Palouse because the Oregon Railroad and Navigation Company would not reroute its track, it was whispered, or because a Pasco owner refused to sell nine sections to the government. The largest landowners of the proposed area were sheep raisers Max and Hans Harder, Colfax bankers E. T. Coman and William Huntley, and the Northern Pacific Railroad.[35]

"The Palouse project has been lied about, jiggered, and flim-flammed to a fair-ye-well," stormed the *Pasco Express,* and so adamant were Palouse proponents that when the Franklin County Development League charged that federal cost estimates had been excessive, the 1913 legislature appropriated $10,000 for another survey. Again there was a favorable report and again the Palouse seemed ready to go, when war intervened and a postwar collapse of farm prices put financing out of the question. Accusations of political artifice and slipshod engineering echoed for years after. The Palouse would not die until the Columbia Basin swallowed it.

The Columbia Basin project—or, as it was long called, the Big Bend—faced the challenge of delivering water long distances and the handicaps of high cost and disinterested federal administrations. The Reclamation Service thought of it as a project for the future, "if hard times should come on . . . and the country would be looking for public works upon which to use large bodies of men who were out of labor," as a senator phrased its view.[36] Except to urge water codes and reclamation surveys, Washington's governors vacillated on irrigation for thirty years, but near the end of Ernest Lister's administration (1913–19) the state energetically pursued development of the Big Bend. The clearest federal espousal of wholesale development of the Columbia River from a national figure was Herbert C. Hoover's speech in Seattle in 1926, three years before his term as president. Once in office, Hoover was less enthusiastic. Western irrigation talk was not popular in eastern states, which feared competition and overproduction.

Even if presidents had been interested, from about 1913 to 1924 changes in policies and personnel tore the Reclamation Service. When Elwood Mead became commissioner of a renamed Bureau of Reclamation in 1924, publicly to advocate screening project settlers and peopling one project before opening another, he sustained the federal policy of creating only family-size farms.

Washington's aspirants for Congress or the state legislature regularly stated their views on the Big Bend. By the mid-1920s, the proposed project was a major issue in eastern Washington political campaigns. Clarence C. Dill, defeated for reelection as a congressman largely for his opposition to United States entry into World War I, unseated incumbent Miles Poindexter for the Senate in 1922 partly because Poindexter (perhaps given no choice by his Spokane managers) favored irrigating the Big Bend by gravity canals. Dill knew little about irrigation, by his admission, but against Poindexter he came out for irrigation by any feasible method, and believed thereafter that his majority of four thousand stemmed largely from the eight to ten thousand Big Bend voters who favored damming the Columbia and pumping irrigation water.[37]

Irrigation of the desert by ditch or by dam generated a thundering controversy that inevitably spilled into the state's affairs, an internecine confrontation in which Spokane anchored the gravity ditch advocates and central Washington the dam proponents. But that is too general to describe adequately the divisions (and shades) of opinions. Both sides wanted commercial development. Rapid expansion of irrigation works in the state had ended: 41.5 percent of the irrigation construction in Washington up to World War II had been completed between 1905 and 1909. Now the Big Bend promised a statewide business revival with new settlement on irrigated farms (Governor Lister estimated fifty thousand new families might come).

For years Spokane's posturing irritated the residents of Yakima, Wenatchee, Pasco, and other central Washington towns. Spokane had backed federal development of the Palouse in preference to Yakima; Spokane regarded the Big Bend project as its private commercial bonanza; the Spokane Chamber of Commerce talked like proprietor of the Big Bend; and the Washington Water Power Company, headquartered in Spokane, favored gravity over a dam to protect its interests in generating sites. The Spokane chamber even renamed the Big Bend, according to James A. Ford, its energetic secretary-manager, whose quick mind and relish for intrigue fashioned much of the publicity for the proposed gravity system. "We realized that Big Bend meant nothing to people in the East," Ford once recalled, "so we went into a back room of the chamber and picked the name Columbia Basin project."[38] Given Spokane's attitude, at least some of the dialectic represented the determination of central Washington to hold onto the project for itself and a chance to snipe at Spokane.

The Big Bend, or Columbia Basin, consisted largely of sagebrush desert, windblown over an ancient basalt base, annual rainfall from six to ten inches, settled here and there and then abandoned; its few dryland farmers harvested every second year (a crop failure for them meant four years without income). Nearly 80 percent of this forlorn land was privately owned, 9.5 percent by the federal government, 6.1 percent by the state, and 3.4 percent by railroads. Unlike Washington's earlier large irrigation projects, in this one no owner held enough ground to step forward as chief developer or beneficiary.[39]

Although the Big Bend would be a federal project, if built, a private irrigation man, Elbert Blaine (who grouched that private companies could have built Yakima's canals cheaper than the government), revived interest in the project while acting as an adviser to Lister. Blaine so enthused the governor and Spokane businessmen with the possibility of a canal to the desert from the Pend Oreille River that two weeks before Christmas 1918 the state's hydraulic engineer, its geologist, and a caravan of volunteer Spokane automobile drivers bumped overland in snow from Albeni Falls on the Pend Oreille to Davenport and Rock Lake to be sure, by barometric readings, that the proposed canal route really was all downhill. It was, and Lister advanced a gravity canal for the Big Bend in his 1919 message to the legislature, predicting that the project would "carry Washington into the front rank as a leading agricultural state."[40]

Earlier in 1918, by chance, the kinetic editor and publisher of the *Wenatchee Daily World*, Rufus Woods, had printed the surmise of William H. Clapp, an Ephrata attorney, that the Big Bend could be irrigated from a reservoir behind a dam in the steep-walled Grand Coulee. "The last, the newest, the most ambitious idea in the way of reclamation," Woods called Clapp's idea.[41]

Stirred by a prospective revival of immigration, the 1919 legislature appropriated $100,000, and two years later $50,000 more, for studies. Already twelve reports had appeared on aspects of the basin—five on the Palouse project alone—and thirteen more would follow before 1930, one in 1924 by the Federal Power Commission on electrical generation outlook for the Columbia and another in 1925 on irrigation by the Bureau of Reclamation. The state's 1919 report estimated that 1,753,000 acres could be watered by a gravity system from the Pend Oreille (Clark's Fork).

But an eminent engineer, Hugh L. Cooper, who had come to Washington twenty years earlier as bridge builder for D. C. Corbin's railroads and later built the Muscle Shoals and Keokuk projects, endorsed a Grand Coulee dam. Cooper doubtless gave an engineer's judgment, but he may have enjoyed the moment, for he had little regard for Spokane's opinions and may have still been piqued by the refusal of some Spokane residents to return his family silver service and household goods after he sold them at auction to pay his bills.

If Cooper endorsed the dam, Spokane would hire its own expert. Through the Washington State Department of Conservation and Development, Spokane engaged General George W. Goethals, builder of the Panama Canal and wartime quartermaster general, an authentic national hero, whose six-day inspection of the canal route, damsite, and arid lands was a triumphal tour. Wilson Creek flew flags for him; Ephrata staged a rabbit drive; and everywhere on his route, Goethals was surrounded by farm people who sidled up to see this great man. A story goes that the general called the Grand Coulee "a perfect damsite," adding, "If I were twenty years younger, I'd like nothing better than to tackle the job." But his report, relying on earlier inquiries, endorsed the gravity plan as less costly, simpler, and covering more acres.[42]

In 1926 Washington lagged Idaho and Oregon in acreage under federal irrigation. The federal Reclamation Service had constructed the Umatilla and Klamath projects in Oregon; the Minidoka, King Hill, and Boise in Idaho; and it had learned a great deal. The service was now experienced in irrigation in fifteen western states and had completed dams that combined irrigation and generation—the Roosevelt in Arizona and the Boise River in Idaho. The army engineers, with a drumroll of publicity, were planning a series of dams for the Columbia to generate electricity, despite protests from barge companies calling for an open river for navigation.

If Spokane was one camp, and central Washington another, in the debate over a gravity or a pumping system, the farmers already settled on Washington's reclamation projects made a third camp. They thought that new irrigation should be put off. The Sunnyside Valley Irrigation District, for one, told Senator Jones that it opposed "any extensions of activities in reclaiming arid lands . . . until conditions show a need for such construction," alleging that all but one of the state's irrigation districts were insolvent and their members delinquent in water payments.[43] Albert Goss, state Grange master, told a congressional committee the project was "badly timed," and the state director of conservation and development thought new reclamation "neither wise nor necessary," saying the farmers' problem was to market crops already produced. The U.S. secretary of agriculture worried about surplus farm products.[44]

But influential men of the state saw the Big Bend as a way to quicken business and bring new settlers. Two agencies clamored for irrigation, although they disagreed on the method: the Columbia Basin Irrigation League (its first secretary, Jim Ford), which backed the gravity canal, and the Columbia River Development League, which favored the dam and pumping. A tall, hard-working former Ephrata attorney, James O'Sullivan, had written a number of newspaper articles for the dam, and as the campaign between the two leagues heated, the pumpers brought him back from Michigan where he operated a family contracting business, as chief publicist. Paid a lump sum of $500, O'Sullivan tirelessly crisscrossed the state in an open car over dirt roads, jouncing to any hamlet where a group would listen to him explain the advantages of a dam. When Arthur Powell Davis, director of the Reclamation Service from 1914 to 1923, visited Washington, O'Sullivan (poking habitually at his pipe) got Davis aside to talk about the dam to him. Davis later denied that O'Sullivan had swayed him, but possibly he saw in the dam a way of preserving the service's stake in the Columbia in competition with the generating plans of the army engineers.

When Congress appropriated funds to study the best uses of the Missouri River, Jones persuaded Dill to go with him to talk with President Hoover, who agreed to $600,000 for a similar study of the Columbia. According to Dill, Jones quietly advised the army to spend most of the money on the Grand Coulee site. The army used $400,000 there and its report called for the dam. (The gravity canal proponents cried political influence.) Reclamation Commissioner Elwood Mead declared the Columbia Basin "the largest and finest compact body of land feasible of irrigation remaining undeveloped in the United States. . . . As a conservation measure this ranks among the greatest yet attempted in this country." Rather than lose the giant irrigation project, Spokane, and even the Grange, accepted the dam, the Grange stipulating that electricity from Grand Coulee must develop industry that in turn would create "a legitimate demand for more land."[45]

Congress approved the dam in December 1930, but Hoover refused to request funding because the federal budget showed a deficit. Dill meanwhile had elicited a promise from Franklin D. Roosevelt that, if elected president, he would build Grand Coulee dam. And it was Roosevelt who demanded that the dam be included in a public works appropriation bill to begin the work that would remake the face of eastern Washington.[46]

CHAPTER 6

Red Apples: Big Business

For ten years, 1908 through 1917, Spokane staged an annual National Apple Show to publicize Washington's surging apple commerce and ensure a luminous place in the business. Apple-growing districts surrounded the city in 1908 (northern Idaho, the valley of the Spokane east of the city, Kettle Falls and Arcadia to the north, the Palouse, Walla Walla, and Clarkston to the south, and Yakima, Wenatchee, and Okanogan to the west), but in the show's ten years, Washington's irrigated orchards bordering the Columbia River emerged as the prime producers of commercial varieties. Growers in other districts pulled out millions of trees, and the growers who persevered saw that only by shrewd marketing of exceptional apples would they prosper. Apple consumption was declining in the United States when the apple show opened, and Washington stood sixteenth among apple-producing states. As the state's position improved, the show's deteriorated: it closed, in debt, the year that Washington vaulted into first place among apple states.[1]

During its seasonal runs—always dependent on citizen subscriptions and railroad gifts—the show bulged in a temporary canvas arena attached to the armory and evolved into a week-long winter carnival attended by thousands, until war dulled the country's holiday spirit. Walla Walla in 1917 exhibited a patriotic flag of dried apples, and Yakima's Commercial Club displayed a shield of colored apples surrounding portraits of President Wilson and Food Administrator Hoover.[2]

One decade of intense planting that ended in 1914 rooted Washington's great apple orchards. More than one million trees were set out in 1908 alone. Nearly every section of eastern Washington planted orchards, including its driest counties. Whitman County, for one, held nearly 240,000 trees and produced one distinctive variety, a comparatively small, reddish, yellow-streaked apple, the Palouse; Spokane and Stevens counties together counted nearly a million trees.[3] At least three dozen kinds of apples went to market, but even as orchards advanced like orderly skirmishers across eastern Washington, selling agents realized that a few superior varieties, cultivated by irrigation in the long growing seasons (up to two hundred days) of Yakima, Wenatchee, and Okanogan, were capturing the commercial apple business. The Wenatchee and Okanogan growing areas, together about seventy-five miles long, devoted approximately half of their tillable acres to apples; the Yakima Valley, one hundred miles, produced a variety of other fruits and field crops. From 1910 on, grafting desirable varieties onto existing trees was common practice.

With its apple show, Spokane held a convention for producers to ventilate their problems. At the 1909 meeting, the delegates adopted grades—extra fancy, choice, and orchard run—little heeded but indicative of the direction the business was heading. At every convention, orchardists called for unified marketing to expand sales of Washington apples and protect them against fluctuations (and manipulations) of demand and price. The 1910 parley, devoted to selling, resulted in a growers' conference at Portland early in 1911, attended by Washington producers, to consider a Pacific Northwest "central selling agency." At later meetings in Walla Walla, growers adopted a plan modeled on the California Fruit Growers Exchange, which sold citrus fruits across the nation. This ambitious Northwest scheme failed, partly because districts continued to compete and partly because, in the evolving character of the apple business, individuals then felt that by uniting they were giving up too much. The *Yakima Republic* summed it up: "Why talk about organizing the fruit men of three states, when we have not . . . formed a working association in any single valley or neighborhood?"[4]

Rather than dealing as a group, growers at the time sold individually to cash buyers or commission men who descended on the apple towns at harvest to bid for crops—buyers usually better informed than farmers about prospects and prices in competing areas. The cash buyer paid for a grower's apples and took them; the commission man agreed to sell for a percentage of the sale price and usually shipped his apples to auction markets in Chicago, New York, or Boston. Sometimes he advanced a grower money against anticipated sales. Under the pressure of trading before buyers left town, farmers often concluded that they had been rushed into selling cheaply. And as more apples came on the market, buyers selected more carefully, rejecting varieties or sizes unlikely to sell at retail. Buyers constantly warned Washington growers to strive for quality. A Minnesota commission buyer said in 1908: "Poor packing and bad grading will ruin the market." As early as 1895 St. Paul buyers urged Yakima orchardists "to see that their output is properly . . . prepared for the wholesale trade of the East." The business changed. No longer, as they had in earlier years when apples were scarce, did buyers come before harvest to deposit sealed bids with banks.[5]

Meanwhile the Hood River (Oregon) Apple Growers Union sold 90 percent of their district's fruit cooperatively, and the famed Wellhouse orchards of Kansas (at fifteen hundred acres, said before 1900 to be the world's largest orchards) prospered by meticulous handling, grading, and packaging. Taking note, the Yakima Commercial Club set up apple displays in eastern cities, thinking Hood River's higher prices resulted from fruit shows.[6]

No one preached quality more diligently than that slow-moving bear of a man, the Pittsburgh commission buyer James S. Crutchfield, drawn to Washington to find apples for the eastern luxury market. He took fifteen carloads in 1903 and returned thereafter each year, lumbering through Wenatchee, a soft-spoken earnest missioner from the temples of commerce with one gospel for growers: "You're three thousand miles from the market—there is no place in your business for anything but the finest quality." In his persistent way, "Crutch" sold the strategy eventually adopted by Northwest growers: quality fruit produced by careful growing and quick harvest, rapid transportation, and cold storage. "The market is bigger than anyone," Crutch intoned over and over. "You can't quarrel with the market."[7]

In 1910 the volume of apples rose swiftly (past 5.8 million bushels, double 1906) to more than the sales system could handle, and competition was intense. Crutchfield moved to be sure that his company, Crutchfield and Woolfolk, would be in front. With financial assistance from a Seattle financier, R. H. Parsons, Crutchfield hired W. F. Gwin, a veteran Northwest commission man, to open a selling agency at Portland (soon moved to Seattle), the Northwestern Fruit Exchange, and the exchange in turn encouraged local growers' associations to grade and pack apples to its standards. (With about thirty affiliated associations, the exchange would also function as a training ground for men who shaped the business, such as Gwin, who eventually left to form Gwin, White and Prince, a private marketing firm, and A. Z.

Wells of Wells and Wade, once a purchaser for the American Fruit Exchange.)[8]

Crutchfield's business in the Northwest was not confined to Wenatchee. His exchange handled fruit from growers throughout the Pacific Northwest, providing them with aggressive selling, systematic distribution (through the North American Fruit Exchange), and intimate knowledge of the marketplace. Yet many growers continued to sell on their own, preferring to speculate for a big profit every few years and relying on itinerant cash and commission buyers they had learned individually to trust.

A major stockholder in the North American Fruit Exchange, an international produce marketer, Crutchfield in 1919 broke away to form the American Fruit Growers, Inc., a stock company of eastern commission-house operators, and through American purchased his own orchards—fifteen thousand acres of bearing trees worth perhaps $2 million in the Wenatchee and Yakima valleys (and vegetable and fruit-growing farms in nine other states), selling under the Blue Goose brand name through jobbing houses and brokerages in two hundred American cities and exporting to world markets.[9]

Following the example of California citrus and raisin producers promoting their Sunkist and Sunmaid trademarks, the Northwest fruit business emphasized brand names for two decades. Growers who dealt with Blue Goose agencies had to meet stringent standards for handling, grading, and packing, and could sell only Delicious, Jonathan, and a few other varieties. In 1912 and again in 1914, when new orchards flooded apple markets, sending the price plunging, Crutchfield's people met the emergency by opening new markets while scores of independent growers went out of business.

As the market faltered with too much fruit, Gwin lashed the growers for "reckless promotion" and "bull speculation in land," calling the apple-market plunge "the inevitable period of reaction." Orchardists made their problems, he asserted; they did not understand the apple trade; they must tear out their seventy-nine varieties and concentrate on eight or ten, and adopt the methods of manufacturers and marketers. Apples are a specialty item, he went on, to be sold for quality to those who buy luxuries.[10]

The apple glut forced marginal districts out of the trade. "Once the irrigated areas became able to supply the entire market, dry-land orcharding was unable to meet the competition," agronomist Leonard Hegnauer explained, and "acres upon acres of large spreading apple trees were cut down . . . to make room for wheat . . . fine applewood for fireplace burning."[11]

Crutchfield and Gwin determined to advertise Northwest apples with an exclusive brand name; they adopted the trademark Skookum, suggested by a Peshastin woman in a contest, levied ten cents a box on growers for campaign funds, and bought New York streetcar placards in 1913. The crop sold quickly to one wholesale buyer.[12]

As a pattern of selling began to take shape, so did a cycle of production, crops up one year and down the next, that would last from 1909 through 1935 (except for 1916–17 and 1925–26). Advertising seemed to improve sales so surely that in 1916, Wenatchee orchardists who wanted to capitalize on the name Skookum formed themselves into the cooperative Skookum Packers Association, as their articles of incorporation said, "to secure control of the registered brand or trademark for fresh fruits known as Skookum; to establish the standards, rules and regulations under which individual growers' associations may pack and ship . . . under such trademark," and control brand advertising. In exchange for the name, the association appointed the Northwestern Fruit Exchange its exclusive agent for selling Skookum fruits.[13]

With J. B. Adams, Leavenworth, as president, the Skookum Packers took in large growers from all parts of the Northwest: Walla Walla, Weiser, eventually Payette, Yakima, Spokane, Hood River, and others. The association soon hired O. Thomas Clawson to enforce grading and packing standards; his grades would be recognized unofficially for all Wenatchee-affiliated growers, if not for those of Yakima. Grading was a sore point between Wenatchee and Yakima for years. Clawson rode to orchards in a Ford touring car over rutted roads—and sold shares in the car to state inspectors who covered the same area.[14]

Skookum placed color ads in national magazines—*Saturday Evening Post, Good Housekeeping, Literary Digest,* and *Sunset*—at a cost to growers of five cents a box. For a short time, the association also peddled Indian "Skookum" dolls and sponsored an Indian singer who appeared on radio programs. As the Skookum brand attracted loyal patrons, the association's general manager let it be known immodestly that Skookum's "plan and purpose . . . is to stabilize the whole industry."[15] That would be a large order.

Without the nagging of a Crutchfield, Yakima's growers had formed a marketing cooperative, the Yakima Horticultural Union, begun informally in 1902 and reorganized the next year as a stock association which rented a warehouse and hired a manager. By World War I, the union represented perhaps one hundred and fifty growers—half of the producers in the Yakima Valley—selling under the Blue Ribbon and

Red Ribbon brands. Much of the rest of Yakima's apples sold through a loose federation of growers' associations, each with its own warehouse, formed between 1909 and 1911 as the Yakima Fruit Growers Association, modeled on California's Sunkist growers, and managed by J. H. Robbins, who had been in business in Oakland, California.[16]

While he had no experience in fruit, Robbins proved astute and energetic. He relied on California friends for advice and warned Yakima growers that they faced enormous competition when trees already planted began to bear, carrying his ominous message to growers' meetings throughout the valley, speaking in packing sheds, warehouses—wherever listeners gathered.

By and large, older orchardists of Yakima remained independent of union or association, relying on their established trade contacts, but newer growers joined the association, nearly six hundred of them in its first year.[17] Now Robbins, facing the familiar vexing variations in packing, hired traveling inspectors to enforce grades and packing for apples sold under the association's Big Y trademark. His first year almost ended in disaster, almost sinking the Big Y—with heavy crops, railway delays, and grower defections. Robbins, obliged to sell at low prices, persuaded his remaining members to take proportionate shares of the association's disappointing income. As more growers talked of breaking away, Robbins held the association together by the device of sending his most influential members on tours to see selling conditions for themselves.

As might be expected of two large organizations side by side, jealousies hampered both the horticultural union and the association. Growers, bankers, sellers, and buyers constantly counseled the two to merge.

Contention, in fact, dogged the entire apple industry. Camps of competing sellers scrambled for the best markets and highest prices. As the dimensions of the disastrous 1912 glut had become clear, the Spokane Chamber of Commerce convened nearly two hundred and fifty growers, bankers, and railway representatives from Northwest states to consider again a central sales agency for fruit from the entire region, confident that such an agency offered "a practical solution for handling and financing the apple crop." At the meeting, an Atlanta speaker described united selling in Georgia's peach business; Crutchfield called for "confidence in each other . . . absolutely essential to establishing the apple industry on a sound business basis," and scolded the bankers for "rates of interest . . . that would make a commission man blush," pleading with them to "protect" the fruit business.[18]

From this pep-rally conclave emerged the Pacific Northwest Fruit Distributors, attracting such men as H. F. Davidson of Hood River, W. T. Clark, the Wenatchee canal builder and nurseryman, Robert E. Strahorn, the reedy, secretive Harriman railroad promoter who chaired the meeting, and most important, W. H. Paulhamus, recently out of the governor's race ("Pennsylvania Dutch . . . an organizer and orator by nature," *Sunset* called him), the Puyallup grower who had organized the raspberry business. A one-time state senator, and president and manager of the Puyallup Fruit Growers Association, Paulhamus was accomplished at one of the arts of fruit selling—suing the railroads. As a grower remarked, "before the war, claims against railroads were a big part of the apple business."[19]

The new distributors' cooperative pirated Robbins for its manager and Davidson for its president (which precipitated the withdrawal of Clark and his Wenatchee friends, because he had hoped for the presidency). As attorney, Strahorn proved to be a liability; his Harriman connections soured the Great Northern and Northern Pacific, the principal railroads in apple country.[20]

Despite these handicaps, the Pacific Northwest Fruit Distributors started strong, claiming eight thousand growers, including the Yakima Fruit Growers Association, the Hood River Apple Growers Union (soon to withdraw), and subsidiaries such as the Central Idaho–Washington Fruit Growers Association with members' orchards in counties known chiefly for grains. The distributors even sold the Palouse apple, using the more common name of Red Bellflower. Aided by a short eastern crop, they sold roughly half the fruit shipped from Northwest states in 1913, more than twelve thousand carloads in twenty-eight months, spreading $8 million among the members.[21] With Ben A. Perham as sales manager (a former Seattle fruit broker hired away, like Robbins, from the Big Y), the distributors, faced with surplus fruit in the abundant 1914 season, pushed Northwest apples into hundreds of new markets. Perham's heroic performance in new markets prevented heavy financial losses, even though some of the crop had ripened so fast it was not shipped.[22]

But bickering, perhaps predestined by the ambitions of its founders, and the reluctance of "well known growers" to join, sapped the organization, and uncertain quality in its apples drained its sales prospects. Its officers berated growers for dumping cull apples on the market, while a by-products committee tried, "without any funds and with very little help," complained Paulhamus, to promote canneries at Spokane, Yakima, and Wenatchee to process low-quality fruits.[23] The organization's officers furnished fancy office suites and paid themselves generous salaries, ostensibly to impress prospective buyers, but Paulhamus believed these costly trappings eroded growers' confidence in the management.[24]

By the middle of 1915, the Pacific Northwest Fruit Distributors had closed two eastern selling offices and cut its Spokane staff. Davidson, incensed at Robbins's salary, resigned as president. Within three years the regional central marketing agency and the high hopes for it were gone, despite an attempt to save it by forming a growers' council of twenty-five to impose "some semblance of authority to call the marketing agencies together and insist on such rules for the game as would make it possible for the industry to live," Paulhamus told friends. But without funds and an "evangelist" to inspire members, the council gave up.[25]

To be sure, the Pacific Northwest Fruit Distributors had handled apples that could not compete directly with those of Yakima or Wenatchee-Okanogan, and had been undersold by independent growers, but it had saved its affiliates money by central purchases of wrapping paper, boxes, and other supplies and by arranging for cold storage for apples delayed by railcar shortages or low prices. Perhaps without its internal rivalries, these services would have sustained the distributors, but the fact remained that there were too many growers and too many apples, and in their desperation to stay in business, growers either sold cheaply in competition with central sales agencies or defected when prices rose.

The failure of the Pacific Northwest Fruit Distributors went beyond dissent. The distributors coalesced the frustrations of a business that had reached its turning point, a climax delayed by war. In less than twenty years, Washington had risen to first in volume among apple states, from 1.2 percent of U.S. production to 15 percent, while the earlier leader, New York, fell from 20 to 14 percent, despite New York's closeness to the eastern markets for fancy apples.[26]

Although the distributors failed, the luxury sales had been captured almost wholly by cooperative sellers in Yakima and Wenatchee-Okanogan. One-third of Washington's crop—and nearly all its eastern sales—moved through the union and cooperatives (and a handful of smaller ones) in these two districts. The irrigated orchards and ideal climates of Yakima and Wenatchee-Okanogan drove other Washington areas out of the apple business. Millions of trees would be ripped out in the twenties. Within a decade after World War I, only three other commercial districts remained: Spokane, producing 3 percent of the crop and selling through Skookum; Walla Walla, 2 percent; and White Swan, across the Columbia from Hood River, 1.3 percent.[27]

Washington's distinctive large, well-colored, paper-wrapped, boxed apples—hawked on New York streets as Yak-EYE-ma apples—were almost entirely the creation of Yakima and Wenatchee-Okanogan. They advertised and sold extra-fancy apples, setting their own standards for high quality. Eastern growers traditionally sold smaller, unwrapped apples in barrels. For Washington, apples had become almost as important as lumber. In some years apple returns exceeded those of lumber, and nearly all of eastern Washington's economy rested on apples and wheat in one way or another.

Yet the apple business faced huge difficulties. It needed storage to wipe away the seasons, reliable cheap transport, sprays against fruit diseases, and new markets, because, as refrigeration improved, competitive fruits from the southwestern United States and foreign countries also reached the best apple markets. At its turning point, Washington's apple business reached for technical solutions—improved sprays, mechanical sorting, orchard heaters, and other devices. But there remained 60 percent or more of the annual crop without trustworthy markets—those lesser grades suitable for local sales, canning, juices, and cider, but not for quality buyers.

The success of Yakima and Wenatchee-Okanogan as commercial apple districts rested partly on their partnership with the railroads, the Great Northern at Wenatchee and the Northern Pacific (and later, Union Pacific) at Yakima. Wenatchee publisher Rufus Woods scolded them for this: "Fruit men are not always going to get through by leaving it all to God and the Great Northern." Before the war, railroads were chronically short of freight cars; immediately before the war, other railroads shorted the Great Northern 6 to 8 percent of its cars, and the Northern Pacific, 10 to 25 percent.[28]

Railroads began supplying refrigerated cars as early as 1902 and increased their number rapidly until by 1915 U.S. railroads and private express companies operated more than 110,000. The seasonal competition for these cars was severe among producers of perishable products, but railroads were almost as careless about returning refrigerator cars as any others. Northern Pacific refrigerator cars sometimes were loaded with grain. Over objections of the American Association of Railways, which until then had regulated freight cars, the federal Interstate Commerce Commission in 1917 ordered railroads to speed their return of refrigerated, ventilated, heated, and insulated cars.[29]

Refrigerated cars were expensive to build and operate. A typical one weighed about ten tons more than a customary boxcar and had ice bunkers at either end, each holding a ton of ice. Railroads established icing stations along their lines to re-ice apples six to eight times between Washington State and Chicago. For years before 1918, railroads furnished apple growers with refrigerated cars for only the freight charge. Consequently, when the railroads imposed special fees, shippers protested.[30]

But from October 15 through April 15 each year, when the weather was cold, the railroads heated apple cars or permitted shippers to heat at the shippers' risk. Heated cars, insulated with paper and equipped with false floors and walls for air circulation, at first warmed with steam from the locomotive, then used special stoves fueled from beneath the car, burning coal, oil, charcoal, or wood. A shipper who heated his own car sent along a caretaker (whom the railroad returned free), but apple shippers gradually delegated icing and heating to railroads and express companies.

By the end of World War I, an expensive fleet of refrigerated and insulated cars, with a network of icing stations, moved western apple crops—great trains of forty or fifty refrigerator cars leaving every day. Space was precious, so railroads ignored overloading. Shippers customarily put thirty-seven thousand pounds or more on cars built for thirty-five.[31] The Great Northern ran lightweight "red ball" apple expresses—six days and two hours from Wenatchee to Minneapolis. Yet many refrigerated cars were fifteen years old, and fewer than half were insulated two inches thick (as federal rules required). As the railroads replaced old cars with larger ones hauling 756 boxes compared with 630 previously, they handed the refrigerated car business to subsidiaries: the Pacific Fruit Express (1906) controlled by the Union Pacific and Southern Pacific, the Northern Car Company owned by Northern Pacific, and Western Fruit Express formed in 1923 as a Great Northern auxiliary. Western express companies interchanged cars with the southeastern Fruit Growers Express Company; between them, they operated twenty-four thousand refrigerated cars, about one-fifth of those in the United States.[32] With the change in management, shippers' complaints against the railroads gradually shifted from services to costs.

In costs, the government played a pivotal role for a dozen years. Railroad presidents objected that after the panic of 1907 the federal government had denied them rate increases for higher labor costs, repairs, new tracks, and equipment, but during the war, when the government seized a "rusty and demoralized" railway system (the railroads' phrase), the federal director general had suddenly and drastically raised rates. The Washington State public service commission sued the government for lower rates, charging that the increases added $2.5 million a year to the costs of marketing Northwest fruits and vegetables. And while the government operated the railroads, from December 26, 1917 to March 1, 1920, it bought equipment, passing the debts along to railroads when federal control ended. The wartime rates continued after the war, and Washington's apple growers—and shippers of all kinds—protested. They wanted to return to prewar rates.[33]

Higher rates enabled railroads to pay for their new equipment, but opened them to competition for apple freight from steamship companies using the Panama Canal. Apples brought Northwest railroads an estimated $18 million a year in revenue. Exporters had sent a few apple shipments through the canal before the war, but after railroad rates went up, Seattle and Portland shippers sent more and more apples by sea, and growers who hoped to expand their markets into Europe and South America preferred water routes.[34] Seattle held an annual fruit exposition at a water terminal beginning in 1921, directed by the Wenatchee orchardist and politician John A. Gellatly, assisted by the Seattle photographer Asahel Curtis, who owned an orchard near Grandview. In 1921–22 an estimated 30.2 percent of the exported apples moved through the canal; by 1930–31 the volume would rise to 73 percent.[35]

For the railroads in Washington State, the twenties were a decade of nearly continuous contention over rates—while competition increased. By the late twenties, auto truckers were hauling apples to the Coast, at first to fill empty space in their trucks, at low rates. Truck freighting, then not large, would grow while railroads complained that unregulated truckers hauled for whatever the shipper would pay. At the same time, apple-marketing associations, singly and jointly (on occasion with state agencies), sued railroads before the Interstate Commerce Commission for rate cuts, but the Seattle and Portland chambers of commerce advocated higher rail than water rates, arguing that revised rates would deprive them of "locational advantages."[36] Railroads also filed petitions for rate changes.

The ICC, however, generally held to the 1920 rates and, as the twenties wore on, observed that apple growers earned "reasonably satisfactory" returns. Railroads reduced their operating costs and increased revenues in the Northwest, so that while they lost tonnage to water carriers and trucks, they seemed in good financial condition. The ICC allowed minor adjustments in the complex origin-and-destination groupings that determined rates and set maximums ($1.73 a box inside the United States); the commission also conceded that freight rates often were "varying and inconsistent," but concluded that "due largely to water competition and the desire to stimulate and develop the fruit-growing industry of the Pacific Northwest, rates on apples, as well as other fresh deciduous fruits, have been maintained on a low basis." [37]

When railroads could not supply enough cars to move apples quickly to market, growers had to store their fruit. Storage could also lengthen the selling season. Consequently, growers and scientists experimented with warehousing. In early days, orchardists stored apples in barns or cellars; some buried fruit for the winter under straw covered with dirt—a large version of the earthen root cellar of every farm home. Experiments to find reliable apple-storing methods began before 1910—tests to learn when to pick, storage temperatures, handling, and the storage characteristics of apple varieties. (For a time, the Yakima Fruit Growers stored in transit at Council Bluffs, Iowa.) The nation's meat packers had developed chains of refrigerated and heated branch warehouses by 1900; United Fruit Company moved its sales of imported bananas westward from Atlantic ports with a similar system of warehouses. But until World War I, the costs of large-scale storage were too high for Washington's apple producers. To help out, the Great Northern winked at warehouses and sheds built on its right-of-way and lent perhaps $800,000 at low interest during the twenties to encourage construction of refrigerated warehouses. [38]

Early mechanical cooling systems used ammonia in pipes as a coolant, and the warehouse crew controlled temperatures simply by opening or closing doors and hosing aisles for a humid interior. At 30 to 40 degrees, apples kept reasonably well. Sellers hastily peddled fruit that softened. Shortly before the war, on the advice of the Department of Agriculture, growers tried insulated warehouses opened at night to cool air with exhaust fans and closed during the day. During the twenties, the extension service and a few growers' cooperatives experimented with further mechanical coolants, such as carbon dioxide.

But whether they were ventilated or mechanically cooled, stored apples developed fungus and mold. Oiled wrapping papers helped deter deterioration. As Yakima and Wenatchee-Okanogan enlarged their storage during the twenties, they tested harvesting, handling, and cooling methods to prevent rot. Research centered on Delicious, Winesap, and other best-selling kinds. Such types as Ben Davis, early popular in Washington, were discarded as uncompetitive despite a thick, russeted skin that kept for long periods. By the end of the twenties, one-half of a normal crop would be stored each year for orderly marketing. But storage received little publicity. The apple customer thought that storage costs escalated prices. Actually storage averaged about nine cents a box, compared with sixty-eight cents for freight, forty for packing, and eleven for selling. But Washington's producers did not want to be known for stored apples. Their advertising emphasized size, color, quality, and crisp freshness.[39]

In the mid-twenties, British protests of arsenic residue on apples threatened to close off Washington's largest export market. Lead-arsenate sprays had been widely used to control the coddling moth (a worm) since Yakima and Wenatchee-Okanogan seriously entered commercial orcharding. The coddling moth, generally believed to have spread across Washington from Walla Walla orchards, so frustrated Walla Walla growers that many tore out thirty-year-old trees to convert to wheat as Washington's great apple expansion started. The state agricultural experiment station, using some of these abandoned trees for testing, produced apples nearly worm-free by spraying. Some truly imaginative attacks on moths were suggested: importing songbirds to eat worms, killing moths with electrical charges, and cold-storing ladybug beetles for release against aphids—actually tried in Wenatchee orchards.[40]

Although the state regulated pesticides as early as 1901, and the federal government published rules for their use, these reflected a simpler time of paris green, lime, and sulphur solutions. The state horticultural service inspected orchards and advised growers before the war, but the legislature repealed the authority of county commissioners to fund these programs, and many absentee orchard owners ignored rules or advice, allowing pests and blight to ravage their trees and spread to neighbors'. In such cases, the counties eventually sprayed without permission and billed the owner. A second insect, San Jose scale, also a migrant from Walla Walla, seemed immune to the usual lime-sulphur sprays, requiring new poisons.[41] (In 1902, the city of Yakima cut every cottonwood tree in town as a scale breeder.)

After the war, growers fell into a routine of spring spraying against fungus and tree insects, importing bees in May (at blossom time) for fertilizing, spraying calyx and thinning in July, several lead-arsenate sprayings (two pounds to 100 gallons of water) for moths in August, and harvesting early in the fall. Most growers also "color" picked (harvesting apples by color rather than picking an entire tree at once).

A spraying outfit commonly consisted of a tank on a horse-drawn wagon (or as time went by, on a light tractor) with pumps and hose. As the twenties passed, permanent spray systems were installed with pipes underground from central tanks and pumps. (At least one stationary plant had been used in Wenatchee as early as 1912.) When moths persisted, growers strengthened lead-arsenate solutions,

fish-oil and mineral-oil carriers that
er washings at packing.[42]
rsenate residue might endanger human
Drug Administration and Department
1927 federal conference on spray res-
erances, and Senators Joseph Cannon
Agriculture Secretary H. C. Wallace to
public health service, somewhat lower
ug agency. But Washington's growers,
uld shut off 40 percent of their export
d sent delegations to plead with the
moth control and spray removal.[43]
ler and Fred Overly, moved to Wen-
h partial support from growers' orga-
problems. (In 1937 the legislature es-
t station at Wenatchee.) Fortunately,
increased washing—using several in-
almed the British, who continued to
buy apples while growers sought improved practices from research.
From this time, hot water for washing sent clouds of steam from packing sheds.[44]

Growers striving to produce quality apples were not much interested in deliberately producing apples for canning or by-products. The
ideal, for them, was selling every apple in luxury and export trades,
although in reality half or two-thirds of each crop would be rejected
for discoloration, small size, damage in handling, insect mars, or similar flaws. Housewives bought low-grade apples for home canning—
those frazzling summer days in steaming kitchens squeezing fruits
through cheese-cloth cones to make jams and sauces, using apple juice
as a fruit pectin—and cull apples sold briskly in most markets in competition with higher grades. For years, W. J. Hays and L. G. Hays of
Yakima sold cull Stayman and Winesap apples in Scotland and other
foreign countries for better prices than they could get at home. Railroads carried culls at lower cost, too, bulking them loose on beds of
straw in boxcars.[45]

An Entiat grower, S. L. Packwood, was astounded to find only culls
selling in western Washington, where "dealers made more money selling the poor stuff . . . at $1.85 to $2 a box." Echoing the North Pacific
Distributors a decade earlier, Packwood begged distributors to ban
shipments of culls. Paulhamus and his coterie had tried to promote
local canneries to take rejected apples, but, except for the ubiquitous

cider mills that pressed wormy and rotting fruit in every country town, there were few by-product factories. Canneries ran seasonally at Sunnyside, Wenatchee, Grandview, Spokane, Asotin, and Yakima. The Libby, McNeill, and Libby cannery at Yakima, opened in 1917, brought half its fruit to Yakima from other districts, because its contracts for apples, cherries, peaches, pears, and apricots there fell short of the tonnage needed for a season's run—more than six hundred tons of cherries in 1919 and 730 in 1920.[46]

For a time, evaporating plants operated at Yakima, Wenatchee, Cashmere, Zillah, Grandview, Walla Walla, and Chelan. An apple concentrator made apple bricks for sauce and apple butter in Wenatchee, but the plant burned and was not rebuilt. Evaporated fruits never became popular (possibly because the fruit was dipped in boiling lye washes) and for years commercially canned fruit was suspect. Tales circulated of metallic taste, poisoning from cans, inferior fruits, foreign matter, and botulism. No matter that they canned—actually, jarred—in their homes, housewives distrusted commercial canning. At any rate, by-products used only a small part of the apple crop. In 1919, for example, when Yakima's crops were worth an estimated $42 million, processors bought $552,000 worth. Year after year, farmers simply threw culls and wormy apples into the river. Growers regarded canneries as a dumping ground. The Spokane Chamber of Commerce, trying to contract for 300,000 pounds of cherries to justify a cannery, got pledges for only 75,000.[47]

The big money in fruit raising flowed from selling extra fancy apples of preferred varieties: Delicious, Winesap, Jonathan, and Rome Beauty. Nearly 90 percent of the Yakima and Wenatchee-Okanogan output consisted of those four types—Winesaps about 40 percent, Delicious 22, Jonathans 15, and Romes 10 percent of a typical harvest. Growers whose apples graded extra fancy could average 29 cents a box higher than the profit on any other grade.[48]

Some early experiments with commercial frozen fruits took place in western Washington where a Denver investor, H. S. Baker, successfully froze strawberries in 1911. In association with Paulhamus and the Puyallup growers Davis produced barreled frozen fruits after the war, but the market did not understand his product, and the distribution system was not equipped to handle it. Clarence Birdseye, simultaneously developing frozen foods in New York, went bankrupt, tried again, and launched a campaign to educate the public to frozen foods as the thirties approached. A major step toward public acceptance was conversion to home-size packages.[49]

With the approach of the thirties, Washington's apple business was closing its experimental period: its selling varieties, orchard and harvest practices, handling (increasingly mechanized with conveyor belts and sizers), and marketing were established. Except for seasons of malign weather, Wenatchee-Okanogan produced about twenty thousand carloads and Yakima produced about fifteen thousand in the good years. Half the crop was usually stored, and shipments were scheduled every month of the year. In the very best years, perhaps 40 percent of the crop was graded extra fancy—the best. Despite a falling rate of national apple sales, the northwestern boxed-apple states had increased their markets 150 percent over prewar years and were recognized around the world. Skookum ads in 1928 produced requests for informational pamphlets from five hundred United States cities and from Sweden, England, Holland, Peru, China, Scotland, Cuba, Hawaii, Argentina, Newfoundland, Australia, Bermuda, Brazil, Finland, Mexico, South Africa, Puerto Rico, Germany, Panama, New Zealand, Honduras, the Fiji Islands, Switzerland, and Java.[50]

No one could doubt that the terraces of those narrow river valleys feeding the Columbia dominated the state's commercial apple trade. In the decade after the war, more than 3.5 million bearing trees were cut in other parts of eastern Washington, one-third of the producing trees in Washington. New plantings virtually stopped in 1931, while Yakima and Wenatchee-Okanogan growers learned to increase the yield from each tree.[51]

The business, celebrated by an annual Wenatchee apple blossom festival begun in 1920, was ruled by four powerful marketing groups, who among them sold more than 85 percent of the Washington apples in commercial channels (one in every four apples consumed in the United States): the Yakima Horticultural Union and Yakima Fruit Growers Association, the Skookum Packers, and the Wenatchee District Cooperative Association, this last formed in 1921 with a million-dollar bank loan and Aaron Sapiro's connivance to free its members from their bondage to Crutchfield's Northwestern Fruit Exchange.[52] The Northwestern, of course, grew and marketed apples for itself, and in the Wenatchee district perhaps thirty independent growers and a dozen small, clannish cooperatives fended for themselves. And the merger of the Wenatchee-Beebe Orchard Company with American Fruit Growers placed the nation's largest fruit company in Washington.[53]

Dozens of brand names beckoned from colorful box-end labels: Blue Goose, Wenoka, Siwash, Dainty Maid, Hi-Yu, Skookum, Red Winner and Blue Winner, Snoboy, Jim Hill—and some modish names such as Radio and Electric. Wenatchee and Yakima, in 1916 and 1917, had organized traffic associations to improve railcar supplies and shipping schedules; these gradually took over marketing information, packing and grading standards, and shipping negotiations with water carriers.

Growers' associations, in addition to joint purchases of supplies and equipment, warehouse management, advertising, and selling, acted as credit banks for their members. The Yakima Fruit Growers, for one, discounted its members' notes with the Spokane federal intermediate credit bank for money to advance to growers waiting for their apples to sell, and the Wenatchee District Cooperative was among the first in Washington to obtain a loan from the federal farm board, $40,000, to market Winesaps.[54]

Around the apple business mushroomed a structure of service and manufacturing businesses dependent on it. Boxmaking, for instance, consumed low-grade softwoods to make the twenty-two to twenty-six million apple boxes used each year; a Pine Box Manufacturers Association, organized in 1922, standardized boxes. Perhaps three dozen mills sawed from 50,000 to 140,000 feet of box lumber daily. Among the largest were Biles-Coleman, Omak; Schmitten, Cashmere; Cascade Lumber, Yakima; Western Pine Manufacturing and D. J. Wilson, Spokane. Washington makers also sold to midwestern box buyers, and southern factories sent boxes to Yakima and Wenatchee.[55]

So important had the apple commerce become to Washington that the state director of agriculture led in organizing a Boxed Apple Bureau (collecting fees from growers) to advertise Washington apples. He spent $100,000 for Christmas handbills distributed by jobbers in forty cities, stickers on Northern Pacific dining car menus, and foreign-language newspaper ads as well as the customary mass-circulation magazine and newspaper advertising of the business. And the state director of horticulture, to protect the reputation of Washington apples, sued alleged shippers of culls, "shined up, packed and sold under false labels," to expose them.[56]

The red apple, beguiling, shiny, crisp in the grocer's bin, had become big business.

CHAPTER 7

Bankers and Farmers

The man in charge of money, more than anyone, was Daniel Webster Twohy, a slender, bald banker with a proper, almost pious, manner, who was installed in 1902 as president of Spokane's Old National Bank by his brothers—Denis, James, and John, railroad contractors. With associates, the Twohys bought the bank from its founder, Stephen S. Glidden, once operator of the Tiger-Poorman mine in the Coeur d'Alenes, who named his bank "old" because he didn't care to be second, and there had already been a First National and a Spokane National in the city.

Until the depression of the thirties, banking in Spokane could almost be divided into two eras—before Twohy and after Twohy. Even the Dutch lenders, who virtually owned downtown Spokane by foreclosure in 1896 and continued to invest millions in rural eastern Washington until World War I, did not mark Spokane finance as indelibly as Twohy.[1]

Twohy's effect on farmers and their money was indirect. He was not much interested in farmers except as aggregate capital; neither was he given to posturing or to party politics. He was devoted to finance, big money, and to promoting Spokane to build his bank. Twohy was one of six bank presidents in Spokane, and he was the one who would revolutionize banking in the city. He changed its forms and practices, bought other banks, and secured reserve status for Spokane to compete with Portland, which, until the early nineteen hundreds, dominated Spokane's finance as it dominated Spokane's commerce. Twohy was, of course, a right man at the right time, in a national emergence of banking in a new century. Perhaps half a dozen bright youngsters had been sent by their Oregon fathers to be eastern Washington bankers when settlers poured in; they started strings of country banks, and, because Twohy made Spokane a financial center, they came eventually to Spokane.

A thirty-eight-year-old bachelor (he did not marry until he was forty), Twohy had risen from credit manager in a family store to bank president in West Superior, Wisconsin. His brothers prepared him for Spokane's booster spirit and the rich prospects of its tributary country, but he was perhaps surprised by lack of imagination among the city's bankers. Conservative, reserved, they had not made loans to their legal limits, possibly haunted still by the collapse of seven of Spokane's ten banks in 1893, although recovery was magnificent: in 1896 Spokane's bank clearings were one-third higher than those of Seattle or Tacoma. Neither had they taken advantage of Congress's reduction in 1900 of capital requirements for national banks. Most bankers, also directors of other companies, seemed to regard finance as personal business among social and pecuniary peers.

In Twohy's opinion, Spokane could move toward a central position in banking while it grew as an inland wholesale distribution center. He remarked quite soon after his arrival, alluding to the law requiring national banks to deposit 60 percent of their reserves in designated banks, that "many great cities became reserve centers for their trade areas." Portland at the time was the only reserve city in the Northwest. Twohy offered to pay 2 percent on country bank accounts placed with the Old National. The lordly members of the Spokane Clearing House Association, who paid no interest but competed for country bank funds (and privately called Twohy "that upstart from Wisconsin"), summoned him to appear before them for that transgression. And he opened the first savings department among national banks in the Pacific Northwest, paying interest, another innovation. He rewrote his bank's legalistic promissory note as a forthright pledge and charged interest consistent with collateral, observing, "If the borrower's interest is legitimate and sound, he is entitled to a fair rate, and if it is not legitimate and sound, the bank will not lend its credit at any price."[2]

In flushing fresh air through Spokane banking, Twohy advanced the Old National. He soon reported that its deposits had increased a million dollars in one year. Using subsidiaries, he bought other banks (he had perhaps analyzed chain banking in Minnesota), and within seven years the Old National, through its Union Trust Company and then Union Securities Company, controlled twenty-four banks, acquiring a dozen by absorbing those of J. D. Bassett, the Ritzville banker (and onetime state senator), naming Bassett a vice-president of Union Securities, and giving him $500,000 to buy other banks in eastern Washington and adjacent Idaho. The banks Old National owned would grow to thirty-four by 1912 but shrink to twenty-two by 1929 with mergers and consolidations in the twenties.[3]

When Union Securities bought a bank, Twohy's examiner appraised its loans—country banks then did not have savings accounts—and within a day or two, bought or backed away. If he bought, Twohy paid perhaps 3 percent for the deposits and 2 percent for time deposits, assumed the "good" loans, and "let the fellow who was selling collect the other loans as he could." Or Twohy might buy out stockholders and pay cash for deposits, as he did at Reardan, where he merged two banks.[4]

He did not buy Levi Ankeny's country banks, but Twohy snared them by bringing Ankeny onto the Old National Bank board in 1903 to sit beside others of an impressive directorate: Thomas Humbird, the Weyerhaeuser-connected lumberman; Peter Larson and Thomas Greenough, Montana railroad contractors and Idaho mine owners with substantial real estate in Spokane; and J. D. Farrell, the Wisconsin lawyer and banker who moved to Seattle as a formidable railroad lobbyist. Twohy maintained the confidence of this group partly by paying his stockholders 10 percent dividends for twenty consecutive years and amassing undistributed reserves. With their support and his growing string of country banks, he rose quickly to be one of the powerful men of eastern Washington.

In less than a year after Twohy's arrival, Spokane banks increased their volume of promissory notes (many discounted from country banks) against the coming wheat harvest, drawing even more business from the grain counties than Portland. Using the expanding wheat commerce as his main argument, Twohy led other Spokane bankers in 1908 in persuading the comptroller of the currency to designate Spokane a reserve city (Tacoma became one the same year; Seattle had been since 1906), cutting the matriarchal tie to Portland. Smaller banks could place reserves and up to 9 percent of their demand deposits with reserve banks.[5]

Spokane's other leading banks, which had followed Twohy in paying interest on country-bank deposits, also opened their boards to men with business interests outside the city. When the mining promoter Charles Sweeny, erstwhile banker, moved to New York, he sold the Exchange National Bank's stock majority to Edwin T. Coman, the Colfax lawyer turned banker, whose associates included Lillis Smith, called by newspapers "the wheat king of the Palouse," William Huntley, Montana stockman and Palouse wheat grower, Harry L. Day, manager of the Hercules mine in the Coeur d'Alenes, and Frank M. Rothrock, whose dividends from the Hercules had been spent to establish him as a leading sheep and cattle breeder. (The Exchange thereafter loaned heavily in livestock.) Coman also increased the Exchange's capital—"the first million-dollar bank between Minneapolis and the Pacific Coast."[6]

About the time Twohy entered the Old National, the Traders National sold a large share of its stock to A. Fielding McClaine, Alfred Coolidge, and Aaron Kuhn, among others. McClaine and Coolidge, sons of banker fathers in Silverton, Oregon, owned majority shares in half a dozen Washington country banks. Kuhn, a pioneer Palouse merchant, grain buyer, and moneylender (his loans were small and careful), bought and merged as the Kuhn Building two bankrupt Riverside avenue buildings, the Holland and Van Valkenburg.[7]

If not its oldest, Spokane's prestigious bank was the Spokane and Eastern Trust, formed by J. P. M. Richards with eastern friends (one a former law partner of Grover Cleveland's), and managed by his brother, Henry Richards. Through interlocking directorates, the bank was intimately connected with the Washington Water Power Company, other city banks, and real estate development. Enlarging its board from nine to nineteen in 1908 and 1909, it added such men as the Coeur d'Alene mine operators A. B. Campbell and John A. Finch; F. F. Johnson, president of the First National Bank, Wallace, Idaho; F. W. Kettenbach, president of the Lewiston National; Fred Phair, a prominent Spokane contractor; William Thompson, cashier, State Bank of Wilbur; C. W. Winter, cashier, Bank of Colville, and partner in several other country banks; and E. F. Cartier van Dissel, president of the Phoenix [lumber] Mill Company, Spokane. Five years later, the trust company absorbed the Traders and the Northwest Loan and Trust, founded by the brewing brothers, Samuel, Julius, and Adolph Galland.[8]

Linked by directors to rural Washington, Spokane banks inspired clannish conformity for the area's cluttered banking. Banks had been started or purchased by men who settled in growing towns for that purpose—Ankeny, McClaine, Coolidge, David P. Thompson (an officer of seventeen national banks between 1879 and 1891), and F. X. Wade, to mention a few—and by local merchants whose entry into banking certified their economic importance in their towns: D. F. Percival, storekeeper, Cheney; Dorsey Baker, physician and railroader, Walla Walla; Ben Snipes, cattleman, Ellensburg; F. D. Mottet, sheepman turned banker, Connell; R. C. McCroskey, wheat farmer into banker, Pullman; and others. Some bankers who prospered in one town expanded to others (Charles P. Coey, Rockford and Fairfield, for example), creating small networks of country banks.

The largest number of Washington banks before World War I were chartered by the state, although until the state instituted examinations in 1907, no one was sure of their condition. "The state banks' reporting was so incomplete," alibied the state's first examiner, "that I am unable . . . to offer any comparisons with previous years."[9] Private banks, a few dating from territorial times, came and went with casual regulation. Only a handful would remain by 1915, when the state legislated them out of existence. National banks, chartered by the federal government, tended to be largest and regarded as the most secure. Banks moved from one type to another; in 1907, when Washington codified its banking laws, twenty-four state banks opened—eighteen previously private—and seven converted to national banks. Most of the state banks then reported capital of $10,000 to $15,000.[10]

Several pioneer banks had been started primarily to transfer funds between towns. Others were started as sidelines (a merchant might call a corner of his store a bank, keep accounts in his spare time, and hide his strongbox under the floor); and nearly all owners managed their banks, or at least set policy. The young man bent on a banking career bought some stock in a bank, went to work there at menial tasks, and advanced—perhaps by marrying the banker's daughter.[11]

Few farmers traveled to Spokane to bank, although their cooperatives or associations might. Farmers and their country bankers fused in a precarious balance. A farmer nearly always needed credit to sustain him until his next harvest, when he would pay up loans and debts—unless his crop failed. George H. McCroskey joked that town bankers "kept paper tough as whalebone" for farmers' loan contracts, but banks more often failed by overextending to help farmers than by adhering to prudent practices. Wealthier men in a town might do their business mainly with a city bank, leaving the local banker to deal with smaller merchants and farmers. And "whenever farmers failed to pay off their notes, the reserve of the bank fell and the bank's liquidity was impaired," lamented a banker. To a creditor in a hurry for repayment, farmers could be exasperatingly mulish, as a cashier in wheat country grumbled: "None of them want to sell on a falling market; then when the market begins to pick up a little none of them seem disposed to sell on a rising market and so the story goes year in and year out."[12]

Farmers known as frugal and reliable often received bank loans without security. Some country bankers disdained chattel mortgages as "indications that the borrower's credit was over-extended or his character not sound."[13] The town banker usually knew his several score customers well; in fact, he frequently served as trusted adviser in business and personal affairs. Tellers often made out checks for customers to sign, wrote their deposit slips, and allowed farmers "promiscuous overdrafts against invisible balances." More than one country banker pleaded with his farm customers to confine their banking to the hours his bank was open.[14]

As settlement gathered force in eastern Washington, the Walla Walla land office estimated that the average homesteader growing wheat on 160 acres earned about $450 a year. Although the value of farmland appreciated 419 percent between 1900 and 1912, until farmers held equities of perhaps $7,000 and mortgages averaging 22 percent of the land's value, dealing with farmers was not often enriching, but it was time-consuming, uncertain, and personal. For years bankers pressed farmers to be businessmen. Twohy's man, W. D. Vincent, surveying rural banking and credit, could insist that "when the farmer operates his business on a business basis, he will get the same credits as a business man," but he did not deal with many farmers. The Washington Bankers Association distributed farm accounting forms published by the state college; its members agreed that "farmers as a rule do not keep books—the least that any farmer should do is keep a cash book."[15]

In these unfolding years for eastern Washington, banking services and credit for farmers, dependent on a banker's mood and a farmer's repute, were opportunistic and changeable. Neither state nor national banks could lend on the security of real estate, and the small capital of country banks usually ruled out large, long-term loans. As a Thornton banker explained: "Sound banking procedure required that most loans should be repaid annually so that recurring demands for each year's wheat crop could be met." In one year, he extended only six loans to farmers beyond their initial expiration.[16]

As collateral, the farmer offered his chattels: his crop, his house, his animals, his machines, or anything else of value. One offered 150 feet, 7 inches of three-ply rubber machine belting. His sources for loans narrowed to friends, banks, moneylenders, and merchants. If he impressed his banker as reliable, he might receive a credit line—"We will guarantee up to $50 a month for groceries," his banker might tell his storekeeper—to be paid up when his crop sold. Country bankers were forever petitioned to subrogate their interest in crop loans by creditors who sold a farmer gas, oil, repairs, and equipment for his harvest. Regularly in the middle of each month, an assistant cashier in a country bank mailed his form letters beginning, "Your account is overdue and we request that you stop in. . . ." [17] Town merchants might extend credit, but farmers shared a general impression that merchants sold on high margins to insure themselves against defaulting patrons.

Implement dealers, driven by promotional competition, were usually keen to sell on credit, writing a series of two- and three-month promissory notes, each bearing 12 percent interest, stipulating that the farmer pay the home office or a national bank. Loan company agents took chattel mortgages at 2 or 3 percent a month; for a crop mortgage the lender usually required the farmer to harvest, sack, and deliver wheat properly marked to a warehouse.

The mortgage records of eastern Washington counties during this period show the slow emancipation of Washington from Portland. Between 1900 and World War I, the counties increasingly recorded loans by lenders in Washington towns or by Spokane branches of large companies: the Provident Trust, Vermont Loan and Trust, Lombard Investment, and similar firms. One lender, the Northwestern and Pacific Hypotheekbank, owned principally by Dutch investors in Amsterdam and Rotterdam, lent millions on the security of real estate in Washington's most productive wheat and fruit districts. In 1910, for instance, its loans of $4,498,349 concentrated in Adams, Douglas, Lincoln, and Spokane counties. A second company formed by the same investors, DeTweede Northwestern and Pacific Hypotheekbank, in 1911 loaned $1,114,660, one-third of it in Washington's leading wheat counties, although its largest single investment was in irrigated tracts near Twin Falls, Idaho. [18] Private trust and mortgage companies in 1914 reported more than $7,250,000 lent with farm real estate as security in the vicinity of Spokane. [19]

Spokane's trespass into rural banking, sitting city directors on rural boards and sending bright young city bankers to learn their trade (and impress the home office) by managing country accounts, the expanding investment in agriculture by impersonal loan companies with directors in Holland or North Dakota or New York, the legislative closure of private banks, the emergence of trust companies as bankers and insurance companies as lenders, and the constraints of national and international commerce—all of these, joined with the farmer's growing investment in his business, closed out the personal era of country banking and stiffened the requirements to conform, to keep books and offer collateral. And where personal banking lingered, rather than treasuring it, bankers acted embarrassed by their seeming laxity.

Under such conditions, many farmers could not get money from a bank. As a result, inadequate farm credit in Washington, and in the nation, grew larger as a political issue. Only in the direst situations would bankers rally to the farmer, as after the 1907 depression when Seattle and Inland Empire bankers financed wheat shipments from inland warehouses to revive the export trade.[20] Princeton's president, Woodrow Wilson, addressing the American Bankers Association in the twilight of the 1907 panic, conveyed the "hostile attitude of plain men" toward bankers. President Theodore Roosevelt's Country Life Commission underscored the urgent need for farm credit. At his inauguration as U.S. president, Wilson called for credit "suited to practical needs" of farmers. Washington's new governor, Marion E. Hay, at his inauguration, echoed Wilson, declaring farm districts "retarded" because "farmers cannot secure money at a low enough rate of interest or on long enough time."

Three Washington state members of a federal American Rural Credits Commission that studied European farm credit produced a 100,000-word report advocating "very long-term farm loans," collective security, and reduced interest rates. Other than appreciative editorials in country newspapers, nothing came of this document, because Congress, less than a year later, passed the Federal Farm Loan Act of 1916, the first of the measures that erected a farm-credit structure fostered by government. There would be federal land banks, federal joint stock-land banks, federal intermediate credit banks, federal cooperative banks, changes in federal reserve regulations to ease restrictions on agricultural paper, state crop-credit associations, and state farm-marketing cooperatives—the dawn of a politicized era that sometimes helped and sometimes further burdened farmers.

City bankers generally expected little change in credit for Washington's farms from federal legislation in 1916; they declared lending procedures cumbersome and operating expenses high, or felt with Edwin Coman that farmers "operated upon such strictly individual lines that cooperative pledging of assets does not appeal to them."[21] Nevertheless, when Spokane was given the regional bank for Washington, Oregon, Idaho, and Montana, and the postmaster was named the bank's temporary agent, sacks of mail piled up and farmers organized the cooperative associations required as local lending agents under the federal act.[22]

Perhaps as a related effect, interest rates charged by bankers and lenders in some wheat districts fell from 10 or 12 to 8 percent.[23] But city bankers remained cautious: the Okanogan Growers, soliciting a $10,000 loan for a warehouse, were turned down in Spokane, because, said the Okanogan banker Harry Kerr, "financing a warehouse for cooperative apple growers . . . was a new thing . . . not strictly a banking proposition." Seattle's National Bank of Commerce, however, agreed to a three-year note for Okanogan. On the other hand, the Traders and Fidelity national banks of Spokane split a $25,000 unsecured loan to the North Pacific Fruit Growers to pay its members.[24]

Any immediate effect from government-sponsored credit was blunted by court challenges of the act's constitutionality and by war in Europe. As European farm production buckled, Washington farmers (with nearly every other agricultural area of the United States) harvested large crops. Despite clogged wartime railways and unpredictable sea schedules, buyers bought Washington produce for domestic and foreign delivery. Prosperity rolled across the Pacific Northwest. Banks were full of money, as the state examiner observed, from "the largest increase in deposits in the history of the state. The farming communities have enjoyed good crops and exceptionally high prices."[25] Farmers paid old debts and contracted new ones; they bought more land, machines, and automobiles. Many increased production—some on marginal land. The federal government stabilized the wheat price as a war measure, removing uncertainty from the market for the time being.

When the United States entered the war, even with young men depleting farm labor by military service and hundreds of families moving out of inland Washington to coastal war plants, farm profits rose even higher. Banks then strained to meet their four Liberty Loan quotas to provide the government with funds for war, and a Victory Loan for reconstruction. Bank deposits shrank as patrons withdrew their savings to buy Liberty issues—a turnabout, the banks losing money, the farmers making it. "Nearly 75 percent of the third Liberty Loan subscriptions . . . were made from funds borrowed from the banks," reported a country cashier, recommending that the government first sop up all the money in manufacturing centers "whereby withdrawal of funds in agricultural communities would be deferred."[26] His was not so much a protest as a bray of frustration. Banks traded gold for reserve notes, sending their gold to regional Federal Reserve banks. Daniel Twohy reported "all of the banks of Spokane withholding gold coin and gold certificates from circulation. . . . We have reached the point where anyone wanting gold it is self-evident that it is for . . . hoarding."[27] The metallic base of the monetary system slipped away, and paper took its place.

Farmers cared little for the intricacies of bank systems, which, with ancient suspicion, they felt discriminated against them. They had reached their best credit position in years, the climax of a painfully slow advance since the panic of 1893. Farmland values in 1918 were 60 percent higher than 1912–14, and business seemed to be getting better after the war. Deluded that prosperity would continue, many farmers bought new machines and more land, taking the ground of those who seized the opportunity to pay off their debts and move to town. Business prospects seemed so rosy that Twohy stepped aside as president to become chairman of the board of his three related companies, the Old National Bank, Union Trust, and Union Securities.

A good many farmers stayed away from commercial banks but flocked to the Spokane federal land bank for long-term loans. Thirty months after it opened (with a former Montana state senator, D. G. O'Shea, as president), the Spokane bank reported lending $48 million to 17,500 borrowers—about half those who applied for loans—on the security of first mortgages on their land.[28] In the four states of the Spokane bank's district, 451 local farm associations formed. Among the earliest, locals in fruit-raising districts, Cashmere, Okanogan, Sunnyslope, and Wenatchee, all organized in December 1916. The average loan rose from roughly $2,500 in 1917 to more than $4,200 by 1920, increasing the ratio of debt to land value approximately 8 percent. Forced to suspend, after a heartening start, until the U.S. Supreme Court upheld constitutionality of the banks, the Spokane bank resumed in the spring of 1921.[29]

In the prosperous months right after the war, commercial banks needed outlets for deposited funds, and although they continued to favor city merchants, a number approved larger, if not longer, loans to farmers. "A plethora of deposits resulted in a corresponding increase in loans," Coman explained, and added ominously, "In the desire to get the money working, the banks sometimes lost sight of the prime requisite of a good bank loan—and that is liquidity." Too many country bankers belatedly realized that their generous loans had depleted funds for short-term lending to farmers who needed to pay their harvest costs.[30]

Under federal sponsorship, the tide of credit that had consistently run against the farmer seemed to be flowing his way. The land banks steadily increased their share of the farmers' mortgage debt, from perhaps 5 percent in 1921 to more than 20 percent by the thirties. Some of this business represented refinancing of older mortgages.[31] In promotional literature, the Spokane bank boasted that it "liberated the farmer from three to five-year loans and 8 to 10 percent interest."[32] And after ten years of operation, the chairman of the Spokane board would amiably chide the Washington Bankers Association, saying that his bank seemed to have passed its "early stages . . . when it was re-garded rather as an interloper in the financial scheme, and a great many had grave doubts as to the wisdom of the act, and whether the thing would, after all, survive."[33]

Good times soon soured for the nation's farmers. Sharp cuts in government spending and the end of federal price guarantees hastened a postwar collapse. Farm prices in general had risen steadily until May 1920, when they stood nearly two and one-half times higher than 1910–14. But in the summer of 1920 this artificial prosperity deflated. By June 1921, farm prices had shriveled almost to prewar levels. The markets evaporated for livestock, wheat, and small apples. Banks called loans. Farmers paid, went out of business, or mortgaged land to pay operating expenses. By 1930 the farm mortgage debt would be 295 percent of its prewar level.[34]

And the Pacific Northwest was parching with prolonged drought. In the Big Bend, grain seeds scorched and blew out of the soil. The land bank approved 6,149 seed-grain loans worth $1.9 million. Ten years of dry weather destroyed upland orchards and range livestock. Yet when neighbors sold out, farmers who had—or could borrow—money continued to enlarge their holdings. But in the marginal districts, farmed only when the weather was favorable and prices high, cheat grass and sand crept on abandoned farms.[35]

The rural debacle strained an overgrown banking system. Through the first twenty years of the century, as Spokane solidified its central position under Twohy's goading, a network of banking emerged, not only by expanding city bank boards to take in rural directors and the acquisition of country banks but also through interlocking managements. E. T. Coman, for example, was president of the Exchange National of Spokane, the Bank of Farmington, the Farmers State at Newport, and the Rockford State banks. A Twohy man, J. K. McCornack, a vice-president of Old National, was president of the Bank of Edwall, the Security State of Palouse, and the First National, Wenatchee. And Twohy was president of the Yakima National Bank.[36]

The growth of eastern Washington's larger towns contributed to an increase in the number of banks, but state and national banks also started up in small towns, unruffled by the failure of three related Seattle banks in 1917—a failure that persuaded the legislature to enact a deposit and guaranty system, a voluntary insurance plan that expired four years later with the closing of Washington's largest state bank.

During 1919, thirty-one new state banks opened, twenty-two of them in eastern Washington (eight in Yakima County alone), a flurry of charters greater than any preceding year, enlarging Washington's system to 286 state and 84 national banks. In more than a dozen smaller towns, already mummifying because of urban migration and motorcars, competing banks started. They were shipping points with a few stores and a railroad station—such hamlets as Addy, Asotin, Cashmere, Chelan, Connell, Coulee City, Grandview, LaCrosse, Odessa, Tekoa, and Toppenish. In most of these places, banks could not do enough business with merchants to survive; they dealt with farmers. As farm prices fell and markets closed, scores of small banks teetered at the edge of failure, overcommitted to farmers who could not pay back loans and who could not sell to meet their debts as land values declined. The stable, well-managed country banks borrowed from correspondent city banks as others sank.[37]

Eleven closed in 1921, including banks at Yakima, Othello, Lind, Connell, and Mansfield; the next year, those at Withrow, Waterville, Ephrata, and Grandview; in 1923, Coulee City, Colville, Northport, and Bridgeport.[38] Outside the cities, banking stagnated. Money borrowed by banks—brisk borrowing a sign of brisk business—showed decreases each year. By the end of the decade, fifty-one state and thirteen national banks had failed in Washington, most of them in rural communities of eastern Washington, nearly all destroyed by farm depression and weak management.[39]

City bankers thought—in an impersonal way, for they, too decried human suffering—that losing weaker banks strengthened the system. The decade was prosperous for cities. "In the industrial communities, there is a superabundance of money," remarked the state's bank supervisor. In the cities, Calvin Coolidge's presidency, 1923 to 1929, would be remembered as years of "Coolidge prosperity." With new automobiles, jazz, bootleg booze, and money in their pockets, city people could not comprehend what farmers were fussing about.[40]

The immediate postwar years not only wiped out a number of country banks, they widened the gulf between banker and farmer. The president of a Colville bank felt obliged to refute "the charge that bankers denied proper credit facilities. . . . A reading of the statements of the banks . . . particularly in the country districts, will show that they have strained themselves to the utmost to take care of their customers." The Yakima Valley Bank ran newspaper advertisements with information about bank practices to allay "an unreasonable prejudice . . . in the minds of many farmers against banks."[41] Farmers saw another source of help. They turned to government.

Although politicians told themselves that farmers lacked cohesive political strength, a groundswell of guilt at treatment of the farmers had been building in national and state governments. The Federal Reserve's wartime "easy money" policies and its 1916 authorization for banks to accept and rediscount warehouse receipts showed this spirit, but they were gestures largely lost on farmers who believed, a speaker told the Washington Bankers Association, that Federal Reserve regulations "curtailed the ability of small country banks to finance the farmer." And the federal Joint Commission of Agricultural Inquiry reported that "the banking machinery of the country is not . . . adapted to the farmer's requirements." [42]

Senators Wesley Jones of Washington, Charles McNary and Robert Stanfield of Oregon, Frank Gooding of Idaho, and Representative John Summers of Washington, among others, saw that farm rescue was again a popular issue. Both the national and state Republican and Democratic parties campaigned on postwar platforms that included establishing the legal rights of farm marketing associations, studying farm costs, and expanding the federal loan system. Perhaps Washington State fostered some of this revived concern for the farmer; the state's Grange had joined Oregon, Colorado, Maine, Pennsylvania, and Kentucky to pay a lobbyist in Washington, D.C., and participated in a farmers' war council which became the National Farmers Council. In 1918 and 1919 the National Board of Farm Organizations and the national Grange also opened offices in the national capital. [43]

Despite the efforts of these competing farm organizations, the real rural political muscle belonged to congressional delegations from farm states and the agricultural extension service. Montana, however, was the only Pacific Northwest state represented in Chicago during November 1919 at the American Farm Bureau Federation's organizing convention. The federation launched a massive organizing campaign: by the following December, thirty-seven states were affiliated; by July 1921, forty-two. Washington was among the last. [44]

Farm leaders and congressmen shared a consensus that farmers' selling cooperatives would solve farm problems. And in 1921, the most powerful cooperative force among Washington farmers was the stocky attorney from California, Aaron Sapiro. He counseled the state's wheat and fruit growers, telling them that by joining, farmers could control their markets. Sapiro impressed the 1921 legislature, overwhelmingly Republican because the westside Farm-Labor party had split the Democrats. Sapiro helped draft House Bill 255, authorizing farm marketing cooperatives, and in midsession addressed the House on the bill's merits. Offered by the House Committee on Agriculture, the marketing bill (affording a rare occasion for eastside and westside agricultural counties to collaborate) passed on the last day of the session, after a conference committee spent a Sunday with George Jewett of the wheat growers and other eastern Washington spokesmen.[45] Incidentally, if bankers seemed aloof in their counting houses, the bankers in the legislature supported the farmers handsomely: Coman, a senator, voted for farm bills and F. J. Wilmer, a Rosalia banker, was a leading Senate proponent. The governor had appealed for a farm marketing law (several states passed similar laws), but regulation of cold storage facilities, which he also wanted, was scuttled.[46]

Within three years, thirty-three farm marketing cooperatives were organized. Those on the westside were largely associations of dairy, poultry, or berry producers, and on the east, chiefly fruit growers (among them, the Wenatchee District Cooperative Association). In the director of agriculture's opinion, the most successful were "those which handled products every month" rather than seasonally.[47]

With the American Farm Bureau Federation feeding them polls of farmers' preferences and occasionally flooding Congress with telegrams, the farm bloc (congressmen from farm states) moved ahead. Senator Arthur Capper of Kansas sponsored a federal act to exempt farm cooperatives from antitrust prosecution and cosponsored one of several bills intended to strengthen country banks (through the Federal Reserve) to serve farmers better. And Congress accepted the War Finance Corporation as the federal agency to finance postwar farm exports. The corporation, revived in 1921 over President Wilson's veto as a temporary agency to give credit to European buyers of American farm products, was extended by the Agricultural Credits Act of 1921 to make one-year cash advances to commercial banks and cooperative associations on the security of agricultural paper—warehouse receipts, bills of lading, mortgages on livestock—up to 75 percent of value.[48] Particularly in wheat and livestock states, the corporation's welcome funding enabled banks to extend existing loans or make new ones to farmers.

Committees of local bankers and businessmen administered regional offices. Autocratic R. L. Rutter, next to Twohy Spokane's most prominent banker and president of the Spokane and Eastern, served as chairman of the Washington agricultural loan agency. In one of his comradely letters to Eugene Meyer, Jr., chairman of the War Finance Corporation, Rutter observed that "all we can get out of this work . . . is the satisfaction of work well done."[49] Rutter had been a wool buyer early in his career; in Spokane, he was known as an energetic organizer, impatient with people or systems that did not perform smartly.

Rutter's agency, in fewer than three years (it began liquidating at the end of 1924), advanced $1,065,731 to seventeen Washington banks—all rural and most small—to the Washington Growers Service Corporation of Yakima, and the cooperative Okanogan County Livestock Association, secured by their notes. The new money helped them survive. The Washington agency repaid all the federal advances and foreclosed none of its loans, but with the Okanogan association and five banks, repayment was touch and go. The First National Bank of St. John failed despite War Finance Corporation aid, and at one time Okanogan had thirty-six delinquent of fifty-nine loans to members. The livestock association and most banks pulled through (Washington's bank failures fell from twelve in 1921 to five in 1922 and five again in 1923). Bank advances ranged from $12,000 to the doomed St. John bank to $47,500 for the Pullman State, and among the banks assisted were some of the smallest in Washington, for example, Palouse, Marlin, Odessa, Molson, Endicott, and Valleyford.[50]

The Washington agricultural loan agency received sixty-six applications and approved twenty-four (twenty-one advances to banks, one to a cooperative, and two to livestock associations), venturing into perilous financial territory because small banks often were in depressed districts. Rutter looked down on small-town bankers, remarking to Meyer that "any man who would accept the position of cashier of a bank in a little town like that [Winthrop], it is fair to assume does not amount to much."[51]

The War Finance Corporation relieved city bankers of any duty they may have felt to ease the plight of rural bankers, and, with other federal agencies, reduced the farmers' reliance on the banking system. Bank loans for agriculture declined after 1920 throughout the United States, partly because farmers could not offer acceptable security, of course, but also because federal and state agencies, which took agricultural paper, passed much of the lending function to warehouses and cooperative associations. By contrast, commercial banks had steadily increased their agricultural loan volumes between 1914 and 1920 (in other areas more substantially than in Washington). The uneasy partnership between bankers and farmers unraveled from 1920 onward.[52] Bankers could console themselves that rural banking would have shrunk in any event because motorcars sped the few well-to-do farmers to banks in bigger towns.

Country banks continued to fail—two or four or six each year—

until 1931, when twenty-two collapsed. In the middle of the twenties, the state supervisor of banking had begun to discourage new banks, because "over-banking has contributed more to bank failures than has the general business depression." As the Coolidge years neared their end, Spokane's banks saw their business slowly stagnate. The Old National, which had paid dividends of 10 percent each year between 1904 and 1924, paid none in 1925, 2 percent the next two years, and 7 percent in 1929, when business, even farming, seemed to be swinging upward again.[53]

The Spokane land bank nearly suffocated from its landslide loan business. It had lent more than $24.5 million to 9,201 borrowers by the end of 1921, and in the next two years, more than $38 million to nearly 11,000. But, forced to foreclose many of its early loans, by 1924 the bank held thousands of bankrupt acres that would not sell for the appraisals on which loans had been based. Most delinquencies dated from the immediate postwar months. In Adams County, for instance, dryland farms that averaged $37 an acre in 1920 fell to $22 by 1925; in Douglas, from $40 to $28; and even in Whitman, the best wheatland in Washington, from $98 to $62.[54] For Whitman, Lincoln, and Walla Walla county land, buyers appeared, smelling bargains in the farmers' distress, but in the Big Bend counties, where farmers relied on government grants for seed, production costs remained relatively constant while no substantial crops grew in six searing years. The fine soil lay unturned, sifting against vacant farmhouses. Farmers assigned their mortgages or sold out to neighbors, who took only the best land to operate with machines at lower unit cost.[55]

George C. Jewett, the wheat cooperative manager, became president of the Spokane land bank in 1925 to rescue it. He managed to sell twenty foreclosed farms in one month, the bank's best sales period. Three years later, with the bank still numbed by foreclosed acres, Jewett left to help form a national grain marketing cooperative. He was succeeded by E. M. Ehrhardt. From 1924, a year after it moved into its own terra cotta office building in Spokane, the bank's loan average slipped to about $4.7 million a year. Eventually a rescue commission from the nation's eleven other farm loan banks accepted mortgages from the Spokane bank to tide it over as the depression of the thirties shrouded Northwest farmers.[56]

Through the trying twenties, commercial bankers tried to help farmers, within the bounds of prudent fiscal practices. Nearly every city banker and businessman cajoled the farmer to be more efficient, and between 1920 and 1927 wheat farmers supposedly increased their efficiency by an estimated 27 percent, using tractors and fewer men for large-scale cultivation.[57] Efficiency was a chimeral statistic on the farm, but the war had elevated everyone's impression of efficiency's virtues.

The war had also heightened bankers' concern for their public relations. They had been stung by their strong-arm promotions of war bonds and, shortly after the war, imposed service charges for the first time. In 1925, urged by the American Banking Association, the Washington Bankers Association appointed "key" bankers in twenty-five agricultural counties to assist farmers. Under the leadership of Joseph W. Bradley, a vice-president of Twohy's Old National Bank and chairman of the bankers' state agricultural committee, key bankers sat with farmers to discuss finances and cooperation. The association sponsored short courses on farming for bankers and, with railroads and the state college, underwrote demonstration trains—one for livestock breeding in 1927, and another for general farming that visited forty-one farm communities during 1929. Stevens County bankers supported dairymen in forming an Inland Empire Dairy Congress, and Kittitas bankers helped raise $50,000 to promote local land settlement. Bankers sponsored purebred cattle herds for farms in Stevens, Chelan, and Yakima counties.[58]

Near the end of the twenties, many bankers thought they detected encouraging economic signs. E. E. Flood, vice-president of the Exchange National (which sold to Old National in 1929), opined, "The farmer is paying off his mortgage. . . . This is especially significant as the condition in Spokane is largely dependent on the condition of agriculture." The Washington director of agriculture called 1929 the best year for farmers since the war. A Colfax banker observed that Whitman County land values had risen $10 an acre within a year and that many farmers had paid off a large part of their debts within the past two years. Three Colfax banks, in annual reports, remarked that the liquidation of farmers' debts was better than they had expected.[59]

By this time the commercial banks' investment in farmland had fallen substantially from ten years earlier. Most national banks invested instead in government and corporate securities, although bank assets varied by area; in such farm-reliant counties as Spokane, Yakima, Whitman, Walla Walla, Okanogan, Columbia, Chelan, and Benton, banks reported roughly twice the national average of loans, discounts, and overdrafts.[60] Some Palouse country bankers had introduced real estate and farm-loan departments, advertising, "no association to join, no capital stock to buy," affording a borrower up to thirty-two years to pay.[61]

Possibly the bankers' public relations efforts to reach farmers improved the understanding of the problems of both, for a consensus wafted through Washington's farm counties that, regardless of the shortcomings of the banking system, tariffs and taxes really lay at the bottom of the farmers' economic problems. The tariff was an elusive, complex issue. While the *Colfax Commoner* blamed the high prices of farm machinery on the tariff, the *Colfax Gazette* editorialized that wheat prices would rise "if the . . . government would impose a sufficient tariff to protect the price fixed against importations of foreign grain."[62] These were political viewpoints, of course, one for lower, the other for higher tariffs, both speaking to the farmer.

As a matter of fact, the federal government, dominated by protectionists in a Republican Congress and inspired by economic nationalism, exercised the highest general tariffs in fifteen years, which afforded no real advantages to western farmers. But if tariffs seemed simply a convenient scapegoat, taxes truly burdened the Washington farmer.

Like many other states, Washington had a revenue system resting on property taxes that most heavily affected landowners. The state constitution required that real and personal property be assessed at equal and uniform rates. City real estate, appraised on improvements, offered loopholes, but rural appraisals valued the land itself. "In Whitman County . . . taxes are one of the principal causes of depression," Senator F. J. Wilmer contended. "Land values and farm prices have fallen to 1914 levels but farm taxes are three times what they were in 1914." A state tax commission reported that assessments were "inaccurate and unequal," with farm property "more effectively and accurately assessed" than that of merchants, manufacturers, and large corporations.[63]

The state farm bureau and taxpayers' associations demanded lower government costs and a revised tax structure, portraying citizens as "thoroughly aroused." In Asotin County, cited as typical, farmers sold wheat for less than their taxes, forcing them to borrow. During the scorching years in Douglas County, a citizens' committee convinced the commissioners to cut taxes in half to see farmers through.[64] Governor Hartley, continuing his predecessor Hart's penury in state government, which he called "constructive economy," created a commission in 1925 to distribute taxes more equitably. (One of Hartley's economies stopped the state college from mailing extension bulletins to farmers. And he vetoed a bill to provide seed wheat.) For five years Hartley's tax commission held dreary hearings full of stifling statistics that revealed the sectional discriminations among the taxed; it raised some assessments on public services and large corporations, which were challenged in the courts. For the farmer nothing changed. A state examiner, visiting Colfax five years after the commission started its work, declared, "The tax problem . . . is the most serious and acute in the history of the state. Under recent decisions of the supreme court affecting banks and railroads . . . there is clearly indicated the shifting of a much greater burden to the farmer, the homeowner, and the local businessman."[65]

The tax commission acknowledged that Washington had imposed "fairly constant annual increases" in taxes between 1922 and 1930. The legislature created a special tax investigating commission for more study (chaired by Dorsey M. Hill, Walla Walla wheat farmer and treasurer of Whitman College), and the electors in 1930 passed a constitutional amendment to classify some properties for tax purposes. But the incoming governor in 1933, Clarence D. Martin, called the tax program "a failure." While Washington struggled to invent alternative taxes that would ease assessments on property (the Grange advocated taxes on cigarettes, butter substitutes, and income), the depression of the thirties, and passage in 1933 of a 40-mill limit, crippled the property tax as a revenue source.[66]

Meanwhile, Congress mirrored the farmers' frustrations and the farm bloc lost ground. Congress had passed the Intermediate Credit Act (1923) to allow farmers to borrow against their crops from short-term credit agencies run by farm land banks, but the cooperatives and country banks supposed to be panting for intermediate loans proved surprisingly cool. The Spokane intermediate credit bank loaned on wheat, wool, beans, dried prunes, canned fruits and vegetables, cold-pack fruits, certified alfalfa seed, apples, and honey, but in half a decade used only 11 percent of its lending capacity. After ten years the Spokane bank had served fewer than three dozen cooperatives: fourteen fruit and vegetable associations, twelve grain, six dairy, and a handful not limited to one product. To these the bank lent $1.5 million, of which $696,000 went for buildings. Nine farmers' credit organizations, which acted as credit banks for their members, took intermediate loans and discounts—all but two of them in eastern Washington and six of them exclusively for fruit growers. In the same ten years, perhaps thirty small credit associations failed.[67]

The farm bloc's main proposal, to reduce farm surpluses through a government export corporation that would buy at artificial prices and sell abroad at market prices—the McNary-Haugen idea—was defeated or vetoed five times between 1924 and 1928. Farmers had formed state export corporation leagues to push this plan. A short-lived Washington league, started in 1923, raised $3,187 to send delegates to the capital when McNary-Haugen proposals were debated. Both Coolidge and his secretary of commerce, Hoover, believed that private, rather than government, associations could solve farmers' difficulties.[68]

Debates on McNary-Haugen bills drew a picture of the farmers' distress for the whole country, however, and Hoover, as president, called a special session of Congress to pass the Agricultural Marketing Act of 1929, creating a federal farm board to underwrite national private cooperative associations as export agencies. Seventy-five farmers formed the North Pacific Grain Growers for Washington, Idaho, and Oregon, and a number of locals organized and took over most of the twenty-year-old farmers' union cooperatives that owned elevators.[69]

Albert Goss, master of the Washington Grange, declared the 1929 act "the most substantial aid ever given cooperative farming," adding that cooperative financing had resulted from "the refusal of chain banks to extend credit to agriculture at reasonable rates."[70] This was a biased view, no doubt, but clearly as federal legislation had evolved in the twenties, the government and government-supported farmers' associations had taken the place of the banking system in farm finance. Even bankers saw that. "Farm relief legislation is looming large in Washington," D. W. Twohy observed after visiting the capital. "Some way will be found . . . to keep the exportable surplus of our basic farm commodities from depressing prices below the cost of production."[71]

The farm bloc stirred now and then. Summers's charges of collusion between millers and exporters to hold down Washington wheat prices resulted in a Department of Justice inquiry that turned up "some ground" for his allegations. Gooding tried to rally twenty-five Republican senators as a tariff bloc to "put people back to work by restoring an American market for their products." And Gooding also championed new long-haul rate regulation.[72]

But the farmers' political unity in Congress had frayed again. The American Farm Bureau Federation, maimed by its ejection of Sapiro and his cooperative movement in 1924, lost its power, and the Washington State bureau, in debt, dissolved the following spring, although it reorganized within a year with headquarters at Colfax (moved to Yakima in 1930) to continue to lobby in state and national capitals and sell insurance to members.[73]

By the last years of the 1920s many pioneers of farming and banking in Washington were gone or, like Twohy, approaching retirement. Spokane now held a central position in inland Washington's banking structure. Farm credit had evolved from a personal chat between a country banker and his neighbor to a national political issue. And farmers, who had endured depression since 1920, were about to have the company of a nation in misery.

CHAPTER 8

Machines

*I*n the open reaches of grain and stock country, isolation was as tangible as dust sifting on the wind. The flat land, fenced, occasionally shaded by a lonesome stand of Lombardy poplars and a barn marking a farm home, repeated its tedious pattern to the horizon—silent land where bird and animal calls and the wind's whine carried distinctly.

Farm families there lived reclusive lives, one day like another. Men and women turned leathery and hardhanded in their fields. Two out of three of their children did not go regularly to schools, but learned the ways of animals and weather; they knew little of other people, dressed in the same bib overalls every day, and talked in the cadences of their parents, sounding like the rubes city folk took them for.

In these districts, the drudgery of life on the soil evaporated slowly. They were more than forty years into the twentieth century before running water or electricity transformed their homes. The farm husband saw practical use for an automobile and a telephone. His wife might yearn for running water in her kitchen, but, by 1920, when nearly half the farmers owned cars and phones, less than a third had indoor running water and one in ten had electricity or gas for cooking. In ten more years, nearly everyone would own cars and telephones.[1]

Until the chugging gas-powered automobile dusted the countryside, rural travel was confined to rutted wagon trails. In some seasons, mud mired wagons and even horses. In hilly districts, steep and winding trails with switchbacks—"turntables" in country parlance—for negotiating sharp turns made wagon travel slow and even dangerous. Wenatchee residents forded the river twice to reach nearby Cashmere;

their road to Ellensburg was so steep that they cut small trees to fasten to the rear wagon axle to prevent wearing out brakes.[2]

For a few rural towns and farms within an easy drive of stations, electric railroads whirred for a fleeting decade before the automobile took over. For fewer than twenty years, gaudy electrics radiating from Spokane raced through the Palouse, hauling freight and passengers, rapid transportation to the city and home again, with as many as six trains a day. One electric, the Spokane and Inland Empire, sped south from Spokane as far as Moscow, Idaho, and east to the railroad owners' resorts at Liberty, Hayden, and Coeur d'Alene lakes. A second, the Interurban operated by the Washington Water Power Company, ran green, plush-seated cars to Medical Lake and Cheney. The Yakima Valley Transportation Company operated a 44-mile system to valley towns, and the Walla Walla Valley Railway Company, a shorter line.

The Spokane and Inland Empire erected bungalow stations at towns and trackside sheds where farmers could tie their teams while they rode the train; it ran "theater specials," late homeward trains on Saturday nights. For sixty cents or less, it sped its riders over a rough roadbed from Spokane to the lakes, carrying as many as thirty thousand passengers a day—brash derbied blades in celluloid collars leaning from car steps with as much aplomb as they could muster in a fifty-mile-an-hour wind. Farm families found the rapid, frequent runs convenient for shopping in larger towns, a chance to get away from the farm for a day, to luxuriate in wicker seats, electric lights in petal-glass shades, shiny brass fittings, and a rear observation platform.[3]

With a generating plant at Nine Mile Falls, the Spokane and Inland Empire operated thirteen locomotives and sixty passenger cars; it carried large consignments of freight and, with parcel post, brought mail-order houses close to the farms. (For years, country editors pleaded with their readers to patronize home merchants.) The electric delivered its Spokane passengers to a yellow stucco terminal only one block from the Auditorium theater and no more than three or four from stores and restaurants.

For the railroad's first five years, it made money—revenues of more than $1.2 million in 1908. But in 1909, as crowded special trains highballed to Coeur d'Alene, carrying excited bidders for Indian reservation lands, two trains collided, killing fifteen and injuring more than seventy-five persons. Damage claims strained the company's finances (despite a book value of $24.8 million) and the road was sold to the Great Northern. The Great Northern would run the electric until 1930, carrying mostly freight.

The Palouse farm family that rode to Spokane could not fail to compare itself with fashionable men and women in the city, their dusty roads with brick pavement, their clapboard buildings with brick and granite buildings lining Riverside Avenue. In theaters, cafes, and stores they saw urban ease unlike their dutiful labor. Farm visitors usually thought of city people as impudent and artificial; and city residents, however much they agreed that agriculture was the backbone of the nation, treated farmers as unlettered hayseeds, for Spokane was a city with airs, social castes, and ambitions, confident of its luminosity in the cosmos of smaller towns around it.

The automobile that ended the era of electric trains burst on the nation in clouds of smoke and dust, its noise and breakdowns obscuring the revolution it would work, generally looked on as a sporting machine for the wealthy whose chauffeurs bumped through roadless country in endurance and speed contests. Spokane's first cars were an 1898 Locomobile steamer and a Haynes-Apperson with rear motor and tiller steering, marvelous and novel.

Before automobiles, when railroads provided long-distance hauling, roads between towns could be ignored, and Washington's campaign for improvement aimed first at better local wagon roads. The Spokane businessmen who had raised road funds by subscription in 1884–85 thought a road "an important factor in winning back the county seat from Cheney and bringing trade into town." (Spokane took the county seat the next year—politics, not roads.) Colfax macadamized its main street to lay dust in 1902; other towns put down a few yards of plank, brick, or wood-block paving; and in rural districts, farmers working out road taxes built straw roads packed by iron wagon wheels; they graded, scraping toward the center, and dumped wagonloads of straw six inches deep until the straw mixed with mud for a tough surface. Wide-tired wagons, it was said, packed roads better and hauled bigger loads. (A Spokane good roads association advocated four-inch rims.) Counties and businessmen's associations bought "drags"—half logs fitted with horse harness—to lend to farmers for smoothing rural roads. Thus a crude road network crept painfully across eastern Washington—a road system intended mainly to get the farmer to the nearest town. But dust browned the summer countryside, and in wet seasons, wagons sank, horses slipped, and farmers cursed.

Each county built and maintained its roads, often completing unconnected sections of so-called state highways from "nowhere to nowhere." These "little roads were considered one of the perquisites" of a commissioner's office. For a time Chelan County required those who petitioned for roads to negotiate right-of-way. But Washington was not far behind other states: when the state appointed its first highway engineer in 1905, only thirteen other states had highway departments.[4]

In the campaign for better roads, the compelling voice at first was that of Sam Hill, a Great Northern officer, born of Quaker parents in North Carolina, trained for the law, husband of pouty Mary, eldest daughter of James J. Hill. He moved to Washington in 1898, a man of extraordinary reputation: world traveler with changes of clothing in forty foreign clubs, friend of statesmen, crusader for peace and for good roads. Self-confident, wealthy, his largish head crowned with a shock of graying hair, Hill on September 14, 1899, in Spokane with fourteen men, organized a Washington Good Roads Association to launch an educational drive. County associations sprang up. But when he visited the national capital, senators told Hill that hard-surfaced roads were for "sporting fellows." Even so, Hill's timing was sure, for the common people were rapidly seeing what automobiles could do. Cross-country trips proved the automobile's durability and speed. By 1903, when Henry Ford opened his motorcar company, most Americans knew that the automobile was going to replace the horse.[5]

Surprisingly, good roads meetings attracted few. "So little interest," clucked the *Colfax Commoner*, pointing out that despite the costs of roads "there are only a few miles . . . which do not have to be worked over every few months." This was the nub of citizen attitudes: roads took heavy taxes and fell apart quickly. Five minutes of applause followed a lady's shout at a meeting on road taxes: "We raise thousands every year—and the roads are impassable!"

To show road construction methods, the Great Northern Railway and U.S. Department of Agriculture sponsored a good roads train to towns in Washington, Oregon, and Idaho in 1902. Sam Hill thought it "not a successful venture," and it was not repeated. Object-lesson roads, funded near experimental farms by the Agriculture Department, located in Washington at Pullman and Walla Walla, showed solutions to local construction problems. Yet these were fundamentally wagon roads. A decision to design roads for automobiles was not reached until 1909. In 1912, the city of Spokane still laid brick paving on inclines because horse drivers preferred it.[6]

With Hill as patron, a consulting engineer, Samuel C. Lancaster, traveled Washington, Oregon, and Idaho teaching road building in 1907 and 1908; near Hill's mansion, Maryhill, he and Hill designed and built a stretch of highway to show engineers and public road officials. But Hill's preeminence soon faded, blunted by a falling out over roads (and politics) with Governor Hay, 1909–13.[7] North of Spokane near his estate, Waikiki, the organizer of the Spokane and Inland Empire electric, Jay P. Graves, laid three miles of demonstration road and offered cash awards for improved designs.

In 1905 five Spokane bicycle dealers also sold automobiles; in 1907 Lorenzo L. True opened a gas station; the city recorded a fatal car wreck in 1908; and by 1910 twenty-one firms were selling only automobiles and 9,300 Washington residents owned one. The pioneer Spokane dealers, Guy and Dee Riegel, taxicab men, rented a basement storeroom and lowered display cars into it through sidewalk doors. Hundreds flocked to new automobile showings, including the introduction of Ford's 1908 Model T (four-cylinder, pedal-shifted with two forward speeds, it could hit forty miles an hour and sold for $850). Shining with black leather seats in black tub body and folding windshield, the Model T was the car Ford meant to make—durable, simple to operate and fix, mounted high to travel country roads. For years Ford owners believed that if the car stopped, rest it a few days and it would run again. Chauffeurs might still drive prestigious cars, but the common man's automobile—Ford, Buick, Oldsmobile, and a score of others—had come.

Enclosed bodies and self-starters encouraged women to drive. Detroiters with self-starters reached Spokane in 1914. When Dodge publicized its original car, the Riegel brothers wrote two hundred orders with down payments before a display model arrived. Guy Riegel warned buyers not to drive their cars from Detroit, alerting them to "bad roads and unscrupulous farmers" who dug mudholes and then charged to pull out cars with their teams.[8]

Makers built cars for bad roads, however, and no matter how poor the roads, farmers drove their twenty-horsepower Fords with planetary transmissions and buggy tops. Between 1910 and 1920, a Washington State highway system of 1,146 miles, with 141 miles of improved (scraped) roads, expanded to 3,079 miles with 1,944 improved (scraped and graveled). By 1930 there were 3,500 miles with 3,239 improved (oiled and, in some places, concrete lanes). The Spokane County good roads association, managed by lank Frank Guilbert (a sales agent for home builders), promoted a new highway eastward, the Great Apple Way, thirty feet wide, graveled, lined to Idaho with trees, and another westward, asphalted, with a magnificent view of Spokane at its crest above the city. The association opposed roadside advertising. By 1917 thieves were stealing an average of ten cars a day in Washington. Juveniles were reprimanded and told not to do it again.[9]

Businessmen's clubs in towns once secure on rail lines now called for improved auto roads. Even the best wagon roads could not stand up under automobile travel. "With automobiles in large numbers tearing through the country at 30 miles an hour, the matter of better county roads is becoming a vital question," declared the *Cheney Free Press* in an editorial typical of many. "It is an indisputable fact that auto traffic cuts great ruts in our country roads, tears them to pieces." Not only wagon roads—its president told the Washington Good Roads Association that a paved Palouse highway, south from Spokane, had broken so badly in five years that most drivers used a parallel gravel road.[10]

As Washington's government struggled to catch up with the surging, bouncing automobile, city and rural residents disagreed over routes and funding. Cities favored an east-west highway across the state (it would enlarge Seattle's trade with eastern counties), branching in eastern Washington to meet regional highways, the Inland Empire and Sunset, where they joined near Ellensburg. Cities also wanted a north-south highway in western and another in eastern Washington—the eastern one to connect with the 449-mile Inland Empire Highway, the "scenic route" that meandered from Ellensburg through Yakima, Pasco, Walla Walla, Dayton, and Colfax to Spokane, and continued north through Colville to the Canadian border at Laurier. (A central Washington highway from Pasco reached Spokane by Connell and Ritzville.) The Sunset went through Wenatchee, crossed the Columbia by toll bridge there or ferry at Vantage, climbed a steep twisting sand-hill to Waterville, and ended in Spokane. By 1916, none of the central had been built, and eighty-four miles of the Inland Empire had been smoothed. Drivers used these routes, nevertheless, following telephone wires, fences, hills, and streambeds between the graded sections.[11]

The cities' plan, converging the state's highway routes on Seattle and Spokane, was predictably adopted by the legislature, but disparaged by rural voters, much as farmers across the United States derided the Lincoln Highway from New York to San Francisco as a "peacock alley" for rich tourists. "The people of this state must not be taxed to build such a road for autos of the wealthy," scolded J. C. Lawrence, Whitman County's fiery Bull Moose, recently resigned from the state railroad commission. "What we want is good roads radiating out from the centers of the agricultural districts so the farmers can reach their nearest towns over good roads." [12]

And eastern Washington grumbled that western Washington wolfed road funds. During its 1913 session, when the legislature voted $1.9 million for roads, eastside lobbyists (calling themselves the Eastern Washington Highway Association) persuaded senate and house covertly to pledge one-third to eastern counties, a division that endured until 1928. [13] Spokane delegations seeking road funds unabashedly cowed legislators in the name of William H. Cowles, publisher of the *Spokesman-Review* and president of the county good roads association from 1912 to 1940.

The Rambler sales manager in Spokane had observed in 1910 (the year that Spokane passed a traffic code) that farmers asked for five- and seven-passenger cars and "were taking their place beside city people as buyers." (A seven-passenger, sixty-horsepower Thomas cost $5,000.) In north central Washington there was one car for every ten residents: 1,937 cars in Chelan County; 229 in Ferry; 2,462 in Lincoln; 690 in Okanogan; 1,249 in Douglas; and an even 1,000 in Grant. Chelan hired a plainclothes cop. Used-car advertisements appeared in the *Spokesman-Review* under the classified heading, "automobiles and bicycles." The Great War slowed road construction but not the automobile mania. At the armistice, "the whole country awoke to a crying need for more roads and better roads," declared the state highway commissioner. Farmers, prospering between 1915 and 1920, bought cars and trucks, and when railroads congested with war traffic, motored their produce to market. By 1921 on Yakima's produce row, three trucks were crowding every horse team. [14]

Wheat farmers of eastern Washington had been domesticating steam and gas-powered machines in their fields for more than a decade; crop loans and installment payments for tractors and combines accustomed them to debt; and every day they confronted the lonely distances that automobiles promised to conquer. Buying a machine with time payments was nothing new to them. Even before the war, cars sold on time contracts, one-third down and twelve months to pay (and buyers clamored for longer pay-out periods). The Guaranty Sales Corporation, organized in New York in 1916, financed purchases of twenty-one makes, including Ford, General Motors, and Dodge. (In 1919 General Motors formed its own credit agency.) By 1921 half the cars sold in America went on installment plans.

Makers of other expensive goods—ranges, washers, furniture—adopted installment purchasing to increase their sales. Farmers with cars could drive to town to shop for such items. "Simultaneously with the advance in the use of the automobile there has been a marked advance in the purchase of . . . luxury goods," President Hoover's Commission on Recent Economic Changes would comment in 1929.

The automobile also conferred status. When the hick motored into town, his car spoke for him. City sophisticates might scoff at the farmer's eccentric driving but not at his car. Rural buyers, conscious of style, ordered handsome vehicles. Cram Motor Company, Colfax, described a Studebaker Victoria sold to an Endicott buyer: "upholstered in the finest quality mohair, with hydrolic four-wheel brakes, glare-proof vision windshield . . . headlights controlled from the wheel, automatic ignition, vanity case, and balloon tires." [15]

The contest between pedestrians and cars prompted a Spokane engineer to suggest waggishly that "unthinking and selfish pedestrians" hogging streets should wear protective pneumatic underwear and carry sirens in their belts. For a time, Granges seriously discussed proposing dirt roads for teams alongside auto roads. In 1921 Spokane's traffic regulations required pedestrians, as well as motorists, to observe traffic semaphores at busy intersections.

The federal government in 1916 had enacted the first of a series of highway-aid programs, initially to improve roads for the postal service, and between 1917 and 1929 allocated $12.4 million to Washington. At the end of the war, the government had distributed surplus construction equipment to states, sending Washington 266 trucks, five Holt tractors, tools, explosives, and instruments. Washington's automobile ownerships passed 145,000 in 1920. [16]

Although the federal government continued its highway program, Washington's road plan lugged through the twenties, stalling with political disputes and frequent departmental shifts. For several years a $30 million bond issue for highways was a controversial political issue; known as the Carlyon bill, it was strongly opposed in eastern Washington. The state, forming highway districts, gradually took over the management of state roads; the state advocated concrete surfaces for permanence, but county commissions favored gravel and crushed rock, cheap and easy to repair.

As automobiling spread, critics asserted both that it solidified family life by family outings and eroded family life by freeing youngsters in cars from parental supervision. A state senator from Spokane warned that automobiles encouraged people to spend beyond their means, contributed to the delinquency of the young, and "took away the calm and contentment of the American home." [17] If moral effects were arguable, the economic effects showed everywhere—in automobile sales rooms, repair shops, insurance agencies, accessory dealers (including those selling dust-protective coats and headgear), and by 1912 the entry of American Gasoline Company (Shell) stations into the Northwest to compete with Standard Oil of California. At first, automobile garages and general stores with a pump by the door sold gasoline, but by 1919 bulk plants were liberally scattered through eastern Washington to supply chain service stations. These new businesses created jobs for boys leaving the farm. By 1930, one in every twenty-nine men employed in Washington worked in a business directly related to automobiles, a ratio that (outside the largest cities) was about the same in urban and rural counties.[18]

In his 1919 message, Governor Ernest Lister called for completing the east-west highway along a trail broken through Snoqualmie Pass four years earlier. (There had been an abortive scheme once to finance the road by a lottery of the Yesler Mill and other Seattle property to raise $80,000.) Lister rode in a seventeen-auto caravan from Seattle that met groups from Yakima and Ellensburg to dedicate "the first passable thoroughfare between east and west-side counties," and twenty-five cars crossed the pass that day. To finance road expansion, the legislature created a motor-vehicle fund and in 1921 (following Oregon, New Mexico, and Colorado in 1919) enacted a tax of one cent a gallon on gasoline that would rise to five cents within the decade. By 1925, gas taxes had passed in nearly every state and, with license fees, were taking the place of levies for highway construction.[19]

But at his inauguration as governor in 1925, Roland H. Hartley, an opinionated lumberman from Everett, raised again the shibboleth of roads for recreation. Highways cost too much, Hartley cried. "The public demand for good roads is but the echo of the clamor of the cement crowd, the material men, the machinery folks, the contractors, the auto club secretaries. . . . It's not the farmer but the joyrider upon whom we are expending most of the money!" So many citizens owned cars that Hartley's views impressed most as dated, but everyone wanted lower taxes. In rural areas and eastern Washington towns, a strong sentiment surfaced for pay-as-you-go highway funding. The Carlyon bill, submitted as a referendum, was voted down. Albert Goss, master of the Washington Grange, told the Washington Good Roads Association, "We vigorously oppose any plan which contemplates departing from a pay-as-you-go policy. . . . No policy . . . should be considered which ignores the farm-to-market road."[20]

Hartley installed a pay-as-you-go road program, persuaded the legislators to repeal the last of the highway levy laws, and spent for roads only the funds raised from license fees, gas taxes, and federal aid. He brushed aside imperious Sam Hill, rushing to "rescue" Washington's highway program by spending his personal funds for an audit of Highway Department books that he believed would quiet the state-wide uproar over fiscal policy. Hartley's austere road program, in effect until 1933, marked Washington as one of the few states without bonded indebtedness for highway construction. The next administration, taking office during the Depression, immediately passed a $10 million bond issue for highways as a relief measure, specifying in contracts that builders use hand labor.[21]

Under Hartley the state built roads at a modest pace. In 1929 the state adopted a policy of heavy oiling for county roads and concrete for state highways. Washington's engineers followed closely the pavement testing conducted by the Federal Bureau of Public Roads and the state of Illinois. But as highway design improved, manufacturers produced bigger, faster cars. Despite a cautious state program, driving improved for the motorist. Good roads associations, counties, oil companies, and businessmen put up directional signs. (The Inland Automobile Association in 1912 erected nine-foot white signs with black crossboards and orange letters on Trent Road near Spokane, for example.) The Colfax Chamber of Commerce erected 400 signs reading, "To Colfax." Counties set out warning signs, and before the end of 1928 the Inland Automobile Association had marked 1,477 miles with signs pointing to the nearest town. The association also listed clean restaurants and issued maps. If the road ended, the maps advised "follow river" or "follow wires." (Fifteen years earlier the Pathfinder Company had used a Locomobile equipped with compass, gradometer, and other devices to produce tour maps.) The IAA would continue its signing until 1946, twenty-three years after the state adopted standard markers made in the penitentiary. Nearly every car on the road in the twenties carried a tow rope, cannisters of gas and water, and a tire-repair kit. Quite a few drivers complained that gas stations and hot-dog stands used flashing red lights for attention, like railroad crossings.[22]

The automobile shrank the geographic isolation of the Washington farmer but did not make him prosperous, for while car ownership rose steadily throughout the twenties, agriculture was depressed. Car prices fell lower than before the war: a Ford roadster cost $485 delivered in Spokane; a Chevrolet, $642; and both could be bought with weekly payments. And if the farmer had imagined that the car would imbue rural life with the better aspects of city life, he was disappointed. The automobile extended cities, eliminated the one-room schoolhouse, obliterated most small trading centers, and gradually took over much of the freight hauling. Small town merchants protested that speed cops, lurking near their outskirts, discouraged shoppers. Between 1920 and 1930, almost three-fourths of the villages in wheat counties declined in population and business, although some survived by boosterism, and by amenities such as clean public restrooms. "The car and good roads made the way to the city too easy," lamented the *Oakesdale Tribune,* "and the former customers and patrons of the small town liked the sensation of buying where large selections of goods were available."[23]

The automobile also stretched the distances farmers traveled weekly. And at the end of the twenties, when the state speed limit had been raised to forty miles an hour on the best highways, country roads remained dusty and rutted. Many simply followed section lines regardless of terrain; and because few roads were open in winter, farmers rested their cars on blocks until spring. Cars still stuck in the mud, but every road cost more than before. An Odessa couple, in May among the season's first to cross Snoqualmie Pass from Seattle, reported that they had made the trip in ten hours despite deep mud at the top. For farmers, too, speed and endurance in their cars mattered.[24]

Rural citizens who embraced personal cars balked, even though they patronized, motor passenger and freight service, fearing that buses and trucks would pillage their trains—and that is what happened. Stage lines sprang up in eastern Washington around 1910, novelties like five-passenger White touring cars for hire in good weather between Ephrata and Soap Lake or thirty-passenger motor buses paralleling electric railroad tracks and schedules from Spokane to Millwood in the Spokane Valley. Motor freight routes ran mainly north and south because no reliable highway crossed the Cascades. Trucking grew, haphazard, in a gypsy way: "Any operator able to buy any sort of a second-hand auto on instalments . . . could enter the field and skim off the cream of business when the weather was fair," complained the director of public works. "When the unprofitable season arrived, the irresponsible competitor withdrew . . . and left the original operator with ultimate bankruptcy staring him in the face."[25]

In 1920, buses in the state collected an estimated $750,000 in fares. A caravan of seventy-five trucks toured eastern Washington towns, accompanied by the Fort George Wright army band, promoting "ship-by-truck week." A new business was taking root. The next year the legislature regulated it, requiring operators of regular lines to secure certificates of convenience and necessity and issuing approximately fifty, mostly to companies in western Washington.[26]

But antagonism toward commercial motor vehicles continued.

"The heavily loaded, solid-tire truck is . . . responsible for most of the damage done to highways," a highway engineer charged. Railroad companies routinely protested certificates for motor carriers, and for a time the state pondered whether to allow trucks on routes parallel-ing rail lines. Country editors chimed in. "Just why these [truck] lines should be granted certificates when they are tearing up roads, violat-ing speed laws, hogging the roads, and committing misdemeanors is an open question," stormed the *Colfax Gazette*. Opposition by Tekoa, Farmington, Garfield, Palouse, and Potlatch, all railroad towns, per-suaded one truck-line applicant to withdraw.[27]

Certificated routes in eastern Washington settled early into a pattern centering on larger towns: one truck network spread like wheel spokes from Yakima, another from Wenatchee, from Walla Walla, and from Spokane. Yet county commissioners might close their roads to heavy vehicles in winter, "for the purpose of eliminating stages," and assert that "these lines are taking the cream of passenger and freight business without paying a cent for construction of roads."[28]

Despite resistance, and although postmen and deliverymen in cities clung to horse-drawn wagons, motor-truck lines spread inexorably across the open countryside, and by the mid-twenties the railroads were going into the truck business, the Great Northern with its sub-sidiary Northland Transportation (sold within five years) and the Union Pacific with Union Pacific Stage Lines. Now, sighed the mayor of Colfax, "four stages of great size . . .[are] making a depot of Main street."[29] With nearly two hundred truck and stage companies in busi-ness, Spokane merchants arranged a union terminal in 1928. Some of the motor lines had grown large by then: The Washington Motor Coach Company connected Yakima, Ellensburg, Wenatchee, Coulee City, Oroville, Walla Walla, Pasco, and Spokane; the Columbia Gorge System linked southeastern Washington with Salt Lake City. Like the personal car, the motor bus and truck could not be denied; they were fast, convenient, and competitive. Yet fly-by-nights remained until 1935, when the legislature tightened regulation to put them out of business. By then the electric railroad through the Palouse was virtu-ally liquidated and steam railways had embarked on a policy of cut-ting routes and service.[30]

Before the automobile, the telephone had begun dispelling rural iso-lation like sunshine melting a morning fog. On the party line Saturday evenings a farmer near Oakesdale played records on his new phono-graph; switchboard operators everywhere gave weather forecasts; the hand-rung, shiny wooden cases with magnetic clapper and two black bells on top delighted youngsters who, recalled one, "took down our phones to gossip" when the operator went off duty at eight o'clock. (They called that "rubbering.") Each house answered its distinctive ring—two shorts and a long or three shorts or another combination—and because the phones were all hooked together, anyone on the line might eavesdrop for information and entertainment.[31]

Telephone systems grew in two ways: by the organization of mutual or stock companies in neighborhoods where farmers wanted to talk to each other or call into town, and by the progressive consolidation of systems to provide long-distance calling.

Walla Walla installed telephones in 1884, and the lines followed settlement northward. In the fall of 1886, Charles B. Hopkins (a founder of the *Colfax Gazette*) strung lines in the Palouse and bought Spokane exchange equipment. Yakima had phones by 1889; Davenport, 1890; Chelan, 1891; Tekoa, 1892; and exchanges continued to spread, hampered only a little by the panic of 1893. Between 1900 and 1910 telephone systems blossomed like spring flowers. In 1920, Washington's independent exchanges (those neither licensed by nor connected with National Bell) increased from 3.6 percent of the systems to 30 percent, and the number rose from 191 to 881, a flowering of user-owned telephone companies. For a time, Washington was second among states in the number of telephones per hundred citizens. The cities had phones first, of course, but by 1907, two-thirds of Washington's phone companies were mutual or independent and 15 percent of its phones were rural.[32]

Urban companies merged before rural ones, many joining Pacific Telephone and Telegraph. In 1921, of fifty-six telephone companies in eastern Washington, 70 percent served only one town and five still had the word "Farmers" in their names—the Farmers Telephone and Telegraph, Wenatchee, or the Bluecreek Farmers Telephone Association, Chewelah, as examples.[33] These small companies often contracted with Pacific for long-distance connections, and Pacific inserted a contract clause giving it first refusal to buy the exchange.

Telephone equipment was varied. A number of manufacturers sold it, and their salesmen stalked the countryside peddling complete systems. Medical Lake, for one, installed Baird "secret service" instruments allowing the operator ("central") to cut off everyone but the party called. The Kellogg Switchboard and Supply Company of Chicago advertised (in Yakima) that its "farm telephone is standard—it can be attached to any telephone exchange, whether Bell or independent." Kellogg delivered a switchboard, wire, and instruments with instructions for users to hook the system together.[34]

While mergers connected Spokane telephones with Portland and Salt Lake City, and those with San Francisco and San Diego, rural lines spread: Yakima's switchboard in a hotel lobby was spliced in 1900 into the Valley Telephone Company to reach Grandview, Sunnyside, and other nearby towns; fourteen Dunkard farmers (the Christian Cooperative Telephone Association) each paid $50 for life interests in a line between Mabton and Sunnyside. Pacific States Telephone had wired Wenatchee in 1900, but within three years, in protest of its rates, forty-five users formed the Farmers Telephone and Telegraph, bought the Wenatchee franchise from Arthur Gunn (who had not used it) and contracted with Pacific for long-distance service. Pacific's rates fomented rebellion elsewhere. Independents continued to pop up: James H. Porter, Loomis, alone tended 140 miles of wire and a switchboard; A. H. Brown and his sons formed the Kennewick Valley Telephone Company for Kennewick, Richland, and Benton City; at Davenport, John Hanson sold telephones to farmers, hooked them to barbed-wire fences, then to his switchboard, and thus saved most of the cost of lines; and so it went. These were typical, not singular, enterprises.[35]

In the nineties, callers rang the operator to signal the end of a conversation, hence the enduring expression, "ringing off." Counting 325 telephones in Colfax and 25 more on the line to Union Flat, Pacific States' manager in 1903 observed, "The telephone is coming more and more into use in the rural districts and the farmers find it of as much convenience as do merchants and business people in towns."[36]

The mechanical quality and management of farmers' lines was predictably variable, disruptions frequent, and downed or broken lines common. The *Chesaw News* remarked that "you could start a telephone message at Conconully and overtake it with an 18-year-old cayuse." Farmers soon wanted bigger and better systems, and they found selling their company easier than expanding it or fixing it. Pacific Telephone and Telegraph, which would emerge as the giant in western telephone service, succeeded Pacific States in 1906, and eventually formed regional operating companies, taking in many lines that farm stockholders wanted to sell. Pacific grew inland from coastal cities while Inter State Telephone, formed in Montana, extended westward into Washington under management of an industrious young salesman, Thaddeus S. Lane, who sold bonds to farmers and merchants to raise capital and used Inter State as a holding company to acquire ten systems in northern Idaho and eastern Washington, including the Home Telephone Company, Spokane, which offered dial service.[37]

For a while, some towns were divided between competing telephone systems, as was Spokane with Home and Inland, the latter organized by William S. Norman to operate, as telephone lines, two abandoned government telegraph wires, one through Davenport to Spokane and the other to the Coeur d'Alene mining district. Norman soon sold to Sunset, formed in 1883 as a Pacific subsidiary to operate long-distance lines.[38]

Thaddeus Lane symbolized one of three forces shaping telephone service; he represented the entrepreneur who hoped to profit from a local company. A second force, Pacific, sought comprehensive systems for economies of scale and connections between cities. And the third, user-owned companies, simply wanted the convenience of telephoning. With their slim finances and meager technical knowledge, many cooperative companies failed—Davenport, for instance, overwhelmed by a $500,000 bond issue to renovate and expand—and others survived by ingenuity. The Cowiche company's manager charged ten to fourteen-cent tolls on all calls because "no line can give adequate service if free gossiping is allowed."

Pacific Telephone and Telegraph, as early as 1911, allowed subscribers to charge telegrams to their telephone bills, designating Yakima, Spokane, and Walla Walla as all-night telegraph stations. By superior connections and by advertising, Pacific became dominant within a few years. In 1915 it acquired the Spokane system; by 1917 it owned most urban systems in the West. Using large-gauge copper wire and vacuum-tube repeaters, Pacific transmitted calls from the Pacific to the Atlantic coast—although conversations often had to be shouted—advertising "this triumph of science" in country newspapers in 1915.[39]

Many companies outside the Pacific system affiliated with the Interstate Utilities Company, successor to Inter State, which would become General Telephone. Interstate, formed of north Idaho exchanges after a court halted Pacific's acquisitions there as restraint of trade, expanded at first by leasing exchanges from Pacific. It also bought local systems: Tekoa in 1923, Pullman in 1925, Medical Lake, Reardan, and Davenport in 1926, Kettle Falls in 1928, Garfield and Farmers of Wenatchee in 1929, Waverly in 1930, and so on.[40] Nearly all these town systems were connected with farmer exchanges around them. Rockford, for one, had formed a telephone association of half a dozen farmer lines. Interstate connected its companies for intercity calling and exchanged calls with Pacific. But it fought territorial skirmishes well into the thirties, emerging with an inland territory that included most of rural eastern, northeastern, and northcentral Washington and northern Idaho.

Not long after telephones jangled across eastern Washington, the federal government experimented with country mail service on twelve rural free delivery routes, one originating in Yakima, and after its three-month trial, continued the service in response to rural petitioners. (Along one route, it was whispered, farmers addressed letters to their cows to make a showing of large patronage.) The Yakima run handled more than three thousand pieces of mail the first month. The service grew steadily: parcel post started in 1913; by 1915 Washington had 356 rural mail routes. Country postmasters had been slow to approve the system, thinking it would eliminate their jobs, and town merchants cried against mail-order competition, but the *Colfax Commoner,* no doubt speaking for most rural citizens, counted "four things essential to the farmer," rural free delivery, parcel post, good roads, and a telephone.[41]

Formerly a farmer rode to town occasionally to collect his mail. Now it came every day, brought by a friend, the rural carrier. The farmer offered the mailman gifts, invited him to dinner, and gave him messages for others along the route. Farmers became avid newspaper readers. The mail service encouraged numbering houses in towns and improving country roads. But most of all, it embraced the farmer in a world beyond his horizons.

With rural free delivery, parcel post, good roads, and a telephone, the farmer still lacked electricity, and it took him a long time to get it. Some along electric railroads or transmission lines hooked up quietly, without leave—the farther from the direct-current generating station, the dimmer the lights. Farmers on irrigation projects often used electric current from water pumps or waterwheels in ditches. Like the spread of telephones, cities were wired for electricity first, local plants served smaller towns, and large companies busily swallowed smaller ones. Unlike the telephone, however, electrical generation was complex and required a power plant, so that few neighbors were able to get together to build their own systems.

Two major electrical utilities shared eastern Washington (and parts of neighboring states): the Washington Water Power, based in Spokane, and Pacific Power and Light, Portland. Incorporated in 1889 to consolidate hydroelectric sites in Spokane, Washington Water Power was nearly wrecked in 1893, and rescued by a creditors' committee headed by the Brooklyn investment broker, William Augustus White, who ruled the company for three decades. White sent the diffident twenty-six-year-old son of family friends, David Lynde Huntington, to be his man in Spokane. Huntington was general manager until 1910, and president until his death in 1929.[42]

Pacific Power and Light, the 1910 fusion of seventeen existing electric, gas, and water utilities in Washington and Oregon by a holding company, American Power and Light, was run until 1933 by a reserved former railway executive, Guy W. Talbot. Pacific and Washington Water Power were fortuitously linked by Josiah Richards, a twenty-nine-year-old Spokane accountant named a Pacific director at its organization, who was the son of imperial J. P. M. Richards, founder of the Spokane and Eastern Trust and a director of Washington Water Power from its founding to his death in 1924. And by "gentleman's agreement," Washington Water Power pledged not to extend south of Colfax or Palouse, leaving that territory to a Pacific subsidiary.[43]

Huntington at first intended simply to light Spokane, but the citizens of Hillyard, a suburb, and then the owners of mines in northern Idaho, approached him for current. With the construction in 1903 of a long line into the Coeur d'Alene mines, Washington Water Power adopted a policy of long-distance transmission. Spokane had electric street lights by 1885—visitors gaped at its dozen twinkling arcs—and preferred residential districts were lighted by 1888, but the company lost money and made up deficits from a flour mill acquired in merging river rights. Walla Walla sparkled with electricity by 1889; Colfax 1890; Yakima 1891; Waitsburg 1896, with combined water and steam generation; and between 1900 and 1915 most towns in eastern Washington strung electric systems, using power from a local stream or buying current from one of the large utilities.

As Washington Water Power and Pacific divided eastern Washington, Pacific served the ten southeastern counties—the Yakima Valley, Pasco, Dayton, Pomeroy, Walla Walla, and Lewiston-Clarkston. Washington Water Power took the rest. Between 1910 and 1930, Washington Water Power would buy eighty-five distribution systems owned by twenty-eight companies; by 1930, it would serve 101 towns in eastern Washington. Its first rural transmission lines ran through the Palouse in 1905, and to the Big Bend in 1907. Yet these lines served towns—not farms even near the transmission lines. (On the other hand, Washington Water connected farms along its interurban railway from Spokane to Medical Lake and Cheney, and served Vera and Opportunity on the Spokane and Inland Empire.) No rural grid existed; none was contemplated.[44]

One reason utilities did not reach farms was that scattered farms would not repay the costs of construction; for a time, another reason was limited current. Both Pacific and Washington Water Power built and bought power sites and plants to supply their expanding systems,

Pacific through a subsidiary, Inland Power and Light. Pacific generated current on the Naches, Snake, Columbia (Black Rock site), Walla Walla, and Yakima rivers and from steam plants; Washington Water Power, with Coeur d'Alene Lake as a reservoir, used the Spokane at Monroe Street, Post Street, Upper Falls, Long Lake, and Nine Mile dams, and the Pend Oreille and Chelan rivers—thirteen generating sites and one steam plant, by 1930 a total of 206,384 kilowatts.[45]

The two utility companies occasionally swapped service area (the Lewiston-Clarkston sold to Washington Water Power in 1930, for example) and during 1917 connected their transmission systems at Lind for reciprocal sales of surplus current. (Later they also interconnected at Taunton and Pomeroy.) Pacific connected its Yakima-Pasco and Walla Walla–Pendleton systems in 1911, using some increased capacity to extend service to more Yakima Valley towns, and enlarging its service area there in 1917 and again in 1926.

Washington Water Power's lines to the Palouse and Big Bend carried current that was wholesaled to smaller utilities, allowing them to offer twenty-four-hour service. The company's first purchases were the Colfax and Big Bend water power companies in 1910.

For the first years, electricity went mainly for commercial use, motors, store-window lights, and nighttime home illumination. But as early as 1902 one utility, the Yakima Water, Light and Power, offered daytime service, with a warning, "As the same circuit will be used for power as is now used for the lights, the success of the day service will depend largely on those using electric lights in their homes, in seeing that they are turned off promptly in the morning, and not permitted to burn throughout the day."[46] At Waitsburg, the generating plant night operator burned a carbon-filament lamp over his cot; when the filament glowed brighter, he knew that lights were going off in homes for the night and reduced the water flow; when his lamp dimmed in the morning, he opened the penstock. Quite a few plants ran in such uncomplicated ways. Where they could, plant operators simply looked out a window to see lights coming on or going off in town.

At Wilson Creek, the owner of the local gas-powered plant furnished current from sunset to midnight and half a day Tuesdays for ironing. At Ephrata, where the generator ran on diesel oil, the utility rented an electric vacuum cleaner to housewives for twenty-five cents a day. Soap Lake used three or four kerosene street lights before acquiring a gasoline electric generator in 1920. Quincy was lighted from a generator run by a Model T Ford engine. Townspeople were delighted, therefore, to have Washington Water Power's twenty-four-hour current.[47]

Utility companies did not advertise appliances strongly until after 1910, when they enlarged their generating capacity, and then sales lagged because few homes had electric outlets. Wiring usually consisted of a single drop-cord from the ceiling in each room. Spokane's newspapers promoted appliances, however, offering table lamps for new subscriptions. The first Washington Water Power ads, for "daylight" kitchens, promoted 100-watt frosted globes to replace the customary clear glass ones. In a residential district without electrical service, salesmen paid on commission occasionally persuaded residents to petition for street lights and thus extend power lines to their neighborhood. For several years, Washington Water Power allowed homeowners to use a refrigerator free through the winter, finding that the user generally purchased it at the end of a trial period. By such simple means, the company doubled the use of electricity in Spokane homes between 1914 and 1918.[48]

Pacific Power and Light demonstrated electric cooking from railroad cars, and there is a legend in the company that an energetic Pacific sales manager at Pomeroy revived a flagging Thor washing machine company with his order for a carload.[49] A Washington State College demonstration train toured the state to promote electrical use on farms. Speakers at women's meetings declared that "women are not going to milk cows and make butter without modern conveniences with power." But, in fact, not many farms had electricity.[50] Some farmers installed gas-powered generators; in Whitman County, for example, 103 gas generators were in use immediately after the war, about one hundred farm homes were connected with the Washington Water Power, and twenty-five owned an electric range or water heater.[51]

Because a number of families moved away from Spokane during the war for industrial jobs, the Washington Water Power launched a heavy advertising program after the war to use the current it was generating. The campaign sold 469 new ranges in seven weeks, and by 1925, 4,075 homes in Spokane and 2,788 in adjacent rural areas used electric ranges. In Spokane, that was roughly one in nine homes.[52]

Even farm homes near towns could not simply hook up. Municipalities were not authorized to sell surplus current outside their limits, and to avoid raising rates to pay the cost of rural extensions, towns supported ratio-to-cost revenue regulations that, observed a Washington Water Power sales manager dryly, "did not permit wide distribution to sparsely settled areas." Farmers who contracted for electrical current were required (by a company policy approved by the state) to guarantee a stipulated return to the company either by cash payments or by buying enough appliances to run up their bills. A four-mile power line to forty-two rural homes near Spokane was built only after "about twenty customers ordered electric ranges, pumping equipment, etc., while others . . . paid a portion of the line cost." Such guarantees of revenue for the utility relaxed only slightly in 1931, when the State Public Service Commission permitted one utility to lower its requirement for cash advances because farm customers supplied the poles and labor.[53]

Under such conditions, electric service reached farms at a maddeningly slow pace. The Washington Grange, impatient with rural service and rates, had begun as early as 1916 to advocate public ownership of utilities, envisaging small cooperative companies of farmers. The private power companies, needless to say, worked vigorously against public ownership. In the 1921 legislative session they defeated a bill authorizing Seattle, Tacoma, and other city systems to sell current outside their corporate limits, and in 1924 persuaded voters against an initiative for public utility districts. When Washington Water Power extended service to Ephrata and Moses Lake in 1922, it was accused of timing its press releases to blunt the public power campaign (and discourage talk of a dam at Grand Coulee). Allegations aside, rural people wanted current: Grant County residents guaranteed annual sales of 1,200 horsepower to get a Washington Water Power line, because they believed the company's rates would cut their pumping costs in half.[54]

Washington's six private utilities spent $175,000 to defeat the 1924 public power initiative. During the campaign, Washington Water Power asked its municipal customers to sign fifty-year franchises, but their victory proved hollow. Surveying prospective rural customers in Yakima and Benton counties, Pacific concluded that "less than half the people . . . think in terms of electrical energy." (They wanted indoor bathrooms first.) Washington Water Power's primary lines, accounting for 60 percent of construction costs, ran $735 to $818 a mile to build. At those prices, a private or public utility could not afford to serve isolated rural homes.[55]

Farm families wanted electricity at costs comparable to those of city customers. Clarence Dill, running for office, told them on the radio that was their due. For Pacific, especially, rates had been a constant problem. Washington public service accountants charged that Pacific relied on its Washington income for profit in its entire system. Ordered in 1915 to reduce rates for Walla Walla and Yakima, Pacific justified higher rates to rural users in the Yakima area on the basis of line costs.

Ten years later, frustrated Walla Walla customers, joined by others, forced a reduction in Pacific's rates in a suit that went to the state supreme court.[56] Both Pacific and Washington Water Power occasionally lowered rates voluntarily.

While power lines inched slowly across the Pacific Northwest, farmers nationwide demanded electrical service, not only for their homes but for pumping, poultry houses, spraying, and similar uses. The social pressures for electricity changed during the twenties, too, as appliance makers and dealers replaced utility companies as the leading advertisers of home uses. The American Farm Bureau Federation organized a national study in which twenty-two states, including Washington, took part through state committees that investigated farm use and promoted rural service. After its organizing meeting at Spokane's Davenport Hotel, the Washington committee in 1925 (chaired by E. O. Holland, president of the state college, and including Huntington) surveyed fifteen systems. It reported that Washington Water Power served 2,491 rural customers, Pacific 4,795, and that about 10 percent of Washington's homes were electrified—the largest proportion in western Washington fruit-growing districts. Eleven of eighteen farm homes surveyed near Pullman used electricity (and had fifty-three appliances among them); twenty-five of thirty-two near Colfax; eight of eleven near Wilbur; nine of twenty near Neppel (Moses Lake); and eighteen of twenty near Cashmere. Electric appliances sold briskly to farmers, prompting the *Yakima Morning Herald* to say that Washington was well above the national average of 7 percent of farm homes with electricity and 10 percent with running water, "but still extremely low for a region that boasts of such extensive hydro power sites."[57]

On the basis of the statewide study, utility companies could claim that they had not wholly neglected rural users, and in 1928 (when it sold more than $1 million worth of appliances) Pacific appointed an agricultural agent to promote rural use "where adaptable." Thus the electrical age dawned on farms, and so did another: in 1930, Pacific erected a nine-mile distribution line for airway beacons and runway lights.[58] Isolated farm homes would not receive current, however, until the Rural Electrification Administration brought it with federal subsidies—some not until after World War II. In 1928 American Power and Light bought Washington Water Power—a year after the death of William Augustus White, shaper of the company's acquisitive policy. And when Huntington died in 1929, on the eve of the Depression, the company was handed to Frank T. Post, long its chief counsel, as a caretaker president. The company virtually stopped expanding as the erosion of private by public utilities began. A melancholy little man, sardonic, combative Homer T. Bone, a Tacoma attorney, gave public power a razor voice, and in 1930 Washington voters passed an initiative for public power districts which, in time, would strip Washington Water Power of its systems in Okanogan, Douglas, Grant, Pend Oreille, and Chelan counties.[59]

If electricity had been slow to reach farms, plumbing for water and waste disposal was even slower. Rural sanitation offered a staple topic for health association meetings for years, but as the state health report said in 1914, "the health board is doing nothing to help the farmer." And the farmer's precious automobile posed a health hazard as camping became popular—auto tourists, "nomadic, camping on the roadside, drinking contaminated milk and water, polluting both the ground and the water, carrying contagious diseases from town to town."[60]

For all its mechanical advances, the countryside, and many towns, remained woefully primitive in sanitation. Disease and contamination were not well understood. Swarms of flies from privies and manure piles landed on uncovered foods. Flies seemed everywhere, thick and noisy. (In one way the automobile helped: as cars and tractors replaced animals, manure piles disappeared.) A federal study of typhoid among soldiers in the Spanish-American War awakened the nation's health officers to the hazards of flies, and Washington State distributed pamphlets warning of fly-borne diseases as early as 1904. Towns held monthly fly-swatting campaigns—a winner in Cheney produced 277 squashed insects—yet the flies persisted in plagues, and few houses had screens.[61]

As Washington's population grew, its health problems naturally increased. Systems for handling water supplies and disposing of waste were inadequate. This was a national problem, but the federal government took no general responsibility for pollution control. (In 1913 the government would, however, regulate sanitary practices on trains crossing state boundaries.) Even after Washington organized a health department, statistics were so casual and reporting so erratic that no systematic prevention was practical. In the absence of terrifying epidemics, not many people cared. Town voters monotonously turned down bond issues or levies for sanitary improvements, and when they passed one, the municipality's taxing power was likely to be challenged.[62] Many people resisted toilets with an unfounded fear that "sewer gas" from pipes carried diseases. As one state sanitarian wryly observed, "The fact that a serious outbreak of . . . diseases has not decimated the population of this state is probably due to the proverbial good luck of the westerner."[63]

The state constitution provided for a board of health and a bureau of vital statistics, but no effective health work started until 1903, when the legislature appropriated $5,000 for a sanitary program and authorized the appointment of county health officers, a gesture to rural sections. (Although the legislature had enacted various health bills, it had also consistently cut appropriations for them until 1903.) Of an 1899 act for a "pure water supply," a health officer remarked that "none of the cities have . . . facilities nor . . . technical knowledge for determining whether provisions of the law are being violated." The federal Public Health Service Act, authorizing investigations of diseases related to water pollution, would not pass until 1912.[64]

Well into the thirties, the state's health program focused on the most populous areas—cities—except for attempts to improve sanitation in public schools with vaccinations, educational programs, and wolverine toilets (a chemical toilet), but the customary water bucket with two cups stayed. The Health Board (a department after 1921) regarded typhoid fever as its most compelling challenge—607 died from it between 1913 and 1917—and strove to regulate dumping of raw sewage into the rivers that also supplied domestic water. "The prevelance of typhoid fever may be considered an index of sanitary conditions of any locality," declared the board, and by that standard, rural Washington was unsanitary indeed. With few exceptions, eastern Washington towns drew their water from flowing streams. Yakima drew from the Yakima River, Wenatchee from the Columbia, Walla Walla from irrigation canals, and Spokane from the Spokane—all waterways also used as the most convenient means of discharging sewers.[65]

The popular notion held that flowing water purified itself every seven miles. Tests on the Snake and Spokane rivers in 1913 led health officers to conclude that the rivers "show a practically complete degree of self-purification by natural processes" in approximately seventy miles. Farms and small towns used wells for water and outhouses for disposal, and because cities could hardly keep up with growing populations, many urban residents also took water from wells that might be contaminated by privies or cesspools. As a consequence, typhoid broke out every year; the disease was endemic in towns of the Yakima and Columbia valleys where farmers took domestic water from irrigation ditches contaminated by animals and privies, washed milk cans and foods in canals, and dumped waste into them. Nearly everyone believed that impure water tasted and smelled bad.[66]

Yet conditions improved slowly. Spokane, for one, had begun a municipal water distribution system in 1884, taking water upstream from sewerage discharge. Four years later the city council required that water closets on sewer lines be hooked up, affecting only a small business district along Main, Riverside, and Sprague. It adopted a Waring disposal system, which ostensibly purified wastewater by running it over a series of gravel benches. Neither water nor sewerage disposal reached outlying residences; homes north of the river did not have city water until 1908 or sewer lines until 1915. Many of the city's finest homes used cesspools; the others, outhouses. In nearly every city, residents balked at taxes for water and disposal systems. At the suggestion of a Chicago lender, Spokane in 1895 issued special warrants payable from revenue to finance its water system, apparently the first time a city had tried such a financial device. Perhaps that was a way to restore public credit after the panic of 1893. At any rate, it stimulated the idea of special improvement districts in which the residents who benefited paid for the improvement, and it also stimulated a long series of court tests of municipal taxing powers and debt limitations.[67] Partly as a revenue measure, and partly for health, Spokane closed private wells in 1904 wherever city water was available. Not until 1908 did the city change its municipal water source to wells, because Coeur d'Alene started dumping sewerage into the Spokane River. The wells changed Spokane from soft to hard water.[68]

Perhaps a dozen eastern Washington towns bought chlorination systems to purify water before World War I, among them Clarkston, Dayton, Ellensburg, Kennewick, Newport, Pasco, Prosser, Republic, Walla Walla, Wenatchee, Yakima, and Spokane. This was a step forward, but no security for families using well water—and certainly beyond the reach of rural residents. By 1930, sewerage and water were still problems. In 1942 a national review called "the pollution of waters in a number of areas of the Pacific Northwest . . . a growing menace," from sewage, industrial wastes, and mining wastes. "Quite generally, the cities and industrial plants . . . discharge raw sewage into streams," the report continued, naming Yakima, Spokane, Wenatchee, and Walla Walla among cities where sewage treatment plants were "badly needed." Spokane would not construct a disposal plant until after World War II, and then only under duress from the state.[69]

If pure water and human waste disposal stood as continual and expensive problems, garbage disposal also posed difficulties. Rural residents could dump garbage in hollows and feed table scraps to hogs. On the other hand, cities often allowed garbage to pile up until streets and alleys were impassable, then hauled it a few yards from town and dumped it. Spokane burned its garbage beginning in 1907, but Walla Walla, more typically, relied on a private contractor, who resigned when his hogs died in 1922. Seattle's method of spreading garbage in layers covered by dirt—"sanitary fills"—gradually took hold in other cities after 1914.[70]

As they learned more about diseases, state and local health officers reduced the number and severity of epidemics. For years, quarantining was the accepted way to prevent the spread of an infection: ominous yellow or red placards were tacked to infected houses, whose occupants were forbidden to leave. After septic sore throats, typhoid, and diphtheria had been linked with contaminated milk, cities enacted milk ordinances with standards for cleanliness and inspected dairies. Some truly imaginative measures were tried: Spokane, for example, sterilized its library books. But by 1920 only Spokane and Yakima counties in eastern Washington were employing full-time health officers, and generally nothing short of a severe epidemic would arouse public concern, such as the dramatic outbreak of venereal disease among soldiers in Northwest training camps which persuaded the legislature belatedly in 1919 to authorize public controls. Among its efforts, the state circulated a public health service film, *How Life Begins,* to public schools to "break the conspiracy of silence" about human reproduction.[71] But prostitution continued to be tolerated by most towns as a necessary evil that went with itinerant harvest hands, loggers, and railroad gangs.

In this regard, isolation helped the farmer. He alleviated his loneliness with auto, telephone, mail, and radio, and while distance was no guarantee that he would escape sickness, it was at least a barrier against contamination.

CHAPTER 9

"Marvellous Treasure": The Mines

*I*n a paneled federal courtroom in Portland, Oregon, Edgar L. New-house's affidavit set out the real conditions of Inland Empire lead-silver mining. Before formation of his company, American Smelting and Refining, no smelter in the United States could handle all the ore from Idaho's Coeur d'Alene mining district, and after its formation, American became the only practical market for ore. From a dominant position astride the lead-silver industry, American ("the smelter trust") felt justified in requiring long-term ore sales contracts, setting prices and mine production quotas, and regulating the lead available for sale—all to stabilize a chancy industry.[1]

Among the trust's officers, Newhouse, the senior vice-president, was perhaps the most credible to mining men. But his view from the top of the industry collided with theirs from the bottom: most mine own-ers and managers considered American Smelting and Refining oppres-sive and greedy. Those conflicting attitudes drew the trust to this courtroom in Oregon in 1917 to assert again its control of the indus-try in a suit to prevent the Bunker Hill and Sullivan Mining and Con-centrating Company, prince of the Coeur d'Alenes, from smelting its ores not contracted to American.

The lawsuit, dismissed when the trust and Bunker Hill agreed out of court, brought to a climax six momentous years in the Coeur d'Alenes, the fattest of the mining districts surrounding Spokane. Those six years began in 1912 when the Hercules Mining Company pressed its temporary advantage, the trust's need for Hercules ore to mix with dry ores in smelting, to get an unusually lucrative return from smelting. As the Hercules contract neared renewal in May 1915, rumors circulated, soon confirmed, that American intended to raise smelter rates for everyone and drive out competing ore buyers. Bunker Hill, demanding terms as favorable as those of the Hercules, charged that the trust "warned the independent smelting companies that if they entered into any contracts," the trust "would make it impossible for said other companies to thereafter do business in the Coeur d'Alene mining district."[2]

A mining company dealt with the trust or took the risky course of building its own smelter. Two major companies of the Coeur d'Alenes dared the risk: the Bunker Hill by erecting a smelter in 1917 at Kellogg next to its principal mine; the Hercules by renovating an abandoned copper plant at Northport, Washington, on the Columbia River and buying the independent Pennsylvania Smelting and Refining Company at Carnegie, Pennsylvania, as a refinery and sales agent.[3]

A mining district newspaper called construction of the Bunker Hill smelter "the most important event in the history of mining in the Coeur d'Alene district," because the plant treated low-grade ores from mines that would not bear the cost of long shipments. Shipping and smelting were essential for lode mining, for unless ores were shipped to a buyer who smelted them into salable metal, no income could be realized from lead, silver, zinc, or copper. Gold was different. A miner could spend or bank gold dust and be rich with ounces; lead, used mainly for paints and sheeting, had to be smelted into pigs weighed by the ton.

Gold had been the trigger that set off the Coeur d'Alene mines, as gold propelled mining rushes elsewhere in the West. Hearing whoops of "gold," waves of prospectors lapped over the forested mountains of northern Idaho, deep with snow in the last months of 1883, bound for streams flowing into the north fork of the Coeur d'Alene River. "Six or seven men took out $600 in one day . . . working this claim in the bed of the creek. It is not over two feet deep," one wrote his hometown newspaper. And reading of $600 a day, more prospectors dashed to Idaho. "The ground was all taken up in 20-acre lots: creeks, gulches and everything," wrote another.[4]

The placer claims lay on bedrock—shallow, unpromising. Amid rumored riches, money flowed. Claims changed hands at an average of $1,600 a claim. And as prospectors emptied their pokes, merchants and suppliers raked in quick profits. Flour sold for fourteen dollars a sack, bacon for forty cents a pound. Tent hotels in shack camps charged a dollar to sleep on the ground. Contract carriers demanded fifty cents to deliver one letter. Many gold seekers rode the Northern Pacific to Idaho, pausing in Spokane to buy tools and beans at fancy prices. Miner's whisky, remarked a newspaperman at the mines, made a man "lie worse than a Spokane outfitter." Thus Spokane early acquired its reputation in the mining country for gouging and sharp dealing.[5]

In the long run, there were too many men and too little gold. As prospectors realized that north-fork gold would not enrich them, some fanned over the hills to the Coeur d'Alene River's south fork. There on Canyon Creek in May 1884 two staked a lead-silver claim, the Tiger, and soon sold the ground to Stephen S. Glidden, a Montana grocer. In September 1885, downstream at Milo Gulch, Noah S. Kellogg, a prospector using a borrowed mule, claimed lead-silver outcroppings and called this the Bunker Hill. Kellogg's find set off a new rush. Eventually the courts ordered him to share his discovery with partners, the mule's owners and saloonkeepers Dutch Jake Goetz and Harry Baer, who had grubstaked him.

Milo Gulch and Canyon Creek would be the twin centers of lode mining in northern Idaho. The Bunker Hill's diverse owners leased their claim to a self-promoting salesman, James F. Wardner, who forced their hand by cannily filing on their water supply. Wardner also leased the adjacent Sullivan, working it and the Bunker Hill from trenches and mixing their ores for the best mineral showing. Glidden's crew meanwhile piled ore near the Tiger portal and packed sacks of it over the mountains for assays. Separately, Glidden and Wardner talked up their claims to men allied with Samuel T. Hauser, governor (1885–87) of Montana Territory, investor in Montana banks, railroads, mines, and a smelter at Wickes, and intimate of Northern Pacific directors—in their judgment, the capitalist most likely to build them a railroad or perhaps buy their claims, for Wardner and Glidden were more interested in money than mining.

Not long after, consequently, "a gentleman on a good-looking mule," as Jim Wardner described him, rode into camp, introduced himself as Daniel C. Corbin, and asked to be shown around. Short, lean, beak-nosed, Corbin carried impressive credentials: he was a Hauser man, surveyor, freighter, banker, mine and smelter investor, and brother of the noted New York banker and railroad man, Austin Corbin. Corbin inspected Milo Gulch and Canyon Creek, now blanketed with mining claims, collected a sack of ore samples, listened politely—uncharacteristically, for Corbin was not much of a listener—and trotted off to start a railroad. "It all impressed me forcibly," he said later, "and I concluded a connection with the Northern Pacific . . . would pay."[6]

With sanction of the Northern Pacific, Corbin and Hauser's satraps laid a hastily built narrow-gauge track, the Coeur d'Alene Railway and Navigation Company, from the mines to Old Mission on the Coeur d'Alene River, where trains met Coeur d'Alene lake steamers that connected with another Corbin road, the Spokane Falls and Idaho, running from the lakefront to the Northern Pacific main line. The Bunker Hill built a spur to the Corbin line, and Glidden built a steep narrow-gauge railroad down Canyon Creek to the Corbin terminus at Wallace. By transfers, sacked ore moved over rail and water to the Wickes and other smelters, starting late in 1886. "The entering wedge which opened the marvellous treasure of the Coeur d'Alenes to the world," Idaho's governor called Corbin's road. In its first full year of operation, the Coeur d'Alene Railway and Navigation Company carried roughly $3.5 million worth of ore and concentrates. And by a chance of law, Corbin connected Spokane to the mines, for Northern Pacific attorneys warned him that under Idaho laws a Montana company probably could not build legally from Montana westward into Idaho as Corbin intended. Therefore, he formed his railways as Washington corporations, built eastward from Hauser Junction near Spokane, and fixed Spokane uncontestably as principal supplier of the mining country.

Transportation and proven mines altered the Coeur d'Alenes rapidly. Wardner soon rustled a buyer for the Bunker Hill and the Sullivan, the Portland magnate Simeon G. Reed, who resold to Darius O. Mills and William H. Crocker, San Francisco bankers, and John Hays Hammond, a renowned engineer. John A. Finch, a onetime steel executive, and Amasa B. Campbell, miner, foraged as partners staking and buying claims for one speculators' syndicate in Youngstown, Ohio and another in Milwaukee. Patrick Clark, once Marcus Daly's mine foreman in Butte, claimed the Poorman across Canyon Creek from Glidden's Tiger and sold stock to cronies. By 1890 two dozen mines produced ore. Glidden sold and moved to Spokane to found the Old National Bank; his son-in-law and mine manager, Frank R. Culbertson, would stay in the mines until 1904, when he, too, moved to Spokane to open a variety store.

To take the growing mining business for itself, the Northern Pacific leased Corbin's railroad for 999 years, issued bonds to pay his debts, spent half a million widening the narrow to standard gauge, and soon extended the line to Montana to eliminate lake transfers of ore. The bonds amounted to twice the value of the railroad, which drove the Coeur d'Alene Railway and Navigation into insolvency, and someone at the Northern Pacific and Corbin diverted to themselves $465,000

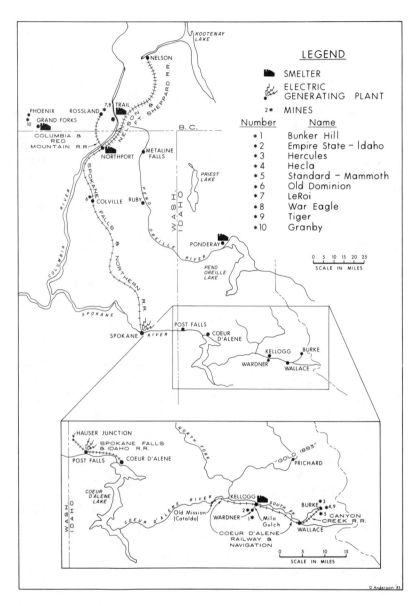

The principal mines and smelters tributary to Spokane up to 1930 and the pioneer feeder railroads connecting the city with them. Electric generating plants of the Washington Water Power on the Spokane River provided steady power for the Coeur d'Alene district. (Map by David Anderson, Eastern Washington University cartographic laboratory.)

worth, more than half the issue. The Union Pacific reached Milo Gulch through its subsidiary Washington and Idaho. Within a decade of Noah Kellogg's claiming of the Bunker Hill, most major Coeur d'Alene mines belonged not to their discoverers but to stockholders scattered across America.[7]

With business development, family homes and robust civility crept into the district. Three main towns sprang up: Wardner (soon to be overshadowed by Kellogg), near the Bunker Hill; Burke, on Canyon Creek; and Wallace, at the crossroads between them. On their fringes, Finns, Irish, Swedes, and other national groups huddled in enclaves. Wardner merchants rather regarded Burke as a nest of rowdies, the wellspring of workmen's discontent. Wallace saw itself as the district's financial, social, and intellectual center, particularly after it captured the Shoshone County seat. Managers and laborers drew apart, losing their easy comradeship of earlier days. Yet this remained a masculine, roisterous camp pandering to men who toiled in continual peril underground. These were seasonal mines, many with primitive equipment, many sifting low-grade ores, often financed by speculators buying penny stocks, and some managed by men who had never before had a mine and were wary, protective, and fearful of losing this one chance to be rich.

Fantasies of wealth drove men across other parts of the Inland Empire, and some found minerals (lead and silver in 1885 in mountains near Colville, silver in 1887 on the Salmon River in the Okanogans south of the international border, in 1896 lead and zinc in the Metaline district of northeastern Washington, and, shortly after that, gold in the rocky crags of the Buffalo Hump country east of Grangeville, Idaho). Such discoveries set off new cries for roads and machines. The newspapers throbbed with mineral strikes, proposed railroads (most never built), and the possibility of a Spokane smelter.

Within weeks after sale of his Coeur d'Alene Railway and Navigation Company, D. C. Corbin took command of a projected railway north from Spokane through Colville to the Columbia River, the Spokane Falls and Northern, and just about the time he started to build it, a mining rush swept across the mountainous country of British Columbia west of Kootenay Lake. By the time Corbin's railroad reached the Columbia, another rush galloped to Red Mountain, west of the Columbia. By splitting his line at Northport, Corbin reached both camps. He built the Nelson and Fort Sheppard to Nelson on the west arm of Kootenay Lake and the Columbia and Red Mountain into Rossland, igniting genuine fears among Canadians that the United

States might annex southern British Columbia, and establishing Spokane as chief supplier for both districts.

Rossland's best mines sold to Spokane men and, as the panic of 1893 faded, spewed ore. The LeRoi, purchased for $30,000 by Spokane attorneys George M. Forster and William Ridpath, who formed a company with George Turner, Valentine Peyton, and others, disgorged $84,000 worth of ore a day while its stock rocketed from 25 cents to $7.50 a share. Finch and Campbell, with Isaac N. Peyton, Patrick Clark, Corbin's son, Austin II, and his chief engineer, Edward J. Roberts, opened the War Eagle. Like Charles Sweeny, erstwhile Spokane storekeeper whose strategy in the Coeur d'Alenes had been to encircle desirable claims and who now ballyhooed Rossland, they all touted cheap stocks to prospective buyers in the eastern United States, Canada, and London.

Cut off from the rest of Canada by mountains, Rossland was an American camp—owned by Americans, mined by Americans, linked to Spokane by railroad, its ores treated at the Trail smelter built by F. Augustus Heinze on the heights above the Columbia. Heinze was a New York engineer who had dazzled Butte by digging a profit from the "exhausted" Rarus mine. Encouraged—perhaps coerced—by D. C. Corbin, the LeRoi erected its own smelter at Northport beside the Spokane Falls and Northern. Between them, the Trail and Northport smelters polluted the Columbia and shriveled riverside orchards.

British and Canadian financiers determined to drive Americans out of Rossland. To that end, the Canadian Pacific bought out Heinze, a Toronto syndicate took the War Eagle, and a British speculator, Whitaker Wright, the LeRoi. With their shares of $5 million in cash from Wright, Turner built Spokane's Columbia Building, Ridpath, the Ridpath Hotel, Peyton, the Peyton (on the burned skeleton of the Great Eastern), and two other men bought the Hyde Block, one of the city's major downtown structures.

Rossland had paid off at a time when a number of Spokane men desperately needed money to avoid losing mortgaged homes, businesses, or investments. Such prominent men as F. Rockwood Moore, president of the Washington Water Power, whose fine new native stone home on Seventh Avenue was mortgaged, and the old-timers A. M. Cannon and James N. Glover, went under during the panic. No one knows how many were saved by selling Rossland mines. The Spokane periodical *Northwest Mining Truth* declared that with sale of the LeRoi, "a blanket mortgage upon almost all the downtown city was lifted." Though not true, the comment fit the spirit of the times. George Turner bought Moore's home. Austin and D. C. Corbin built mansions on snobbish Seventh Avenue in 1898, and A. B. Campbell and Patrick Clark, castles in Browne's Addition, designed by the fashionable architect, Kirtland K. Cutter. Campbell's house had a basement game room where he played poker noisily with comrades, to his refined wife's chagrin.[8]

Large, low-grade copper deposits, discovered in 1895 in the Boundary district (on the United States side of the border southwest of Rossland), belonged largely to the Granby Mining, Smelting and Power Company, formed with Canadian capital by Jay P. Graves and Aubrey L. White of Spokane. A reedy, fastidious, soft-spoken man, Graves had seen his real estate business falter four years earlier. But when a mining engineer, A. B. W. Hodges, concluded that an experimental process probably would smelt Boundary copper, Graves plunged. Financed with ten-cent stock and White's persuasion, Granby started digging in 1896 and opened a 4,000-ton smelter at Grand Forks, British Columbia, two years later. Granby also renovated Phoenix, a forgotten mining town overgrown with brush. The Canadian Pacific and the Great Northern built spurs to reach the Granby and other companies at Boundary. As his mining company flourished, Graves was building his electric railroad from Spokane and, on land bought from a man involved in a shooting, fashioning a magnificent country estate, Waikiki, north of Spokane. One of three brothers who had moved from Illinois to Spokane, Graves would be a wealthy man of consequence in the city for twenty-five years.[9]

By 1900, however, many of the mining districts of the Inland Empire had been snuffed out: the Colville, which sustained only one important metal mine, the Old Dominion, and a maladroit smelter; the Salmon River; and the Buffalo Hump, audaciously promoted by Charles Sweeny. The low-grade lead-zinc mineral belt of the Metaline, which extended northward into Canada, lacked transportation, an inconvenience Patsy Clark glossed over in 1899 when he sold Montreal men his Republic Mine there for $3 million.

The Coeur d'Alenes needed reliable electric current for year-round production rather than generators on seasonal streams; the mines profited but ran at half-capacity from 1890 through 1899, hobbled by depression, strangled with litigation over rights to ore bodies, and obstructed by work stoppages and violent protests of their labor force over wages, working conditions, company stores, and union recognition. For labor troubles, the unions and some mine managers blamed the Bunker Hill and Sullivan, which not only refused to bargain with

A Washington Water Power Company demonstration truck showing the household uses of electricity, about 1915. Miss Cowgill demonstrated the then-novel electric range and oven in many towns of eastern Washington. (Eastern Washington University)

Small boys posed on the donkey that "discovered" the Bunker Hill claim in the Coeur d'Alene mining district. The youngest of three Day brothers, Jerome, sat backward on the donkey in a Wardner street in 1887.

A well-known mining engineer snapped this picture during one of the "peaceful" years between periods of martial law to suppress Coeur d'Alene labor unions in 1892 and 1899. The printing reads: "Two Western Federation of Miners that was out to get a deput[y] sheriff at Gem. Photo taken by Fredrick Burbidge, 1893."

Never to be seen again, a river of logs—the Potlatch company's log drive on the north fork of the Clearwater about fifteen miles upstream from Asahka, Idaho. Logs decked along riverbanks in winter were driven downstream to mills in the spring. (Photo: Paul Seiffert, Orofino. University of Idaho Library, Special Collections, A. B. Curtis Collection 13-6).

A steam donkey stacking logs near a logging railroad in the St. Joe district of northern Idaho, undated. Loggers often worked out of sight of the donkey, using whistles to signal the cable operator. (Washington State University: Manuscripts, Archives, and Special Collections 70-097)

"The biggest mill I ever heard of," in the phrase of William Deary, its first manager—the Potlatch Lumber Company mill, looking from the southwest, at Potlatch, Idaho, 1907. Note company houses on the hill, right background. (Washington State University: Manuscripts, Archives, and Special Collections 70-448)

Bunkhouse interior at a Potlatch Lumber Company logging camp, 1907. Workers supplied their own bedding and slept on straw mattresses on wooden bunks. Such quarters, and a lack of washing and bathing facilities, contributed to the loggers' dissatisfaction during the Wobbly union period. (Washington State University: Manuscripts, Archives, and Special Collections 80-023)

The Potlatch company store interior, 1907, showing the shoe, crockery, and grocery departments. The "Merc," as it was affectionately known, drew shoppers from miles around as well as families of lumber company employees. (Washington State University: Manuscripts, Archives, and Special Collections 70-497)

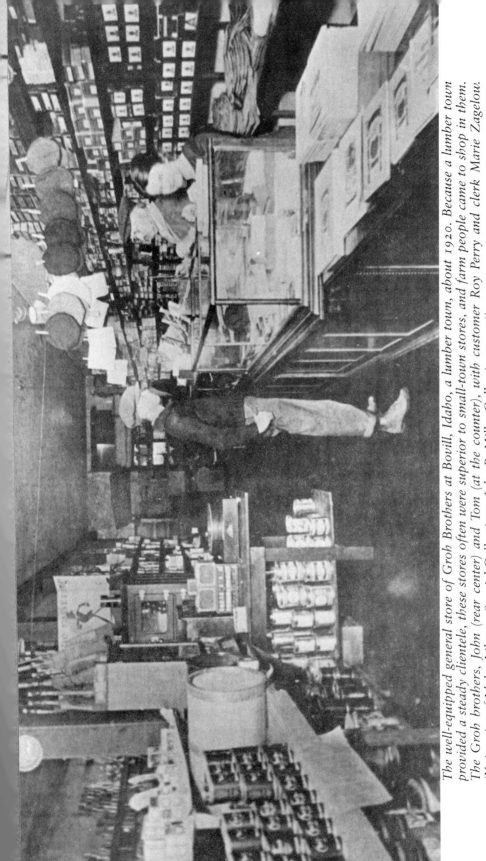

The well-equipped general store of Groh Brothers at Bovill, Idaho, a lumber town, about 1920. Because a lumber town provided a steady clientele, these stores often were superior to small-town stores, and farm people came to shop in them. The Groh brothers, John (rear center) and Tom (at the counter), with customer Roy Perry and clerk Marie Zagelow. (University of Idaho Library, Special Collections, John B. Miller Collection 12-96)

More famous than Spokane, the Davenport Hotel was opened in 1914 by Louis Davenport, who started as a restaurant proprietor. His noted restaurant, foreground, was renamed the Italian Gardens in 1922, and another wing was added to the hotel. (WWP)

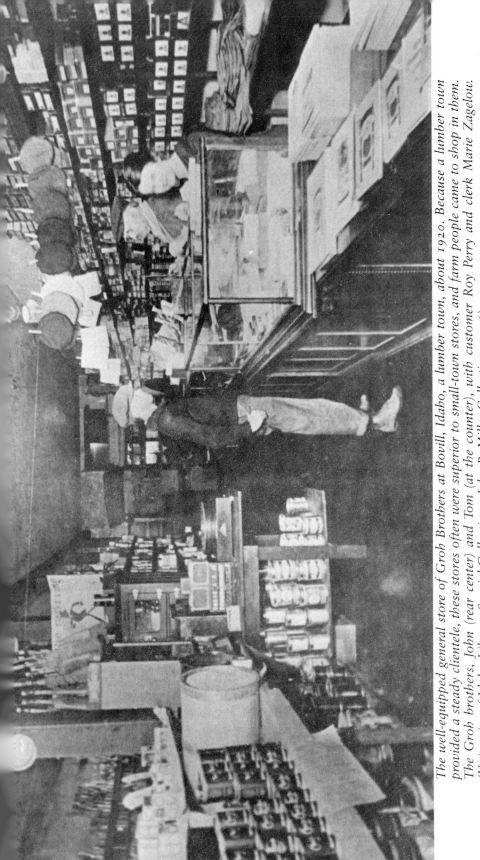

The well-equipped general store of Grob Brothers at Bovill, Idaho, a lumber town, about 1920. Because a lumber town provided a steady clientele, these stores often were superior to small-town stores, and farm people came to shop in them. The Grob brothers, John (rear center) and Tom (at the counter), with customer Roy Perry and clerk Marie Zagelow. (University of Idaho Library, Special Collections, John B. Miller Collection 12-96)

The funeral procession of James S. "Cashup" Davis in June 1896, winding past a crossroads schoolhouse near Steptoe Butte in the Palouse. The photo shows the roads, fencing, terrain, and the distances in Whitman County, perhaps the most desirable district for settlers. (Washington State University: Manuscripts, Archives, and Special Collections 70-077)

Cannon Park on Mission Avenue, Spokane, in 1912, one of the city's most complete playgrounds, purchased and developed with a bond issue passed by Spokane voters to carry out Olmsted Brothers plan for a park system. Only boys seem to be wading. (Spokane Park Department)

More famous than Spokane, the Davenport Hotel was opened in 1914 by Louis Davenport, who started as a restaurant proprietor. His noted restaurant, foreground, was renamed the Italian Gardens in 1922, and another wing was added to the hotel. (WWP)

Blackfeet Indians pitched tipis along Riverside avenue in 1925 when they attended the Indian Congress, while tourists gawked. (Eastern Washington State Historical Society)

Spokane Interstate Fair, 1914, one of the largest eastern Washington fairs. Although it appears prosperous, businessmen had to subscribe $13,000 to keep the fair going, and fairs everywhere competed with airplane stunts, racing, and other attractions. Derby Day, the largest racing meet of the Spokane fair, drew thirty thousand. (Eastern Washington State Historical Society)

Almost every town had its outdoor market where nearby farmers sold fruits and vegetables from their wagons. This is the Spokane farmers' market, about 1915. Most towns established a traditional day for the market, and farmers also sent their children to peddle produce door to door in residential sections. (Eastern Washington State Historical Society)

Miss Spokane, Margaret Motie, holds the key to the city, standing between the Spokane and the United States flags. The picture was snapped by Frank Guilbert at the Spokane Interstate Fair in 1913. (Eastern Washington State Historical Society)

unions but maintained two companies of state militia made up of men loyal to the company.

After the governor of Idaho imposed martial law in 1892 to suppress union disorders, an uneasy truce—a union-dominated peace—lasted until the unions, demonstrating against the Bunker Hill again in 1899, dynamited its concentrating mill. Martial law returned. Under military sway, the mine managers, organized as the Mine Owners Association, adopted work permits and a central hiring agency that would check unionism in the mines until World War I.[10]

Thus by 1900 mining in the Inland Empire had virtually shaken out; the region's people knew the money-making districts and the others that could profit with roads and mills. They knew where to find magnesite, marble, clays, and other deposits. Nearly every section of the Inland Empire had been examined, with here and there a transitory boom—gold on the Palouse River, on the sandbars of the Columbia, in the Cascades near Wenatchee, at weathering Ruby on the Pend Oreille—leaving a few lucky men, isolated mines, ghost towns, and deserted flumes.

By 1900 migrants were streaming into Spokane. The city's very size and variety of merchants and suppliers pumped it as the regional distribution center. A mining exchange, opened in 1890 in a vacant storeroom, briskly traded mining stocks. Spokane's people thought of the mining areas, the farms, and small towns, as satellites. The chamber of commerce puffery regularly claimed the orchards of Yakima and Wenatchee, the wheat fields of the Palouse, and the mines of the Coeur d'Alenes for the "Spokane country," portraying Spokane as the jewel of its universe—superior airs that miffed other towns. Rural newspapers delighted in potshots at Spokane. The Spokane mining exchange, wrote a Wallace editor, "is and has been for some time, a serious menace to the development of the Coeur d'Alene district, and their petty larceny method of dealing in stocks has done as much to retard the development of meritorious properties as any other public leech we know of."[11]

The first ten years of the new century cast silver-lead marketing in the mold that shaped mining for the next fifty. At first, Coeur d'Alene companies had sold ores or concentrates on short-term tonnage contracts to a dozen or more smelters, doing business wherever they could. The Bunker Hill's owners bought the smelter at Tacoma for it and their Alaska mines. But this random pattern changed with formation of American Smelting and Refining Company (Asarco).[12]

Asarco was organized in 1899 by giants of corporate finance—Henry H. Rogers, Leonard Lewisohn, and John D. Rockefeller, Jr.—to combine eleven companies that owned sixteen smelters, eighteen refineries, and some mines, for the purpose of reducing competition and stabilizing profits in the erratic smelting industry. Known from its start as the "smelter trust," Asarco gathered in every large smelter except those of Meyer Guggenheim's four sons and half a dozen independent plants. The trust proved unwieldy and within a year appealed to the Guggenheims for help on terms so favorable that the Guggenheims took control. The brothers streamlined American by closing obsolescent plants, renovating or relocating others, and scheduling ore shipments and railroad routes from mines to use Asarco's combined plant capacity most efficiently. Asarco began to prosper.[13]

The mine managers of the Coeur d'Alenes balked at the trust's manipulation of the ore market, but they dealt with Asarco because smelters outside the trust could not handle the district's output. The managers jockeyed for favored treatment in quotas and prices as individuals and as a group, and in competing to sell their ore, inevitably gave up too much.

To some mine managers, however, the trust offered a model. A merger of mines to end debilitating competition made sense. Nimble Jim Wardner had proposed merger to Sam Hauser in 1888. *Engineering and Mining Journal* in 1899 heard consolidation was in the wind. In 1901 Campbell and Finch tried to join the Standard, Mammoth, and Hecla but could not come to terms. And merger occurred to Charlie Sweeny, too.[14]

A big talker but shrewd, Sweeny used the Last Chance Mine above Wardner to invade adjoining ore bodies, tried to cut off the Bunker Hill, and relied on a rotund, stumpy lawyer, Weldon B. Heyburn, to justify him in court. Sweeny persuaded Rockefeller's people (who brought in Jay Gould's heir, George) to underwrite a merger of Coeur d'Alene mines that would also extricate Rockefeller from unwanted investments in the puny Monte Cristo mines in northwestern Washington and the wan Everett smelter. With George Turner negotiating for him, Sweeny in 1903 bagged most of the major mines (the Standard, Mammoth, and Morning in the upper end of the district and of course his own Empire State-Idaho, mines clustered near Wardner in the lower end) for the Federal Mining and Smelting Company, a Delaware corporation. Sweeny might have taken the Bunker Hill and Sullivan as well, but he squeezed too hard and talked too much. Even so, for roughly $15 million in Federal stock and Rockefeller cash, Sweeny combined most of the Coeur d'Alenes' major producers of the time.

He surely relished the *Spokesman-Review*'s comment that he was "the dominant power in the Coeur d'Alenes." In 1904 Federal produced 21 percent of the domestic lead of the United States.[15]

When Sweeny talked boldly of Federal smelting its own ores, the Guggenheims dispatched Bernard M. Baruch, then a New York broker, to buy the Everett, Tacoma, and Selby (San Francisco) plants; then Daniel Guggenheim, obviously with Rockefeller's leave, bought stock control of Federal. The Bunker Hill and Sullivan, to ensure future sales, had contracted to deliver its ore to the trust for twenty-five years. Now Federal signed a twenty-five-year contract.

After Federal, combining mines became a way of life in the Coeur d'Alenes. Merging promised economies of scale and ore production large enough to impress even the trust.

But north Idaho would no longer be the private preserve of mining men. New actors came on the scene: a power company and lumbermen. Sweeny, Campbell, Finch, and others bought the power site at Post Falls on the Spokane River to generate electric current for mining twelve months of the year. When they could not interest General Electric or Westinghouse, they sold their rights to the Washington Water Power Company, which built a Post Falls plant and enlarged its Monroe Street station in Spokane to electrify the mines late in 1903 with current from outside the district.

And lumbermen moved in—well-financed large companies—to claim north Idaho's forests and do a high-volume freight business. Lumbermen would be formidable political adversaries; they sought favored tax treatment, concessions on waterways, and special rates from railroads. Towns flowered outside the mining district, and Spokane courted new bankrolls. If Spokane bankers had been slow to invest in mines after the panic of 1893, as *Northwest Mining Truth* asserted, they were not slow to put money into lumber or to invite lumbermen to sit on their boards.[16]

One of the few mines that Sweeny had failed to sweep into Federal, the Hercules, lay in the hills above Burke. The mine had been discovered and was now managed by Harry L. Day. He brought into a guarded partnership the men who had worked in the Hercules for twelve years before finding its vein: a railroad engineer, Levi W. (Al) Hutton; a dairy hand, August Paulsen, and his employer, Sylvester Markwell; a butcher, Frank M. Rothrock; Charles "Dad" Reeves, a barber; and a Burke storekeeper, Damian Cardoner. Wary, stubborn, articulate, and rather stocky, Day had come to the Coeur d'Alenes as a young man with his father, a pioneer Wardner merchant. He had worked in mines, joined the union, hired out as a bookkeeper, and kept his faith in the Hercules. So had his sister, Eleanor, who put much of her schoolteacher's pay into the mine. The Days and their partners, who had seen other men lose mines when raiders bought up stock or cut off access, protected the Hercules as part of the family. "The Hercules was our child, our career," Harry once said. On June 2, 1901, Paulsen, digging alone in the Hercules, swung his pick into the richest silver-lead vein in the Coeur d'Alenes.

Harry Day's struggle to sell Hercules ore without capitulating to the trust, and the protective wall he built around his mine (a bank, newspaper, foundry, custom mill, political connections), elevated him to power. He would be one of the most influential men in the Coeur d'Alenes for the next thirty years. Day first sold ore to American Metal, a small New York buyer, and next to the independent Selby. He and Selby's president united in opposing Asarco, until the trust bought the Selby. Then Day indignantly cut off shipments. Despite the pinch of finding smelters outside the trust, Day kept the Hercules churning: in 1905 the mine yielded dividends of $43,000 a month; in 1906, $60,000; and in 1907, a depression year, more than $87,000. Bonanza paydays, these, to men who worked on a railroad, in a dairy, a barbershop, and in stores.[17]

The Hercules partners cavorted while Day guarded the mine. He did move from Burke, however, to congenial Wallace, where the Hercules built a large custom mill in 1911. As Harry hired miners banished from antiunion Wardner, Canyon Creek continued to be a haven for union men, many married, stable, experienced miners. And Day expanded his ground, buying likely claims—the Tamarack, Custer, and Sherman among them—in the hills around Burke.

Day's standing among mine managers rested on his firmness and his persuasive powers. At the other end of the Coeur d'Alenes, Stanly A. Easton owed his prestige to position and bearing. A majestic six feet, five inches, a graduate of the University of California in mining engineering, Easton came to the Bunker Hill and Sullivan as general manager in 1903. He would hold the position thirty years. Austere and capable, Easton set the course for the Coeur d'Alenes as nearly as any one man.

Political opposites, Day preeminent among north Idaho's Democrats, and Easton among Republicans, the two nonetheless traded mining information and acted in concert against the trust, taxation, tariffs, railroads, unions, and all the other menaces to mining. They cooperated in a scheme to import electric current from Montana cheaper than Washington Water Power would sell it. They were reserved confederates, not warm friends, and their confidential exchanges stopped when Harry Day stunned the mining district in 1912 by taking the presidency of Federal. His chief task was to find new properties to sustain the company. Day's shift to Federal coincided with a trust contract to buy Hercules ore on terms extremely profitable to the Hercules, because Asarco temporarily needed the ore for flux in its smelters. That was fortunate for the Hercules, because mining had been in the doldrums after 1907. Edgar Newhouse of Asarco said bluntly that the trust would never again write as good a contract for anyone.[18]

Naturally the Bunker Hill demanded terms as favorable; its president, F. W. Bradley, and general manager, Easton, threatened to build their own smelter unless they got rates like those of the Hercules. On the other hand, the trust prepared to impose new contracts in 1915 raising its charges for all its Coeur d'Alene customers.

When the trust closed the Coeur d'Alenes to competitors by threats, the Bunker Hill and Sullivan built a smelter at Kellogg. Its long contract with the trust had specified that Asarco was to receive concentrates carrying between 30 and 70 percent lead. Beginning in 1917, consequently, the Bunker Hill smelted its own concentrates containing less than 30 and more than 70 percent lead, and operated a custom smelter to treat ores of others, making profitable the low-grade lead mines of the district.[19]

Asarco sued, alleging breach of contract, and in a paneled Oregon courtroom a revealing beam of publicity played briefly over the U.S. lead mining industry. The settlement out of court allowed the Bunker Hill to smelt those concentrates not covered by its Asarco contract and, by inference, to treat the ores of other mines.

Like the Bunker Hill, Harry Day and his brothers, Eugene and Jerome, concluded that they must knuckle under to the trust or smelt their own ores. They quietly bought the idle Northport smelter and the Pennsylvania Smelting and Refining Company and arranged preferential freight rates with the Great Northern. Almost to the day in 1916 when he and his brothers started up their renovated Northport plant, Harry abruptly resigned from Federal.

Within months, war in Europe, with disruption of world shipping, forced upward the demand and the price of lead. In 1917 lead reached its highest price quotations in forty years. During the war—the Idaho Mining Association was later to say—Coeur d'Alene mines made 48 percent of their profits between 1903 and 1922. Everyone in the lead industry—miner, smelterer, refiner, and manufacturer—was overwhelmed with business. The Bunker Hill, Federal, Hercules, Hecla, and other companies—some had closed their mines when prices were low—reached peaks of production during World War I. And Harry Day, Bradley of the Bunker Hill, and Edward Brush of Asarco served together on a federal committee formed by Bernard Baruch, an adviser to the Council of National Defense, to allocate wartime lead supplies.[20]

As military service and war industries took men, a shortage of experienced miners persuaded the Bunker Hill and the Hecla, the two remaining patrons, to close the district hiring bureau in January 1917. Union organizers took this as a signal to reenter the Coeur d'Alenes, demanding to negotiate wages and hours, particularly an eight-hour workday. (Ten hours had been standard.) Their efforts might have been less threatening had mine managers not feared that disgruntled union men—or enemy agents, of whom rumors abounded—might dynamite mines or mills. Barbed-wire fences, revolving searchlights, and armed patrols protected mines and mills to prevent sabotage. The managers worried about the belligerent Industrial Workers of the World, the Wobblies, and sought prosecution of its members as criminal syndicalists.

Despite fears, none of the mines or mills was openly attacked, and a military conciliator arranged relatively peaceful labor relations throughout the war with his appeal to patriotism. After the armistice, unions struck the major mines. But as mines closed in a declining metals market, the strike petered out. Mine managers, including the Days, reopened their hiring bureau (it would remain until its manager, George T. Edmiston, retired in 1947), and, with the menace of a gun-toting deputy sheriff, Jack Foster, again throttled unionism. "The firm attitude of the operators in maintaining the 'open shop' system, together with the activity of the peace officers," reported *Engineering and Mining Journal,* "have combined to bring about a very satisfactory condition" in the Coeur d'Alenes.[21]

The war-puffed metals market inevitably deflated with the return of peace, although the Pittman Act, to restock the nation's silver trove, sustained some lead-silver mines until October 1923. The war spread a preoccupation with mortality, both of men and mines. Some old mines had been reopened, and some with limited ores, like the Interstate-Callahan, had profited spectacularly during the conflict, but many old mines had bottomed—the Frisco at 1,500 feet down, the Standard-Mammoth at 1,650, and the venerable Tiger at 1,800 feet. Yet some ore bodies continued to unexpected depths, well beyond the predictions of geologists and engineers, and a few of them surprised mining men—the Sunshine, for example, an old shaft driven deeper to rich silver by Yakima investors new to mining. But Coeur d'Alene operators in general were in a mood to measure the probable life of each mine and to husband its mineral resources after the war.

Consequently, the twenties passed in cautious vigilance. Mines opened when lead prices rose, as in 1925—there seemed a general, if timid, trend upward throughout the decade—and closed when prices fell. In the postwar realignment of the lead industry, the Days reached an accord with the trust and sold Asarco their Northport smelter, which was dismantled for equipment to renovate the East Helena plant.

The effect of Inland Empire mines, mainly those of the Coeur d'Alenes, on Spokane is not precisely measurable. The city served as principal distribution point for equipment and supplies almost from the beginning; miners spent their rolls in its hotels, saloons, and gambling resorts; Wobblies made their headquarters in Spokane to the outspoken displeasure of mine managers; and the Spokane Hotel for years drew mining men as gathering place. Men who had made fortunes from mines invested in businesses in Spokane (the Union Iron Works, for example, which manufactured a notable line of mining equipment), and they served on the boards of the city's banks and businesses, built homes, and erected central office buildings. Mine litigation enriched Spokane attorneys, men like Myron A. Folsom who counseled August Paulsen, the Bunker Hill, and the Hercules, and for a time acted as the Bunker Hill's marketing manager.

Wealthy from the Hercules, Frank Rothrock promoted Spokane as a livestock marketing center. A stock exchange flourished in good times and endured in bad. Although Jay Graves resigned from the Granby in 1916 and its operations moved to the British Columbia coast, the Metaline district continued to yield lead, zinc, and silver. And who can count how many industrious citizens first came to Spokane with visions of quick riches from mines and settled for lesser dreams? By 1920, however, the editors of *Northwest Mining Truth* complained that Spokane was turning its back on mining; in an editorial they recalled the city's mining heritage and in a feature article recounted the past of this "mining-built metropolis." [22]

Of the men who guided the Coeur d'Alenes from the turn of the century, few remained. John Finch, Mace Campbell, Charles Sweeny, D. C. Corbin, and scores of others were dead. Stanly Easton, Harry Day, and James F. McCarthy of the Hecla spoke as the district's elder statesmen. When the metals market crashed with the stock market in 1929, the mines slowly closed down to wait for better days.

CHAPTER 10

Lumber: Great Lakes Invaders

Fred Herrick was a wiry, restless man of the woods. While he prevailed, superlatives grew as thick as the trees he mowed. He was said to be the second largest owner of white pine timber in the world, the largest independent lumber operator in the Inland Empire, and the darling of the lumberjacks who took his rubber checks with a smile. Like nearly every other major lumberman in the inland Northwest after 1900, Herrick migrated, a latecomer in 1909, from the fading forests of the upper Midwest to buy thousands of acres of Idaho stumpage. At fifty-five he moved to St. Maries to cut his trees.[1]

From the turn of the twentieth century to the depression of the thirties, the lumber business around Spokane was like Herrick—combative, opportunistic, exploitive, rising and falling, booming and busting with large hopes and small realizations.

Until almost 1900, lumbering in the interior Pacific Northwest consisted mainly of sawmill operators who followed surges of settlement to cut lumber for new towns and farmers. Pioneer mills whined at Spokane Falls, Colville, Deer Park, Post Falls, Harrison, Rathdrum, St. Maries, Coeur d'Alene, Sandpoint, Colfax, Walla Walla, Yakima, and elsewhere, ready to move if settlers shifted or the trees ran out. They used streams and lakes to float logs from forest to mills and river current to turn their saws. The *Colfax Commoner* described them all with its comment that William Codd, a Wisconsin native who built a mill at Colfax in 1877, drove logs on the Palouse River "for half the buildings in Whitman County." In the same way, the other pioneer mills built the districts around them. To the end of the nineties, sawmills at Colfax, Palouse City, and Elberton, to name a few, cut timber from riverbanks—until they peeled the shores and then had to skid logs on winter snow for spring river drives.[2]

Local mills bought trees from settlers, the government, or the Northern Pacific. And boundaries were not always clear, or respected. Mills got a good deal of their wood from someone else's land. (The Northern Pacific, itself, was a prodigious timber user. The federal government strove to confine the railroad's cutting to lands it could legitimately claim, but the Supreme Court let the company cut where it might.) They stripped the land to open it for farming or they selected only the best trees, leaving ragged, spindly growth behind them. For years farmers spent their off-seasons blasting stumps on logged land and, in winter, hitching their teams to drag logs for sheds and fences they built in the spring. So many trees. No one thought of saving forests. In the distance stood more. In the Palouse, loggers and farmers cut the timberline back eight to twelve miles. In mining districts, forests disappeared underground as mine timbers. A mill at Sandpoint specialized in flawless square beams for English warships.[3]

The Palouse pioneer George H. McCroskey remembered five- and six-day trips to the hills for timber before railroads came—those railroads that radiated from Spokane to ensure the city's place in the lumber business of the Inland Empire. Beside the Spokane River lay two of the larger mills before 1900: Frederick Post's, lipping the canyon at Post Falls, and the Sawmill Phoenix at Spokane on a dammed river channel, acquired through foreclosure by Dutch lenders, and dedicated with champagne, whistles, and cheers. Managed by Spokane's perennial parade marshal, dapper Eli F. Cartier van Dissel, refugee from a defunct California orchard colony of wealthy Hollanders, the Phoenix brought logs over the Spokane Falls and Northern Railroad from 10,000 acres near Springdale.[4]

The railroads lowered their lumber shipping rates in 1894 to lure business, enticing a few mills to send lumber as far as eastern Montana and the Dakotas, but the vast inland forests were hardly shaved five years later when Washington State lumber, chiefly from Puget Sound, sold in Great Lakes states, where the timber was nearly played out. Great Lakes lumbermen looked south and west for new stumpage, courted by the railroads and western states soliciting commerce. Many evenings in St. Paul, James J. Hill lectured his politely nodding neighbor, Frederick E. Weyerhaeuser, on abundant Northwest timber, perhaps telling Weyerhaeuser nothing new, for Weyerhaeuser, a major shareholder in important Great Lakes lumber companies, had turned down an 1885 Northern Pacific offer of a Tacoma millsite and coast timber.[5]

By the late nineties, Weyerhaeuser and other Great Lakes lumber-men were determined to move to the Pacific Northwest; their crews sampled its timber, cruised its forests, and asked concessions from state administrations. Idaho politicians assured Weyerhaeuser agents that a law requiring state lands to be logged within twenty years would be relaxed and hinted that forest taxes would be low—pledges they did not keep. Washington required timber on its state lands to be cut within five years, lengthened to ten in 1905, but sold little state timber because the land commissioner thought the trees worth more than the prices bid for land.[6]

As grabbing the best timber turned into a race, Weyerhaeuser formed a syndicate among friends (some turned him down) to buy large tracts from the Northern Pacific, gambling $1.8 million in 1900 on 900,000 acres of the railroad's Douglas fir forests in ten western Washington counties, one of America's largest land sales. And as Wey-erhaeuser and the other midwest princes bought trees, the federal gov-ernment moved fast, lashed by a developing conservation policy and Gifford Pinchot, first chief of the Forest Service (then known as the Bureau of Forestry). The government send young foresters to survey forest boundaries and designated treed public land as reserves. By 1909 the government had set aside the Kaniksu, Coeur d'Alene, Cab-inet, Colville, Palouse, Chelan, Wenatchee, Clearwater, Pend Oreille, and Nez Perce national forests and by 1911 had added the Selway, St. Joe, and Okanogan. This amounted to about half the forested land of the region—not all of it, incidentally, commercial timber.[7]

The Weyerhaeuser syndicate, including Frederick's sons, bought Idaho timber through subsidiaries between 1898 and 1910: the Clear-water Timber Company acquired huge tracts, paying in railroad scrip, when its man purloined a rival's special train to win a race to file land descriptions; the Humbird Lumber Company bought timber and sev-eral going companies, including the Sandpoint Lumber Company on Lake Pend Oreille; the Bonners Ferry Lumber Company had woods operations in Idaho, Montana, and British Columbia (although Can-ada banned log exports before it started cutting); the ill-starred Rut-ledge Lumber Company bought 200,000 acres in Bonner, Boundary, and Kootenai counties and 29,440 acres of old-growth pine along the St. Maries River from the Northern Pacific; and the Potlatch Lumber Company purchased 30,000 acres of state school lands, raising cries of collusion and favoritism. Some Clearwater and Rutledge purchases were given the Northern Pacific as lieu lands when the government set aside Mount Rainier National Park and the Pacific Forest Reserve. For a generation, private owners and governments swapped lands to fill gaps in their holdings. They called this "blocking in."[8]

Henry Turrish, a Wisconsin lumberman competing with Weyerhaeuser, bought 13,000 forest acres in Latah County and 11,000 in southern Shoshone County (the Elk Creek drainage) from the state. He and Charles Weyerhaeuser, one of Frederick's sons, soon merged to form the Potlatch Lumber Company, which, in turn, absorbed the Palouse Lumber Company (and its 180,000 acres near Elk Creek) shortly after the Palouse took 14,700 acres along the Palouse River from the Spokane Hypotheekbank for less than seven dollars an acre.[9]

During 1902 the Northern Pacific sold much of its stumpage north of Spokane. The Phoenix bought 10,000 acres; Holland-Horr, 15,000; the Buckeye Lumber Company at Denison on the Spokane Falls and Northern, 46,000; Spokane Lumber, 28,000; the Washington Mill Company, Spokane, 4,000; Consolidated Lumber, 7,000; Standard Lumber, Deer Park, without a mill, 5,000; and the Bradley Company, Wisconsin, 100,000 acres—sales that totaled about 215,000 acres (rounded), the genesis of large-scale logging in northeastern Washington. The names of the companies, familiar then, and many of the trees, would be gone within twenty years. About thirty mills then lined the Spokane Falls and Northern, the largest that of Edwards Bradford at Elk, owned by Omaha, Nebraska, people. Sensing the whirlwind pace of changes in their business, thirty lumbermen organized the Eastern Washington and Idaho Lumbermen's Association with van Dissel as president, a short-lived trade group that presaged the associations soon formed to sell lumber, lobby, and prevent forest fires.[10]

In a rush of sales, one-third of the forested land of the Inland Empire changed ownership in the pivotal years from 1900 to 1909. By 1910, the Northern Pacific and Weyerhaeuser between them owned 34.6 percent of the merchantable timber of Washington. Nine years later the railroad's land commissioner would report the Northern Pacific's best timberlands sold, the remainder hard to reach or lower quality. Most of Weyerhaeuser's stumpage stood in western Washington, 85 percent of it bought from the railroad. The state government was investigating the management of its land office with allegations of "fake" sales of westside timber to Weyerhaeuser agents, but, for all the sensational charges, the legislature refused to impeach Land Commissioner E. W. Ross, and the accusations quieted.[11]

In twenty-four months, Idaho peddled state timber for nearly one million dollars. Not all of Idaho's trees went to lumber companies, for the inland Northwest boiled with new settlers, and not all the settlers' timber claims were homesteads, for dark whispers of land fraud circulated. Stories were told of settlers hired by lumbermen to build shanties at the intersection of four timber claims to qualify for all four, and there were reports of bogus entrymen and false swearings. The "rankest fake homesteads," an investigator called them, in Shoshone, Kootenai, and Nez Perce counties. A resolution offered in the U.S. House of Representatives alleged that Rutledge and others formed an "unlawful combination" that interfered with settlers' rights, forced down the market value of timberlands, employed claim jumpers, and subverted state agents. Nothing came of that.[12]

In Montana a prominent businessman, R. M. Cobban, was indicted for conspiracy to bribe citizens to enter false timber claims in Missoula and Powell counties. Cobban would be elected president of the Missoula chamber of commerce six months before a jury found him innocent.[13]

A Forest Service man who saw north Idaho's forests before large-scale cutting started described long stretches of old-growth white pine, unscarred by fires, broken now and then by the log house and barn of a homesteader in a small natural meadow. He saw among the "endless" pines some large mature larch, fir, cedar, and occasionally spruce—the cedar, abundant, fit for seventy- to ninety-foot poles. There were trees as far as he could see in the distance.[14]

Soon the cutting began. With more than four hundred square miles of trees in the Coeur d'Alene–St. Joe district, Weyerhaeuser's Potlatch company erected a mill that its manager, William Deary, a hardheaded Irish Catholic lumberman from Minnesota, called "the biggest mill I ever heard of"—thirteen connected buildings, a sixty-five-acre drying yard, the Palouse dammed for a millpond, capable of producing 350,000 board feet in one ten-hour shift. The story goes that Deary chose the millsite by jabbing his pencil through a map, brushing aside Moscow's aspirations for the mill with the remark, "There isn't enough water in Moscow to baptize a Protestant bastard!" Neither was there much water in the seasonal Palouse. Farmers along the river sued to remove the company's dam. Courts in Washington and Idaho denied them, knowing their states' hunger for industry. As an Idaho justice observed, "For many years the said timber area lay undeveloped; . . . the county derived no taxes from it."[15]

Eighteen miles north of Moscow the company built a comfortable workers' town, Potlatch, on hillsides overlooking its mill, with brick bank, mercantile store ("the Merc") and four classes of family housing—hilltop managers' homes that rented for $40 a month, descending to the smallest dwellings for Greeks, Italians, and Japanese, a community church and a Catholic church, and tree-shaded board sidewalks. (The trees were planted after those already there had been cut for a townsite.) Four years later the company built a smaller mill and another town deeper in the woods at Elk River. (It planted trees there, too.) As one resident described it, "Elk River stood virtually in a hole cut out of a dense forest cover of mature white pine." The town lasted for about twenty-five years, its houses of green timber warping, the Bulgarian workmen who excavated its mill yard and built forest railroads long scattered.[16]

But Weyerhaeuser's men were not alone in the forests. By 1909 more than three hundred mills roared in the Inland Empire, and to the region drifted a new breed of lumberjack, Great Lakes men wearing mackinaws and stagged pants, to work beside Northwest loggers in long overcoats.[17]

The inland lakes and streams formed a competitive arena for lumbermen, the rivers a transportation network and the lakes storage ponds, the cheapest way to move and hold timber. Lumber companies dredged streams to remove obstacles, then applied to collect tolls from other users. They built flumes, tramways, and railroads, but they preferred water haulage. Competing for water sites divided lumbermen, but sharing waterways brought them together. A "first class" millsite, opined the Coeur d'Alene lumberman and banker William Dollar, was level ground with water on one side and a railroad on the other. Such ideal spots were scarce. On Coeur d'Alene Lake, Rutledge owned the best.[18]

By conservative estimate, 8,091,000 acres of commercial forest stood in Idaho north of the Salmon River and 5,498,000 acres in Washington east of the Cascades. (Montana's forests were in a pocket in Lincoln, Flathead, and Missoula counties.) Of this the federal government reserved 53 percent in Idaho and 45 percent in Washington. Perhaps 1,078,000 acres in Washington and 2,605,000 in northern Idaho belonged to private owners; of this private timber, lumber companies owned roughly half. Nearly 90 percent of Idaho's commercial timber stood in Nez Perce, Clearwater, Latah, Shoshone, Kootenai, Benewah, and Bonner counties; about two-thirds of Washington's on the Cascade slopes of Chelan, Kittitas, Yakima, and Klickitat counties, and one-third in Okanogan, Ferry, Pend Oreille, Stevens, and Spokane counties. Although a variety of species towered here (hemlock, fir, cedar, larch), pine dominated the lumber trade: in Washington a yellow or ponderosa pine, rising perhaps 125 to 140 feet with a two- to four-foot trunk, used for light construction (and in the twenties, boxes); in Idaho and Montana a white pine, used for interior woodwork, pattern-making, and eventually, matches—the commercial woods of the Inland Empire.[19]

By and large the lumbermen who marched into this battleground between 1898 and 1910 were seasoned, mature, and armed with money. They practiced integrated lumbering: each company owned its stumpage, transportation, mills, and sales agency. The Northern Pacific declined to lay a branch where Potlatch Lumber wanted it, forcing Potlatch to build its own—the Washington, Idaho and Montana. A paradigm of the Inland Empire lumber business consisted of three elements: integration, absentee stockholders or parent company, and progressive absorption of established mills by the largest, growth by feeding on competitors. (Stockholders also customarily sent their sons to work in the mills.) A company with a good millsite but declining stumpage, or with financial problems, or with timber but no mill, was a prime target for takeover, and in mergers some of the noted old names disappeared: the Phoenix, B. R. Lewis, and scores of others. All of the biggest mills (except the Lewiston mill in 1926) had been built by 1911, so that the Inland Empire's mill capacity did not change materially for thirty years despite changes in ownership. And almost none of the mills ran regularly to capacity.[20]

Many smaller mills cut their timber and quit, and when the easy-to-reach timber receded, only large companies could afford to continue. Some small ones survived as logging contractors for big ones. And as lumbering expanded, north Idaho's production leaped from 56 million board feet in 1899 to 728 million a year by 1911. Shipments of machinery and supplies poured through Spokane. Little wonder that the chamber of commerce chose as its first honorary member a builder of feeder railroads, Daniel Chase Corbin.[21]

For Weyerhaeuser, the bristling Deary set the style in Idaho, and in the giant's shadow, F. A. Blackwell set it for everyone else. (Herrick came seven years after Blackwell.) They virtually ignored a second arena, the borderlands of Spokane's empire, the eastern Cascades and northwestern Montana: Biles-Coleman at Omak, Cascade Lumber (organized by Oklahoma investors) at Yakima, Neils at Libby (in 1911, and later in Klickitat County), and dozens of others.

A native of Pennsylvania, a lumberman since age seventeen, a sober, reserved block of a man, balding with brush mustache, Blackwell at fifty invested $190,000 in Idaho state timber in 1902 and continued to buy. Eventually he held 100,000 acres or more in northern Idaho and northeastern Washington, including the eastern slopes of Mount Spokane, logged with a giant flume that shot into a creek leading to Spirit Lake.[22]

Before cutting timber, Blackwell promoted an electric railroad from the city of Coeur d'Alene to Spokane to serve the lake mills, the Coeur d'Alene and Spokane Railway, Ltd., a company consisting of a principal stockholder in Wisconsin; Dollar, the ubiquitous Coeur d'Alene banker; C. P. Lindsley of Lindsley Brothers, Spokane, Chicago, and Portland, shippers of cedar and poles; and Coeur d'Alene merchants. In its second year, the railroad merged with the Spokane and Inland Empire, Jay P. Graves's electric system to the Palouse and to north Idaho lake resorts.[23]

Then Blackwell turned to the business that brought him West. He organized the Panhandle Lumber Company with 125,000-feet-a-day sawmills at Spirit Lake and Ione and a connecting steam railroad from Coeur d'Alene, the Idaho and Washington Northern. Panhandle's stockholders included Dollar, Lindsley, a group of Pennsylvanians, and Frank J. Davies, manager of the Rutledge Timber Company, a Weyerhaeuser affiliate. (Davies held 80 of 550 issued shares, perhaps as a personal investment, but no one could say the Weyerhaeuser camp didn't know what Blackwell was up to.) When it began to log, Panhandle cooperated in spring drives on Priest River with others, including Humbird, Dalkena, and later Diamond Match.[24]

As he bought timber quietly (some at twenty-five cents a thousand), the taciturn Blackwell surveyed his railroad. The 106-mile line met the Northern Pacific at McGuire's near Coeur d'Alene and angled northward to Metaline Falls. It opened in November 1907, "spick and span, gleaming brass and black" trains (fourteen engines) to haul logs, lumber, and passengers. And with it, the low-grade-lead mining business of northeastern Washington came to life. While Blackwell penetrated northeastern Washington from Coeur d'Alene, Corbin built from Spokane through northern Idaho, the Spokane International, to connect with the Canadian Pacific.[25]

In the usual manner of Inland Empire entrepreneurs, Blackwell enveloped his domain. His company owned timber, railroad, townsites, mills, and a cement plant at Metaline Falls. Blackwell was a director of banks at Spirit Lake, Ione, Coeur d'Alene, Newport, and Usk. And he groomed his reserved son, Russell, a business college graduate who had managed the Coeur d'Alene and Spokane and, at twenty-eight, now managed the Idaho and Washington Northern.

Despite his prominence, Blackwell was running into mounting problems. In retrospect, his investments in Idaho would prove to have been badly timed. The railroad was financed by bonds secured by a mortgage to the Illinois Trust and Savings Bank, Chicago, but Blackwell could not sell the bonds and was forced to agree to a supplemental mortgage and a second mortgage to secure funds. Falling behind, he borrowed from the Panhandle Lumber Company and then turned to the Chicago, Milwaukee and St. Paul Railway, which was particularly interested in access to the Coeur d'Alene lakefront. The Milwaukee agreed to assist in exchange for capital stock, acquired more stock when Blackwell defaulted an interest payment, and at the stockholders' annual meeting of the Idaho and Washington Northern in July 1914, the Milwaukee voted a majority of the stock and elected its own directors. The Milwaukee was now in control of the Blackwell line, and two years later, when the Blackwell railway was foreclosed, the Milwaukee acquired it physically. With transfer of the railroad, Russell dropped out of his father's businesses to open a Reo automobile dealership in Spokane.[26]

Yet Blackwell appeared to prosper, and Spokane clubs solicited him to join. He became an Old National Bank director and entered Spokane real estate speculation with Fred B. Grinnell, who with Blackwell was a director of Graves's electric system. But Blackwell kept his home in Coeur d'Alene, a three-story Victorian frame on Sherman Avenue, the main street. Perhaps Grinnell served as intermediary when the Blackwell Lumber Company, formed in 1909, took over the bankrupt B. R. Lewis mill on Coeur d'Alene Lake.[27]

For timber to supply his mill, Blackwell signed a contract for a rumored billion board feet of pine (actually it was 625 million) belonging to the Menasha Wooden Ware Company, a Wisconsin manufacturer of wood products founded in 1849. For $500,000 in Blackwell company capital stock and a series of promissory notes to be paid off within three years, Blackwell acquired the right to cut 100 million board feet a year from Menasha's timber holdings in Shoshone, Latah, Kootenai, and Benewah counties (some of it fronting on the Milwaukee main line). As he started logging, Blackwell found that (as with his railroad) he could not sell his lumber company stock or produce lumber fast enough to meet payments on his notes. In 1911, Blackwell Lumber Company issued $1.5 million in additional (preferred) stock, giving the stock to Menasha Wooden Ware to retire promissory notes, and negotiated an extension of the timber agreement to ten years. "On account of the general business depression and the very dull lumber market, together with the scare created by the forest fires of last season," Blackwell told his stockholders before they voted on the new agreement with Menasha, "the management has found it impossible to dispose of the common stock in the treasury, or any considerable amount of the five year term notes which we offered some months since." He declared that the new arrangement "puts the company in a very much stronger and better position."[28]

But the lumber business did not improve. In 1916, the Menasha company elected a majority of the directors and, in effect, assumed management of the Blackwell Lumber Company.[29]

Blackwell was nearing seventy years (and the end of his life, for he died in 1922) when Diamond Match snatched a considerable block of stumpage at his back door near Ione by quietly pyramiding the modest purchases of smaller firms and successfully contested a Blackwell water right. In 1921 Diamond acquired 14,500 acres in northern Idaho from the Northern Pacific for $578,000, and in 1926 bought nearly all the railroad's remaining stumpage in the Kalispell Creek drainage near Priest Lake—only to see it burn a few weeks later. (In this area, logging and fire scalped forested hills, which were eventually replanted with ponderosa.) Now logging what had been a Blackwell preserve, Diamond built a two-and-one-half mile tram to the west branch of the Pend Oreille River, took over the Humbird mill near Newport, bought cutting rights to state timber near Priest River, and played a major role in the Inland Empire's lumber business—huge wood operations for small boxes of commonplace matches.[30]

Unlike lumbermen who built empires, when he and his associates moved the McGoldrick Lumber Company from Minneapolis to Spokane in 1904, James P. McGoldrick bought a ready-made realm for $450,000: the months-old A. M. Fox Lumber Company, then the largest mill in eastern Washington, with its pond on the Spokane River south of Gonzaga College. At forty-six, McGoldrick ruled his forests in Benewah and Shoshone counties, and his mill, as he ruled his office. He was a brisk, erect man smoking a triple-loop pipe, striding from front to back of the office to scrutinize each desk, scooping handfuls of wooden matches from a bowl.[31]

McGoldrick might pop up anywhere in logging camps or mill. A story goes that while he watched his crews drive logs in chilling weather, a cheeky lumberjack asked if he had some whiskey to warm them. McGoldrick sent his wagon to town for two gallons. The son of a lumberman, McGoldrick typified an era of personal management, an era of companies dominated by one man, staffed with friends and their likeliest sons, companies that rarely survived the succeeding generation.[32]

Early in the century, loggers often cut every tree, but between 1910 and 1915 they began to agree that selective cutting was cheaper; clear-cutting felled small, unusable trees or unsalable species. Logs and poles were skidded by horses to sleigh trails, decked there to be hauled over rutted, snowy roads, and dumped at river landings for spring drives. Crews sanded steeper forest roads to avoid crowding horses moving downhill, and often competed to see which camp could move the biggest load.[33] Long after the thirties, loggers drove the winter's cut on rushing spring streams, but hydroelectric dams slowly closed the rivers and several old millsites became more valuable for irrigation or powerhouses: Dalkena, Post Falls, the upper falls of the Spokane, tributaries of the Yakima, and others.

And as the timber receded from the riverbanks, the lumber companies laid short logging railroads to their cutting sites. At various times, Humbird operated forty-two miles of forest railroad; McGoldrick, thirty-five; Herrick's Milwaukee Lumber, seventy-eight; Ohio Match, forty-eight; Panhandle, thirty; Winton (Coeur d'Alene and Rose Lake), fifty-nine miles—spurs leading to rivers or to common carrier railroads. Where they did not lay rails, lumber companies strung tramways, flumes, and wagon roads to move logs.[34]

Mining companies contested river-dredging and tolls imposed by lumber companies; landowners frequently sued for damages to river-front property—and sometimes won. One collected from Dalkena and Humbird for shattering his fields by blasting stumps, windfalls, and debris to clear Priest River. When Blackwell sued for right-of-way, however, the courts reaffirmed the economic boon of the lumber business to Idaho: "The natural resources of the state cannot be completely developed without . . . the right of eminent domain," and noted that the 1903 legislature sanctioned eminent domain for storing and floating logs on nonnavigable Idaho streams. Yet by 1914, after ten years of battle in which booms were sometimes dynamited, the Idaho supreme court banned log drives on the Coeur d'Alene River.[35]

Roughly one-third of the men employed in lumbering worked in logging camps, and another third in sawmills. Logging camps traditionally closed for the winter sometime between November and January and reopened in April or May. Camps moved as the forest was cut. Lumberjacks worked six days a week, ten hours a day; they carried their own bedrolls, slept on straw mattresses in frame (or canvas) bunkhouses, and hung their wet socks and clothing around the bunkhouse barrel stove. Camps rarely offered bathing or laundry tubs, but stoves heated water for washing. Most lumberjacks wore two-piece woolen long underwear winter and summer. No one who lived in a camp forgot the smells.[36]

The lore of logging endows these primitive camps with masculine mythos, a code of the woods: a man who came into camp got two or three free meals and an empty bunk; he could not ask for work but waited for the foreman to offer it; in the cookhouse, no one talked at table except to ask for food. Eat and get out. Foremen wakened their crews at dawn by kicking open bunkhouse doors. Women in camps brought bad luck.[37]

This gross life would induce loggers to join the Industrial Workers of the World (Wobblies) in the union's campaign for company-furnished clean bedding, mattresses, steel cots, bathhouses, laundries, drying lines, and sanitary food. Logging crews usually combined single men, to whom the forest was a way of life, with local men working for a season's stake to farm or mine. Turnover was high. As an old-timer remarked, one crew always seemed to be coming, one working, and one leaving.

Towns near the timber—Spokane, for one—tolerated "skid roads," decrepit districts of cheap hotels and saloons where lumberjacks nested between seasons. The lumber business fostered castes, the lumberjack at the bottom and mill manager at the top. John Humbird, whose lumberjacks probably received four dollars a day and paid part of it back for forty-cent meals, spent $600 a month for a life-style that suited his post as manager of the Sandpoint mill.[38]

Small, mobile, gyppo mills might set up in a woods clearing until the trees around were cut, dragging logs with horse teams, but large, permanent mills drew their logs from a pond by a bull chain, a continuous belt, to the saw carriage. Sawn boards dropped from the carriage onto the green chain (another belt) for grading and thence into traps for sizing. Next they bumped to a planer for smoothing, then to kiln or loading platform for the drying yard. Experienced men graded by judging the appearance and strength of passing boards. Mill work was arduous, noisy, and dangerous. Men often lost fingers, and accidents costing an arm or leg were not uncommon. Mill towns always saw maimed men on the streets. By 1900, steam and electric power had replaced waterwheels—some of the electricity from railroads that strung electric and telegraph poles along their rights-of-way.

Crews in the woods and mill yards hauled with horses until after World War I, when machines gradually replaced animals except on the steepest terrain. Caterpillar tractors for log skidding puffed near Libby as early as 1913, and an occasional one rumbled through St. Maries camps. By the mid-twenties, Rutledge ran twenty steam donkeys for skidding, reeling 9,000-foot cables to move logs, coordinating the work by whistles because the men might be half a mile from the machines. Donkey boilers ate two or three cords of wood a day. And by the mid-twenties, tractors—"full of sound and fury, confidence and majesty"—rapidly displaced horses and pushed aside haystacks and barns for mechanics, repair shops, and spare parts. Dalkena, for one, switched early to trucks with solid rubber tires for log haulage.[39]

Logging in Idaho started in the north and moved south. The Sandpoint district mills reached their high point about 1910; by the twenties, the center had shifted to the Coeur d'Alene–St. Joe with Blackwell, McGoldrick, Herrick, Rutledge, and others; and in 1927 would migrate southward again to the Clearwater with the opening of Weyerhaeuser's Lewiston mill. As logging moved southward in Idaho, it shifted northward in Washington. Spokane County once held perhaps 700,000 acres of merchantable timber; as it fell, loggers moved on to Stevens County, which by 1925 was furnishing half the logs for Spokane mills, and to Pend Oreille (15 percent). Hedlund Lumber and Manufacturing and White Pine Sash of Spokane both cut Ferry County next. In the mid-twenties, Hedlund bought cutting rights to 129,300 acres in Ferry, about 9 percent of the county's total acreage, and contracted to cut 30 million board feet a year.[40]

In Washington and Idaho, lumbermen found mature forests ready to be cut. States not only required timber to be removed from state lands within a specific period, but their tax systems penalized owners who delayed harvesting trees. And to produce income from their investments—to meet carrying charges and reduce debts—the lumbermen started to cut and sell fast. The migration of Great Lakes lumbermen to the Inland Empire took place at a time when lumber use in the United States had begun to decline and southern pine was coming on the market. Competition for sales became intense. Lumbermen fought for lower freight rates in order to compete in midwestern and eastern markets, and, in these suits, Weyerhaeuser showed its power. Potlatch Lumber in 1908 led in challenging a lumber-rate increase published by the Northern Pacific and Great Northern, to cite an instance, and pushed through a 3.5-cent differential favoring inland over coastal shippers. The railroads also moved Sandpoint into the Spokane shipping group—railroads based their rates on "origination groups" and "destination groups"—and the Interstate Commerce Commission adopted the principle that inland groups were entitled to lower rates because of their costs of logging mountainous terrain, long hauls from timber to mills, and lumber of lesser quality.[41]

For a few years, as settlers bolted into the Pacific Northwest, about one-third of the region's lumber went for local building. One in every eight carloads was sold in eastern Montana. Spokane, which had put up 675 new structures in 1900 as migration accelerated, built 1,500 to 1,900 a year from 1904 through 1909 and supported three dozen lumberyards. The city's population virtually tripled in ten years, while that of eastern Washington more than doubled. Even Walla Walla, which immigrants had thought pretty well settled in the eighties, grew 70 percent. Consequently, lumber companies found a brisk demand for materials virtually at home.[42] Idaho's cedar shingle production increased steadily from 1899 to 1907; its cedar pole exports also grew and, unlike shingles, whose sales dropped off, maintained a steady sales pace into the thirties.[43]

But as transcontinental railroads completed their main lines, they laid off thousands, ending the booming ancillary trade of merchants, bankers, and farmers—nearly every supplier and service accustomed to railroad men's patronage felt the loss—and drought slowed immigration. Building slackened. In 1910 Spokane put up 2,184 new structures worth $5.8 million; in 1912, only 784 units; and in 1914, 420 worth $730,000.[44]

The slackening of home markets wounded a lumber business already hurt by rising costs of production and competition in the Mississippi Valley states that bought nearly half the Inland Empire's exported lumber. In a rush to liquidate stumpage, lumber companies continued to cut even as prices fell, creating surpluses that drove prices down further. Most companies had borrowed heavily to buy timber and build mills—Blackwell as an example. Their stockholders were restless for dividends, and their creditors for payment. For most, their profit margin between 1909 and 1914 averaged little more than 1 percent, well below the 6 demanded—too little to pay interest on their debts. A shakeout started: stronger companies absorbed weaker. Absentee owners seized command. By 1916 the Coeur d'Alene district had passed its zenith. Mills began dropping out.[45]

Before this slowdown, forests of the Inland Empire flared in one of the worst fire seasons in a century—that searing season of 1910 when more than seven thousand fires burned 3.3 million acres in four Pacific Northwest states, destroying old-growth, sound, choice white pine. Idaho, with 744 blazes, suffered the heaviest losses: 1.7 million scorched acres. Washington, with nearly six times as many fires, lost 202,799 acres. Smoke drifted as far as Boston. President Taft sent troops to help hundreds of volunteers manning fire lines with Forest Service and logging company men.[46]

The flames wiped out the stumpage of some companies, contributing to their collapse. While charred trees scarred mountain slopes and the market drooped, the Rutledge Company built a new mill because the time limit was running out on its timber on state land. On 600 acres of Coeur d'Alene Lake waterfront, the Rutledge mill opened in 1916. It would never be profitable. Not only was the market tenuous, but two fires in the twenties would burn its camps, flumes, and much stumpage, and Rutledge would merge within a decade and a half to avoid bankruptcy.[47]

Fred Herrick, James McGoldrick, and others acquired large tracts of fire-damaged timber from the Forest Service between 1911 and 1915, sending their logging crews into blackened skeleton forests where ashes and soot, with the usual dust, sifted over men toiling in summer heat. Although the market already sagged with too much lumber, the Forest Service sold burned timber (at two dollars a thousand board feet) because it felt "morally obliged" to make the best use of damaged trees. The annual cut in the Inland Empire was averaging 750 million to 860 million board feet. The Forest Service's morality loaded the market with 500 million more board feet in 1911 alone. With the new Rutledge mill and federal salvage, the cut passed a billion feet in 1916.[48]

Herrick, a native of Michigan who owned shares in midwestern and southern lumber companies, entered Idaho in 1909, near the end of the boom decade, attracted by the blandishments of the Chicago, Milwaukee and St. Paul Railway, which was eager to promote lumber shipments from the forests on its main line south of Coeur d'Alene Lake. With Herrick and Blackwell, cutting Menasha timber in the same general area, the Milwaukee built a branch from Plummer to Coeur d'Alene in 1910. Although his record in Idaho might suggest that Herrick was backed by the Milwaukee, the Northern Pacific regarded him as their man. But he was nobody's man. He was a loner, a woodsman who detested office routine, and the major shareholder in his companies. In twenty years, Herrick created an empire and a legend. (Herrick was an enthusiastic hunter. A story runs that he liked to introduce visitors to his "board of directors," an office lined with stuffed cougar heads.)[49]

Some of Herrick's money came from selling Mississippi and Alabama lumber holdings. (The Mississippi went to the Denkmanns, onetime Weyerhaeuser associates.) Herrick bought large stumpage rights near St. Maries, including an estimated 100 million board feet on the Coeur d'Alene Indian Reservation, said to be "the largest single sale of standing timber by the government." The man inspired superlatives. The 1910 fires burned a railroad he had started and damaged part of his timber, but he rebuilt the tracks and simultaneously erected the Milwaukee Lumber Company mill at St. Maries. From there, the Milwaukee laid rail fifty miles to Purdue, Idaho.[50]

Distress in the lumber business struck Herrick as opportunity. Although he was said to hold $2 million worth of unsold lumber in his yards, he bought troubled companies: Grant Brothers at Harrison, which he renamed the Export Lumber Company and equipped with machinery from a failed Michigan mill to specialize in mining timbers; in 1919, the Coeur d'Alene mill from the estate of Patrick Largey, Butte; and in 1923, the St. Maries Lumber Company and its stumpage from William Kroll. Herrick's buys cost millions: Largey cost him $1.5 million; Kroll, $1.8 million. For a 54,000-acre timber tract in the St. Joe district, Herrick paid $600,000—twice the Rutledge bid. As he expanded, Herrick's finances tangled; he owed two dozen or more loans to banks at any one time and stretched large lines of credit at his suppliers. A banker characterized Herrick as a "very eccentric, shrewd operator," with a reputation "for drawing checks without funds in the bank." His lumberjacks cheerfully held their paychecks, it was said, until Herrick dealt for money to cover them.[51]

Herrick's town, St. Maries, ignited—figuratively—as a flashpoint in the lumber companies' strife with the Industrial Workers of the World. The Wobblies opened an office there but stopped selling union pamphlets when county prosecutors, trying Wobblies as criminal syndicalists, used the publications as inflammatory evidence. (Ironically, the state supreme court ruled in 1924 that the Wobblies' publicized "sabotage" was not property destruction within the meaning of Idaho's syndicalism act. The IWW definition was striking on the job, lagging at work, a tactic apparently fostered by the union's attorney, George Vanderveer.)[52]

For all its posturing, the IWW proved inept in organizing Inland Empire lumber workers, and the resistance of managers, aided by state and federal governments, was callous. The lumber companies deliberately branded the Wobblies as violent to play on the patriotic fervor of World War I and to impel state and federal suppression of the union. F. A. Silcox, then regional forester (later, chief U.S. forester), lamented that "even the best men in the [lumber] industry . . . lacked the social imagination" to see the workers' side. It suited employers to blame their troubles on union agitation rather than improve conditions in logging camps. When they could not get soldiers to help them, loyal citizens often drove suspected Wobblies out of their towns. The union opposed the war, and the federal government therefore branded the IWW as an enemy. So did the governors of Northwest states. The union saw the war as a time to win its demands, but lies, patriotic opposition, and bad timing cost the union its vigor.[53]

Organization of the Loyal Legion of Loggers and Lumbermen, the 4-L, as a union of patriotic men, introduced the eight-hour workday into the Northwest lumber industry. And the Loyal Legion, regarded as a tool of the industry, demanded clean camps. With the end of World War I, the Loyal Legion faded; it was gone except as a social society from the Inland Empire by 1924. So was the strength of the Wobblies. When the IWW called a strike in 1919, only 250 men walked out of Coeur d'Alene mills, and when managers, refusing to negotiate, announced a wage increase of 2.5 cents an hour, the strike broke. Many of the strikers were already back at work or battling Idaho's worst forest fires since 1910.[54]

Nevertheless, the union's alarms produced two lasting effects: the companies (under the eyes of state health officers) cleaned up their camps, and, having gotten together to throttle the union, the companies continued to cooperate—to fight fires, handle log drives, stamp out tree insects, and promote western lumber sales. Possibly union complaints also hastened contract logging. By contracting with smaller companies, big ones could shift employee protests in the woods to their contractors.

Forest fires, caused by lightning, railroad sparks, or careless men, united the lumber industry as no other hazard. A number of fire-prevention associations had formed in the Inland Empire—the Potlatch, Coeur d'Alene, Pend Oreille, Priest Lake, and North Idaho forest protective associations, among them—before a Spokane meeting in January 1909 of fourteen lumbermen and federal foresters to organize against fire. Urged by Weyerhaeuser's George S. Long, they formed the Pacific Northwest Forest Conservation and Protective Association, which soon took in other members and changed its name to the Western Forestry and Conservation Association. They pooled funds, set out forest patrols to report and fight fires, and lobbied for state and federal fire protection.[55]

The Weyerhaeuser role evoked some public resentment of the association's calls for state and federal assistance. A number of people felt that if Weyerhaeuser wanted its forests protected, it had money enough to hire patrolmen. But the Forest Service and timber owners worked together, without spending much money. (One Forest Service effort was to expand forest roads and trails to reach fires: in 1910 there had been only twenty-nine miles of Forest Service roads in the Northwest; by 1930 there were more than three thousand miles.) In the years immediately after the war, the eastern Washington protective associations spent perhaps $40,000 annually among them for fire patrols and prevention work.[56] In 1924, however, Congress passed the Forest Protection Bill sponsored by Senator Charles McNary of Oregon and Representative John D. Clarke of New York, allocating funds to states and creating a conservation partnership among the federal service, the states, and private timber owners. The Washington state forester reported a "material decrease in fire loss" in the first four years of mutual efforts. The basic prevention program called for slash disposal, forest patrols, devices to prevent engine sparks, and publicity aimed at careless smokers and campers.[57]

Lumbermen cooperated in other ways. Those of the Coeur d'Alene region formed a log owners association in 1919 to operate a sorting boom on the St. Joe River, an arrangement typical of many districts. And northern Idaho used fire protective associations, beginning in 1923, to tear out currant and gooseberry bushes that hosted the destructive blister rust (a parasite fungus) browning Idaho pine. The least durable associations were those to sell lumber. The Western Pine Association, modeled on similar midwestern agencies, set industry standards for lumber that were widely adopted, but its efforts to promote sales were only moderately successful. Over the first three decades of lumber exporting from the inland Northwest, marketing associations formed and broke up—agencies like the Inland Empire Lumber Manufacturers, Western Pine Shippers, Lumber Manufacturers Agency, Idaho White Pine Bureau, and others, fragile, short-lived compacts to publicize and sell the region's lumber.[58]

The Federal Trade Commission charged that lumber producers of Idaho, western Montana, and eastern Oregon, through their Western Pine Manufacturers Association, drove prices upward "by concerted action."[59]

Spokane's postwar role in the lumber industry was not manufacturing but banking, sales offices, and meeting place. Wholesaling and match blocks accounted for the city's largest revenue from lumber. Almost one-fourth of the wood sold was match blocks for perhaps forty years. Lumbermen convened at the Spokane Club and made the Davenport Hotel a lumberman's headquarters, as mining men made the Spokane Hotel theirs. The Spokane chapter of the international fraternal order of the lumber industry, the Hoo Hoo, formed at the Davenport in 1921.[60]

Wholesalers opened offices in the city. Weyerhaeuser rented the entire tenth floor of the Old National Bank Building. But Weyerhaeuser's sales from Inland Empire affiliates did not go well. Potlatch lumber—badly cut—was hard to sell. Neither Deary, who died in 1913, nor his successor, A. W. Laird, was a lumberman; Deary had been a logger, Laird a financier. Independent wholesalers also clustered in Spokane, men like E. F. Wales, who in 1921 formed a company that would last more than sixty years, passing to a third generation.[61]

Spokane was also where most lumber company owners chose to live. Blackwell had stayed in Coeur d'Alene, but Thomas Humbird, Herrick, McGoldrick, George F. Jewett, James Brown, and others owned Spokane homes. Humbird built a handsome house at the head of Lincoln Street, overlooking the city (but in the thirties, when D. W. Twohy divided his home into apartments, Humbird took the lower floor). Jewett bought on Sumner, on basalt cliffs looking down into the city center. McGoldrick and Brown chose to live on fashionable Rockwood Boulevard, where the plat had been designed by the Olmsted Brothers, the Massachusetts landscape architects. (Brown in 1928 acquired the granite and frame house of Frank C. Walker, who moved to New York, and later to Washington, D.C., as Franklin Roosevelt's postmaster general.) Compared with these, the Herrick house on Shoshone was modest, on a winding street of attractive residences.

For a decade after the war, Washington led the nation in lumber production. More than 90 percent of the state's lumber exports originated west of the Cascades. The Inland Empire was small in comparison, but within the Spokane trade zone, lumber was a leading industry. Westside companies more and more relied on ocean routes through the Panama Canal to lay down lumber at Atlantic ports at freight costs far below those of railroads. The cost of delivering Inland Empire lumber by rail was higher than that of western Washington lumber by ocean vessel, and by one estimate, the cost of producing one thousand board feet was $2.50 higher in the Inland Empire than on the coast. To ship a thousand feet of lumber to an eastern city was $4.46 more from the Inland Empire by rail than by vessel from a seaport. (By another estimate, sea delivery was $15 a thousand cheaper.) By 1928 the Panama Canal was handling 20 percent of the lumber marketed in the United States, not quite half the production of northwestern states.[62]

Southern pine producers, midwestern wood-products manufacturers (some using lumber from the Inland Empire), and western Washington lumber interests combined to restrict the market for standard dimensions from the Inland Empire. (Weyerhaeuser's westside mills, in this instance, competed with the company's affiliated inland mills.)

And the center of interior lumber manufacturing shifted southward toward Klamath Falls in southern Oregon, the location of two-thirds of Oregon's private timber east of the Cascades. Even as Spokane area lumber companies increased their production each year, save 1921, Spokane lumber workers drifted into Oregon to find jobs.[63]

Inland Empire companies tried to compete by sending more salesmen oftener into their best selling areas—salesmen, good talkers, who traditionally rode like princes in lumber-train cabooses. And to recapture customers who defected to Oregon mills, the Inland Empire produced lower grades and thinner boards, lighter and cheaper. Some kinds of lumber that could not have been sold a decade earlier now found buyers looking for bargains: hemlock, for one, used for light construction, flooring, and siding; larch, for another, substituted for fir in house building. Spokane's mills also competed by specializing; several manufactured stock frames and sash, and for a time Spokane and Missoula produced about 15 percent of the stock sash sold in the United States.[64]

Large new consumers of white-pine stumpage came into the Inland Empire—the match companies. In the first twenty months after the war, the Diamond and Ohio match companies spent $2.5 million for north Idaho timber, built forest camps and mills, and started making the two-inch blocks for wooden matches, consuming perhaps 75 million board feet of pine a year. Diamond cut mainly in the Priest River district; Ohio, on the north fork of the Coeur d'Alene River, where, during gold rushes less than forty years earlier, prospectors had described forests so thick they had turned sideways to squeeze between trees. For a decade, four match-block companies—Federal, Powell, Ohio, and Diamond—operated near Spokane. If the city could no longer pretend to be a milling center, it could honestly claim the unglamorous title of "match block capital."[65]

But the lumber market continued to dismay. Too much wood. Low prices. Heavy inventories. Rising stumpage costs. Howard Elliott, president of the Northern Pacific, told his people, "The demand for good timber is so great that we do not want to be too 'squeamish' about crowding our prices up." Processing cost more: since the turn of the century, inland mills had air-dried lumber in yards. By the end of the twenties, they were installing kilns. (Western Washington usually shipped green lumber.) Finding lumber surpluses, dealers reduced their inventories, shifting the costs of storage from themselves to the mills. Independent wholesalers might stock no lumber now, but fill orders by telephoning mills or prowling their yards.[66]

Man-made materials reduced the national demand for lumber.

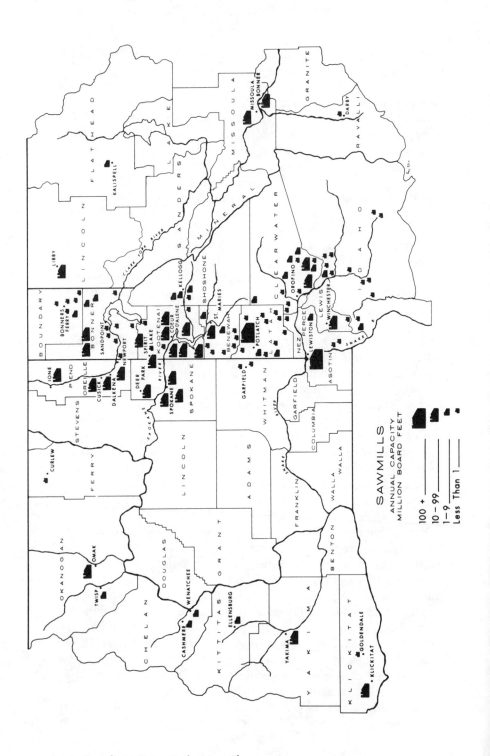

SAWMILLS

ANNUAL CAPACITY
MILLION BOARD FEET

100 +
10 – 99
1 – 9
Less Than 1

Northwest mills experimented with new products: plywood, particleboard, and other building materials made from waste. Between 1920 and 1930, the lumber used for an average house dropped from 18,900 to 15,400 board feet and continued to decline. If any industry governed the lumber trade, it was housing, and in the twenties, housing construction rode a roller coaster. Seattle set new home-building records each year from 1920 to 1927; Portland faltered. The Washington Mutual Savings Bank of Seattle, a prominent mortgage lender, felt obliged in 1926 to publish a survey of Seattle vacancies to dispel a Portland report that Northwest cities had overbuilt. Spokane had overbuilt in 1910; it was relatively stable, building replacement housing and a few new ones; its savings and loan associations extended their lending territories for mortgage contracts, selling even in coastal cities. And building costs in the United States pushed steadily upward. By 1927 the cost of a house was nearly double that of 1913.[67]

In such uncertain times, lumber companies should have pulled back, but they were goaded to cut by indebtedness, competition, time limits on stumpage rights, and the state tax systems. Both Washington and Idaho, relying on property taxes, regarded lumber companies, with railroads and mining companies, as likely targets for tax revenues, because they looked prosperous. Lumbermen continually protested that tax rules prevented orderly cutting, and a 1910 forestry commission appointed by Washington Governor Hay recommended a tax on standing timber at wildland values with a yield tax when cut, but the legislature refused to submit this plan to voters as a constitutional amendment. Timber owners continued to pay annual taxes on generous county assessments of the value of their standing trees.[68]

Faced with their own rising costs, county governments declined appeals for lower taxes on trees. In some eastern Washington counties, railroads squeezed county governments by withholding tax payments until contested assessments were decided by the courts. In nine timbered eastern Washington counties, lumbermen cut as fast as they could; they reduced the private acreage assessed as timberland 22 percent between 1909 and 1919, and in Lincoln County sawed all the private assessable timber. (In two counties, Chelan and Kittitas, siz-

Sawmills in the Inland Empire in 1930, indicating the location of merchantable timber and transportation lines. The two largest, at Potlatch and Lewiston, belonged to Weyerhaeuser company subsidiaries. (Based on Hutchison and Winters, *Northern Idaho Forest Resources and Industries*, p. 24, and annual mill production data from *Timberman*. Drawn by Ray Ellis, Eastern Washington University cartographic laboratory.)

able areas were not then on tax rolls, and by 1930 the timbered areas in these two still made only a small part of the assessment total.)[69]

At the turn of the century, average taxes on timbered land had amounted to perhaps 15 cents an acre. By 1922 the average had reached $2.60, as the assessed valuation on Washington timberlands rose steadily, from about $4.88 an acre in 1905 to $13.35 by 1912 and $21.19 by 1920, when lumber companies cried that 12 percent of the state's real estate tax revenues fell on them. "The whole effect," fretted a university professor who knew the system, "is to hurry the cutting of our forests and prevent any private owner from reforesting cut-over lands." The lumberman's only practical relief from high taxes seemed to be to cut his timber. Washington's voters in 1925 defeated changes in tax laws that would have helped lumber companies, although that was not the cause of the defeat, but in 1930, almost too late, approved classifying property for tax purposes, affording some relief.[70]

Assessors in northern Idaho counties often were torn between lumber and mining companies. Only 4.9 million of 12.5 million acres in northern Idaho were subject to taxes, forcing counties to gouge whom they could. Rutledge, McGoldrick, and others protested Shoshone County valuations of $292,000 on their timber, charging in a petition to commissioners that mining companies escaped proportionate taxes. The formation of new counties in northern Idaho (Bonner in 1907, Benewah and Boundary in 1915) afforded lumber companies new opportunities to woo assessors. The Humbird company had filed a series of suits challenging assessed valuations by Kootenai County before Bonner was split off, and the assessed value of timber was an issue in fiscal transfers when part of Shoshone was annexed by Nez Perce County. Like Washington, Idaho waited until 1930 to change its tax laws to permit owners to designate "reforestation land" and defer yield taxes. By then, the lumber industry of the Inland Empire was near panic.[71]

In the ten years after the war, lumber companies continued to close—those "inadequately financed" companies cited by the Washington Planning Council in a study of the industry, the companies hobbled by "interest rates too high for long-term financing" and a tax system that penalized the lumber operators. A new round of mergers ensued and mills closed at Sandpoint, Bonners Ferry, Spirit Lake, Ione, and Elk. The Menasha owners of Blackwell Lumber rode out the worst of the thirties before selling to Rutledge. One by one, old companies dropped like autumn leaves.[72]

Many surviving companies turned to selective cutting. Herrick's manager, James W. Girard, declared that "it does not pay to cut the ten and twelve-inch trees. . . . Size of timber affects the cost of operation more than any one factor." And he growled, "If forest propaganda would produce trees, this country would be very thickly populated with all of the valuable species. It is easier to talk of forestry than to practice it and in some cases more practical."[73] Girard was doubtless sniping at Weyerhaeuser's publicized early efforts at reforestation, for Herrick regarded the syndicate's companies as rivals.

The Inland Empire cut the largest stock of timber in its history in 1925—1,731,000,000 board feet, most in Idaho, nearly all from private lands. The companies thought that business was getting better. And for many merchants in the Inland Empire, 1925 was a good year. The nation's stock exchanges watched rising quotations. But a perceptible slowdown had already begun. Looking back, businessmen would realize that Washington State's industrial growth lost speed about 1923, and at the same time Oregon's lumber production was rising as Washington's declined, a trend that would hold through the thirties.[74] An alfalfa business was starting on the cutover lands of Boundary, Bonner, Kootenai, and Benewah counties. This was a barometer of the lumber business, in a way, for the more alfalfa land, the less remaining stumpage.

The Weyerhaeusers chose these years to start cutting 200,000 acres of untouched timber in the Clearwater district of northern Idaho, opening a mill on the former county fairgrounds at Lewiston in 1927 and damming the Clearwater River for a 320-acre millpond. The Lewiston mill once more moved the fulcrum of Idaho lumbering southward.

About the time the Lewiston mill opened, Frederick "Fritz" Jewett, who had succeeded Huntington Taylor at Rutledge, finished a review of Weyerhaeuser's inland operations; he concluded that none of the inland companies was secure and recommended their consolidation. F. K. Weyerhaeuser concurred. The company, he said, must "put its house in order" in a "weakened, discouraged" industry. Consequently in 1931 three companies—Clearwater, Rutledge, and Potlatch— merged as Potlatch Forests, Inc. Humbird, nearing the end of its cutting and anticipating profits, was not included.[75]

While the corporate Weyerhaeuser prudently put its house in order, the loner Fred Herrick stretched his empire. Herrick's various companies did not formally trade funds, services, or goods, but he clearly regarded them as one, using the assets of one operation as collateral to finance another, and in 1927 he formed a joint sales agency. The companies' accounts did not accurately reflect dealings among Herrick properties, however, and tended to inflate depreciation and assets. Early in 1923 Herrick had bid approximately $2.2 million to obtain cutting rights to 67,400 acres of pine in Bear Valley, Oregon, the Malheur National Forest, and, expecting a fifty-year harvest, contracted with the Forest Service to lay a railroad from Crane to Burns (connecting with the Oregon Short Line of the Union Pacific) and sixty miles of logging railroad to a mill he would erect at Burns. "One of the finest large compact bodies of yellow-pine timber in the West," the Forest Service's bid prospectus called the stand, estimating a yield of 890 million board feet.[76]

Herrick's finances were shaky before his Oregon venture; he borrowed heavily from midwestern bankers and from the Exchange National Bank, Spokane, which sold his notes to thirteen or more affiliated banks, most of them small. Early in the twenties, Everett E. Flood, Exchange vice-president, had committed the bank to refinancing commercial loans secured by Herrick's personal notes. At that time, the deal seemed a fine stroke of business. But as creditors pressed Herrick, he deftly evaded them. Sometimes no one could find him. At one point, Herrick considered raising new money with a gold bond issue secured simply by his name—Fred Herrick bonds; another time, he proposed a pay-as-you-go contract to cut timber owned by the Milwaukee Land Company, a railroad subsidiary. Knowing that most of his freight went by Northern Pacific, the Milwaukee turned him down. As his schemes deflated and debts mounted, Herrick named Flood his sole financial representative. Flood tried to placate creditors—now exceedingly waspish—and raise money, finding prospective lenders wary.

To Flood, success in Oregon seemed to be Herrick's one chance to shore up his tottering finances. Flood apparently never got a complete accounting from Herrick, but an accounting firm audit showed that only Herrick's St. Maries mill and Export Lumber Company could hope for dividends; the unfunded debts of others, equal to their assets, had to be paid from operations. If Herrick's creditors forced payment, the audit said, he would be bankrupt. Realizing that he must save Herrick to save the bank, Flood took the title of treasurer in the Oregon company.[77]

But the lumber market was slipping away; railroad contractors fell behind schedule; Herrick did not start cutting on time. After acrimonious exchanges, the Forest Service withdrew from the Oregon contract, and the U.S. Senate investigated, among its witnesses William B. Greeley, chief of the Forest Service, who (although he had badgered

Herrick) urged that the government give Herrick more time. But Oregon legislators blocked an extension. Herrick sold his unfinished railroad to the Union Pacific, and the Forest Service rebid the Bear Valley timber, awarding it to the Edward Hines Associated Lumber Interests, a Chicago company owned 30 percent by Weyerhaeuser.[78]

Herrick could not hold on. As claims against him soared past $2 million, he declared bankruptcy, assigning everything but his home, his automobile, and $5,000. Flood was in Chicago negotiating with a large Herrick creditor, the Continental National Bank and Trust, one of thirty-three banks holding Herrick notes; he would return to face charges of embezzlement at his bank, eventually to be acquitted. On October 16, 1928, a somber band of Herrick's creditors convened in the Old National Bank's assembly room to liquidate his property. They counted more than one hundred claims amounting to $4.4 million, respectfully aware that the seventy-four-year-old man whose empire they dismembered owned fifteen companies and was reputed to be the second largest owner of white pine stumpage in the world. Less than three months later, the Exchange Bank failed, carrying down three others—destroyed, an editor thought, by Herrick's failure and Flood's "bad management." The bank's stockholders had refused appeals to contribute fifty dollars a share to save it.[79]

Herrick's creditors could not realize that their melancholy task marked the end of an era, that in the next five years dozens of other meetings like theirs would sift the debris of stricken lumber companies. Herrick fell at a time that Washington's public lands commissioner called "the worst that I have known in my 18 years" as commissioner. (The commissioner himself was soon denying allegations of fraud in the sale of tide and shore lands.) Herrick's collapse was generally regarded as unlucky timing, a gamble confounded by a falling lumber market, and perhaps political intrigue. On this basis, both Congress and the Oregon legislature voted him pensions. The years 1924 through 1926 had been especially damaging to the lumber industry, a trade magazine declared, and 1930 seemed worse. By 1931 the value of stumpage would fall 80 percent, and in another year the average lumber prices at Northwest mills would tumble to their lowest since 1904, with the fewest mills running since the nineties. Herrick's fall was not so much the collapse of one man as the disintegration of an industry. Few would survive.[80]

Elemental Spokane

Aubrey Lee White returned to Spokane late in 1905 after nearly ten years in New York City, where he had sold stock in Jay P. Graves's Granby Mining and Smelting Company and then bonds for the construction of Graves's Spokane and Inland Empire Railway, of which White was now a vice-president. White discovered that the pandemic national fever for city beautification had infected Spokane, and the city roiled with immigrants pouring, hundreds a day, off immigrant railroad trains. An uproar of real estate speculation thrust plats east, north, and south. People bought land they had never seen so they would not miss out.

A dandified, persuasive man, White had served on one of New York's beautification committees, where he had been dismayed by the prices New York paid for parkland it could have bought cheaply earlier. Now he saw Spokane, his adopted city (he had come at age twenty in 1889 following his brothers from Maine) drifting into New York's dilemma, and he went about demanding that Spokane preserve its scenic vistas and land for parks and playgrounds before real estate promoters overran them. Naturally enough, promoters became his strong allies, because buyers' anticipation of a neighborhood park helped sell houses and lots. Another way to sell homes was to provide a streetcar line. Land promoters built six, radiating from downtown. Spokane's outlying residential districts grew up alongside these routes, and the Washington Water Power gradually bought up and merged the streetcar companies.[1]

A young newspaperman, Joseph Smith, who in 1894 thought that a fierce competitive spirit afforded Spokane a metropolitan air, visited the city again shortly after White came back. "Elemental Spokane," Smith wrote in a notebook, "the conservativism of the WWP Co— daring of Graves—low light rate—high house rate . . . the Bohemian spirit—the social life . . . the spirit of civic pride in the federated [men's] clubs . . . the city beautiful—lawns and shade trees and flowers."[2]

A decade after the panic of 1893, elemental Spokane danced with euphoric boosterism. Businessmen thought they could spoon-feed expansion by advertising. A publicity bureau, opened in 1902, had been succeeded by the 150,000 Club in 1905, which aimed to ballyhoo Spokane into a population of 150,000 within ten years. (It failed.) And the club was replaced by the Greater Spokane Committee in 1911, and it by another, and that one by still another, and so on.[3]

Boosters had puffed Spokane since its beginning, to be sure, when James N. Glover sold half of his twenty-two-block townsite to John J. Browne and Anthony M. Cannon, and the three, constituting themselves a townsite company, met trains to collar promising settlers. Boosterism in Spokane has not stilled since. Spokane Falls was incorporated November 29, 1881, a village of seven hundred souls with its plunging waterfall and the Northern Pacific main line. When the first railroad train arrived earlier that year, the official party aboard barely glanced at the huts and false-fronted buildings, but one sniffed that Spokane needed paint.

But in the eyes of Glover, Browne, and Cannon the clapboard town was going to be a great city, because they were going to make it one. Glover had come from Oregon in 1873; Cannon and Browne, five years later. Enchanted by the falls, Glover stared through a sleepless night at the tumbling water and then bought out the homesteaders on the ground. He visualized business houses rising on a "sea of gold," the sun-flowered flat south of the river. And there, in the same two dozen blocks where it started, Spokane's central business district has played its drama of fire, rebirth, and growth.

Nearly all the businesses burned on August 4, 1889, but within a few days Spokane's merchants resolved to build a new city. They overbuilt in high-spending competition, ornate, fire-resistant structures of brick and granite along Riverside Avenue. Oddly enough, although steel framing had been used elsewhere since 1871, not one of Spokane's new buildings used it. Nearly all the builders went heavily into debt. Earlier Spokane had lacked outside capital, but now the Northwestern and Pacific Hypotheekbank, a Dutch-owned mortgage company, lent generously. An imposing city rose. After miles of unpainted, dusty hamlets, railroad travelers came upon Spokane, new six- and seven-story buildings lofting majestically above the rushing river. They were awed as if they had happened upon an oasis of formal gardens in a desert. A Dutch lender wrote home, "I have never seen a small town . . . which offers such an overwhelming impression of monumental buildings. . . . Its people were too extravagant during its early development and many over-reached themselves to force its development."[4] Overbuilt perhaps, but the grandeur of rebuilt Spokane, with its railroad connections, quieted speculation about which city was to be the great one of eastern Washington.

The *Review*'s Oregon owners meant their Renaissance building, seven brick stories with pointed tower, to be the most conspicuous. Cannon and Browne built a grandiose office building and theater, the Auditorium, with their portraits in stained glass, Turkish rugs, and a stage one foot wider and deeper than any in America. At the Auditorium's turreted pinnacle, the gilded goddess Thalia saluted the reconstructed city.

After these classical wonders, visitors might retreat to the Coeur d'Alene variety theater run by Harry Baer and Dutch Jake Goetz, rich from grubstaking prospectors. Roundheaded, mustached Dutch Jake, seeing a man gamble away all his money, would slip him one hundred dollars and courteously tell him to go home. Dozens of lesser saloons lined the streets. In 1888 when the territorial legislature enacted woman suffrage, men feared women would vote for prohibition. A barkeep, Edward M. Bloomer, sent his wife to the polls as a test. She was turned away. The state supreme court upheld her exclusion, and women would not vote again in Washington's general elections until 1910.[5]

Even as Spokane rebuilt from its fire, the nation's economy stuttered. In 1893 a crushing depression fell across the United States, and in the Palouse unseasonal steady rains destroyed crops. Faced with impending bankruptcy in The Netherlands, the Hypotheekbank aggressively foreclosed its mortgages on Spokane's fine buildings. Cannon, Glover, and dozens of other men were ruined. By 1896, when Spokane's assessed valuation stood at $15 million, the Dutch owned $4.7 million in property, generally the best commercial ground. As soon as the panic started to break, the Dutch began selling—only four important buildings had escaped foreclosure—and new owners bought the structures. They were a new generation of influential men for Spokane, men like D. C. Corbin, rich from building feeder railroads; F. Lewis Clark and Charles Sweeny, who made a killing in mining stocks; Patrick Welch, railroad contractor; Aaron Kuhn, Palouse merchant and moneylender turned banker; David T. Ham (with King George V beard and bow tie), real estate investor and political machinist; James L. Comstock and Robert B. Paterson, merchants, whose principal object was to acquire a central site for their store; William H. Cowles, newspaper publisher, who confided to an associate that real estate was the only investment he could make without arousing suspicion that his papers promoted businesses he owned; and others.

If powerful men ran Spokane, they were the men with capital who could afford to buy land after the panic. Coming home to boosting, growing Spokane, Aubrey White, with perhaps half a million dollars of his own, enlisted these men in his campaign to make Spokane a beautiful city with a park no more than fifteen minutes' walk from any residence. Foremost among his allies was a friend from bachelor days, Cowles.

Cowles had come to Spokane at twenty-four in 1891, with an inheritance from his father's estate, to be business manager of the *Spokesman,* and gradually bought his partners' stock to keep the newspaper from failing; he purchased the rival *Review* and merged the two into a morning daily, the *Spokesman-Review,* in 1894. Three years later the *Chronicle's* owners offered him their evening paper and he bought it, combining the mechanical departments but keeping separate editorial staffs for his two papers. Educated at Yale, brought up in a newspaper family—his late father had been a stockholder and business manager of the *Chicago Tribune*—Cowles emerged from the panic of 1893 as publisher of the chief purveyors of Spokane's intellectual and political life, the newspapers. He also bought a good deal of property for future development. Politicians sought his endorsement, businessmen his blessing, and publicists his cooperation.[6]

Cowles's newspapers boosted Spokane as enthusiastically as its chamber of commerce (which Cowles helped found). With A. L. White urging Spokane to wake up and buy parklands before speculators and developers gobbled them, the *Spokesman-Review* boosted parks, too, supporting a successful 1907 campaign by the civic beautification committee of the 150,000 Club to vote in a nonpolitical board of park commissioners. White, appointed to the park board, was elected president at its first meeting and he speedily hired the noted Massachusetts landscape architects, the Olmsted Brothers, to plan a park system for the city (at a fee of $1,000 and $300 expenses). He also persuaded the city council to buy and plant 80,000 street trees in 1908.[7]

White relied on his important friends both to donate and to solicit others to give land for parks. By 1914, his park board had amassed two-thirds of the ground Spokane needed for parks up to 1960, nearly all of the land staked out by the Olmsteds. White's coterie regularly included Cowles; Louis M. Davenport, the soft-spoken restaurant owner who in 1914 opened his notable hotel; John A. Finch; and Robert Lewis Rutter, president of the Spokane and Eastern Trust Company. Cowles and Finch both gave extensively to the park system; both men, with the merchant, Paterson, were trustees of the Davenport Hotel Company.[8]

Spokane citizens who whispered that a clique manipulated the affairs of the city could hardly have named a more likely ruling cluster. White openly called them his "powerhouse," men of consequence who influenced others. Socially they were disparate: Cowles valued privacy, propriety, and breeding; Davenport's origins were ordinary and his instincts those of a showman; Finch, married against his associates' advice to an impetuous, poor, beautiful young wife, regarded his wealth as a public trust (and perhaps mistrusted his future widow's stewardship); Rutter, a Philadelphian, self-made, relished the perquisites of authority.

With White and others, they shared a conviction that they could control their economic and physical environment and, to a lesser degree, their social and natural environment. They believed they could make Spokane the kind of city they chose. Their public lives demonstrated their certitude that they shaped the city, and the Spokane they wanted was prosperous and pleasant—the right kind of people, selected merchants and factories, quiet, green neighborhoods, and an unobtrusive municipal government with low taxes, adequate services, and no monkey business. If their progress toward this consensus ideal sometimes seemed heavy-handed and self-seeking (as it occasionally was), their outlook was benevolent, and, because elemental Spokane was not complex, they achieved much of what they intended.[9]

And residents of Spokane evidently concurred in the conceits of their weightiest men. People who thrived on frolic, nightlife, and artistic inspiration found Spokane dull. Except for a handful who tried to impose their own standards, they generally moved away. Quite possibly Spokane's straitlaced and rather proper prejudices, evident by World War I, were partly a reaction to its rowdy heritage—Dutch Jake, Wobblies storming the city council for the right to speak on the streets, itinerant railroad construction gangs, and lumberjacks, miners, and farmhands seeking an off-season haven. If some of Spokane's new millionaires acquired airs when they shed their seedier days, so did the city. Such archetypal new rich as L. W. Hutton and August Paulsen, who (with partners) had struck a rich mine, invested in real estate and lent their names to benevolent causes, because they regarded these as proper pursuits for wealthy men.

Of course, there was an obverse to the coin of managed progress. The men who fashioned Spokane would not hesitate, working through such agencies as the chamber of commerce and the Washington Water Power Company, to discourage commercial or industrial expansion of the wrong kind—one, for instance, that would import workers undesirable as permanent residents.[10]

Influence varied according to the occasion, naturally, and another power group centered on the city's bankers, among whom Daniel Twohy was preeminent. Before Rutter, J. P. M. Richards ran the Spokane and Eastern Trust while his brother, Henry, served as president of Washington Water Power from 1895 until 1910. Department store owners made up an emerging circle of consequence: Paterson, Comstock, and James L. Paine (whose daughter would marry W. H. Cowles, Jr.) of the Crescent and Spokane Dry Goods companies, Frank Culbertson, and a few others.

Each of these groups tended to communicate horizontally among its members of similar rank and vertically from owner to employees and agents. Other than in their clubs, churches, and social events, the highest levels of one hierarchy did not seem to confer regularly with those of another. At social meetings, where delicate issues could not be debated openly, a raised eyebrow, tone of voice, or nod might pass for agreement. If the event were auspicious (and neutral) enough, however, the groups might get together, as they did for the 1911 Apple Show subscription dinner attended by Twohy, H. M. Richards, Corbin, Comstock, Finch, Cowles, Rutter, and other important men.[11]

Two classes of message bearers—attorneys and real estate men—linked the spheres of power. The law partnership of William J. C. Wakefield and Archibald W. Witherspoon, formed in 1905, served as informal mediator. The discreet Wakefield was a member of the park board, Finch's attorney and next-door neighbor, Davenport hotel trustee, and a director of Twohy's Union Trust Company. The magesterial Witherspoon was Cowles's attorney and director of dozens of companies (he once claimed to be on seventy-five boards). He was a man who savored his connections—bragged of them.

Among real estate men, Arthur D. Jones (like Cowles, he had worked briefly as a Chicago newspaper reporter) stood first. Manager of Cowles's properties, astute, dependable, and close-mouthed, Jones joined Cowles and Finch in promoting the Cannon Hill Park residential district; he represented the Bostonian, Charles Francis Adams II, in Spokane; and participated in the Consolidated Improvement Company and Hillyard Townsite Company with F. Lewis Clark, a wellborn speculator and developer with central downtown properties. Clark's Maine parents gave Liberty Park to the city, and he might have been more commanding if he had been less cantankerous. His wife shooed away guests when she saw him coming home. On a January evening in 1914, Clark put his wife on a train at Santa Barbara, California, and disappeared, never to be seen again.

The city's powerful men ordinarily did not run for political office; they left that grubby task to others. Yet Ham served as county commissioner from 1919 to 1925, Coman (the banker) was a state senate power, and Comstock, Wakefield, and Culbertson lent their names to a ticket for city charter reform in 1910. Cowles's *Spokesman-Review* backed a rival slate that won, largely because newly franchised women voted for it. The charter provided a nonpartisan, five-member commission to govern the city, a municipal structure regarded by civic reformers nationally as modern and representative, a form that flowed from the same wellspring of reason and aesthetics as city beautification, parks, and, eventually, long-range city planning. For those who thought an elite ran Spokane, the charter election of 1910 offered a conundrum—one power group contending with another.

The momentum from its immigrant boom propelled Spokane for half a decade after the rush stalled in 1910. The second decade of the twentieth century began agreeably with 32,000 crowding on New Year's Eve to see the Old National Bank's fifteen-story, white terra cotta building, a tangible symbol of Spokane's progress. Eleven months later Spokane opened a new Monroe Street Bridge with the longest monolithic concrete span in America, 281 feet. (The council shortly after fired its designer, city engineer John C. Ralston, in a street-policy dispute.) Although immigration slowed, Spokane was busy catching up. Nearly every year before World War I at least one large new building went up: a new Spokane Club in 1912, a new city hall and union railroad depot in 1913, renovated Mohawk and Sherwood buildings in 1916 and 1917, and so on. And to pave its major streets, the city spent more than one million dollars in 1910 and again in 1911.

Two buildings tinctured Spokane's future. One, the Davenport Hotel, which opened unfinished on September 1, 1914, became more widely known than the city. With this Florentine structure, twelve stories and four hundred rooms, newspapers asserted that Spokane "underwent the transition from a big country town to a metropolis." The $3 million Davenport, financed largely with a loan from the Chicago, Milwaukee and St. Paul Railway and bonds and stocks peddled by Davenport and Finch, opened without a deficit only because Cowles personally solicited stockholders to assume pro rata shares of a $300,000 shortfall. The governor led a grand march while Blackfeet Indians danced ceremonially to dedicate the hotel—named for a man who had come to Spokane twenty-six years earlier with seventy-five cents.[12]

The other building, Culbertson's department store, split retail shopping from Spokane's financial-and-professional district in and near the Old National and Paulsen buildings. Businessmen felt for years that the city's business district would gravitate toward Washington and Riverside, the "million-dollar corner" with the highest traffic volume in Spokane. Paulsen built his building a block west, Hutton a block south, and the Old National, across Riverside from the Paulsen. Kemp and Hebert moved their department store a block north but bought the Temple Court at Riverside and Washington as a future location. Building managers commonly leased ground floors to banks and retail stores, second and third floors to business and professional men, and upper floors for apartments.[13]

Frank Culbertson wanted the site a block south of the million-dollar corner—across Washington from the Hutton—for his store, but the owners would not sell. Consequently he leased a building Patrick Welch erected for him at Main and Wall. Culbertson's move there in 1914, with the Crescent half a block away and the Palace department store a block away, pulled shopper traffic toward a retail district at Main's intersections with Post and Wall. (The separation was widened late in the twenties with construction of Sears, Roebuck and Montgomery Ward stores one block west and north of the Crescent, and the Paulsen medical and dental building at Washington and Riverside.)

The Davenport helped publicize Spokane—visitors praised its food and service, remembered its shiny washed coins and Moorish patio lobby—and the Old National mailed 10,000 postcards to national banks throughout the country. With unquenchable boosterism, Spokane staged a national country life convention in 1911; in 1914 the chamber of commerce surveyed rural districts for farmers willing to sell eighty acres to immigrants, hoping to revive settlement with promises of fertile land. Washington State joined Oregon and British Columbia in magazine advertisements to attract tourists.

Spokane had grown with a network of overhead wires for electricity, telephones, and trolley cars. Canopied automobiles snorted among the horses on its bricked streets. A gentleman motorist, perceiving a woman driver approaching at an intersection, stopped his vehicle and tipped his hat as the lady passed. Young swains squired their damsels to ice-cream parlors (the Astor, Antlers, or Palm) with latticed booths and ceiling fans, or to stage shows at the Auditorium, Shubert, or Spokane theaters, and if not there, to nickel movies flickering on a cloth screen. Respectable women donned hats and gloves—they "dressed"—to shop downtown. Milkmen, laundry men, and mailmen rode carts drawn by horses that knew the routes, too. The city had built twenty new schools before 1910 as its population swelled, where boys in knickers and girls in gingham marched to classes to the music of a phonograph. Life was unhurried, the faces downtown friendly and familiar.

Despite its placid comport, Spokane itched to grow. For some years the city hankered to become a cattle-trade center, catering mainly to farmers who raised and sold a few animals a year on their grain farms. Between 1914 and 1925 the chamber of commerce (managed in 1914 by Gordon C. Corbaley) orchestrated a campaign that would establish meat packing as Spokane's largest industry by 1925, making products valued at $7.7 million a year.[14]

In 1914 Walter D. Roberts, with generous loans from the Exchange National Bank, organized the Spokane Union Stockyards Company to build a stock-handling yard on twenty-one acres east of the city. A worldwide shortage of beef cattle was driving meat prices upward, and such cattlemen as Frank Rothrock, proprietor of the showplace Hercules farm near Sprague, foresaw no limits to expansion. The bank, of which Rothrock was a director, lent Roberts funds to double his yards in 1917 and joined the Old National, Spokane and Eastern Trust, and the Chicago packer, Armour and Company, in forming the Spokane Cattle Loan Company, an agency to lend breeders money to enlarge their herds. (Armour had stipulated the agency as a condition for opening its Northwest plant in Spokane.) The chamber of commerce convened a stockman's conference in 1917 to explain the profits likely in a rising beef market. Four months later, Armour bought the Spokane packing plant of E. H. Stanton. T. C. Carstens, a Coast packing company, soon came in. With large packers as customers and high beef prices, the Spokane Union Stockyards again doubled its yard size; it handled $10.5 million worth of cattle in 1919, an increase of $3 million over the previous year. But in 1920 the cattle market collapsed worldwide.[15]

Deliveries of cattle slowed as prices fell. The stockyards showed deficits, and the Exchange Bank learned from an auditor that the stockyards company was insolvent. Bank examiners warned the Exchange that its loans to the stockyards (and to Fred Herrick) were "excessive." Yet the bank stalled until 1926, when it foreclosed, finding office furniture gone and the yards deserted and awash in rubbish. The stockyards limped in receivership until 1930, when Rothrock, certain a well-managed yard could maintain Spokane's regional preeminence in packing, organized a new company, the Old Union Stockyards. By then, the Exchange had closed, its assets sold to the Old National.[16]

World War I enriched farmers and mining companies but drained Spokane. Thousands moved away to work in war plants, the cost of living shot upward 80 percent, and foodstuffs and materials usually distributed through city wholesalers were diverted to war use—slowing nonmilitary commerce.[17]

Women took jobs as stenographers and store clerks, posts then usually filled by men. "The demand for girls . . . is so great," sighed one employer, "that it has apparently gone to their heads, as they are asking much more money than ever before." Three Spokane women were appointed railway mail clerks. By 1920 more women than men lived in the city.[18]

War taught neighbors to mistrust one another. The Federal Reserve Bank of San Francisco warned members to keep "a close look-out for any suspicious account or transaction which might be interpreted as involving enemy funds or money used for enemy propaganda," and be secret about it. Patriotic committees (councils of defense) maintained card files of their neighbors' contributions to Liberty Bond and Red Cross drives, spied on those suspected of sympathy for the German side, and harassed "slackers," sometimes acting clandestinely, savagely. Schools dropped the German language. Rural patriots could be as ugly as urban. In a typical incident, a husband and wife sued Winona's United War Work Committee for slander and assault; they had declined to pay eight dollars assessed them for bonds, were forcibly hauled to a citizens' meeting for censure, and ostracized. The court awarded them one dollar. They closed their house and moved away.[19]

When the veterans came home, their insular innocence was gone. Family ties had loosened. Not many people came through the war without a taint of cynical acquisitiveness. Women did not readily give up the jobs they had taken. Nearly every school and business had at least one who "lost her man in the war" and now proposed a career rather than a family. The war wove the fabric of a generation's common experience and it lived in parades, political speeches, motion pictures, Gold Star Mothers, the American Legion, children's toys, and games. Even though Civil War Union veterans, white-haired, bent, with ribboned medals on old blue jackets, still paraded and visited schools on Memorial Day, to the people of the twenties, "the war" was the war just past. A. L. White chaired a civic committee to build an auditorium as a memorial to Spokane's war dead, but the fund campaign was dropped to avoid conflicting with city bond issues.

The 1920 census dismayed Spokane's boosters; it showed that since 1910, the city had gained a net thirty-five souls. Spokane seemed to be standing still. Spokane's boom years to 1910 had jingled with a carnival atmosphere; now the sober twenties rattled with organized schemes to sell Spokane to new industry, new immigrants, and tourists through agencies, chiefly the chamber of commerce and its committees, bureaus, and associations. Spokane continued to hope for large manufacturing payrolls. The chamber of commerce called Spokane the "city of sunshine and power," but electric energy had not yet become an overriding locational factor for manufacturers, and the city could not match the economies of scale offered by western cities with established industrial clusters.

The men who had captained Spokane after 1900 approached comfortable middle age, and some were gone: Finch fell dead at his Hayden Lake home in 1915, leaving a $3 million estate; Henry Richards died in an accident in 1913; Coman, the banker, moved to California in 1922. Jay P. Graves had been sapped by the 1909 wreck of his trains and market reversals. And Aubrey White had lost his tidy fortune; in 1921 he gave up his park board presidency, and three years later took a sinecure as garden editor of the *Spokesman-Review*. Moreover, the city had diversified. Perhaps by 1920 it was too complex to be shaped only by the consensus of wealthy men. Their style of leadership changed; now they worked through lieutenants and organizations.

But leading men continued to subscribe to managed progress, not only in Spokane but across the nation. Eastern and California cities had set up planning commissions before the war to centralize, by fiat, the commercial and aesthetic conduct of urban growth. Spokane established its planning commission in 1917 with a broad "power to investigate and make recommendations to the city council in respect to all matters pertaining to living conditions in the city." For its first years, the commission was largely an adjunct of the park system, but as planning evolved away from its reformist roots and toward professionalism, and with the appointment of Benjamin H. Kizer, the attorney, as commission chairman in 1928, and Harry F. Aumack as planner in 1929, the commission took on tasks once performed by consensus and opinion: it separated commercial from residential districts, preserved aesthetic sites, regulated building heights, and even carried out such mechanical tasks as ensuring that continuing streets in separate plats bore the same name. Kizer voiced the conventional view: the commission offered "a flexible, orderly program for the development of Spokane."[20]

The city's businessmen now financed a phalanx of publicists, foremost among them James A. Ford, a former newspaperman (and one-time secretary to Senator Miles A. Poindexter), who stepped in as managing secretary of the chamber of commerce in 1917. Ford brewed much of Spokane's growth strategy for the next three decades, including its promotion of the Columbia Basin irrigation project, and created a metropolitan midway: an annual Sportsmen's and Tourists' show set in a man-made forest and twenty-foot waterfall under the Union Pacific's black steel viaduct; acquisition of Spokane's own mountain, Mount Carleton ("Old Baldy"), ceremoniously renamed Mount Spokane and in 1927 designated a state park; an annual Indian Congress in 1925 and 1926, when tribes pitched tepees in the Riverside Avenue parkway (which closed when Indian leaders declared their people demeaned by dressing as natives to entertain gawkers); automobile and home-industry shows, a certified seed-potato growers' association, and so on.[21]

In 1923 the railroads, the Great Northern, Northern Pacific, and Burlington, mounted a three-year $1,240,000 advertising campaign in national mass magazines (*National Geographic, Literary Digest, American,* and others) to entice industry, immigrants, and tourists to the Pacific Northwest. To continue the campaign, Spokane in 1926 launched its own magazine ads, joining Los Angeles, San Diego, San Francisco, Oakland, Portland, Tacoma, and Seattle in trading advertising space. Spokane's ads puffed "the city alluring" with "intriguing motor roads" to seventy-six lakes and "majestic Long Lake dam with a fall higher than Niagara."[22]

Saying that businessmen solicited him, Louis A. von Wasmer (who soon dropped the "von") packed Seattle radio station KHQ into his car to move it to two draped studio rooms in the Davenport Hotel. He went on the air on October 30, 1925, as Seattle stations, telling their listeners to tune in Spokane, silenced for an hour. Delegations from Inland Empire communities sent their singing groups and boosters, during the twenties, to broadcast tributes to their towns. The national air derby raced from New York to Spokane in 1927, and, the next year, pilot Nick Mamer and Mrs. Clarence I. Paulsen flew from Spokane to St. Paul (eleven hours and twelve minutes) to show that airmail could fly a northern route.[23]

By the last years of the twenties, eastern Washington business conditions were pocked with odd blemishes: farmers cried depression while rural sales of implements and cars remained brisk; in the city, savings accounts grew. Farm distress sounded no echoing slowdown of urban commerce, perhaps because farm and lumber surpluses meant steady work for distributors, wholesalers, and laborers. Tourism to Spokane grew 26 percent in one year, bringing $1.6 million into city stores. Urban bank deposits in 1926–28 stood 7.8 percent above 1923–25; bank clearances, 15 percent. Spokane manufacturers increased capacity one-third and the Union Pacific and Milwaukee railroads jointly spent $300,000 to develop thirty-seven acres in east Spokane for trackside industrial sites. Mining, lumbering, and farming might be pinched, but money flowed and spirits buoyed in Spokane. Publicly and privately, businessmen acknowledged that times were good. A savings and loan, for example, enjoyed its largest savings growth in twenty years in 1927.[24]

Municipal taxes stayed comparatively low (an average of $60.45 a year on a single-family house) despite the city's constant straining to keep up with demands for improvements and services. Spokane had sold seven bond issues between 1898 and 1909 for water, waste disposal, and bridges, nearly exhausting its borrowing capacity, and citizens challenged local improvement districts in the courts. The automobile, freeing residences from streetcar lines, created new calls for street grading and paving, and the new houses, for water and sewer pipes. As an indicator of construction activity, Spokane sewer permits numbered more than one thousand in 1922, remained steady at five- to six-hundred a year from 1924 to 1928, and rose again in 1928 and 1929. Through it all, city finances were precarious. "The city of Spokane . . . has admittedly over $1,000,000 of street improvement bonds in default of both principal and interest and with little prospect of the poor suckers who thought they were investors ever receiving a dollar," an investment broker told bankers, adding that his brokerage bought no municipal paper from any Washington city because of "the attitude of moral evasion and repudiation held by a very large proportion of the people . . . of Washington."[25]

The people of Washington were far more enchanted by new clothing styles than municipal bonds. Women abandoned corsets for loose-fitting, casual styles and a boyish silhouette—the "flapper" look.

Doubtless more bankers were shocked by their wives' bobbed hair than tottery city finances. Skirts shortened, hats clung to the head (cloche, the French bell); the hobble skirt, in which women could hardly drive an automobile or dance the Charleston, hung in their closets.

As clothing styles changed, so did housing. Many of the new houses seemed peculiar to the twenties—bungalows of frame or stucco, one or one-and-a-half stories, low-pitched roofs, a plain design from California, or a more enduring colonial, a two-story oblong house with dormers. Bungalows squatted beside turreted Queen Anne houses of the nineties with their arched windows and spindled railings, their wide porches for summer life—swings, hammocks, and family gatherings. Bungalows' tiny porches, with hardly room for a chair, typified mobile living—auto tours in summer. Functional and easy to maintain, bungalows and colonials attracted the families of working men, "houses of a type which in other cities would belong to the wealthier class," bragged the chamber of commerce. A smugness had set in. Spokane people were fortunate to live in Spokane.

And with ample money, a good many speculated in stocks. After all, ran a saying, a true Spokane native bought penny stocks and made a trade a day. No matter that the pioneer broker, Walter J. Nichols, failed in 1924 (he would come back). Sam J. Wilson, a swashbuckling mining-stock salesman, seemed swimming in money. No matter that the Spokane Stock Exchange denied Wilson membership because one of his stocks was demonstrably worthless; he started his own exchange, the Standard, taking eleven leading brokers with him, nearly sinking the older Spokane.

Wilson exuded success. He drove expensive cars, flew a private airplane, owned three houses in Spokane and a 360-acre estate near Olympia. Eager to profit from Wilson's hunches, some Spokane citizens tossed envelopes of money over his transom to buy twenty-five-cent stocks before their inevitable rise. And rise they did, until the thirties. Another broker, Eldon J. Gibson, could afford to commute from Hayden Lake, where he promoted a country club. The market rose as Wilson counseled, "Treat mining as a business and you will find it is not a gamble."[26]

When the New York stock market crashed, Spokane seemed insulated from disaster. Businessmen forecast a quick recovery. The city was in the midst of a new commercial building splurge—construction between 1928 and 1931 of a second Paulsen building, a downtown ramp garage, a Fox theater, a new Chronicle building with terra cotta gargoyles grinning from its parapet, Montgomery Ward and Sears, Roebuck stores, a Kress dime store, and a chamber of commerce building.

Spokane's unfolding in half a century had been typical of the West, where cities founded as commercial ventures based on railroads and real estate were laid out in rectangular grids, dominated the economic structure of their tributary regions, and developed by private enterprise riding on the back of federal land policy. But true Spokane believers, nevertheless, considered it a unique place; they listened with parochial impatience to visitors who favored any other city. They savored the ambience of parks, tree-lined avenues, hills, the river, lakes, warm days and cool nights, and leisurely living, and summed up their heritage in a homely truth, "It's a nice place to live."

Notes

CHAPTER 1 *An Influx of Strangers*

1. *Walla Walla Union,* Feb. 16, 1878. For settlement 1858–79, see D. W. Meinig, *Great Columbia Plain,* pp. 201–53.

2. *Walla Walla Union,* Dec. 21, 1878 (odors), and March 1, 1879 (rector).

3. H. H. Bancroft, *Works,* 31:202 (Perkins), 308 (Comegys), and 310 (McCroskey).

4. *Walla Walla Union,* Feb. 7 and May 1, 1880.

5. Burke to Waldo M. Yorke, Dec. 15, 1881, quoted in R. C. Nesbit, *He Built Seattle,* pp. 30–31.

6. *Walla Walla Union,* Oct. 4, 1879. See Charlotte Shackleford, "Donation Land Claims."

7. W. M. Yeager, "Pioneer's Problems of Land Acquisition," pp. 31 and 86.

8. *Record* quoted in the *Walla Walla Union,* Dec. 25, 1880; F. J. Yonce, "Public Land Disposal in Washington," pp. 131 and 146–53; Yeager, p. 86.

9. A. C. McGregor, "Agricultural Development of the Columbia Plateau," pp. 28–29; *Walla Walla Union,* March 11, 1882 (cattle drives); G. L. Jackson, *Remembering Yakima,* pp. 1, 20; *Kettle Falls Pioneer,* Sept. 14, 1893 (sheep); J. S. Cotton, "Report on the Range Conditions of Central Washington," p. 19 (overgrazing). Before this period, see E. S. Osgood, "Cattleman in Agricultural History."

10. *Walla Walla Union,* Dec. 20, 1879 (quotation), and March 27, 1880 (Pomeroy); *Colfax Commoner,* June 14, 1895 (black).

11. *Palouse Gazette,* May 18 (superior justice) and June 15, 1883 (jumper); *Years Ago,* p. 5; *Colfax Commoner,* May 27 and June 3, 1892 (stockmen).

12. *Colfax Commoner,* Jan. 7 and 14 and March 30, 1898.

13. *Palouse Story,* p. 84; *Colfax Commoner,* Nov. 20, 1891.

14. Yeager, pp. 105, 110, and 117; W. W. Baker, *Forty Years a Pioneer,* p.

98; J. O. Oliphant, "Readings in the History of Eastern Washington," 5:130; *Tekoa Story*, pp. 169, 182, and 221; K. R. Williams, "Memoirs," n.p. See Marvin Moore, "Palouse Hills Farmstead Architecture, 1890–1915."

15. Yeager, p. 120; Joseph Smith diary, 18:144; *Colfax Gazette*, May 25, 1883.

16. *Palouse Story*, p. 17; *Colfax Commoner*, Jan. 13, 1893.

17. *Globe* quoted in *Colfax Commoner*, March 21, 1890.

18. Leonard Hegnauer, "Eighty-six Golden Years," p. 276; *Spokane Daily Chronicle*, Aug. 3, 1914 (Dennis recollections).

19. Catherine Harder Peot in *Franklin Flyer* 9, no. 3 (January 1977):3.

20. *Palouse Story*, pp. 17 and 35–36; diary of Cora Salnave, Cheney, 1889.

21. *Palouse Story*, p. 36.

22. *Palouse Story*, pp. 14 and 35.

23. *Yakima Herald*, Oct. 1, 1891 (watermelon); *Colfax Commoner*, June 28, 1928, analyzing a church survey.

24. Special Reports of the Bureau of the Census: *Religious Bodies 1906*, pt. 1, p. 368; E. de S. Brunner and J. H. Kolb, *Rural Social Trends*, p. 363.

25. Lt. Thomas W. Symons to Philip Ritz in *Walla Walla Union*, Sept. 4, 1880; B. Hunter et al., "Review of the Agriculture of the Big Bend Country," p. 9.

26. E. L. Zimmerman, "An Introductory Study of the Development of Agriculture in Eastern Washington," p. 15.

27. *Grant County Journal*, Aug. 27, 1953; interview with E. J. Roberts, Nov. 23, 1948; D. Hoefel, *Hoefel Family Album*, p. 67; Eleventh Census, 1890.

28. Jackson, *Remembering Yakima*, 1:12; *Yakima Herald*, Jan. 23, 1896; W. I. Lince in *Yakima Herald*, Dec. 22, 1898.

29. W. D. Lyman, *History of the Yakima Valley*, pp. 277–78.

30. William Cassar recollections, *Yakima Morning Herald*, Jan. 7, 1915 (quotation); William Wiley recollections, *Yakima Sunday Herald*, May 6, 1923.

31. According to the *Yakima Sunday Herald*, Sept. 10, 1922, the Northern Pacific established its own town when speculation raised land prices near the anticipated depot site in the older town. See 12 Supreme Court 283 (1885), a suit by Yakima County to compel the railroad to build a station at Yakima City, which the court decided for the railroad. *Yakima Herald*, June 11, 1891, and Feb. 15, 1900; and *Yakima Morning Herald*, Jan. 10, 1926 (Union ditch).

32. *Yakima Herald*, Dec. 22, 1898.

33. Kirk Monroe, "Eastern Washington and the Water Miracle of Yakima," *Harper's Weekly*, May 19, 1894, p. 466 (dust); George Vance recalling winter of 1891, *Yakima Morning Herald*, Jan. 9, 1921.

34. *Yakima Herald*, April 18 and Oct. 24, 1889, Dec. 6, 1896, July 19, 1900, and Feb. 23, 1908; *Dictionary of American Biography*, 9:324–25 (Hubbard).

35. *Spokesman-Review*, June 10, 1918 (Field); *Spokane Daily Chronicle*, April 14, 1909 (Read et al.), and Sept. 7, 1977 (California Land Company).

36. *Colfax Commoner*, March 14 and Nov. 28, 1890.

37. *Review* quoted in *Colfax Commoner*, Nov. 28, 1890.

38. *Colfax Commoner*, Aug. 21, 1891 (Chicago price), and May 3, 1895 (Fair). Gordon B. Ridgeway, "Populism in Washington," *Pacific Northwest Quarterly* 39, no. 4 (October 1948): 285 (mortgage rates); *Yakima Herald*, June 1, 1891 (taxes), and May 5, 1892 (Northern Pacific).

39. *Colfax Commoner*, Oct. 13, 20 and 27, 1893. *Dayton Chronicle*, Oct. 21, 1893, quoted in F. A. Shaver, R. F. Steele, and A. P. Rose, *Illustrated History of Southeastern Washington*, p. 335. Wallace (Idaho) *Press-Times*, Feb. 1, 1911 (banker).

40. *Colfax Commoner*, Oct. 27, 1893 (Pullman), April 27, 1894 (Palouse City), Jan. 5, 1894 (bidding), March 2, 1894 (skull and crossbones), Aug. 9, 1895 (mob), and Sept. 13, 1895 (judges). Williams, "Memoirs," p. 7.

41. *Colfax Commoner*, Nov. 3, 1893 (cash sales), March 2, 1894 (quotation), and March 9, 1894 (Mason). Lyman, *History of the Yakima Valley*, p. 342 (Snipes).

42. *Yakima Herald*, Nov. 8, 1894 (quotation); N. R. Knight, "History of Banking in Washington," p. 184; *Colfax Commoner*, Feb. 8, 1895 (warrants); W. H. Lever, *Illustrated History of Whitman County*, p. 125; *North West*, May, 1895, p. 28 (settlers) and p. 156 (bureau); *Colfax Commoner*, March 8, 1895, and Aug. 21, 1896.

43. *Yakima Herald*, Oct. 22, 1896; *Colfax Commoner*, Jan. 8, 1897 (quotation).

44. *Colfax Commoner*, Jan. 8 and July 30, 1897, Oct. 6, 1899.

45. Lever, *Illustrated History of Whitman County*, pp. 129–30; *Post-Intelligencer* quoted in *Colfax Commoner*, July 18, 1902; *Spokesman-Review*, April 5 (quotation) and Sept. 15, 1903.

46. *Yakima Herald*, July 14, 1898; H. I. Shotwell, *Shotwell Story*, pp. 24–25 and 42; Nesbit, *He Built Seattle*, pp. 141–42; *Wenatchee Daily World*, Oct. 6, 1942, commenting on Bruce Mitchell's study of Burke's promotion of the Wenatchee townsite.

47. Zimmerman, "An Introductory Study of the Development of Agriculture in Eastern Washington," pp. 18–19; Hunter et al., "Review of the Agriculture of the Big Bend Country," p. 9. The *Colfax Commoner*, Sept. 12, 1924, reports that 1896–97 was the wettest with 31.03 inches of precipitation compared with a thirty-year Palouse average of 21.14, according to F. J. Sievers, Department of Soils, Washington State College.

48. J. E. Ballaine, Colfax, to *Illustrated American*, Aug. 7, 1893, quoted in C. M. Gates, *Readings in Pacific Northwest History*, p. 272; *Pasco Herald*, Oct. 28, 1930 (Frey); N. W. Durham, *History of the City of Spokane and Spokane Country*, 2:134–35 (Dorman); *Yakima Herald*, Oct. 25, 1894 (Benson); *East Washingtonian*, May 2, 1891.

49. A. M. Richmond, "Promotion of the Northwest," p. 36; *Yakima Herald*, Feb. 27, 1896, Nov. 18, 1897, and July 14, 1898; R. D. Scheuerman, "From Wagon Trails to Iron Rails," pp. 37–50; *Spokane Daily Chronicle*, July 12, 1895. C. F. Reuss, "Pioneers of Lincoln County," says immigration to

Lincoln County was largest from Illinois, next from Missouri, and third from Germany. He reports 27.6 percent of the county's pioneers were foreign born.

CHAPTER 2   *The Railroads: Beneficent, Malignant, Fickle*

1. *Walla Walla Union*, Jan. 24, 1880. See J. B. Hedges, *Henry Villard and the Railways of the Northwest*.

2. W. W. Baker, *Forty Years a Pioneer*, pp. 72–73 and 77. Baker had done some banking as early as 1863.

3. *Walla Walla Statesman*, Nov. 22, 1879, quoted in F. A. Shaver, R. F. Steele, and A. P. Rose, *Illustrated History of Southeastern Washington*, p. 309.

4. S. Mickelson, "Promotional Activities of the Northern Pacific's Land and Immigration Departments," pp. 65–66, citing the railroad's 1883 annual report, p. 38. See J. B. Hedges, "Promotion of Immigration to the Pacific Northwest by the Railroads."

5. Newport to Thomas Oakes, Oct. 18, 1881, quoted in Mickelson, p. 211.

6. The railroad subsidized Smalley by buying 5,000 copies of each issue, according to a letter, Smalley to President and Land Committee, Feb. 13, 1884, in Mickelson, pp. 60–64. A. M. Richmond, "Promotion of the Northwest," pp. 56–57.

7. *Walla Walla Union*, Feb. 28, 1880; *New York Times*, May 14, 1887, quoting the *Oregonian*.

8. Equity case E4389, United States v. Northern Pacific Railway Co., et al., 275–92; 16 *Stats.* 291, 305.

9. *New York Times*, May 14, 1887. F. J. Yonce, "Public Land Disposal in Washington," describes land regulations, especially pp. 146–56.

10. R. L. Rosbach, "Lieu Land Controversy in Eastern Washington," pp. 63–64; *New York Times*, May 1, May 14, and April 28, 1887; 7 LD 100; *Colfax Commoner*, March 31, 1893.

11. Rosbach, pp. 75–76; *Colfax Commoner*, July 14, 1893; 17 LD 8.

12. 47 Law Edition 106, 406 (1903).

13. 29 LD 632; *Colfax Commoner*, July 14, 1893.

14. Mickelson, p. 76.

15. *Spokane Falls Chronicle*, March 28, 1882; Hedges, *Henry Villard*, pp. 129 and 131.

16. Equity case E4389: defendant's exhibit no. 9.

17. *Colfax Commoner*, June 25, 1897.

18. Equity case E4389; Winter profile, *North West*, July 1896, p. 19.

19. Equity case E4389. A useful summary of railroad land litigation appears in 311 U.S. 317 (1940). See R. R. Cotroneo, "Western Land Marketing by the Northern Pacific."

20. Hedges, *Henry Villard*, pp. 78–79.

21. *Walla Walla Union*, June 4, 1881.

22. *Weekly Missoulian*, Sept. 21, 1883; C. M. Gates, *Readings in Pacific Northwest History*, p. 206; *Oregonian*, Sept. 9, 1923.

23. Hunt biography, *North West*, October 1889, pp. 14–17.

24. 44 Washington Reports 124 (1906); Shaver et al., *Illustrated History of Southeastern Washington*, p. 329.

25. *Walla Walla Union*, Aug. 13, 1881.

26. *Regulation of Stock Ownership in Railroads*, H. Rept. 2789, 71st Cong., 3d sess., pt. 3, p. 1335.

27. Albro Martin, *James J. Hill and the Opening of the Northwest*, pp. 458–59 and 464.

28. J. G. Pyle, *Life of James J. Hill*, 2:37.

29. 37 Law Edition 686 (1893), the Yakima suit.

30. Mickelson, p. 192.

31. Fourteenth Census, *State Compendium: Washington*, table 1, p. 11; table 5, p. 23; *Census of Agriculture*, table 1.

32. Annual reports of the Spokane building inspector; city directories, 1900–1905; J. J. Hill to D. S. Lamont, July 17, 1898 (Hill Library, St. Paul).

33. Author's analysis of city directories, 1900 and 1910; A. D. Butler, Spokane city engineer, "Advance Programming and Advance Budgeting of Capital Improvements," Dec. 15, 1939, p. 20 (city clerk file 950-NI-1).

34. Based on M. Mitchell, "Washington Newspapers: Territorial and State."

35. *Spokesman-Review*, Aug. 8, 1965 (Malden); *Spokane Daily Chronicle*, March 1, 1908.

36. Session Laws of 1891, chapter 1; D. O. Smart, "History of Railroad Rate Regulation in the State of Washington," pp. 29–37.

37. *Colfax Commoner*, Jan. 20, 1899.

38. *Finding of Facts by the Railroad Commission of Washington Relative to the Valuation of Railroads in the State of Washington*, passim; A. Berglund, "Valuation of Railroads in the State of Washington," pp. 343–44. Joseph Smith's notebook, jotted during a joint session of the legislature Jan. 30, 1907, cites Fairchild's speech on the railroads' response to commission requests for information.

39. *Finding of Facts by the Railroad Commission*, and *Finding of Facts . . . Relative to the Valuation of the Oregon Railroad & Navigation Company* (1909), p. 52.

40. R. V. Scott, "American Railroads and Agricultural Extension," p. 75; 52 Washington Reports 17, 33 (1909); Berglund, "Valuation of Railroads in the State of Washington," p. 343, points out that determining rates based on the costs of service was "at variance with the views of railroad economists generally."

41. The ICC grain-rate study was, of course, a response to the Hoch-Smith resolution in Congress directing the commission to prescribe the lowest practical rates. *Great Northern Railway Company, the Northern Pacific Railway Company: A Review of Their Operations in the Period 1916–1923*, p. 31

(quotation); L. D. Cannell, "Freight Rate Structure and Its Effect on the Price and Movement of Northwest Wheat," pp. 25–27.

42. *Daily Missoulian,* Jan. 15 and 29, 1907 (Hill); Washington Session Laws of 1921, chapter 3. The railroads laid their financial difficulties in part to the "retardation" of the Pacific Northwest, as their view is expressed in *Great Northern . . . Northern Pacific:. . . . 1916–1923,* pp. 21–24.

43. Washington State Tax Commission, *Third Biennial Report* (1929), p. 35.

44. 144 Washington Reports 505 (1927); Washington State Tax Commission, *Fourth Biennial Report* (1932).

45. Abandonment as a policy is discussed in D. C. Jones, "Strategy of Railway Abandonment: The Great Northern in Washington and British Columbia."

CHAPTER 3   *The Grain Trade*

1. Muir to Elijah Smith, president of the Oregon Improvement Co., Sept. 11, 1884 (OIC roll 31), and to Goodall, Perkins and Co., San Francisco, Feb. 11, 1884 (OIC roll 30), microfilm in the University of Washington special collections.

2. W. S. Lewis, *Story of Early Days in the Big Bend Country,* p. 18.

3. *Seattle Times* quoted in the *Colfax Commoner,* Nov. 8, 1901. Leiter's 1896 raid from *Yakima Morning Herald,* May 18, 1930.

4. Washington State Agricultural Extension Service *Bulletin 355,* 1937, p. 8; Washington Bureau of Immigration and Statistics, *Abstract,* 1918; J. B. Watkins, "Wheat Exporting from the Pacific Northwest," Washington State Agricultural Experiment Station *Bulletin 201,* May 1926, p. 52 (fleet).

5. Herman Steen, *Flour Milling in America,* p. 380; *Oregonian,* Dec. 5, 1930, July 17, 1938, and March 27, 1962; *Spokesman-Review,* Aug. 8, 1901, and July 26, 1912. See Watkins, *Bulletin 201,* p. 43.

6. Steen, *Flour Milling,* pp. 381–82; *Oregonian,* April 1, 1918, Aug. 4, 1918, and June 14, 1928; *Spokesman-Review,* March 12, 1901; W. H. Kensel, "Economic History of Spokane, Washington, 1881–1910," pp. 155 and 157.

7. *Oregon Journal,* June 11, 1953; Spokane City Directory, 1910.

8. Steen, *Flour Milling,* p. 283; *Oregon Journal,* March 27, 1962; H. W. Scott, *History of Portland, Oregon,* p. 428.

9. "History of Albers Brothers," *Carnation* 10, no. 1 (February 1930):1–6, supplied by Robert C. Hare with letter, Sept. 5, 1967.

10. *Spokesman-Review,* March 10, 1918, and April 27, 1921; Poor's *Industrials 1918,* p. 283.

11. Biennial Report of the State Department of Agriculture, 1927–28, p. 25; Watkins, *Bulletin 201,* pp. 52–53; [J. S. Davis], *Pacific Northwest Wheat Problems and the Export Subsidy,* p. 353.

12. Based on Davis, *Pacific Northwest Wheat Problems,* table 10, p. 29,

and "Wheat Supply and Distribution in the Pacific Northwest," Oregon Wheat Commission, *Statistical Bulletin 1*, pp. 49 and 52.

13. *Spokesman-Review,* June 2, 1904.

14. *Seattle Times,* Sept. 21, 1950 (review of Seattle milling).

15. P. Burke, "Struggle for Public Ownership: . . . Port of Seattle," *Pacific Northwest Quarterly* 68, no. 2 (April 1977): 60–71.

16. W. E. Hardesty, "Municipal Grain and Freight Port Terminal at Portland, Oregon," *Engineering News-Record* 84, no. 4 (Jan. 22, 1920): 179–82; *American City* 29 (August 1923): 178–80.

17. H. T. Lewis and S. I. Miller, *Economic Resources of the Pacific Northwest,* p. 366.

18. *Cheney Free Press,* Feb. 4, 1912; Washington Bureau of Statistics and Immigration, *Manufacturing Opportunities in the State of Washington* (1918), pp. 206–16.

19. W. A. Rockie, "Some Important Effects of the Summer Fallow System on Farming and Soil Erosion in the Pacific Northwest," *Northwest Science* 6, no. 1 (March 1933): 19–22. See also J. F. Shepherd, "Development of New Wheat Varieties in the Pacific Northwest," *Agricultural History* 54, no. 1 (January 1980): 52–63.

20. E. F. Gaines, "Primary Considerations in Developing New Wheats in Washington," *Northwest Science* 9, no. 1 (February 1935): 8–12.

21. Ibid., p. 10.

22. *Dakota Farmer* quoted in H. C. Filley, *Cooperation in Agriculture,* pp. 127–28. His observation did not hold true for national averages. Washington wheat nearly always brought a price lower than the national average between 1909 and 1930. Before the war, when Washington wheat sold at perhaps 80 cents a bushel, the national average was 89 cents; from 1916 to 1920, the national price averaged 6 cents higher than in Washington; but the gap almost closed between 1921 and 1930, when Washington wheat averaged $1.05 a bushel and the nation $1.06. Oregon Wheat Commission, "Wheat Supply and Distribution," *Statistical Bulletin 1*, pp. 68 and 70.

23. E. F. Gaines and E. G. Schafer, "Wheat Varieties in Washington in 1939," Washington State Agricultural Experiment Station *Bulletin 398.* See J. A. Clark and K. S. Quisenberry, "Varieties of Hard Red Winter Wheat," USDA *Farmers Bulletin 1585.*

24. Based on Oregon Wheat Commission, "Wheat Supply and Distribution," *Statistical Bulletin 1*, pp. 5, 6, 9, and 53–54.

25. D. Hoefel, *Hoefel Family Album,* pp. 72–74.

26. Watkins, "Wheat Exporting," pp. 42–43.

27. Gov. Ernest Lister's inaugural message, 1913, in *Washington Documents 1911–12,* pp. 14–15.

28. Quotation from *Spokesman-Review,* Jan. 26, 1918.

29. Colfax dateline story in *Yakima Herald,* Aug. 12, 1902.

30. On Lind union, see J. Fahey, "Wheat Whiz," *Spokane* 4, no. 6 (June 1980): 38–42.

31. *Spokesman-Review,* Jan. 1, 1906; *Yakima Morning Herald,* April 4,

1909; USDA Farmer Cooperative Service, "Farmer Cooperatives in the United States," *Bulletin 1*, p. 80; *Cheney Free Press*, Dec. 17, 1915, and Aug. 24, 1917; Report of the Office of Farm Markets, *Washington Documents 1919–20*.

32. Second annual report, State Department of Public Works, pp. 147–50, in *Washington Documents 1921–22*.

33. Report of the Office of Farm Markets, p. 12, in *Washington Documents 1919–20; Yakima Morning Herald*, Jan. 14, 1920; *Colfax Gazette*, Feb. 27, March 5, and March 12, 1920.

34. *Colfax Gazette*, Dec. 16, 1921.

35. *Colfax Commoner*, Jan. 11, 1924; *Colfax Gazette*, Sept. 21, 1923; Washington Wheat Growers Association v. Irvin T. Leifer, 132 Wash. 602 (1925); R. H. Elsworth, "Statistics of Farmers' Cooperative Business Organizations, 1920–1935," Farm Credit Administration, Cooperative Division, *Bulletin 6*, 1936, p. 57; Filley, *Cooperation in Agriculture*, pp. 127–28.

36. *Yakima Morning Herald*, Aug. 26, 1922, and Jan. 6, 1928; O. M. Kile, *Farm Bureau through Three Decades*, p. 86; Filley, *Cooperation in Agriculture*, pp. 127–28; *Colfax Commoner*, Dec. 7, 1928.

37. J. W. Gaffney and C. Jans, *History of Sprague, 1880–1962*, p. 61; *Told by the Pioneers*, pp. 95–96.

38. *Colfax Gazette*, Sept. 5 and Oct. 3, 1884; *West Shore*, 13:209 (1887); C. McCormick, *Century of the Reaper*, p. 99.

39. *Colfax Commoner*, Sept. 8, 1893.

40. J. L. Deaton, "Adoption and Diffusion of the Combined Harvester-Thresher in the United States," pp. 7–8; *Spokesman-Review*, Jan. 7, 1928, memories of Gordon Klemgard; *Colfax Commoner*, Aug. 3, 1906; Joseph Smith diaries, Aug. 15, 1894.

41. J. T. Schlebecker, *Whereby We Thrive*, p. 192.

42. *Colfax Commoner*, Jan. 27, 1911; *Spokesman-Review*, March 5 and Oct. 12, 1904, Jan. 20, 1911, Feb. 13, Nov. 7, and Dec. 10, 1913, May 19, 1918; J. Fahey, *Days of the Hercules*, pp. 125–26; T. B. Keith, *Horse Interlude*, passim.

43. *Spokesman-Review*, May 31, 1902, and Jan. 1, 1903.

44. B. W. Currie, *The Tractor*, pp. 138 and 176; McCormick, *Century of the Reaper*, pp. 154–55; *Colfax Gazette*, May 19, 1916.

45. McCormick, *Century of the Reaper*, pp. 114–15; *Spokesman-Review*, Jan. 22, 1910.

46. *Colfax Commoner*, March 17 and 24, 1911.

47. *Spokesman-Review*, June 15, 1902, Oct. 18, 1903, June 10, 1907, Nov. 9, 1909, Jan. 9 and March 13, 1910, and June 11, 1910.

48. Based on my review of chattel mortgage records in Spokane, Whitman, and Chelan counties; *Spokane Daily Chronicle*, May 4, 1913 (Holt).

49. *Spokesman-Review*, March 6, 1916, and May 30, 1918.

50. *Spokesman-Review*, Aug. 18, 1911.

51. *Spokesman-Review*, Aug. 11, 1910, and July 25, 1914; *Spokane Daily Chronicle*, May 26, 1912.

52. *Colfax Commoner,* Aug. 29, 1913; *Spokesman-Review,* Aug. 6 and 7, 1914; Washington State Agricultural Experiment Station *Bulletin 117* (1914); *Colfax Gazette,* Aug. 14, 1914.

53. *Spokane Daily Chronicle,* July 5, 1915; *Colfax Gazette,* Aug. 10, 1923.

54. Spokane and Eastern letter quoted in *Colfax Gazette,* March 24, 1922; *Colfax Gazette,* Sept. 23, 1921; Oregon Wheat Commission, "Wheat Supply and Distribution," *Bulletin 1,* p. 68.

55. Report of the State Supervisor of Banking, 1921, pp. 5–6.

56. Quotation from *Colfax Gazette,* Aug. 16, 1918; Biennial Report of the Commissioner of Public Lands, 1923–24, p. 4; *Colfax Commoner,* March 6, 1925.

57. Watkins, "Wheat Exporting," p. 84.

58. Steen, *Flour Milling,* pp. 74–76 and 123–24; duplicated synopsis of Centennial history furnished by J. D. McClenaghan, Aug. 15, 1967.

59. *Colfax Gazette,* May 19, 1922.

60. *New York Times,* Dec. 16, 1923.

61. *Colfax Commoner,* Jan. 11, 1924.

62. Report of the State Supervisor of Banking, 1924; *Colfax Commoner,* Oct. 3, 1924.

63. Oregon Wheat Commission, "Wheat Supply and Distribution," p. 9; R. M. Turner, *The First Forty-Five Years,* p. 50 (Waterville).

64. Report of the Commissioner of Public Lands, 1923–24, p. 4.

65. Report of the Commissioner of Public Lands, 1923–24, p. 4; *Colfax Commoner,* March 6, 1925.

66. P. H. Landis, "Fifty Years of Population Growth in Washington," Washington State Agricultural Experiment Station *Bulletin 419* (1942); Bureau of the Census, *Fifteenth Census* (1930), *Agriculture,* vol. 1, *Population,* vol. 3, pt. 2, pp. 1223–25; *Abstract,* p. 704, table 149; p. 648, table 89; and p. 590, table 37; *Census of Agriculture, 1935,* vol. 3, pp. 912 and 916–17; Report of the Washington State Board of Equalization, 1930, p. 12, schedule A, table 1.

67. *Colfax Commoner,* May 15, 1930.

68. USDA, *Yearbook of Agriculture, 1931,* pp. 26–29.

69. *Literary Digest,* June 6, 1931, pp. 5–6.

CHAPTER 4   *Barefoot Schoolboys*

1. J. Fahey, "Wag behind Winston's Weekly," *Spokane* 3, no. 11 (November 1979): 40–41, 65.

2. T. W. Riddle, "Old Radicalism in America: John R. Rogers and the Populist Movement," pp. 121–97. C. H. Wooddy, "Populism in Washington," and K. D. Bicha, "Peculiar Populist," analyze Rogers's political strength and philosophy.

3. *Seattle Times,* Jan. 22, 1933.

4. *Winston's Weekly,* Sept. 12, 1903.

5. *Spokesman-Review*, Feb. 16, 1895, and March 14, 1896; House Journal, 1895, especially pp. 275 and 901. Gandy tried to sink the bill by moving that the House reject Senate amendments.

6. *Spokesman-Review*, Aug. 16, 1895.

7. Interview with J. D. Urquhart, recalling his mother's arrival in Lind.

8. *Spokesman-Review*, March 27, 1892. For one, Hartline charged tuition of $6.75, according to the *Spokesman-Review*, Sept. 4, 1904.

9. F. E. Bolton and T. W. Bibb, *History of Education in Washington*, p. 83, table 8.

10. *Spokesman-Review*, June 14, 1902.

11. *Spokesman-Review*, March 10, 1895 (Yakima), and April 4, 1900.

12. Bolton and Bibb, *History of Education in Washington*, p. 125, table 13, from which I calculated 40 percent to arrive at approximate figures for eastern Washington.

13. *Colfax Gazette*, April 21, 1916; *Spokesman-Review*, Jan. 25, 1904, Jan. 27 and March 28, 1909, Sept. 3, 1910, Aug. 15, 1911, June 14 and Aug. 17, 1913, and Jan. 7, 1917.

14. Bolton and Bibb, *History of Education in Washington*, p. 125, table 13; *Spokesman-Review*, April 16, 1914; Biennial Report of the Superintendent of Public Instruction, 1921–22, p. 126, table: "Disorganization of school districts, 1921–22."

15. *Spokesman-Review*, April 16, 1914; Biennial Report of the Superintendent of Public Instruction, 1915–16, p. 19; H. Johnson, *Washington Schools in the Good Old Days*, pp. 14–16; Bolton and Bibb, *History of Education in Washington*, p. 116.

16. R. M. Turner, *The First Forty-Five Years*, p. 9.

17. Gov. Hay's third message (1913), pp. 24–25; Biennial Report of the Superintendent of Public Instruction, 1927–28, p. 28.

18. *Grange News*, July 4, 1923.

19. Biennial Report of the Superintendent of Public Instruction, 1921–22, p. 119.

20. Biennial Report of the Superintendent of Public Instruction, 1927–28, p. 28.

21. *Grange News*, June 20, 1925. The Federal Trade Commission was investigating undercover operations of private utility publicists. See *Spokesman-Review*, Oct. 12, 1928.

22. State Department of Education Report, 1928–36, p. 60; Biennial Report of the Superintendent of Public Instruction, 1929–30, pp. 13–21.

23. S. V. Foran, "Oregon Grange," pp. 18–19.

24. H. A. Crawford, *Washington State Grange, 1889–1924*, pp. 12–13; E. A. Scott, "Grange Movement in Oregon," pp. 16–17; *Grange News*, Oct. 5, 1928.

25. *Colfax Commoner*, Sept. 27, 1889.

26. F. R. Yoder, "Farmers' Alliance in Washington," p. 124; *Colfax Commoner*, May 23, 1890, quoting the *Seattle Press*.

27. *Colfax Commoner*, Dec. 5, 1890, and Oct. 30, 1891; Olympia *Weekly*

Capital, July 15, 1893; D. O. Johansen and C. M. Gates, *Empire of the Columbia*, p. 416.

28. *Yakima Herald*, June 15, 1893; *Colfax Commoner*, Dec. 2, 1892, and Sept. 7, 1894.

29. Proceedings of the Grange convention, 1890, pp. 7–9, quoted in Crawford, *Washington State Grange*, p. 74.

30. H. Cravens, "History of the Farmer-Labor Party," pp. 23–26; C. M. Gardner, *The Grange—Friend of the Farmer*, pp. 138 and 198–99; *Grange News*, Sept. 20, 1928.

31. *Colfax Commoner*, May 3, 1907, Feb. 14, 1908, and Jan. 28, 1910; *Spokesman-Review*, May 31, 1909; O. M. Kile, *Farm Bureau through Three Decades*, pp. 17–19; E. Wiest, *Agricultural Organization in the United States*, p. 475.

32. Gardner, *The Grange—Friend of the Farmer*, pp. 318 and 465–67; C. A. Schwantes, "Making the World Unsafe for Democracy," describes the Walla Walla lockout; *Grange News*, Feb. 5, June 20, and Dec. 5, 1921, May 20, 1922, June 20, 1923; Cravens, "History of the Washington Farmer-Labor Party," pp. 154–56; *Colfax Gazette*, Nov. 25, 1921.

33. Gardner, *The Grange—Friend of the Farmer*, pp. 465–67; *Grange News*, Oct. 5, 1923, June 3, 1924, and Nov. 20, 1929. In seventeen years, Goss reported, the Washington Grange membership expanded 125 percent.

34. M. R. Benedict, *Farm Policies of the United States*, pp. 176–78; *Yakima Morning Herald*, Aug. 6, 1919.

35. G. McConnell, *Decline of Agrarian Democracy*, pp. 55–57; Wiest, *Agricultural Organization*, p. 523; *Colfax Commoner*, July 6, 1928, and Jan. 17, 1929.

36. Wiest, *Agricultural Organization*, p. 352; *Grange News*, Dec. 5, 1924. See *Rural Leaders*, Washington State Agricultural Extension Service *Bulletin* 257 (1931) for proportions of leaders among men and women (75 percent of officers are men) and ages (leaders average 47.2 years).

37. *Grange News*, June 20, 1924.

38. Turner, *The First Forty-Five Years*, p. 29.

39. President Enoch A. Bryan quoted by *Colfax Commoner*, April 7, 1911.

40. Washington State Agricultural Extension Service *Popular Bulletin 1* (January 1908), p. 1; *Colfax Commoner*, July 31, 1908.

41. L. Hegnauer, "Eighty-six Golden Years," p. 292.

42. Ibid., pp. 156–57.

43. *Colfax Commoner*, Aug. 18, 1911; *Yakima Morning Herald*, Jan. 10, 1912.

44. Report of Washington Director of Agriculture, 1913–14, p. 56; E. K. Vandervere, "History of Irrigation in Washington," pp. 139–40; Turner, *The First Forty-Five Years*, p. 29. Donating the land at Prosser allowed the Northern Pacific to select the station's location.

45. R. K. Bliss (Iowa), *Proceedings*, Association of Land-Grant Colleges, 1920, p. 136.

46. Hegnauer, "Eighty-six Golden Years," pp. 154–55.

47. *Grange News,* July 4, 1923.

48. Report of the Agricultural Committee, Washington Bankers Association, *Proceedings 1929,* p. 97.

49. F. A. Shaver, R. F. Steele, and A. P. Rose, *Illustrated History of Southeastern Washington,* p. 174. H. H. Bancroft, *Works,* 31:345, gives the Walla Walla date as 1867; *Walla Walla Union,* Aug. 28, 1880; W. H. Lever, *Illustrated History of Whitman County,* p. 125; *Spokesman-Review,* May 16, 1950.

50. *Spokane Daily Chronicle,* Aug. 3, 1914 (recollections), May 8, 1901, Sept. 26, 1909, and Oct. 25, 1913; *Spokesman-Review,* Nov. 21, 1930, and May 16, 1950; N. W. Durham, *History of the City of Spokane,* 1:152; *Yakima Sunday Herald,* Sept. 17, 1922; *Yakima Herald,* Sept. 30, 1902.

51. *Yakima Herald,* July 26 and Sept. 27, 1894.

52. *Yakima Herald,* Jan. 21, 1903; *Yakima Morning Herald,* Jan. 5, 1907; Washington Attorney General's Opinions, 1917–18, pp. 61–62.

53. *Grange News,* Oct. 20, 1927.

54. *Colfax Commoner,* Nov. 10 and Dec. 22, 1899.

55. *Colfax Gazette,* Sept. 26 and Oct. 3, 1913 (with photo); *Spokane Daily Chronicle,* Aug. 25, 1913; *Spokesman-Review,* Nov. 15, 1915.

56. David Brown, quoted in *Spokesman-Review,* Nov. 15, 1915; *Spokesman-Review,* Nov. 16, 1913, and Oct. 28, 1914; *Colfax Gazette,* March 6, 1914.

57. Hegnauer, "Eighty-six Golden Years," p. 298; F. W. Clemens, *Balanced Farming for the Inland Empire,* p. 2.

58. Clemens, *Balanced Farming,* pp. 5–6.

59. Hegnauer, "Eighty-six Golden Years," p. 302; *Yakima Morning Herald,* June 4, 1930; *Grange News,* April 5 and July 5, 1929.

CHAPTER 5 *Irrigation*

1. *Yakima Morning Herald,* Feb. 16, 1930. The article cited is one of a series on Yakima irrigation in the *Herald* by H. P. Barrett in 1930.

2. *Yakima Herald,* March 27, 1892.

3. *North West,* May 1895, p. 19; W. D. Lyman, *History of the Yakima Valley,* pp. 796; *Yakima Herald,* April 25, 1895; *Yakima Morning Herald,* Feb. 23, 1930.

4. George T. Reid, assistant to the president, Northern Pacific, speaking to the Washington Irrigation Institute; see the institute's *Proceedings 1914,* pp. 104–5.

5. The foreclosed Sunnyside canal sold for $335,000 to the sole bidder, who deeded it to the Washington Irrigation Company. The *Yakima Herald,* March 8, 1900, identifies the bidder as the San Francisco Loan and Trust Company; the *Yakima Morning Herald,* March 2, 1930, identifies him as J. Dalzell Brown. Blaine recalled his involvement in Sunnyside in remarks recorded by a stenographer at the fifth annual meeting of the Columbia Basin

League, Aug. 21, 1926 (James A. Ford scrapbook, used before Ford's death).

6. *Yakima Morning Herald*, April 11, 1904.

7. *Collier's*, Aug. 22, 1908; W. S. Forth, "Wesley L. Jones: A Political Biography," pp. 46 and 99; and Jones's views, 35 *Congressional Record* 1751–57.

8. *Spokesman-Review*, Dec. 22, 1903; USBR, Yakima Project History, rolls 210 and 223; *Winston's Weekly*, Dec. 26, 1903.

9. Newell to Jones, printed in the *Yakima Herald*, May 27, 1903.

10. *Yakima Morning Herald*, March 9, 1930.

11. Lyman, *Yakima Valley*, pp. 549–50, 788; USBR, Yakima Project History, roll 223. See Nelson A. Ault, "McWhorter Papers," pp. 85–118.

12. The U.S. Geological Survey opened a Spokane office in 1903 with Noble in charge. Yakima Project History, roll 223; *Yakima Herald*, Nov. 8, 1905 (cartoon).

13. F. H. Newell, "Reclamation of the West," p. 827.

14. See "Reclamation and the West via Arthur Powell Davis," pp. 78–101, in G. M. Gressley, *Twentieth Century American West*.

15. First annual report, Reclamation Service, p. 291; fourth annual report, p. 341; *Yakima Morning Herald*, April 6, 1930.

16. *Yakima Herald*, July 12, 1905; Jones to Yakima irrigation committee, Dec. 12, 1905, printed in the *Yakima Herald*, Dec. 20, 1905.

17. C. B. Coulter, "National Irrigation in the Yakima Valley," p. 117; *Yakima Morning Herald*, Jan. 29, 1906 (extra); district engineer to engineer in charge, July 12, 1906, in Yakima Project History, "Legal History," pp. 73–76 (roll 223). Sunnyside construction began May 7, 1906; Tieton, April 12, 1906.

18. District engineer to chief engineer, June 15, 1906, Yakima Project History, "Legal History," pp. 149–50 (roll 223); *Irrigation Age*, October 1911; Washington Irrigation Institute, *Proceedings 1914*, p. 106; in an advisory to members dated Nov. 13, 1914, the Investment Brokers Association of America warned of risks in irrigation bond issues.

19. H. J. Kerr, *History of Okanogan*, pp. 108–9; Project History 1916, p. 76, and memo, board of engineers to director, June 9, 1912.

20. 38 *Stats*. 687.

21. Wenatchee *Daily World*, Sept. 15, 1928; B. Mitchell, "Flowing Wealth"; L. M. Hull, ed., *History of Central Washington*, pp. 541 and 588–89; J. A. Gellatly, *History of Wenatchee*, pp. 44–46; Gunn to Clark, April 7 and 11, 1902, in Thomas Burke papers, University of Washington; Clark to Chase, Nov. 22, 1905 (lent by Clifford Chase).

22. G. M. Allen, *Irrigated Lands of the State of Washington*, p. 49; Hull, *Central Washington*, 1:570–74; Wenatchee *Daily World*, Nov. 8 and 15, 1907; Clark to Chase, Nov. 22, 1905 (lent by Clifford Chase).

23. Fourteenth Census, *State Compendium for Washington* (1924), pp. 87 and 89.

24. In Mally v. Weidensteiner, 88 Washington 398 (1915), for example, the court defended its decisions as harmonious but acknowledged claims of

inconsistency by counsel for the appellant. The landmark case for riparian rights is Brown v. Case, 217 Pac. 23 (1913). See C. Horowitz, "Riparian and Appropriated Rights to Use of Water in Washington," 7 *WLR* 197. Horowitz's notes 52, 53, and 54 list significant cases. Johncox, 17 Washington 277 and 139 Washington 84.

25. 164 U.S. 112 (1896). Oregon and Idaho also copied the Wright Act.

26. Senate Journal, 1889–90, p. 240.

27. Chapter entitled "Irrigation and Irrigation Ditches," 1890, amended 1899, 1901, 1905, 1907, 1911, 1913, and 1915.

28. For a sketch of the doctrine of beneficial use in Washington, see Hunter v. Langenour, 250 Pac. 41 (1926).

29. Chapter 117, session laws 1917, established the second-foot as the unit measure, eminent domain for beneficial use, the appointment of water masters, procedures for appropriating water and establishing reservoirs, etc. Amended 1919, 1921, 1925. The 1921 amendment changed the title of hydraulic engineer and name of the department until another change in 1951 (chapter 7, session laws 1921). An early challenge to Chase's authority was West Side Irrigation Co. v. Chase, 115 Wash. 146 (1921). On beneficial use, see Horowitz, "Riparian and Appropriated Rights," p. 215. On assessments, see Roberts v. Richland Irrigation District, 169 Wash. 156 (1932).

30. J. Fahey, *Inland Empire: D. C. Corbin and Spokane*, pp. 201–8.

31. Lawrence Stark, "Lewiston-Clarkston Improvement Company," pp. 60–64.

32. *Yakima Morning Herald,* Jan. 5, 1913.

33. The Arcadia discussion is based on Spokane County civil suit 72903; Arcadia articles of incorporation, Spokane County 169537, 230288, and book J, 167; and *Spokesman-Review,* Feb. 3, 1910. A copy of the prospectus is in the files of the Eastern Washington State Historical Society.

34. Thomas Means to Noble, April 13, 1905, telling the results of the survey; C. E. Grunsky to C. D. Walcott, director, USGS, San Francisco, March 10, 1906. Both are in U.S. Bureau of Reclamation files, loaned by Rupert B. Spearman, area engineer, Upper Columbia Development Office, USBR.

35. The Grunsky to Walcott letter includes a handwritten list of ownerships by quarter sections.

36. Senator Fred DuBois to Harry L. Day, Feb. 3, 1905 (loaned by Henry L. Day).

37. Interview with Dill, April 24, 1948.

38. Interview with Ford, April 28, 1948. Some say Henry Landes, state geologist, suggested the name Columbia Basin.

39. Washington Columbia Basin Survey Commission, "Columbia Basin Project" (1920), p. 31.

40. There are a number of discussions of the dam versus canal. See B. C. Harding, "Water from Pend Oreille: The Gravity Plan for the Columbia Basin." G. Sundborg, *Hail Columbia,* is a biased account drawn largely from James O'Sullivan's papers at Gonzaga University. J. Fahey, "Spokane's Grand Plan to Pre-empt Coulee Dam," mentions the automobile caravans. *Spokes-*

man-Review, Dec. 18, 20, and 22, 1918, reports the barometric survey.

41. *Wenatchee Daily World,* July 18, 1918.

42. *Spokesman-Review,* Feb. 3–9, 1922; W. W. Hindley, "Story of Grand Coulee Dam," *Spokesman-Review* Progress edition, Jan. 25, 1942; "Columbia Basin Irrigation Project," report of G. W. Goethals and Co., Inc., Washington State Department of Conservation and Development, 1922.

43. Sunnyside Valley Irrigation District to Jones, Dec. 12, 1923, quoted in Forth, "Wesley L. Jones," p. 472. In 1931 Washington State appropriated $1,250,000 to refinance districts and reconstruct irrigation works. Congress amended the reclamation act in 1924 to change the annual assessment to 5 percent of each farmer's gross income. The Tieton in 1947 and Sunnyside Valley in 1952 were the first and second projects in the United States to repay their construction costs.

44. Goss is quoted in the *Colfax Commoner,* Sept. 30, 1927; Erle J. Barnes, director of conservation and development, in the *Yakima Morning Herald,* Jan. 27, 1927; and Secretary of Agriculture Jardine's views in an editorial supporting basin development in the *Yakima Morning Herald,* Jan. 3, 1926.

45. Mead's remarks from "Columbia Basin Project, Washington," hearing before the Senate Committee on Irrigation and Reclamation, June 21, 1932, 72d Cong. 1st sess. p. 6.

46. Interview with Dill, April 24, 1948.

CHAPTER 6   *Red Apples: Big Business*

1. N. W. Durham, *History of the City of Spokane,* 1:605–8; *Better Fruit,* Jan. 1910, p. 22; O. E. Anderson, *Refrigeration in America,* p. 166; Washington State Agricultural Extension Service *Bulletin 131* (1916); Report of the Washington Director of Agriculture, 1917–18, p. 131; M. T. Buchanan, "Washington Apples on the New York and Chicago Fruit Auctions," p. 8, table of production by western states, 1889–1938.

2. *Spokesman-Review,* Nov. 19, 1917.

3. *Spokesman-Review,* June 17, 1909; O. M. Morris, "Fertilizers and Cover Crops," Washington State Agricultural Extension Service *Bulletin 217* (1927). The *Colfax Commoner,* Oct. 10, 1891, credits J. T. Arrasmith with growing and naming the Palouse apple.

4. J. W. Ellison, "Cooperative Movement in the Oregon Apple Industry," pp. 77–81; H. H. Maynard, *Marketing Northwestern Apples,* pp. 74–76; *Yakima Morning Herald,* March 1, 1894, Jan. 21, 1897, Jan. 12, 1899, and Feb. 4, 1902. There had been a Northwest Fruit Growers Association in the nineties devoted to cooperative marketing, pest control, uniform packing, and inspection when most growers shipped their apples by express companies, but it declined as Yakima's growers abandoned it.

5. *Yakima Herald,* June 27, 1895; *Yakima Morning Herald,* Jan. 14, 1908. Commission men were licensed and bonded in Washington (chapter 139, ses-

sion laws 1907), and a 1923 amendment (chapter 134, session laws 1923) required accurate accounting and limited commissions to 10 percent of the selling price. See 131 Wash. 394 (1924).

6. Ellison, "Cooperative Movement," p. 71; P. S. Creager, "Wellhouse Apple Orchard," pp. 498–503, an article furnished me by Robert B. Townsend, science librarian, Kansas State University; *Yakima Morning Herald*, Sept. 23, 1903 and Jan. 1, 1909. The Skinner papers in the national archives contain a good deal of information about Hood River.

7. Interview with Earl Barnhill, May 22, 1964; Skookum Packers Assn., *Fiftieth Anniversary Report*, April 30, 1963; *Spokesman-Review*, Nov. 18, 1903.

8. On the volume of apples, see E. L. Overholser, "Production and Marketing Problems," p. 87.

9. Maynard, *Marketing Northwestern Apples*, p. 150; Crutchfield biographical material from *Pittsburgh of Today*, p. 898.

10. Gwin address to the 1913 Washington State Horticultural Association convention, reported in *Yakima Morning Herald*, Jan. 19, 1913.

11. L. Hegnauer, "Eighty-six Golden Years," pp. 195–96.

12. Barnhill interview; Skookum, *Fiftieth Anniversary Report*.

13. Skookum Packers, articles of incorporation, May 11, 1916; memo of agreement with exchange, June 3, 1916; minutes of Skookum executive committee, July 6, 1916 (all in Skookum files). The cycles of production, Buchanan, "Washington Apples," p. 8, table 1.

14. Barnhill interview.

15. *Spokesman-Review*, May 25, 1919; Maynard, *Marketing Northwestern Apples*, p. 161; Barnhill interview.

16. Maynard, *Marketing Northwestern Apples*, pp. 62–63, 65, 66–67; C. B. Coulter, "Big Y Country," pp. 474–76; *Yakima Morning Herald*, June 17, 1902 and Jan. 17, 1909.

17. Coulter, "Big Y Country," pp. 477–78.

18. Ellison, "Cooperative Movement," pp. 84–85; *Spokesman-Review*, Dec. 12, 1912; *Spokane Daily Chronicle*, Dec. 16 and 20, 1912.

19. W. V. Woehlke, "What Ails the Big Red Apple?" pp. 916–25; *Yakima Morning Herald*, March 14, 1908; Barnhill interview.

20. Paulhamus to Bassett, Moomaw, and Kerr, USDA Department of Markets, Jan. 7, 1916 (NA).

21. *Spokesman-Review*, Nov. 14, 1915.

22. *Sunset*, January 1915, pp. 49–50.

23. Paulhamus to J. C. Skinner, n.d. (NA).

24. Paulhamus to Bassett, Moomaw, and Kerr, USDA Department of Markets, Jan. 7, 1916 (NA).

25. Ibid.

26. 185 ICC 299 (1932); an unfinished manuscript history by Barnhill.

27. C. C. Hampson, "Trends in the Apple Industry," Washington State Agricultural Experiment Station *Bulletin 277* (1933).

28. "Car Supply Investigation," 42 ICC 657 (1916–17).

29. S. Thompson, *Railway Statistics* (1930), p. 44; 42 ICC 567, 657 (1916–17).

30. "Perishable Fruit Investigation," 56 ICC 449 (1919–20); 40 ICC 191 (1916); *Yakima Morning Herald*, Oct. 27, 1911.

31. Barnhill interview; 185 ICC 299 (1932).

32. D. M. Street, *Railroad Equipment Financing*, p. 13; 56 ICC 449; *Better Fruit*, Aug. 1929, pp. 9 and 36. The Transportation Act of 1920 extended ICC jurisdiction over rates, valuations, services, etc., and although the act was amended eight times between 1921 and 1930, no significant changes in ICC powers were enacted until the depression of the thirties. By turning refrigerated cars over to subsidiaries, railroads avoided ICC regulation of securities to pay for them.

33. Thompson, *Railway Statistics* (1930), pp. 46–47; 68 ICC 676; 83 ICC 71; Street, *Railroad Equipment Financing*, pp. 31–32. In Wenatchee Valley Fruit Exchange v. Northern Pacific et al. (83 ICC 71) the exchange specifically asked for restoration of rates in effect before 1918–20, a request the ICC denied. By increasing car size, carriers increased their revenue approximately 20 percent. State's lawsuit, *Spokesman-Review*, Aug. 10, 1918.

34. 83 ICC 71 (1923).

35. Western Fruit Jobbers, "Statement to the National Transportation Committee (1933)," p. 15, exhibit 7.

36. 181 ICC 579 (1932).

37. 185 ICC 299 (1932) and 204 ICC 443 (1934).

38. The discussion of storage is based on: *Better Fruit*, Dec. 1917, pp. 8–10, a summary of USDA *Bulletin 587*, "Storage of Apples in the Pacific Northwest"; *Yakima Morning Herald*, Oct. 27, 1911; Barnhill interview; Anderson, *Refrigeration in America*, p. 164; E. L. Overholser, "History of Fruit Storage in the United States"; G. Porter and H. C. Livesay, *Merchants and Manufacturers*, pp. 168–78. See also W. V. Hukill and E. Smith, "Cold Storage of Apples," USDA *Yearbook of Agriculture, 1943–47*, pp. 867–70. In an interview with C. E. Chase, Wenatchee, April 23, 1964, Chase described his talk with Ralph Budd, president of the Great Northern, who approved loans at 6 percent—a 1 percent reduction in the usual rate—for warehouses on Great Northern land at Okanogan, Pateros, Chelan, Sunnyslope, Wenatchee, Cashmere, Monitor, and Peshastin.

39. Anderson, *Refrigeration in America*, pp. 238–41; Overholser, "Production and Marketing Problems," p. 101 (figures rounded by me). *Better Fruit*, Aug. 1929, p. 10, lists warehouses in operation.

40. *Yakima Morning Herald*, Nov. 19, 1901, reported scale in most orchards, appearing within the past eight years; A. L. Melander, "The Wormy Apple"; *Spokesman-Review*, Jan. 29 and Feb. 1, 1910; Wenatchee *Daily World*, April 17, 1919; *Better Fruit*, June 1949, p. 8.

41. Report of Washington Department of Agriculture, 1914, pp. 10 and 54–55; *Yakima Morning Herald*, May 1, 1923; USDA Yearbook, *Insects*, p. 318. Until the legislature withdrew authority, counties paid assistant inspectors who worked with state inspectors.

42. Wenatchee *Daily World,* July 19, 1912; F. L. Overly et al., "Lead and Arsenate Spray"; L. L. Mabbott, "History of the Wenatchee-Okanogan Apple Industry," p. 42; H. L. Garver, "Rural Electrification in Washington," p. 54.

43. Chase interview.

44. J. A. Gellatly, *History of Wenatchee,* p. 124; Washington State Agricultural Experiment Station *Bulletin 226* (1928) and *Bulletin 229* (1928); Report of the Washington State Department of Agriculture, 1925–26, p. 10.

45. *Yakima Morning Herald,* Jan. 6, 1914.

46. *Spokesman-Review,* March 9, 1917, Jan. 17, 1918, and Aug. 20, 1920; Fifth Biennial Report of the Washington State Department of Agriculture, 1921–22, pp. 80–81.

47. *Yakima Herald,* Nov. 3, 1898; *Yakima Morning Herald,* Jan. 1, 1920, Jan. 2, 1923, and Jan. 2, 1925; *Spokesman-Review,* March 2, 1917.

48. Washington State Agricultural Experiment Station *Bulletin 326,* p. 16; Overholser, "Production and Marketing Problems," p. 97: Delicious brought the best average prices in 1921–26, accounting for 25 percent of shipments.

49. S. E. Boyle, "Some Economic Aspects of the Frozen Food Industry," pp. 2–4 and 37–38.

50. Harry Miller annual report, June 30, 1928 (Skookum files).

51. Washington State Agricultural Experiment Station *Bulletin 326,* p. 26 (grades); Hampson, "Trends"; *Yakima Morning Herald,* Oct. 4, 1924 and Jan. 11, 1930 (storage). Overholser, "Production and Marketing Problems," gives 1926–30 car averages as 19,764 cars a year for Wenatchee, 15,234 for Yakima, or Wenatchee 53 percent and Yakima 42 percent of Washington shipments.

52. *Spokesman-Review,* Feb. 27, March 11, and May 8, 1921.

53. *Yakima Morning Herald,* April 6, 1930.

54. E. F. Dummeier, "Financing Cooperative Marketing," p. 38; *Yakima Morning Herald,* Feb. 8, 1930. The Yakima Valley Traffic Association was originally called the Yakima Valley Traffic and Credit Association.

55. A directory of western box factories, *Timberman,* October 1932, pp. 36–48. *Timberman,* April 1931, p. 92; Wenatchee *Daily World,* July 22, 1922.

56. Report of the Washington State Department of Agriculture, 1925–26, p. 35; *Yakima Morning Herald,* Jan. 2 and Nov. 19, 1929, May 28, 1930. The last cited article reports Bureau ad expenditures as $48,000 in 1928, $71,000 in 1929, and $100,000 subscribed for 1930. Quotation from an editorial in *Yakima Morning Herald,* Oct. 31, 1929.

CHAPTER 7 *Bankers and Farmers*

1. For an essay on the Dutch lenders in Spokane, see J. Fahey, "When the Dutch Owned Spokane."

2. *Spokesman-Review,* July 29, 1901, Jan. 1, 1903, Nov. 5, 1922 (magazine section), and Twohy obituary, July 15, 1954.

3. Interview with B. L. Jenkins, Aug. 31, 1967; *Spokane Daily Chronicle,* May 19, 1912; *Yakima Morning Herald,* Oct. 2 and 4, 1929.

4. Jenkins interview; F. E. Rowland to Chris Hughes, June 3, 1930, in Farmers State Bank of Reardan records, Eastern Washington University, container 56:2.

5. C. A. Campbell, "Old National Bank of Spokane," pp. 85–86; N. R. Knight, "History of Banking in Washington," p. 225. Under an 1887 amendment to the National Banking Act, the comptroller could designate reserve cities of 25,000 or more population upon application by three-fourths of the national banks in a given city.

6. Exchange National Bank, thirtieth anniversary statement, 1919.

7. *Colfax Gazette,* Feb. 13, 1903.

8. Spokane County articles of incorporation, amended, 198738 (1908); 227900 (1909); undated clipping, *Spokesman-Review* library; *Spokesman-Review,* July 22, 1933; annual reports, Spokane and Eastern, in files of Seattle-First National, Spokane. Under Washington law, trust companies possessed all the ordinary powers of a bank. See H. H. Preston, "Trust Banking in Washington."

9. State Banking Department, First Annual Report, Dec. 31, 1907, p. 1.

10. Ibid., pp. 1–2.

11. O. K. Burrell, *Gold in the Woodpile,* describes a number of country banks. Although he writes of Oregon, his observations fit Washington.

12. F. E. Rowland to H. S. Wilson, Farmers State Bank records, EWU, 55:6.

13. R. G. Comegys, "Country Banking in Eastern Washington," p. 341.

14. E. T. Coman quoted in *Colfax Commoner,* July 28, 1905.

15. W. M. Yeager, "Pioneer's Problems of Land Acquisition," p. 116; D. O. Johansen and C. M. Gates, *Empire of the Columbia,* pp. 445–46; Campbell, "Old National Bank," p. 120 (quoting Vincent); Washington Bankers Association, *Proceedings 1916,* p. 43.

16. Comegys, "Country Banking," pp. 338–40.

17. Based on my review of county chattel mortgage records and files of the Farmers State Bank, EWU.

18. Northwestern & Pacific Hypotheekbank and DeTweede Northwestern and Pacific Hypotheekbank annual reports 1910 and 1911. DeTweede means second.

19. *Spokesman-Review,* Feb. 10, 1914.

20. Knight, "History of Banking in Washington," pp. 242–43.

21. Coman to Prof. George Severance, Pullman, May 1, 1915, in Exchange National Bank records, Washington State University, 20:21.

22. *Spokesman-Review,* June 8, 1919.

23. Washington Bankers Association, *Proceedings 1917,* p. 171.

24. H. J. Kerr, *History of Okanogan,* pp. 98–99; *Yakima Morning Herald,* Jan. 9, 1914.

25. Washington State Bank Examiner, Tenth Annual Report, Dec. 31, 1916.

26. Assistant cashier, Farmers State Bank, Reardan, to E. W. Wilson, director of sales, Federal Reserve Bank of San Francisco, Aug. 12, 1918, EWU.

27. Twohy to John M. Perrin, chairman of the board, Federal Reserve Bank of San Francisco, April 20, 1918, copy in Farmers State Bank files, EWU.

28. *Spokesman-Review*, Aug. 5, 1919 and March 1, 1921. The Spokane bank opened in May 1917.

29. L. A. Jones and D. Durand, *Mortgage Lending Experience in Agriculture*, p. 9; *Spokesman-Review*, March 1, 1921; and debt to land value, Fifteenth Census, II, pt. 3, p. 429.

30. Comegys, "Country Banking," p. 344; *Colfax Gazette*, July 23, 1920, reporting a Coman address in his campaign for governor.

31. E. S. Sparks, *History and Theory of Agricultural Credit in the United States*, p. 436; *Farm Credit Journal*, November 1934.

32. *Farm Credit Journal*, April 1937.

33. R. E. Shepherd, Washington Bankers Association, *Proceedings 1927*, pp. 73–81.

34. *Farm Credit Journal*, November 1934.

35. A. C. Wiprud, *Federal Farm-Loan System in Operation*, pp. 92–93.

36. Report of the State Bank Commissioner, 1919; *Yakima Morning Herald*, Jan. 1, 1920.

37. Report of the State Bank Commissioner, 1919; Comegys, "Country Banking," p. 347; Report of the Washington Supervisor of Banking, 1923, p. 1.

38. Knight, "History of Banking in Washington," p. 374.

39. Report of the Washington Supervisor of Banking, 1923; Report of Comptroller of the United States, 1931, p. 37.

40. Report of the Washington Supervisor of Banking, 1923.

41. George W. Peddycord, Washington Bankers Association, *Proceedings 1922*, pp. 28–29; *Yakima Morning Herald*, Sept. 25, 1921.

42. F. A. Garrecht, eastern Washington district attorney, Washington Bankers Association, *Proceedings 1921*, pp. 70–71; *Agricultural Crisis and Its Causes*, 2:7.

43. Based on A. M. Christensen, "Agricultural Pressure and Government Response," passim.

44. M. R. Benedict, *Farm Policies of the United States*, pp. 177–78; O. M. Kile, *Farm Bureau through Three Decades*, pp. 47–55; *Spokesman-Review*, Sept. 21, 1921 and Dec. 25, 1925.

45. For Sapiro: *New York Times*, Nov. 25, 1959 (obituary); *National Cyclopedia of American Biography*, C:130. *Spokesman-Review*, Feb. 27 and March 3, 1921; House Journal, 1921; chapter 115, session laws of 1921.

46. A crop-credit bill (chapter 121, session laws of 1921) also passed but, according to a letter from Roger L. Roberts, Washington Department of Agriculture, to me, May 6, 1980, no associations formed under it; Senate Journal, 1921. The cold storage measure was HB 152 which failed on third reading.

47. Sixth Biennial Report, Director of Agriculture, 1924, pp. 33–34; *Spokesman-Review,* March 11, 1921. The Wenatchee association was approved by the director of agriculture, Oct. 21, 1921.

48. C. M. Bishop, "Warehouse Receipts as Collateral"; "Liquidation of the War Finance Corporation"; 42 *Stats.* 634. According to personnel of the National Archives, field records of the Spokane office have been destroyed.

49. Rutter to Meyer, Jan. 22, 1924 (NA).

50. *Spokesman-Review,* Dec. 31, 1925; Rutter to WFC, June 6, 1922 (NA); Fiscal Agent, Federal Reserve Bank of San Francisco, to Assistant Treasurer, WFC, Dec. 27, 1922 (NA). The First National Bank of St. John, said by the comptroller to have failed because of incompetent management, paid 95.5 percent of its deposits (report of comptroller, 1931, pp. 312–463, table 46). The Washington agency also assisted several north Idaho banks.

51. Rutter to Meyer, Sept. 30, 1925 (NA).

52. N. J. Wall, "Agricultural Loans of Commercial Banks," pp. 2–5. From 1920 to 1934, bank loans secured by farm real estate decreased 66 percent nationally; personal and collateral loans, 79 percent. Insurance companies apparently were not as active in farm real estate lending in Washington as in midwestern and eastern states. According to Comegys, "Country Banking," p. 348, some rural bankers helped farmers draw the papers to form agricultural cooperative associations.

53. Report of the Washington Supervisor of Banking, 1925; W. O. Thomson, *Thomson's Manual of Pacific Northwest Finance, 1930,* p. 94.

54. *Spokesman-Review,* Sept. 21, 1947, a thirty-year review of the bank; T. S. Pressly and W. H. Scofield, *Farm Real Estate Values,* pp. 66–67.

55. *Colfax Commoner,* Feb. 9, 1923; Jones and Durand, *Mortgage Lending Experience,* p. 128.

56. *Spokesman-Review,* Sept. 21, 1947.

57. Research Committee on Social Trends, *Recent Social Trends,* pp. 99–100.

58. F. C. Forrest, address on the history of the Washington Bankers Association, Pullman, June 16, 1939, in *Spokesman-Review* library; Washington Bankers Association, *Proceedings 1927,* pp. 99–100; *Proceedings 1929,* pp. 91–97; and *Proceedings 1930,* p. 24.

59. *Spokesman-Review,* Jan. 1, 1928 (Flood); *Colfax Commoner,* Jan. 14, 1927; *Yakima Morning Herald,* May 16, 1930.

60. Report of the Comptroller, 1931, pp. 839 and 931–32.

61. *Colfax Gazette,* April 14, 1922; *Colfax Commoner,* June 13, 1924.

62. *Colfax Gazette,* Aug. 10, 1923; *Commoner,* Jan. 18, 1924.

63. *Colfax Gazette,* Feb 17, 1922; Report of the Tax Investigating Commission, 1921, pp. 26 and 28.

64. *Colfax Commoner,* Dec. 15, 1922; *Spokesman-Review,* Oct. 11, 1928.

65. *Colfax Commoner,* Sept. 11, 1930.

66. Report of State Tax Commission, 1932; *Yakima Morning Herald,* Nov. 7, 1929 and April 18, 1930.

67. Benedict, *Farm Policies,* pp. 184–87; *Spokesman-Review,* Jan. 8, 1928; E. F. Dummeier, "Financing Cooperative Marketing," pp. 58–59.

68. Christensen, "Agricultural Pressure and Government Response"; J. H. Shideler, "Herbert Hoover and the Federal Farm Board Project," pp. 712–13. Hoover's views are discussed in detail in J. H. Wilson, "Hoover's Agricultural Policies," pp. 335–61; and G. H. Koerselman, "Secretary Hoover and National Farm Policy," pp. 378–95. For the Washington Export Corporation League, see R. McDonald and R. G. Dunbar, "Initiation of the McNary-Haugen Movement in Montana and the Pacific Northwest," pp. 68–69.

69. *Colfax Commoner,* Aug. 22, Oct. 31 and Dec. 5, 1929.

70. *Yakima Morning Herald,* June 30, 1930.

71. *Spokesman-Review,* Jan. 9, 1927.

72. *Spokesman-Review,* Dec. 29, 1925 (Summers); *New York Times,* April 3, 1922.

73. *Spokesman-Review,* Dec. 25, 1925 and Jan. 3, 1926; *Colfax Commoner,* June 12, 1930; *Yakima Morning Herald,* June 17, 1930.

CHAPTER 8 *Machines*

1. Proceedings of the State Board of Equalization, 1930, schedule A, table 1.

2. J. A. Gellatly, *History of Wenatchee,* p. 59.

3. *Spokesman-Review,* Dec. 5, 1926, May 1, 1927, and July 22, 1933; *Spokane Daily Chronicle,* Jan. 10, 1919; Washington Water Power Company annual reports, especially 1922. The Spokane and Inland Empire, organized by Jay P. Graves of Spokane, combined F. A. Blackwell's electric line from Coeur d'Alene to Spokane, Graves's streetcar line, the Spokane Traction Company, and resort properties into a new company. The Great Northern acquired the road in 1911 and threw it into receivership in 1919. See G. W. Hilton and J. F. Due, *Electric Interurban Railways in America,* for general background of the electric era.

4. *Colfax Commoner,* Oct. 6, 1911; F. C. Guilbert, "Story of the Washington Good Roads Association" (quotation); Gellatly, *History of Wenatchee,* p. 38; E. L. Armstrong, *History of Public Works,* p. 74.

5. J. J. Flink, *Car Culture,* pp. 24–25; *Spokesman-Review,* Feb. 27, March 3 (editorial), and March 8, 1931 (Hill).

6. About 1910, the National Good Roads Association organized "good roads trains," Armstrong, *History of Public Works,* pp. 71–72; *Spokane Daily Chronicle,* Sept. 20, 1912; *History of Highways,* p. 2. H. J. Bergman, "Progressive on the Right: Marion E. Hay," discusses state administration of its early roads program. The U.S. Department of Agriculture established an Office of Road Inquiry in 1893, which originated the "object-lesson roads" with labor and equipment donated locally.

7. Bergman, "Progressive on the Right," p. 48.

8. F. J. Dullanty, "Riegel Brothers."

9. Report of the Secretary of State, 1917–18.

10. Washington Good Roads Association, *Proceedings 1921*.

11. Report of the State Highway Commissioner, 1914–16, pp. 28–29 and 106; *Colfax Gazette*, May 28, 1915.

12. *Colfax Commoner*, Oct. 6, 1911.

13. F. C. Guilbert to R. L. Rutter, March 17, 1919 (Inland Automobile Association files, Eastern Washington University); *Spokane Daily Chronicle*, Aug. 18, 1928; interview with David C. Guilbert, September 1964.

14. *Spokane Daily Chronicle*, May 13, 1910; *Spokesman-Review*, June 5, 1918 (automobile census); *Yakima Morning Herald*, Oct. 15, 1921; report of the State Highway Commissioner, 1919–20, p. 9.

15. *Colfax Commoner*, June 5, 1925.

16. Report of the State Highway Commissioner, 1919–20, p. 167.

17. Harve Phipps quoted in the *Yakima Morning Herald*, Oct. 16, 1919.

18. My calculation from 1930 census data.

19. *Seattle Times*, July 18, 1965.

20. Transcript of a debate on the Carlyon bill, Washington Good Roads Association, Aug. 26.1920, and Washington Good Roads Association, *Proceedings 1927* (Goss), both IAA files, EWU.

21. *Spokesman-Review*, July 23, 1927.

22. *Spokane Daily Chronicle*, April 21 and Aug. 4, 1912; *Spokesman-Review*, Jan. 3, 1926.

23. Washington State Agricultural Experiment Station *Bulletin 360*, pp. 28–30; *Colfax Commoner*, Oct. 6, 1922 and May 4, 1923; *Oakesdale Tribune*, fiftieth anniversary edition, June 16, 1939.

24. "Fifty Years Ago," *Odessa Record*, May 18, 1978.

25. State Director of Public Works Report, 1921–22, pp. 378–79; *Spokane Daily Chronicle*, Feb. 7, 1915 (Millwood).

26. State Director of Public Works Report, 1921–22, p. 380.

27. *Colfax Gazette*, Sept. 30, 1921.

28. *Colfax Commoner*, Nov. 14, 1924 and Jan. 27, 1927; State Director of Public Works Report, 1921–22, contains routes and certification hearings.

29. *Colfax Commoner*, Jan. 27, 1927.

30. *Regulation of Stock Ownership in Railroads*, p. 1393; *Thomson's Manual of Pacific Northwest Finance 1930*, pp. 192 and 265; E. Bates, *Commercial Survey*, p. 103; Report of Commissioner of Highways, 1926–28, p. 28; Report of Department of Public Works, 1927–28, pp. 10–11; *Grant County Journal*, Aug. 5, 1910; *Colfax Gazette*, May 14, 1920; *Colfax Commoner*, May 16, 1924. Chapter 1, session laws 1919, defines an auto stage; chapter 111, session laws 1921, provides for motor carrier regulation through the department of public works. See P. T. McElhiney, "Competition between Motor Freight Lines and Railroads in the State of Washington."

31. *Spokane Daily Chronicle*, Feb. 5, 1967; L. K. Turner, "Patches of History," p. 16.

32. Bureau of the Census, *Special Reports: Telephones: 1907,* tables 21 and 36, and p. 76.

33. My analysis based on Report of the Department of Public Works, 1921–22, pp. 357–61.

34. *Yakima Morning Herald,* Aug. 5, 1911.

35. *Yakima Herald,* March 1, 1900 and March 1, 1953; Gellatly, *History of Wenatchee,* pp. 110–12; H. I. Shotwell, *Shotwell Story,* p. 34; P. Holmes, "First Telephone System," pp. 17–18; *Yakima Morning Herald,* Jan. 12, 1903.

36. *Colfax Gazette,* Jan. 2, 1903.

37. *Thomson's Manual 1930,* p. 234; *Colfax Commoner,* Oct. 18, 1907; N. W. Durham, *History of the City of Spokane,* 2:363 and 3:626; Pacific Tel. and Tel., *History of the Pacific System,* pp. 24–25.

38. R. F Steele and A. P. Rose, *Illustrated History of the Big Bend Country,* p. 85.

39. Pacific Tel. and Tel., *History of the Pacific System,* pp. 24–25; *Yakima Morning Herald,* Jan. 3, 1911 and Jan. 28, 1915.

40. *Thomson's Manual 1930,* p. 201; unpublished historical files of the General Telephone Company of the Northwest, Inc., selected excerpts furnished by Burton R. Green, public information manager, Feb. 12, 1968.

41. *Yakima Herald,* Dec. 8, 1898 and March 18, 1903 (petitions); *Yakima Morning Herald,* Jan. 20, 1909 and Sept. 5, 1915; *Colfax Commoner,* Oct. 28, 1910 and March 10, 1916 (quotation); *Spokesman-Review,* Nov. 13, 1966 (cows).

42. J. Fahey, *Ballyhoo Bonanza,* pp. 117–20.

43. *Spokane Daily Chronicle,* Dec. 10, 1951; *Spokesman-Review,* June 17, 1924 and Oct. 5, 1930; J. Dierdorff, *How Edison's Lamp Helped Light the West,* p. 14; E. H. Libby to Howard Elliott, president, NP, Nov. 14, 1910 (NP papers, Minnesota Historical Society).

44. E. J. Crosby, *Story of the Washington Water Power,* p. 24; M. K. Green, "Politics and Kilowatts," pp. 3–4; Washington Water Power Company, "Statement A: Outline of Origin and Development," passim.

45. Crosby, *Story of the Washington Water Power,* p. 33.

46. *Yakima Morning Herald,* May 13, 1902.

47. Grant County PUD, *Back through the Pages of History,* p. 20.

48. L. A. Lewis, "Commercial Development," pp. 7–8; *Spokesman-Review,* July 27, 1947.

49. Dierdorff, *Edison's Lamp,* p. 28.

50. *Colfax Gazette,* Nov. 14, 1913.

51. *Colfax Gazette,* April 2, 1920.

52. *Colfax Commoner,* Aug. 28, 1925.

53. Lewis, "Commercial Development," pp. 6–7 (manager); *Spokesman-Review,* Jan. 27, 1928 (twenty customers). See 166 Wash. 82 (1931): In 1906 the state supreme court ruled that the sale of surplus power outside its limits was beyond the corporate powers of a first-class city in Farwell v. Seattle, 43

Wash. 141. In 1931 the court overturned this interpretation, but the Farwell decision stood twenty-five years.

54. E. Marple, "Movement for Public Ownership of Power," pp. 61–66; *Spokesman-Review*, Feb. 2, 1922; S. Doc. 92, 70th Cong., 1st sess.

55. "Farm Lines: An Analysis of Construction Practices and Costs"; *Colfax Commoner*, April 11, 1924 (franchises).

56. Marple, "Movement for Public Ownership" (Dill); 143 Wash. 67 (1927); *Yakima Morning Herald*, Jan. 15, 1916.

57. O. M. Kile, *Farm Bureau through Three Decades*, p. 78; H. L. Garver, "Rural Electrification in Washington," p. 53; *Yakima Morning Herald*, April 29, 1930.

58. Dierdorff, *Edison's Lamp*, pp. 114–15.

59. Bone biography, AP Biographical Service, Dec. 15, 1946, in *Spokesman-Review* library.

60. State Board of Health, Tenth Biennial Report (1914), p. 60; State Department of Health, First Biennial Report (1922), p. 40. General background is based on W. G. Smillie, *Public Health*.

61. Smillie, *Public Health*, p. 354; State Board of Health, Eighth Biennial Report (1910), 38.

62. See Tabb v. Funk, 170 Wash. 545, and Dearling v. Funk, 177 Wash. 349.

63. State Board of Health, Thirteenth Biennial Report (1920), p. 34.

64. Chapter 6, session laws 1899; State Board of Health, Eighth Biennial Report (1910), p. 67, and Sixth Biennial Report (1906), p. 15.

65. State Board of Health, Thirteenth Biennial Report (1920), p. 16.

66. State Board of Health, Tenth Biennial Report (1913–14), pp. 40–41 (river tests); Thirteenth Biennial Report (1920), p. 35.

67. D. B. Seney, "Development of Water, Sewer, and Fire Service in Seattle," pp. 63 and 94; Spokane City Ordinance A583; Winston v. Spokane, 12 Wash. 524 (1895); *Spokesman-Review*, Dec. 13, 1908 and Feb. 26, 1967; *Spokane Daily Chronicle*, Oct. 28, 1907. The laws of 1893 authorized cities to build, maintain, and operate water and sewer systems, and the laws of 1899 extended this authority to cities other than first class, with the power to form assessment districts.

68. *Spokesman-Review*, March 3, 1904 and Dec. 13, 1908; *Spokane Daily Chronicle*, Oct. 28, 1907.

69. National Resources Planning Board, "Development of Resources and Economic Opportunity," p. 157; Donald G. Evans, state director of health, to Gov. A. B. Langlie, April 9, 1941, recommending measures against Spokane (Langlie papers, "Health 1941," from state archives, supplied by David Hastings).

70. E. D. Smith v. Spokane, 55 Wash. 219 (1909) (burning); State Department of Health, First Biennial Report (1922), p. 152.

71. State Board of Health, Thirteenth Biennial Report (1920), p. 13 (health officers) and pp. 114–16 (sex); *Spokesman-Review*, Dec. 19, 1911 (books).

1. American Smelting and Refining Co. v. Bunker Hill and Sullivan, U.S. District Court for Oregon, Equity 7555, now Seattle Federal Records Center, box 20340X; W. R. Ingalls, *Lead and Zinc in the United States,* pp. 239–52, discusses American's effect on the lead industry.

2. Defendant's answer, p. 19, A. S. and R. v. Bunker Hill.

3. J. Fahey, *Days of the Hercules,* pp. 166–68 (Northport and Pennsylvania) and pp. 168–69 (Bunker Hill).

4. Letters, *Weekly Missoulian* (Montana), Sept. 28 and Nov. 30, 1883.

5. In his analysis of 2,400 recorded deeds between 1887 and 1891, Fred O. Jones found an average price for placer claims to be $1,600, for lode claims $8,000. See Jones, "A Valuation Study of the Mineral Resources of Lands Ceded by the Coeur d'Alene Tribe of Indians."

6. For a more detailed account, see J. Fahey, *Inland Empire: D. C. Corbin and Spokane.*

7. Northern Pacific v. Joseph H. Boyd, 57 Law. Ed. 931 (1912), describes bond issue.

8. N. W. Durham, *History of the City of Spokane,* 1:487–88, lists homes.

9. *Spokane Daily Chronicle,* June 11, 1905 (Waikiki) and April 27, 1948 (obituary); *Northwest Mining Truth* 4, no. 11 (July 16, 1919): 12, reviews Granby; W. B. Wilcox, "Early History of Granby"; M. Bean, "Waikiki, Beauty Spot on the Little Spokane."

10. Union relations are detailed in J. Fahey, *Ballyhoo Bonanza,* pp. 68–95, and union organization in J. Fahey, "Ed Boyce and the Western Federation of Miners."

11. *Wallace Miner,* Sept. 14, 1911.

12. The name Asarco is used here for convenience, but it did not come into general use until World War I. The company was usually called A. S. and R. for short.

13. The formation of American Smelting and Refining Company is described in a company-sponsored book by I. F. Marcosson, *Metal Magic,* especially pp. 57–83, and its effect on the Coeur d'Alenes in Fahey, *Ballyhoo Bonanza,* pp. 65–66 and 170–74.

14. Campbell's and Finch's attempt appears in letters from Campbell to Tod Ford, July 3, 1901, and others in the Campbell letterbook, 1901–2, in the Eastern Washington State Historical Society library. Campbell wrote T. F. Woodman on July 8, 1901, that Thomas Greenough and Peter Larson, owners of the Mammoth, would not come in.

15. Fahey, *Ballyhoo Bonanza,* pp. 170–84 and 189. For the story from Rockefeller's viewpoint, see J. E. Fell, "Rockefeller's Right-hand Man."

16. *Northwest Mining Truth* 5, no. 8 (June 3, 1920): 6.

17. Fahey, *Days of the Hercules,* p. 62.

18. Newhouse affidavit, A. S. and R. v. Bunker Hill.

19. The terms of Bunker Hill's contract with Asarco and four other smelt-

ers appear in F. W. Bradley's affidavit, A. S. and R. v. Bunker Hill. Bradley also outlines negotiations between the companies.

20. Fahey, *Days of the Hercules,* pp. 169–73 (war) and p. 176 (prices and production).

21. *Engineering and Mining Journal,* Oct. 9, 1920, p. 737.

22. *Northwest Mining Truth* 5, no. 1 (Feb. 16, 1920): 3 and 5.

CHAPTER 10   *Lumber: Great Lakes Invaders*

1. C. C. Strong and C. S. Webb, *White Pine,* pp. 143–47; G. L. Drake and E. R. Maunder, *Forester's Log,* pp. 100–103; *Spokesman-Review,* May 26, 1929 and Jan. 21, 1953; biographical sketch in Exchange National Bank records, Washington State University archives, cage 20, container 25.

2. *Colfax Commoner,* Feb. 12, 1897 and Nov. 17, 1899.

3. F. J. Yonce, "Public Land Disposal in Washington," pp. 245–26 (trespass, Northern Pacific); R. H. Weidman, "Timber Growing and Logging Practice," p. 8 (selective cuts); S. B. Hutchison, "Century of Lumbering in Northern Idaho," *Timberman,* August 1938, p. 26; Strong and Webb, *White Pine,* pp. 11–24 and 170–73.

4. *Oakesdale Tribune,* fiftieth anniversary edition, June 16, 1939 (McCroskey); N. W. Durham, *History of the City of Spokane,* 1:473; *Spokesman-Review,* March 21, 1896; Spokane County civil suit 10592 (mill transfer); 17 Wash. 172 (1897).

5. R. W. Hidy et al., *Timber and Men,* p. 207.

6. Hutchison, "Century of Lumbering," *Timberman,* September 1938, p. 15 (sampling); J. Fahey, *Days of the Hercules,* p. 84 (Idaho promises); R. O. Hoover, "Public Land Policy of Washington State," pp. 165–70 (laws and sales).

7. D. T. Mason, *Timber Ownership and Lumber Production,* pp. 16–17 (Weyerhaeuser); E. Koch, "1903 and 1904 Boundary Examinations," p. 106; *Establishment and Modification of National Forest Boundaries.* E. S. Meany, "History of the Lumber Industry of the Pacific Northwest," p. 223, lists Weyerhaeuser purchases by county. H. K. Steen, *U.S. Forest Service,* reviews the contest between the president and Congress over authority to designate reserves in Washington and other western states. Commercial timber is defined as forest capable of producing salable timber, economically accessible, and open to cutting.

8. Hidy et al., *Timber and Men,* pp. 254–56; C. D. Pike v. Board of Land Commissioners, 19 Idaho 268 (1911); C. L. Billings on Rutledge in the *Coeur d'Alene Press,* April 1, 1940; Hutchison, *Timberman,* September 1938, pp. 15 and 28; Mount Rainier and Pacific reserve from *Lumber Industry,* 1:239, table 57. Roger Billings points out that the volume of marketable stumpage was far more significant to lumbermen than acreage, and believes the acreage statistics unreliable. I kept them in the text, however, for those of us who do

not readily visualize board feet and because, even if unverifiable, they suggest the relative scope of company operations.

9. Hidy et al., *Timber and Men*, p. 255; *Idaho Daily Statesman*, Nov. 20, 1901; *Spokane Daily Chronicle*, Aug. 21, 1902; *Colfax Gazette*, March 27, 1903 (Palouse acres).

10. *Spokesman-Review*, July 22, 1933 (purchases); R. H. Bockmier, "Inland Empire Lumber Industry," p. 13.

11. Yonce, "Public Land Disposal in Washington," p. 257; Hoover, "Public Land Policy of Washington State," pp. 199–204, 215, and 236; Mason, *Timber Ownership*, pp. 16–17; R. R. Cotroneo, "Timber Marketing by the Northern Pacific," p. 122 (best lands sold).

12. D. T. Mason, *Forests for the Future*, p. 25; J. L. Hall, "Policies and Methods," p. 38; *Idaho Daily Statesman*, Dec. 29, 1902; H.R. 807, 61st Cong., 2d sess. (1910).

13. *Daily Missoulian*, Jan. 10, March 17, and Aug. 13, 1905; United States v. W. A. Clark, 125 Fed. 777 (1905).

14. C. S. Webb, "Some Incidents," p. 69.

15. Hidy et al., *Timber and Men*, pp. 254–56; A. D. Decker, "Lumbering Moves West," p. 22; *Colfax Commoner*, May 12 and April 27, 1906; Potlatch Lumber v. H. T. Peterson et al., 12 Idaho 796 (1906), citing an unreported Washington case, Voltz and Metcalf v. Potlatch Lumber Company.

16. R. K. Harris, "Life in Potlatch," pp. 1–9; Webb, "Some Incidents" (Elk River), p. 69.

17. Decker, "Lumbering Moves West," p. 22; *Spokesman-Review*, Jan. 1, 1909.

18. Testimony in Idaho and Western Ry. v. Dollar, *Transcript on Appeal* (1911), p. 159, in Gonzaga University Law School library.

19. Based on W. G. Weigle, "Pulp Woods in the State of Washington"; N. Nybroten, *Idaho Statistical Abstract*, tables I–2 and VI–8; A. E. Thompson, "Forest Resources of Washington," p. 24; Weidman, "Timber Growing and Logging Practice," p. 4. Timber estimates tend to vary. The Washington State Planning Council, in "Master Plan for Forestry," in 1936 estimated 10.4 million timbered acres in eastern Washington of which 3.1 million were privately owned, labeling its figures tentative. *Timberman*, December 1928, pp. 62–63, published estimated timber stands by counties and species.

20. Hutchison, *Timberman*, September 1938, p. 28 (mill capacity); Bockmier, "Mr. Lumber," p. 14 (sons); S. B. Hutchison and R. K. Winters, *Northern Idaho Forest Resources*, p. 21.

21. Hutchison, *Timberman*, September 1938, p. 26; J. Fahey, *Inland Empire: D. C. Corbin and Spokane*, p. 226.

22. Blackwell originally represented the William Howard Land and Lumber Company in Idaho, incorporated in Idaho in 1901, according to the *Idaho Daily Statesman*, Jan. 17, 1901, but the company soon merged with others. *Idaho Daily Statesman*, Dec. 29, 1902; *Spokesman-Review*, March 31, 1937; Durham, *History of the City of Spokane*, 3:458; F. W. Blackwell, "The Inland Empire of F. A. Blackwell," p. 24.

23. Articles of incorporation, Kootenai County no. 89; *Poor's Manual of Railroads 1909,* p. 1300.

24. Articles of incorporation, Kootenai County no. 611. Blackwell, Lindsley, and two Pennsylvania men each held 100 shares. E. D. Hawksett testimony in Idaho and Western Ry. v. Dollar, p. 551 (mill capacities); Strong and Webb, *White Pine,* p. 64; L. Donally, "Tree Planting Projects," p. 183 (drives).

25. Pennsylvania investors and the Illinois Trust and Savings, Chicago, which held the mortgage, owned 82 percent of the railroad's stock; articles of incorporation, Kootenai County no. 372, indicate that of 9,402 issued shares, Blackwell and his son held 1,450. See *Poor's Manual of Railroads 1916,* p. 524. *Spokesman-Review,* March 21, 1937 (quotation).

26. A simplified discussion, based on H. H. Field, *History of the Milwaukee Railroad,* pp. 142–51 (fiscal), supplied by Jim Scribbins, Milwaukee Railroad. In 1914 the Milwaukee voted 26,236 of 31,721 shares; as sole bidder at sale after foreclosure, it took possession on Jan. 25, 1916. See also *Poor's Manual of Railroads 1916,* pp. 510 and 524. A profile of Russell appeared in *Spokane Woman,* Feb. 25, 1926; sketches of father and son, Durham, *History of the City of Spokane,* 3:458 and 616.

27. Blackwell Lumber Co., articles of incorporation, Kootenai County no. 47, amended 1911, 1916, and 1919; *Spokesman-Review,* Feb. 8, 1911.

28. This discussion is based on correspondence and deeds furnished by Mowry Smith, Jr., senior vice-president, Menasha Corporation, from files of the Menasha Wooden Ware Company, especially deeds June 10, 1909 and July 7, 1911, conveying timber tracts, and notice to stockholders, Blackwell Lumber, June 29, 1911. Smith is co-author of a book recounting the history of Menasha Wooden Ware, *One Third Crew, One Third Boat, One Third Luck.*

29. Articles of incorporation, Kootenai County no. 61, amended 1916.

30. R. W. Billings, "Diamond City," pp. 3–10; Cotroneo, "Timber Marketing," p. 124 (14,500 acres).

31. Articles of incorporation, Kootenai County no. 537; *Spokesman-Review,* Nov. 16, 1903, March 23 and Sept. 30, 1904; interview with E. Lee Smith, Dec. 20, 1976. McGoldrick was financed by J. D. Bronson and associates of Stillwater, Minnesota.

32. R. E. Hult, *Steamboats in the Timber,* p. 107.

33. Webb, "Some Incidents," p. 70.

34. K. A. Adams, *Logging Railroads of the West,* appendix; *Spokesman-Review,* Dec. 7, 1947 (flumes); Webb, "Some Incidents," p. 68.

35. J. F. Falk v. Humbird Lumber and Dalkena Lumber, 36 Idaho 1 (1922); Blackwell Lumber v. Empire Mill Co., 28 Idaho 556 (1916); *Spokane Daily Chronicle,* July 2, 1914 (Coeur d'Alene River).

36. *Spokesman-Review,* May 10, 1953 (one-third); *Early Days in the Forest Service* 4 (1976): 191, 199.

37. *Early Days in the Forest Service* 4 (1976):199–200.

38. J. A. Humbird v. Dorothy Humbird, 42 Idaho 29 (1926).

39. Webb, "Some Incidents," p. 73; *Spokesman-Review,* June 26, 1961;

Timberman, Aug. 1931, p. 34 (quotation); Donally, "Tree Planting Projects," p. 183.

40. Hutchison, "Century of Lumbering," *Timberman,* October 1938, p. 26 (Idaho); "Forest Products Industries," Spokane Chamber of Commerce (Washington); State ex rel White Pine Sash v. Superior Court, Ferry County, 143 Wash. 687 (1927), a suit to condemn right-of-way.

41. Potlatch Lumber et al. v. Northern Pacific et al., 14 ICC 41 (1908).

42. Spokane city building permit records; *Population 1880 to 2000;* Fourteenth Census (1920), *State Compendium: Washington;* Spokane city directories, especially 1905 (yards); *Spokane Daily Chronicle,* Sept. 7, 1913 (Montana sales).

43. Hutchison and Winters, *Northern Idaho Forest Resources,* p. 27.

44. Spokane city building permit records.

45. Hutchison, "Century of Lumbering," *Timberman,* October 1938, p. 34; Mason, *Timber Ownership and Lumber Production,* p. 13, estimates the average profit as 1.06 percent from 1909 through 1914.

46. G. T. Morgan, "Conflagration as Catalyst," pp. 182–83; Webb, "Some Incidents," p. 67.

47. Hidy et al., *Timber and Men,* p. 521; Strong and Webb, *White Pine,* pp. 66–67; *Idaho Daily Statesman,* March 8, 1907, one of several premature reports of building plans; *Spokane Daily Chronicle,* Sept. 7, 1913.

48. Webb, "Some Incidents," p. 67; Steen, *U.S. Forest Service,* p. 110 ("obliged"); Western Pine Association production figures from Spokane Chamber of Commerce Annual Report 1924, p. 34, showing production for 1910–23.

49. Milwaukee Lumber Company, articles of incorporation, Kootenai County no. 250, showing Herrick with 749 shares at $100 par; A. V. Bradrick, Spokane, a Herrick manager, 250 shares; and W. A. Barnum, Coeur d'Alene, one share; A. W. Derleth, *The Milwaukee Road,* p. 187 (Plummer); Cotroneo, "Timber Marketing," p. 128 (NP's man).

50. *Spokesman-Review,* July 22, 1910; Derleth, *The Milwaukee Road,* p. 296.

51. W. W. Hindley, "His $20 Log," *Spokesman-Review,* May 26, 1929 (mills); A. E. Victor, "Fred Herrick and Bill Grotte," p. 39; E. E. Flood to Cashier, Rathdrum State Bank, Dec. 11, 1924 ("shrewd"), WSU; Cotroneo, "Timber Marketing," p. 128 (54,000 acres).

52. See R. C. Sims, "Idaho's Criminal Syndicalism Act"; H. T. Lovin, "Moses Alexander and the Lumber Strike" and "World War Vigilantes in Idaho"; H. M. Hyman, *Soldiers and Spruce;* Fahey, *Days of the Hercules,* pp. 183–85, for discussions of IWW. The court's ruling is 224 Pac 662 (1924).

53. E. F. Dowell, *History of Criminal Syndicalism Legislation,* p. 22 n9; F. M. Silcox, "Labor Unrest in the Lumber Industry," p. 3.

54. Hyman, *Soldiers and Spruce,* passim, esp. pp. 62 and 301; R. A. Perrin, "Two Decades of Turbulence," p. 101; Robert M. McWade, federal conciliator, to Labor Secretary Wilson, Sept. 6, 1919 (NA, RG 280).

55. G. T. Morgan, "Fight against Fire," p. 59; *Timberman*, March 1930, p. 36; Hidy et al., *Timber and Men*, pp. 242 and 247 *n*36.

56. Hutchison and Winters, *Northern Idaho Forest Resources*, p. 31 (roads); "Proceedings of the State Forestry Conference 1922," p. 31.

57. *Timberman*, December 1928, p. 36 (quotation).

58. Coeur d'Alene Log Owners Association, articles of incorporation, Kootenai County no. 1347; H. Schmitz, "State Lines vs. a Common Interest," pp. 5–10.

59. *Spokesman-Review*, Feb. 16, 1922.

60. *Spokane Affairs*, September 1929, p. 11; *Timberman*, September 1929, p. 160 (Spokane lumber industry); interview with E. L. Wales and his Hoo Hoo files.

61. Hidy et al., *Timber and Men*, pp. 521–22; Wales interview.

62. 165 ICC 53 (1930) and 183 ICC 191 (1932) concern rates, and the latter gives canal data; "Bunyan in Buckskin," pp. 188 and 190 (cost comparisons); Hidy et al., *Timber and Men*, p. 521 ($15).

63. 183 ICC 191 (1932) sketches competition; Bockmier, "Inland Empire Lumber Industry," p. 16 (Klamath Falls); Wales interview (workers); *Oregon Journal*, April 4 and July 31, 1927 (Klamath Falls expansion).

64. Bockmier, "Inland Empire Lumber Industry," p. 16 (caboose), p.17 (sizes); Thompson, "Forest Resources of Washington," pp.22–24 (species); *Timberman*, May 1931, pp. 67–68 (stock frames). Hutchison and Winters, *Northern Idaho Forest Resources*, p. 10, remark that pine was in general demand but other species went largely to local markets.

65. *Spokesman-Review*, March 1, 1921.

66. Wales interview; Cotroneo, "Timber Marketing," p. 125, quotes Elliott.

67. W. J. Mead, *Competition and Oligopsony*, p. 41, table 7 (house lumber); Washington Mutual Savings Bank, "The Housing Situation in Seattle"; minutes of Fidelity Mutual Savings Bank, Spokane.

68. "Proceedings of State Forestry Conference 1922," pp. 18–26; Hutchison and Winters, *Northern Idaho Forest Resources*, p. 49.

69. Weigle, "Pulp Woods in the State of Washington," p. 6; Proceedings of the Washington State Board of Equalization 1930, schedule B: Chelan assessed property 2 percent timber, 91 percent unimproved; Kittitas, 11 percent timber, 80 percent unimproved.

70. "Proceedings of State Forestry Conference 1922," p. 24; remarks by Prof. Frank J. Laube, University of Washington, p. 18; *Timberman*, November 1929, pp. 80-84, and November 1930, p. 28 (Washington votes). Washington voters in 1930 approved the fourteenth amendment to the state constitution which eliminated the requirement for a uniform tax against all property, and the legislature (chapter 40, session laws 1931) enacted a reforestation act. See 177 Wash. 65 (1934).

71. *Daily Idaho Press*, July 19, 1909 (Rutledge); Weidman, "Timber Growing and Logging Practice," p. 59; 11 Idaho 614 (1905); 11 Idaho 130

(1905); Hutchison and Winters, *Northern Idaho Forest Resources*, p. 18 (4.9 million).

72. Bockmier, "Inland Empire Lumber Industry," pp. 23–25; Hidy et al., *Timber and Men*, pp. 253–54 and 532–33 *n*21 (Bonners Ferry); Washington State Planning Council, "Master Plan," p. 26.

73. J. W. Girard, "Practice of Forestry in Western Yellow Pine," pp. 39 and 41.

74. *Spokesman-Review*, May 1, 1938. The Western Pine Association released different figures—1,865,000,000 board feet valued at $50 million f.o.b. mills—but the peak year was the same (*Spokesman-Review*, April 22, 1928). *Timberman*, October 1930, p. 158, observes that the Montana cut was steady in 1923–29; W. Wolman, *Development of Manufacturing Industry in the State of Washington*, p. 79 (year 1923); *Timberman*, September 1932, p. 53 (comparative production). W. J. Mead, "Forest Products Economy of the Pacific Northwest," states that between 1927 and 1939 Oregon production increased 19 percent, Washington's fell 42 percent.

75. Hidy et al., *Timber and Men*, pp. 522–23; L. B. Richards, "George Frederick Jewett," pp. 2 and 4 (quotations).

76. "Report of Investigation of Herrick Properties," Robinson, Nowell and Co., San Francisco, to Detroit Trust Company, June 10, 1927; Forest Service prospectus 1922 (both WSU Exchange Bank records); *Spokesman-Review*, May 26, 1929.

77. "Report of Investigation of Herrick Properties."

78. *Spokesman-Review*, Jan. 25 and Feb. 19, 1927, May 26, 1929; *Timberman*, November 1928, p. 188; *Oregonian*, Dec. 16, 1927 and June 2, 1928; *Portland Telegram*, Aug. 1, 1928.

79. *Yakima Daily Republic*, Jan. 21, 1929 ("bad management"); *Spokesman-Review*, Oct. 17, 1928; *Oregonian*, June 2, 1929. Congress awarded Herrick $50,000, untouchable by creditors, for his service in opening Malheur timber. He died in 1953 at ninety-eight (*Spokesman-Review*, Jan. 29, 1936 and Jan. 21, 1953).

80. *Timberman*, November 1930, p. 33, and January 1931, pp. 163–66; Washington Commissioner of Public Lands, Twenty-first Biennial Report (1930), p. 3.

CHAPTER 11   *Elemental Spokane*

1. The electrified Ross Park streetcar line ran Pullman cars with plush seats and small coke ovens. Its every fifth power pole twinkled with clusters of colored electric lights.

2. Smith diary, vol. 18, entry 189, and notebook 1906, Smith collection, box 6, University of Washington.

3. See E. R. Hodgson, "Early Spokane's 150,000 Club."

4. I. Jolles, quoted in J. Fahey, "When the Dutch Owned Spokane," p. 3.

5. J. Fahey, "Nevada Bloomer Goes to the Polls."

6. R. E. Dyar, *News for an Empire*, pp. 75–92.

7. *Parks and Open Spaces Plan* (Spokane), p. 90; Fahey, "A. L. White, Champion of Urban Beauty."

8. Interview with Louise White "Burr" Willis, daughter of A. L. White, April 23, 1980.

9. In his study "Leadership in Spokane," Henry D. Kass discounts control by a "tight-knit elite" on the ground that "urban society with complex needs and divisions of labor militates against such an arrangement." His study, conducted in 1960–67, and based on newspaper mentions of individuals, concludes that identified leaders "normally remained concentrated in one or two areas of public policy at any given time." On the other hand, the promotion of Expo '74 seems to me to reinforce the idea of a small group of primary actors in city affairs.

10. Conversations with James A. Ford.

11. N. W. Durham, *History of the City of Spokane*, 1:560 (dinner). I am indebted to Professor Kass for the general framework of an urban power structure expressed here, but the selection of individuals is mine.

12. D. L. Huntington to W. A. White, Dec. 1, 1914, in Washington Water Power collection, box 6, Washington State University (Cowles's solicitation); *Spokesman-Review*, Sept. 2, 1914 (quotation) and Nov. 28, 1935 (Davenport profile).

13. See J. Fahey, "Million-Dollar Corner."

14. *Spokane Affairs*, June 1927, p. 3.

15. *Spokesman-Review*, May 17, 1914, Feb. 23 and Oct. 27, 1917, Feb. 29, 1920, and July 22, 1933; J. Fahey, *Days of the Hercules*, p. 206 (Rothrock); J. Rosine, "Cattle Cycles—Past and Present."

16. A. S. French, general auditor, Department of Agriculture, to J. J. Hughes, Aug. 20, 1923; report of Exchange bank directors' special meeting, March 26, 1923; minutes of bondholders of Spokane Union Stockyards, Jan. 18, 1927; brief, Feb. 18, 1927, all in Exchange National Bank records, Washington State University, cage 20, container 21; Fahey, *Days of the Hercules*, p. 208.

17. L. A. Lewis, "Commercial Development"; H. Cravens, "History of the Washington Farm-Labor Party," p. 52.

18. Cashier, Farmers State Bank, Reardan, to J. F. Duber, Oct. 13, 1913, in bank records, Eastern Washington University; *Spokesman-Review*, Aug. 29, 1918 (mail clerks); Fourteenth Census (1920).

19. Federal Reserve to Farmers State Bank, Reardan, March 4, 1918, EWU (quotation); *Colfax Gazette*, March 12, 1920.

20. Spokane Ordinance C–2292, Dec. 3, 1917; interview with Frank Tobie, City Plan Office, Jan. 9, 1980; *Spokane Affairs*, December 1928, pp. 3–4 (Kizer quotation). Kizer also chaired the state planning commission in 1933–44.

21. J. A. Ford, *This Is Your Chamber of Commerce*. Ford retired as managing secretary in 1951.

22. *Spokane Affairs,* March 1926, pp. 8–9, and December 1928, pp. 10–11.

23. *Spokane Affairs,* November 1925, p. 9 (KHQ); July 1927, p. 3 (air derby); and November 1928, p. 3 (Mamer).

24. *Spokane Affairs,* July 1928, p. 13, reports that agricultural implement dealers' sales rose 83.4 percent from May 1927 to May 1928; *Spokane Affairs,* November 1928, March 1929, and December 1929; Annual Report 1927, Fidelity Savings and Loan Association.

25. A report, "Advance Programming and Advance Budgeting," from City Engineer A. D. Butler to the National Resources Planning Board, Dec. 15, 1939, reports taxes and sewer permits; F. A. Freeman speech to Clark and Skamania county bankers, May 28, 1925, in Governor Hartley's subject files, box 6, Washington State archives (bond defaults).

26. Interview with Ben Harrison, Spokane Stock Exchange, Nov. 26, 1979; *Spokesman-Review,* Oct. 28 and 29, 1926, Feb. 6, 1929, and Feb. 18, 1934.

Bibliography

The following list of sources omits legal reports and public documents that can be located from the information in the notes.

INTERVIEWS

The direction of several chapters emerged from conversations or interviews, differentiated by the degree of formality, with informed men and women. My discussions with these generous individuals are cited in the notes. In addition to helping with this book, the interviews have also been the basis of historical magazine articles. In alphabetical order, these individuals and their topics are:

Harry F. Aumack, city plan director, Spokane city planning.

Earl Barnhill, Wenatchee, retired fruit grower and association man, the apple business. Barnhill also generously showed me personal files and his uncompleted history of Skookum Packers.

Ford S. Barrett, Jr., Spokane realtor, on the physical development of Spokane and some men involved.

Margaret Bean, retired newspaper writer, on her recollections of Spokane men and women and on the city's history. Ms. Bean, daughter of a pioneer family, worked for the *Spokesman-Review,* and has written extensively on Spokane's history.

Roger W. Billings, Wenatchee, retired lumberman, on lumbering.

Clifford Chase, Wenatchee, on the career of his father, Marvin Chase, and irrigation. Chase lent me some of his father's papers and photographs.

Clarence C. Dill, former United States senator, on the Columbia Basin irrigation project, his negotiations with President Franklin D. Roosevelt for a construction start on Grand Coulee Dam, his political career, and public power.

James A. Ford, managing secretary of the Spokane Chamber of Commerce 1917–51, on the Columbia Basin irrigation project, the gravity plan, and on publicizing Spokane and managing its growth.

Charles A. Gonser, property manager, on the physical development of Spokane and his recollections of individuals.

David C. Guilbert, former manager Inland Automobile Association, on his father's career and the good roads movement.

Ben Harrison, stock broker, on stocks and bonds and Sam J. Wilson.

B. L. Jenkins, accountant, on banking in the Twohy organization.

Henry D. Kass, professor of political science, Eastern Washington University, on theories of urban political influence and leadership.

W. Newland "Doc" Reilly, newspaper reporter and political editor, on aspects of political power.

E. Lee Smith, retired building supplies company president, on construction, changes in method, and men he remembered from his career.

Frank Tobie, Spokane city plan department, on the general background of city planning in Spokane.

J. D. Urquhart, wheat broker, on the grain trade and living conditions in settlement of the Big Bend.

Ernest L. Wales, retired lumber broker, on the lumber business and the men involved in it.

Ralph Watson, realtor, on the physical structure of Spokane and the role of Frank Culbertson in the central business district.

Mrs. Louise "Burr" Willis, daughter of A. L. White, on her father's career and her memories of individuals.

UNPUBLISHED

Aldrich, Elizabeth A. "History of Banking in Idaho." Master's thesis, University of Washington, 1940.

Allen, Darrell D., Ross B. Fortner, et al. "Study of Commercial Banking in Walla Walla." Typescript, Whitman College, 1953.

Ankeny, Elizabeth. "History of Dayton." Dayton (Wash.) Community Study, 1955.

Barnhill, Earl. "History of Skookum Packers Association." Incomplete, typescript and manuscript, Wenatchee, n.d.

Bergman, Hermas J. "Progressive on the Right: Marion E. Hay, Governor of Washington, 1909–1913." Doctoral dissertation, Washington State University, 1967.

Bockmier, Ralph H., Sr. "Inland Empire Lumber Industry over a Period of Sixty-Years, 1900–1965." Typescript, R. H. Bockmier Lumber Corp., 1967, in Washington State University archives, cage 387.

———. "Mr. Lumber" (autobiography). Typescript, in Washington State University archives, cage 387.

Boyce, Todd V. "History of the Beef Cattle Industry in the Inland Empire." Master's thesis, Washington State University, 1937.

Boyle, Stanley E. "Some Economic Aspects of the Frozen Food Industry in the Pacific Northwest." Master's thesis, Washington State University, 1955.

Burrier, Arnold S. "Agricultural Settlement and Development in Oregon." Typescript, Washington State University library, 1936.

Carrasca, Romain S. "Storage of Fruits in Artificial Atmospheres." Master's thesis, Washington State University, 1939.

Chouinard, William R. "Economic Aspects of Washington State Highway Development." Master's thesis, University of Washington, 1950.

Christensen, Alice M. "Agricultural Pressure and Government Response in the United States, 1919–1929." Doctoral dissertation, University of California, 1936. (An article based on this dissertation appeared in *Agricultural History*.)

Cravens, Hamilton. "History of the Washington Farmer-Labor Party, 1918–1924." Master's thesis, University of Washington, 1962.

Daniel, Cletus E. "Labor Radicalism in Pacific Coast Agriculture." Doctoral dissertation, University of Washington, 1972.

Davies, Gaylord S. "Pacific Northwest White Wheat Problems." Master's thesis, University of Washington, 1938.

Davies, Gerald K. "Rates and Costs of Grain Transportation by Railroad." Doctoral dissertation, Washington State University, 1972.

Deaton, James L. "Adoption and Diffusion of the Combined Harvester-Thresher in the United States: A Study in Economic History." Doctoral dissertation, North Carolina State University, 1977. (This is largely a study of diffusion theory.)

Dill, Clarence C. "Autobiography." Typescript, 1969. Revised and later published as *Where Water Falls*, Spokane: C. W. Hill, 1970.

Dullanty, Frederick J. "Riegel Brothers—Growing with the Inland Empire." Thesis, Pacific Coast Banking School, University of Washington, 1952.

"Farm Lines: An Analysis of Construction Practices and Costs and Recommendations for Reducing Costs." Electric Bond & Share Co., report F-8, June 1932, in Washington Water Power collection, Eastern Washington University.

Fogle, James L. "Wheat Economy of Walla Walla County, Washington." Thesis, Whitman College, 1972.

Foran, Susan V. "Oregon Grange: The Study of an Interest Group." Thesis, Reed College, 1958.

Forth, William S. "Wesley L. Jones: A Political Biography." Doctoral dissertation, University of Washington, 1962.

Freeman, Otis W. "Human Geography of the Scablands of Eastern Washington." Doctoral dissertation, Clark University, 1929.

Garver, Harry L. "Rural Electrification in Washington." Professional degree thesis, Washington State University, 1927.

Green, Michael K. "History of the Public Rural Electrification Movement in Washington to 1942." Doctoral dissertation, University of Idaho, 1967.

――――. "Politics and Kilowatts: The Washington Water Power Company and Public Power, 1918–1941." Master's thesis, University of Idaho, 1962.

Guilbert, Frank C. "Story of the Washington Good Roads Association." Typescript, c. 1917, in Inland Automobile Association collection, Eastern Washington University.

Hall, Jack L. "Policies and Methods Used by the Weyerhaeuser Timber Company to Acquire Timber Land." Master's thesis, Pacific University, 1953.

Harding, Bruce C. "Columbia Basin Irrigation League: Its Origins and Operations." Master's thesis, Washington State University, 1951.

Haston, Bruce M. "From Conflict Politics to Cooperative Politics: A Study of the Public-Private Power Controversy in the Pacific Northwest." Doctoral dissertation, Washington State University, 1970.

Hegnauer, Leonard. "Eighty-six Golden Years: The Autobiography of Leonard Hegnauer." Typescript, Washington State University archives, n.d.

Henderson, Robert A. "The Spokesman-Review, 1883–1900: A Mirror to the History of Spokane." Doctoral dissertation, Washington State University, 1967.

Hoover, Roy O. "Public Land Policy of Washington State: Initial Period, 1889–1912." Doctoral dissertation, Washington State University, 1967.

Johansen, Dorothy O. "Capitalism on the Far Western Frontier: The Oregon Steam Navigation Company." Doctoral dissertation, University of Washington, 1941.

Jones, Fred O. "A Valuation Study of the Mineral Resources of Lands Ceded by the Coeur d'Alene Tribe of Indians on March 3, 1891." Petitioner's exhibit 139, Coeur d'Alene Tribe v. United States of America, Indian Claims Commission Docket 81. A typescript copy dated May 1956 is in the Spokane Public Library.

Kensel, William H. "Economic History of Spokane, Washington, 1881–1910." Master's thesis, Washington State University, 1962.

Kimmons, Neil C. "Historical Development of Seattle as a Metropolitan Area." Master's thesis, University of Washington, 1942.

Knight, Neil R. "History of Banking in Washington." Doctoral dissertation, University of Washington, 1935.

Kreiss, James K. "County by County Analysis of Voting Trends in the State of Washington from 1920 to 1962." Master's thesis, University of Washington, 1964.

Kuhler, Joyce B. "History of Agriculture in the Yakima Valley, Washington, from 1880 to 1900." Master's thesis, University of Washington, 1940.

"Land Ownership (by Counties): Pacific Northwest." National Resources Planning Board, region 9, Portland, Ore., Jan. 2, 1943.

Lewis, Lewis A. ["Commercial Development of Electric Service by the Washington Water Power Company."] Typescript, Aug. 1, 1947, in Washington Water Power collection, Eastern Washington University.

"Liquidation of the War Finance Corporation." Letter, Acting Secretary of the Treasury to the Committee on Banking and Currency, Washington, D.C., 1943, in National Archives.

MacDonald, Alexander N. "Seattle's Economic Development, 1880–1910." Doctoral dissertation, University of Washington, 1959.

McElhiney, Paul T. "Competition between Motor Freight Lines and Railroads in the State of Washington." Master's thesis, University of Washington, 1954.

McGregor, Alexander C. "Agricultural Development of the Columbia Plateau: McGregor Land and Livestock Company, a Case History." Doctoral dissertation, University of Washington, 1977 (in 2 parts).

Mabbott, L. Laverne. "History of the Wenatchee-Okanogan Apple Industry prior to 1930." Master's thesis, Washington State University, 1940.

Maier, Harvey E. "Economic History of Pend Oreille County." Master's thesis, University of Washington, 1938.

Martin, Robert R. "Inland Empire of the Pacific Northwest, a Regional Study." Doctoral dissertation, University of Washington, 1935.

Meany, Edmond S., Jr. "History of the Lumber Industry of the Pacific Northwest to 1917." Doctoral dissertation, Harvard University, 1935.

Meinig, Donald W. "Environment and Settlement in the Palouse, 1868–1910." Master's thesis, University of Washington, 1950.

———. "Settlement of the Walla Walla Country." Doctoral dissertation, University of Washington, 1952.

Mickelson, Siegfried. "Promotional Activities of the Northern Pacific's Land and Immigration Departments, 1870 to 1902." Master's thesis, University of Minnesota, 1940.

Miner, William D. "History of the Columbia Basin Projects." Doctoral dissertation, Indiana University, 1950.

Mitchell, Marlene. "Washington Newspapers: Territorial and State: A Bibliography and Checklist." Master's thesis, University of Washington, 1964.

Morgan, George T., Jr. "Fight against Fire: Development of Cooperative Forestry in the Pacific Northwest, 1900–1950." Doctoral dissertation, University of Oregon, 1964.

Morrill, Richard L. "An Experimental Study of Trade in Wheat and Flour in the Flour Milling Industry." Master's thesis, University of Washington, 1957.

Oliphant, J. Orin. "Early History of Spokane, Washington, Told by Contemporaries." Typescript, Eastern Washington University, 1927 (typescripts of newspaper interviews with manuscript emendations).

———. "Readings in the History of Eastern Washington." 5 vols. Typescript pioneer reminiscences and newspaper articles, Eastern Washington University, 1926.

———. "Sidelights on the Pioneer History of Eastern Washington." Typescript, Eastern Washington University, 1927 (extracts from newspapers).

Olson, Michael L. "Development of Agriculture in the Walla Walla–Palouse Country, Washington, 1860–90." Master's thesis, University of Washington, 1967.

Perrin, Robert A. "Two Decades of Turbulence: a Study of the Great Lumber Strikes in Northern Idaho." Master's thesis, University of Idaho, 1961.

Pullen, Douglas R. "Administration of Washington State Governor Louis F. Hart, 1919–25." Doctoral dissertation, University of Washington, 1974.

Richards, Laura B. "George Frederick Jewett: Lumberman and Conservationist." Master's thesis, University of Idaho, 1969.

Richmond, Anthony M. "Promotion of the Northwest." Thesis, Reed College, 1958.

Riddle, Thomas W. "Old Radicalism in America: John R. Rogers and the Populist Movement in Washington, 1891–1900." Doctoral dissertation, Washington State University, 1976.

Rosbach, Ronald L. "Lieu Land Controversy in Eastern Washington." Master's thesis, Washington State University, 1957.

"70 Land Use: Breakdown by Age: For Ed, Tract, and City." Computer report on age of buildings in City of Spokane, Aug. 21, 1973, by Spokane County assessor's office.

Salnave, Cora. "Diary." Cheney, 1889, Eastern Washington University alumni office.

Salo, Sarah J. "Timber Concentration in the Pacific Northwest." Doctoral dissertation, Columbia University, 1945.

Scott, Edna A. "Grange Movement in Oregon, 1873–1900." Master's thesis, University of Oregon, 1923. (Also published as University of Oregon thesis series, No. 1.)

Seedorf, Rita. "Building the Big Bend Country: the Saga of the Matthews Family, 1890–1960." Master's thesis, Eastern Washington University, 1980.

Seney, Donald B. "Development of Water, Sewer, and Fire Service in Seattle and King County, Washington, 1851–1966." Doctoral dissertation, University of Washington, 1975.

Silcox, F. M. "Labor Unrest in the Lumber Industry—Northern Idaho and Western Montana." Federal Mediation and Conciliation Service general subject files 1913–48, case 20-473 (lumber), in National Archives.

Smart, Douglas O. "History of Railroad Rate Regulation in the State of Washington, 1883–1920." Master's thesis, University of Washington, 1957.

Smith, Joseph. Diaries, Manuscript Division, University of Washington Library.

Snodgrass, Donald. "Economics of Farm Storage." Master's thesis, Washington State University, 1951.

Stark, Lawrence R. "Lewiston-Clarkston Improvement Company: City Planner in Southeastern Washington." Typescript, Washington State University, 1978.

Swanson, Robert W. "History of Logging and Lumbering on the Palouse

River, 1870–1905." Master's thesis, Washington State University, 1958.

Tattersall, James N. "Economic Development of the Pacific Northwest to 1920." Doctoral dissertation, University of Washington, 1960.

Treadwell, George T. "Port of Seattle: a Case History of Public Port Development." Typescript, Seattle Public Library, 1924. (Treadwell was chief engineer of the port.)

Urquhart, Alexander D. "Role of the State in Regional Development: A Case Study of the State of Washington in the Valley of the Columbia." Master's thesis, University of Washington, 1949.

Vandevere, Emmett K. "History of Irrigation in Washington." Doctoral dissertation, University of Washington, 1948.

Washington Water Power Company. "Statement A: Outline of Origin and Development." Statement to the Federal Power Commission, May 1937.

Watkins, John B. "Development of the Export Market for Wheat and Flour in the Pacific Northwest." Master's thesis, University of Chicago, 1924.

Williams, Kate R. "Memoirs." Typescript c. 1940, Eastern Washington University alumni office.

Yeager, Walter M. "Pioneer's Problems of Land Acquisition under the Public Land Laws in Southeastern Washington, 1850–1883." Master's thesis, Washington State University, 1961.

Yonce, Frederick J. "Public Land Disposal in Washington." Doctoral dissertation, University of Washington, 1969.

Zimmerman, Earl L. "An Introductory Study of the Development of Agriculture in Eastern Washington." Master's thesis, University of Washington, n.d.

BOOKS

Adams, Kramer A. *Logging Railroads of the West*. New York: Bonanza Books, 1961.

Allen, George M. *Irrigated Lands of the State of Washington*. Olympia: Washington Bureau of Statistics and Immigration, 1910.

American Public Health Association. *A Half Century of Public Health*. New York: American Public Health Assn., 1921.

Anderson, Oscar Edward, Jr. *Refrigeration in America*. Princeton: Princeton University Press, 1953.

Andrus, A. Phillip, et al. *Seattle*. Cambridge, Mass.: Ballinger Publishing Co., 1976. An Association of American Geographers comparative metropolitan analysis project.

Armstrong, Ellis L., ed. *History of Public Works in the United States, 1776–1976*. Chicago: American Public Works Assn., 1976.

Averill, Harry B., John M. Henderson, and William S. Shiach. *An Illustrated History of North Idaho*. Chicago: Western Historical Publishing Co., 1903.

Baker, W. W. *Forty Years a Pioneer: Business Life of Dorsey Syng Baker, 1848–1888*. Seattle: Lowman and Hanford Co., 1934.

Bancroft, H. H. *Works*. Vol. 31: *History of Washington, Idaho, and Montana, 1845–1889*. San Francisco: The History Co., 1890.

Barger, Harold, and Hans H. Landsberg. *American Agriculture, 1899–1939*. New York: National Bureau of Economic Research, Inc., 1942.

Bates, Edwin. *Commercial Survey of the Pacific Northwest*. Washington: Government Printing Office, 1932. U.S. Department of Commerce, Domestic Commerce Series, no. 51.

Benedict, Murray R. *Farm Policies of the United States, 1790–1950*. New York: Twentieth Century Fund, 1953.

Bennett, Robert A. *Walla Walla: Portrait of a Western Town, 1804–1899*. Walla Walla: Pioneer Press, Inc., 1980.

Bibb, Thomas W. *History of Early Common School Education in Washington*. Seattle: University of Washington Press, 1929.

Billington, Ray Allen. *America's Frontier Heritage*. New York: Holt, Rinehart, and Winston, 1966.

Bjork, Kenneth O. *West of the Great Divide: Norwegian Migration to the Pacific Coast, 1847–1893*. Northfield, Minn.: Norwegian-American Historical Assn., 1958.

Bolton, Frederick E., and Thomas W. Bibb. *History of Education in Washington*. USDA Bulletin 9 (1934). Washington: Government Printing Office, 1935.

Brief History of the Washington State Good Roads Association. Seattle: Washington State Good Roads Assn., 1939.

Brunner, Edmund de S., and J. H. Kolb. *Rural Social Trends*. New York: McGraw-Hill Book Co., Inc., 1933.

Bryan, Enoch A. *Orient Meets Occident*. Pullman: Students Book Corp., 1936.

Bureau of Corporations. See *Lumber Industry*.

Burrell, O. K. *Gold in the Woodpile: An Informal History of Banking in Oregon*. Eugene: University of Oregon, 1967.

Camp, Oscar A., and Paul M. McGrew. *History of Washington's Soil and Water Conservation Districts*. Everson, Wash.: n.p., 1969.

Campbell, Alice V. *Short History of Rosalia*. Rosalia, Wash.: n.p., 1930.

Carey, Charles Henry. *History of Oregon*. Chicago: Pioneer Historical Publishing Co., 1922.

Carstensen, Vernon, ed. *The Public Lands*. Madison: University of Wisconsin Press, 1963.

Clemens, Fred W. *Balanced Farming for the Inland Empire*. Spokane: Agricultural Bureau, Chamber of Commerce, 1924. (The Spillman lectures in 1924.)

―――. *Three Hundred Years along the Rothrock Trail*. Spokane: F. M. Rothrock Co., 1954.

Collins, Charles W. *Rural Banking Reform*. New York: Macmillan Co., 1931.

Coman, Edwin T., Jr., and Helen M. Gibbs. *Time, Tide, and Timber: A Century of Pope and Talbot*. Stanford: Stanford University Press, 1949.

Cook, Francis H. *Territory of Washington*. Cheney: State Normal School, 1925.

Cox, Thomas R. *Mills and Markets: A History of the Pacific Coast Lumber Industry to 1900*. Seattle: University of Washington Press, 1974.

Crawford, Harriet Ann. *Washington State Grange, 1889–1924*. Portland, Ore.: Binfords and Mort, 1940.

Crumbaker, Calvin. *Transportation and Politics, a Study of Long-and-Short Haul Policies of Congress and the Interstate Commerce Commission*. Eugene: University of Oregon, 1940. University of Oregon Monographs, Studies in Economics, no. 1.

Currie, Barton W. *The Tractor*. Philadelphia: Curtis Publishing Co., 1916.

Davis, Arthur P. *Irrigation Works Constructed by the United States Government*. New York: John Wiley and Sons, Inc., 1917.

Davis' New Commercial Encyclopedia—the Pacific Northwest. Seattle: Ellis A. Davis, 1909.

Davis, Joseph S. *Pacific Northwest Wheat Problems and the Export Subsidy*. Stanford: Stanford University, 1934. Wheat Studies of the Food Research Institute, vol. 10, no. 10.

———. *Wheat and the AAA*. Washington, D.C.: The Brookings Institution, 1935.

Derleth, August W. *The Milwaukee Road: Its First Hundred Years*. New York: Creative Age Press, 1948.

DeVore, Paul T. *Federal Land Bank of Spokane, 1917–1947*. Spokane: Federal Land Bank, June 30, 1947, mimeographed.

Dierdorff, John. *How Edison's Lamp Helped Light the West: The Story of Pacific Power and Light Company and Its Pioneer Forebears*. Portland: Pacific Power and Light Co., 1971.

Donnelly, Charles. *Facts about the Northern Pacific Land Grant*. N.p., c. 1924.

Dowell, Eldridge F. *History of Criminal Syndicalism Legislation in the United States*. Baltimore: Johns Hopkins Press, 1939.

Drake, George L., and Elwood R. Maunder. *Forester's Log: Fifty Years in the Pacific Northwest*. Santa Cruz: Forest History Society, 1975.

Durham, Nelson W. *History of the City of Spokane and Spokane Country, Washington, from Its Earliest Settlement to the Present Time*. 3 vols. Spokane: Clarke, 1912.

Dyar, Ralph E. *News for an Empire: The Story of the Spokesman-Review of Spokane, Washington, and of the Field It Serves*. Caldwell, Idaho: Caxton Printers, Ltd., 1952.

Early Days in the Forest Service. 4 vols. Missoula: Forest Service Region One, 1944–76, mimeographed.

Edwards, Jonathan. *Illustrated History of Spokane County, State of Washington*. Spokane: Lever, 1900.

Emmett, Boris, and John E. Jeuck. *Catalogues and Counters: A History of Sears, Roebuck and Company*. Chicago: University of Chicago Press, 1950.

Engle, Nathanael H. *Marketing in the West.* New York: Ronald Press, 1946.

Erdman, Henry E. *American Produce Markets.* Boston, New York, Chicago: D. C. Heath and Co., 1928.

Fahey, John. *Ballyhoo Bonanza: Charles Sweeny and the Idaho Mines.* Seattle: University of Washington Press, 1971.

———. *Days of the Hercules.* Moscow: University Press of Idaho, 1978.

———. *Inland Empire: D. C. Corbin and Spokane.* Seattle: University of Washington Press, 1965.

Fairfield, Wash., History Committee. *Early History of Fairfield.* Fairfield, Wash.: History Committee of the Town and Country Study, 1960, mimeographed.

Field, H. H. *History of the Milwaukee Railroad, 1892–1940.* Chicago: privately published, 1942.

Filley, H. Clyde. *Cooperation in Agriculture.* New York: John Wiley and Sons, Inc., 1929.

Flaherty, David C., and William H. Funk. *Clear the Waters! A History of the Pacific Northwest Pollution Control Association, 1934 to 1975.* Seattle: Pacific Northwest Pollution Control Assn., 1976.

Flink, James J. *America Adopts the Automobile, 1895–1910.* Cambridge and London: MIT Press, 1970.

———. *Car Culture.* Cambridge and London: MIT Press, 1975.

Ford, James A. *This Is Your Chamber of Commerce.* Spokane: Chamber of Commerce, c. 1956, mimeographed.

France, George W. *Struggles for Life and Home in the North-West by a Pioneer Homebuilder, 1885–1889.* New York: L. Goldman, 1890.

Freeman, Otis W. *Living Geography: Washington Supplement.* New York: Macmillan Co., 1932.

Freeman, Otis W., and Howard H. Martin, eds. *The Pacific Northwest.* New York: John Wiley and Sons, Inc., 1942.

Gaffney, Joseph W., and Celia Jans. *History of Sprague, 1880–1962.* Spokane: Gonzaga University Press, 1962.

Gardner, Charles M. *The Grange—Friend of the Farmer, 1867–1947.* Washington: National Grange, 1949.

Gates, Charles M. *Readings in Pacific Northwest History: Washington, 1790–1895.* Seattle: University Bookstore, 1944.

Gellatly, John A. *History of Wenatchee.* Wenatchee: J. A. Gellatly, 1962.

Giles, Harry F. *Advantages and Opportunities of the State of Washington for Homebuilders, Investors, and Travelers.* Olympia: Washington Bureau of Statistics and Immigration, 1920.

———. *Manufacturing Opportunities in the State of Washington.* Olympia: Washington Bureau of Statistics and Immigration, 1918.

Goethals, George W., and Co. *Columbia Basin Irrigation Project.* Olympia: Washington Department of Conservation and Development, 1922.

Grant County Public Utility District. *Back through the Pages of History: Public Utility District of Grant County, Washington.* Ephrata, Wash.: Grant County PUD, 1967. Silver anniversary publication.

Great Northern Railway Company, the Northern Pacific Railway Company: A Review of Their Operations in the Period 1916–1923 and a Discussion of Some of Their Most Difficult Problems. New York: Wood, Struthers and Co., 1924.

Gressley, Gene M. *Twentieth Century American West.* Columbia: University of Missouri Press, 1977.

Hammatt, Theodore D. *Methods of Merchandizing American Wheat in the Export Trade.* Part I: *Buying Wheat for Export.* Washington: Department of Commerce, 1924 (Trade Information Bulletin 183, Feb. 4, 1924). Part II: *Selling American Wheat Abroad.* Washington: Department of Commerce, 1924 (Trade Information Bulletin 185, Feb. 11, 1924).

Handlin, David P. *American Home.* Boston and Toronto: Little, Brown and Co., 1979.

Hedges, James B. *Henry Villard and the Railways of the Northwest.* New Haven: Yale University Press, 1930.

Hibbard, Benjamin H. *History of Public Land Policies.* New York: Macmillan Co., 1924.

Hicks, John D. *Populist Revolt, a History of the Farmers' Alliance and the Peoples' Party.* Minneapolis: University of Minnesota Press, 1931.

Hidy, Ralph W., Frank E. Hill, and Allan Nevins. *Timber and Men: The Weyerhaeuser Story.* New York: Macmillan Co., 1963.

Highsmith, Richard M., Jr., ed. *Atlas of the Pacific Northwest.* Corvallis: Oregon State College, 1950.

Hilton, George W., and John F. Due. *Electric Interurban Railways in America.* Stanford: Stanford University Press, 1960. Revised edition, 1964.

History of Benton City, Washington, 1853–1959. Benton City: Kiona-Benton City Community Study, 1958–59.

History of Highways. Olympia: Washington Department of Transportation, 1977. Covers only Washington's highways.

Hobson, G. C., comp. *Idaho Digest and Blue Book.* Caldwell, Idaho: Caxton Printers, Ltd., 1935.

Hoefel, David. *Hoefel Family Album.* Ritzville, Wash.: David Hoefel, 1965.

Holbrook, Stewart H. *Machines of Plenty.* New York: Macmillan Co., 1955.

Hull, Lindley M., ed. *History of Central Washington.* Spokane: Shaw and Borden, 1929.

Hult, Ruby El. *Steamboats in the Timber.* Caldwell, Idaho: Caxton Printers, Ltd., 1953.

Hutchins, Wells A. *Selected Problems in the Law of Water Rights in the West.* Washington: Government Printing Office, 1942. USDA Miscellaneous Publication 418.

Hutchison, S. Blair, and R. K. Winters. *Northern Idaho Forest Resources and Industries.* Washington: Government Printing Office, 1942. USDA Miscellaneous Publication 508.

Hyman, Harold M. *Soldiers and Spruce: Origins of the Loyal Legion of Loggers and Lumbermen.* Los Angeles: Institute of Industrial Relations, University of California, 1963.

Ingalls, Walter R. *Lead and Zinc in the United States*. New York: Hill Publishing Co., 1908.

International Competition in the Production of Wheat for Export. Washington: Department of Commerce, 1924. Trade Information Bulletin 210.

Jackson, Gary L. *Remembering Yakima*. 3 vols. Yakima: Golden West Publishing Co., 1975–77. Names of volumes change.

Jackson, Kenneth T. *Ku Klux Klan in the City, 1915–1930*. New York: Oxford University Press, 1967.

Jasny, Naum. *Competition among Grains*. Stanford: Food Research Institute, 1940.

Johansen, Dorothy O., and Charles M. Gates. *Empire of the Columbia: A History of the Pacific Northwest*. New York: Harper and Brothers, 1957.

Jones, Lawrence A., and David Durand. *Mortgage Lending Experience in Agriculture*. Princeton: Princeton University Press, 1954.

Keith, Thomas B. *Horse Interlude*. Moscow: University Press of Idaho, 1976.

Kerr, Harry J. *History of Okanogan*. Okanogan, Wash.: privately printed, 1931.

Kile, Orville M. *Farm Bureau through Three Decades*. Baltimore: Waverly Press, 1948.

Kincaid, Garret D., and A. H. Harris. *Palouse in the Making*. Palouse, Wash.: Palouse Republic, 1966.

Kingston, Ceylon S., and Herman J. Deutsch, eds. *Grassroots Cuttings*. Longview, Wash.: Longview Daily News, 1954.

Kuhlmann, Charles B. *Development of the Flour-Milling Industry in the United States with Special Reference to the Industry in Minneapolis*. Boston and New York: Houghton Mifflin Co., 1929.

Lee, Everett S., Ann Ratner Miller, Carol P. Brainerd, and Richard A. Easterlin. *Population Redistribution and Economic Growth of the United States, 1870–1950*. 2 vols. Philadelphia: American Philosophical Society, 1957.

Lever, W. H. *Illustrated History of Whitman County, State of Washington*. N.p., 1901.

Lewis, Howard T. *Basic Industries of the Pacific Northwest*. Seattle: Lowman and Hanford Press, 1925. Student handbook.

Lewis, Howard T., and Stephen I. Miller. *Economic Resources of the Pacific Northwest*. Seattle: Lowman and Hanford, 1923.

Lingeman, Richard. *Small Town America*. New York: G. P. Putnam's Sons, 1980.

Loehr, Rodney C. *See* Mason, David T.

Lucia, Ellis. *Big Woods*. New York: Doubleday and Co., 1975.

Lumber Industry. 3 parts. Washington, D.C.: Bureau of Corporations, 1913–14. Reprint, New York: Arno Press, 1972.

Lyman, Horace S. *History of Oregon*. 4 vols. New York: North Pacific Publishing Co., 1903.

Lyman, William D. *Columbia River*. 4th ed. Portland, Ore.: Binfords and Mort, 1963.

———. *History of the Yakima Valley, Washington, Comprising Yakima, Kit-*

titas, and Benton Counties. Chicago: S. J. Clarke Publishing Co., 1919.

McConnell, Grant. *Decline of Agrarian Democracy.* Berkeley: University of California Press, 1953.

McCormick, Cyrus. *Century of the Reaper.* New York: Houghton Mifflin Co., 1931.

McVay, Alfred, ed. *Walla Walla Story.* Walla Walla: Chamber of Commerce, 1953.

Marcosson, Isaac F. *Metal Magic: The Story of the American Smelting and Refining Company.* New York: Farrar, Straus and Co., 1949.

Martin, Albro. *James J. Hill and the Opening of the Northwest.* New York: Oxford University Press, 1976.

Mason, David T. *Forests for the Future.* Edited by Rodney C. Loehr. St. Paul: Minnesota Historical Society, 1952.

———. *Timber Ownership and Lumber Production in the Inland Empire.* Portland: Western Pine Manufacturers Assn., 1920.

Maynard, Harold H. *Marketing Northwestern Apples.* New York: Ronald Press Co., 1923.

Mead, Walter J. *Competition and Oligopsony in the Douglas Fir Industry.* Berkeley: University of California Press, 1966.

Meinig, Donald W. *The Great Columbia Plain: A Historical Geography, 1805–1910.* Seattle and London: University of Washington Press, 1968.

Mills, Randall V. *Sternwheelers Up the Columbia.* Palo Alto: Pacific Books, 1947.

National Resources Planning Board. *Development of Resources and Economic Opportunity in the Pacific Northwest.* Washington: Government Printing Office, 1942. Report of the Pacific Northwest Regional Planning Commission to the NRPB.

———. *Long-Range Planning of Municipal Public Works.* Washington: Government Printing Office, 1941.

———. *Pacific Northwest Region: Industrial Development.* Washington: Government Printing Office, 1942.

Nesbit, Robert C. *He Built Seattle: A Biography of Judge Thomas Burke.* Seattle: University of Washington Press, 1961.

Newell, Gordon. *Rogues, Buffoons, and Statesmen.* Seattle: Hangman Press, as presented by Superior Publishing Co., 1975.

New Empire: Oregon, Washington, Idaho. Portland: Oregon Immigration Board, 1888.

Nourse, Edwin G. *Legal Status of Agricultural Co-operation.* New York: Macmillan Co., 1928.

Nybroten, Norman. *Idaho Statistical Abstract.* Moscow: University of Idaho Bureau of Business and Economic Research, 1971.

Official Northern Pacific Railroad Guide. St. Paul: W. C. Riley, 1892.

Ogden, Daniel M., Jr., and Hugh A. Bone. *Washington Politics.* New York: New York University Press for Citizenship Clearing House, 1960.

Olin, W. H. *American Irrigation Farming.* Chicago: A. C. McClung and Co., 1913.

Pacific Telephone and Telegraph Co. *History of the Pacific System*. San Francisco: Pacific Telephone and Telegraph Co., 1928.

Palouse Story. Palouse, Wash.: Palouse Town and Country Study Program, 1962, mimeographed.

Parks and Open Spaces Plan. Spokane: City Plan Commission, 1965. Report 14, City Plan Series 1, part of a comprehensive plan.

Pittsburgh of Today. Pittsburgh: Consolidated Illustrating Co., 1897.

Pollard, Lancaster. *Oregon and the Pacific Northwest*. Portland: Binfords and Mort, 1946.

Pomeroy, Earl. *Pacific Slope*. New York: Alfred A. Knopf, 1965.

Population Distribution, 1875–1975. Spokane: City Plan Commission, 1953.

Population 1880 to 2000: Spokane, Washington. Spokane: City Plan Commission, 1975. Report 10, City Plan Series 2.

Porter, Glenn, and Harold C. Livesay. *Merchants and Manufacturers: Studies in the Changing Structure of Nineteenth Century Marketing*. Baltimore: Johns Hopkins Press, 1971.

Pressly, Thomas J., and William H. Scofield. *Farm Real Estate Values in the United States by Counties, 1850–1959*. Seattle: University of Washington Press, 1965.

Preston, Howard H. *Trust Banking in Washington*. Seattle: University of Washington Press, 1953.

Pyle, Joseph G. *Life of James J. Hill*. 2 vols. New York: Peter Smith, 1936.

Rae, John R. *American Automobile*. Chicago: University of Chicago Press, 1965.

Relander, Click. *Drummers and Dreamers*. Caldwell, Idaho: Caxton Printers, Ltd., 1956.

Renz, Louis T. *History of the Northern Pacific Railroad*. Fairfield, Wash.: Ye Galleon Press, 1980. Based on NP annual reports.

———. *Northern Pacific Railroad: Data Tables*. Walla Walla: L. T. Renz, 1978.

Reps, John W. *Cities of the American West: A History of Frontier Planning*. Princeton: Princeton University Press, 1979.

Research Committee on Social Trends. *Recent Social Trends in the United States*. New York: McGraw-Hill Book Co., Inc., 1933.

Resources and Attractions of Washington for the Home Seeker, Capitalist, and Tourist. Omaha: Union Pacific Railway, 1892.

Robinson, Marilyn D. *Washington State Statistical Abstract*. Seattle: University of Washington Press, 1952.

Rogin, Leo. *Introduction of Farm Machinery in Its Relation to the Productivity of Labor in the Agriculture of the United States during the Nineteenth Century*. Berkeley: University of California Press, 1931.

Rowan, James. *IWW in the Lumber Industry*. Seattle: Lumber Workers Industrial Union 500, 1921.

Ruby, Robert H., and John A. Brown. *Ferryboats on the Columbia River, including the Bridges and Dams*. Seattle: Superior Publishing Co., 1974.

Rural Electrification in the United States. New York: Edison Electric Institute, c. 1959.

Schlebecker, John T. *Whereby We Thrive: A History of American Farming, 1607–1972*. Ames: Iowa State University Press, 1975.

Schmid, Calvin F., and Stanton E. Schmid. *Growth of Cities and Towns, State of Washington*. Olympia: Washington Planning and Community Affairs Agency, 1969.

Schwantes, Carlos A. *Radical Heritage: Labor, Socialism, and Reform in Washington and British Columbia, 1885–1917*. Seattle: University of Washington Press, 1979.

Scott, Harvey W. *History of Portland, Oregon*. Syracuse: D. Mason and Co., 1890.

Seligman, Edwin R. A. *Economics of Farm Relief*. New York: Columbia University Press, 1929.

Settlers Wanted. Olympia: Washington Department of Conservation and Development, 1923.

Sewerage Facilities Plan: Spokane, Washington. Spokane: Department of Public Works and Utilities, 1965. Report 15, City Plan Series 1.

Shaver, F. A., R. F. Steele, and A. P. Rose. *Illustrated History of Southeastern Washington*. Spokane: Western Historical Publishing Co., 1906.

Sheller, Roscoe. *Ben Snipes, Northwest Cattle King*. Portland: Binfords and Mort, 1957.

Shideler, James H. *Farm Crisis, 1919–1923*. Berkeley and Los Angeles: University of California Press, 1957.

Shotwell, Harry I. *Shotwell Story*. Wenatchee: Daily World Printing Co., 1953.

Smalley, Eugene V. *History of the Northern Pacific Railroad*. New York: G. P. Putnam's Sons, 1883.

Smillie, Wilson G. *Public Health: Its Promise for the Future*. New York: Macmillan Co., 1955.

Smith, Mowry, Jr., and Giles Clark. *One Third Crew, One Third Boat, One Third Luck: The Menasha Corporation (Menasha Wooden Ware Company) Story, 1849–1974*. Neenah, Wisc.: Menasha Corp., 1974.

Soap Lake History Report. Soap Lake, Wash.: Town and County Forum Community Study, 1958, mimeographed.

Sparks, Earl S. *History and Theory of Agricultural Credit in the United States*. New York: Thomas Y. Crowell Co., 1932.

State of Oregon, Its Resources and Opportunities. Salem: Oregon State Immigration Commission, 1912.

Steele, Richard F., and Arthur P. Rose. *Illustrated History of the Big Bend Country, Embracing Lincoln, Douglas, Adams, and Franklin Counties*. Spokane: Western Historical Publishing Co., 1904.

Steen, Harold K. *U.S. Forest Service: A History*. Seattle and London: University of Washington Press, 1976.

Steen, Herman. *Flour Milling in America*. Minneapolis: T. S. Dennison and Co., Inc., 1963.

―――. *The O. W. Fisher Heritage.* Seattle: Frank McCaffrey Publishers, 1961.

Street, Donald M. *Railroad Equipment Financing.* New York: Columbia University Press, 1959.

Strong, Clarence C., and Clyde S. Webb. *White Pine: King of Many Waters.* Missoula: Mountain Press Publishing Co., 1970.

Sundborg, George. *Hail Columbia: The Thirty-Year Struggle for Grand Coulee Dam.* New York: Macmillan Co., 1954.

Swain, Donald C. *Federal Conservation Policy, 1921–1933.* Berkeley: University of California Press, 1963.

Taylor, Carl C. *Farmers' Movement, 1620–1920.* New York: American Book Co., 1953.

Tekoa Story, from Bunchgrass to Grain. Tekoa, Wash.: History Committee of the Tekoa Community Study, 1962, mimeographed.

Thompson, Margaret, and Otis W. Freeman. *Conservation of Northwest Resources.* Seattle: Northwest Conservation League, 1950.

Thompson, Slason. *Railway Statistics for the United States of America.* 1927 and 1930 editions. Chicago: Bureau of Railways News and Statistics, 1927 and 1930.

Thomson, W. O. *Thomson's Manual of Pacific Northwest Finance.* Seattle: Thomson's Statistical Service, 1930.

Told by the Pioneers. Olympia: Washington Pioneer Project, 1937.

Travis, Helga A. *Golden Bonanza.* Prosser, Wash.: privately printed, 1963.

Turner, Russell M. *The First Forty-Five Years: A History of Cooperative Extension Work in Washington State.* Pullman: Washington Extension Service, 1961. Miscellaneous Publication 55.

Upham, Cyril B., and Edwin Lamke. *Closed and Distressed Banks, a Study in Public Administration.* Washington, D.C.: The Brookings Institution, 1934.

U.S. Forest Service. *Early Days in the Forest Service.* 4 vols. USDA Forest Service. Missoula: Region One, 1944–76.

Villard, Henry. *Early History of Transportation in Oregon.* Edited by Oswald Garrison Villard. Eugene: University of Oregon Press, 1944.

Vine, Vernon. *Story of Farm Credit Administration.* Spokane: Farm Credit Administration of Spokane, 1944, mimeographed.

Washington State Board of Health. *Studies in Typhoid Fever by the Washington State Board of Health during 1909–1910.* Olympia: E. L. Boardman, public printer, 1910.

Wheat Supply and Distribution in the Pacific Northwest. Pendleton: Oregon Wheat Commission, 1956. Statistical Bulletin 1.

Wiest, Edward. *Agricultural Organization in the United States.* Lexington: University of Kentucky, 1923.

Wik, Reynold M. *Henry Ford and Grass-roots America.* Ann Arbor: University of Michigan Press, 1972.

Wiprud, A. C. *Federal Farm-Loan System in Operation.* New York: Harper and Brothers, 1921.

Wolman, William. *Development of Manufacturing Industry in the State of Washington.* Pullman: Washington State College, 1958. Economic and Business Studies Bulletin 31.

Woods, Rufus. *Twenty-six Year Battle for Grand Coulee Dam.* Wenatchee: Daily World, 1944.

Years Ago. Rockford, Wash.: Standard-Register, 1953.

ARTICLES AND PAMPHLETS

Arcadia Orchards Company, Washington—Irrigated Orchards. Spokane: n.p., 1909.

Ault, Nelson A. "McWhorter Papers." Washington State University *Research Studies* 26 (1958): 85–118.

Ball, Carlton R. "History of American Wheat Improvement." *Agricultural History* 4 (1930): 48–71.

Bean, Margaret. "Waikiki, Beauty Spot on the Little Spokane." *Spokesman-Review,* Feb. 24, 1957.

Berglund, Abraham. "Valuation of Railroads in the State of Washington." *Journal of Political Economy* 21, no. 4 (April 1913): 332–44.

Bicha, Karel D. "Peculiar Populist: An Assessment of John R. Rogers." *Pacific Northwest Quarterly* 65, no. 3 (July 1974): 110–17.

Billings, Roger W. "Diamond City: Timber Down the Hill, 1920–1928." *Big Smoke,* 1972, pp. 3–10 (annual publication by Stuart Bradley for the Pend Oreille County Historical Society).

Bishop, Crawford M. "Warehouse Receipts as Collateral." 2 *Washington Law Review* 23 (1927).

Blackwell, Frederick W. "The Inland Empire of F. A. Blackwell." *Pacific Northwest Forum* 2, nos. 2–3 (Spring-Summer 1977): 24–34. Photo essay with explanatory notes.

Blanchard, C. J. "Call of the West." *National Geographic* 20, no. 5 (May 1909): 411–37.

Boening, Rose M. "History of Irrigation in the State of Washington." *Washington Historical Quarterly* 9, no. 4 (1918): 259–76, and 10, no. 1 (1919): 21–45.

Brown, Arthur J. "Promotion of Emigration to Washington." *Pacific Northwest Quarterly* 36 (1945): 3–17.

Broyles, Glen J. "Spokane Free Speech Fight, 1909–10: A Study in IWW Tactics." *Labor History* 19, no. 2 (Spring 1978): 238–52.

Budd, Ralph. *Pacific Northwest and the Engineer.* Address before the American Society of Civil Engineers, Tacoma, July 8, 1931, published as Northwest History Pamphlet, College of Puget Sound.

"Bunyan in Buckskin: The House of Weyerhaeuser." *Fortune* 9, no. 4 (April 1934): 62–75, 155–90.

Burke, Padraic. "Struggle for Public Ownership: The Early History of the Port of Seattle." *Pacific Northwest Quarterly* 68, no. 2 (April 1977): 60–71.

Campbell, Claude A. "Old National Bank of Spokane." Washington State University *Research Studies* 18, no. 2 (June 1949): 73–208.

Cannell, Lewis D. "Freight Rate Structure and Its Effect on the Price and Movement of Northwest Wheat." *Bulletin* 2, Bureau of Business and Economic Research, Washington State University, June 1945.

Case, J. Herbert. "Preparation for War and the Liberty Loans." *Annals of the American Academy of Political and Social Science* 99 (January 1922): 121–29.

Chapin, Charles V. "History of State and Municipal Control of Disease." In Mazyck P. Ravenel, ed., *A Half Century of Public Health*, pp. 133–60. New York: American Public Health Assn., 1921.

Christensen, Alice M. "Agricultural Pressure and Government Response in the United States, 1919–1929." *Agricultural History* 11 (1937): 33–42.

Clark, Earl. "Rufus Woods: Grand Coulee Promoter." *Montana Magazine of History* 29, no. 4 (October 1979): 38–51.

Comegys, Robert G. "Country Banking in Eastern Washington: A Case Study." *Pacific Northwest Quarterly* 38, no. 4 (October 1947): 335–56.

Cotroneo, Ross R. "Timber Marketing by the Northern Pacific, 1920–1952." *Journal of Forest History* 20 (July 1976): 120–31.

———. "United States v. Northern Pacific Railway Company." *Pacific Northwest Quarterly* 71, no. 3 (July 1980): 107–11.

———. "Western Land Marketing by the Northern Pacific Railway." *Pacific Historical Review* 37, no. 3 (August 1968): 299–320.

Coulter, C. Brewster. "Big Y Country: Marketing Problems and Organization." *Agricultural History* 46 (1972): 471–88.

———. "National Irrigation in the Yakima Valley, 1902–06." *Pacific Northwest Quarterly* 42 (1951): 99–122.

Creager, Phil S. "Wellhouse Apple Orchard—Largest in the World." *Ninth Biennial Report*, Kansas State Board of Agriculture (1893–94), pp. 498–503.

Crosby, Edward J. *Story of the Washington Water Power Company and Its Part in the History of Electric Service in the Inland Empire, 1889–1930 Inclusive.* Spokane: Washington Water Power Co., 1930.

Danbom, David B. "Agricultural Extension System and the First World War." *Historian* 41, no. 2 (February 1979): 315–31.

Decker, Arlie D. "Lumbering Moves West." *Pacific Northwesterner* 3, no. 2 (Spring 1959): 17–24.

Donally, Lloyd. "Tree Planting Projects on the St. Joe." *Early Days in the Forest Service* 4 (1976): 119–201.

Duffus, William M. "Government Control of the Wheat Trade in the United States." *American Economic Review* 8, no. 1 (March 1918): 62–87.

Eldred, Wilfred. "Wheat and Flour Trade under Food Administration Control: 1917–18." *Quarterly Journal of Economics* 33 (1918): 1–70.

Ellison, Joseph W. "Beginnings of the Apple Industry in Oregon." *Agricultural History* 11 (1937): 322–43.

———. "Cooperative Movement in the Oregon Apple Industry." *Agricultural History* 13 (1939): 77–96.

———. "Marketing Problems of Northwest Apples." *Agricultural History* 16 (1942): 103–15.

Fahey, John. "Coeur d'Alene Confederacy." *Idaho Yesterdays* 12, no. 1 (Spring 1968): 2–7.

———. "Ed Boyce and the Western Federation of Miners." *Idaho Yesterdays* 25, no. 3 (Fall 1981): 18–30.

———. "Nevada Bloomer Goes to the Polls." *Spokane* 4, no. 10 (October 1980): 21–23.

———. "Million-Dollar Corner: The Development of Downtown Spokane, 1890–1920." *Pacific Northwest Quarterly* 62, no. 2 (April 1971): 77–85.

———. "Spokane's Grand Plan to Pre-empt Coulee Dam." *Spokane* 5, no. 7 (July 1981): 17–21.

———. "Wag behind Winston's Weekly." *Spokane* 3, no. 11 (November 1979): 40–41 and 65.

———. "Wheat Whiz." *Spokane* 4, no. 6 (June 1980): 38–42.

———. "When the Dutch Owned Spokane." *Pacific Northwest Quarterly* 72, no. 1 (January 1981): 2–10.

Farm Fortunes. Spokane: Chamber of Commerce, 1906.

Fell, James E., Jr. "Rockefeller's Right-hand Man: Frederick T. Gates and the Northwestern Investments." *Business History Review* 52, no. 4 (Winter 1978): 537–61.

Ferris, Joel E. "Early Day Banking in the State of Washington." *Coast Banker,* October 1958, n.p.

Freeman, Otis W. "Apple Industry of the Wenatchee Area." *Economic Geography* 10 (1934): 160–71.

Fruit Growing in Eastern Washington. Spokane: Spokane and Inland Empire Railroad Co., 1911.

Fuller, Wayne E. "Good Roads and Rural Free Delivery of Mail." *Mississippi Valley Historical Review* 42 (June 1955): 67–83.

Gaines, E. F. "Primary Considerations in Developing New Wheats in Washington." *Northwest Science* 9, no. 1 (February 1935): 8–12.

Gates, Paul W. "Homestead Law in an Incongruous Land System." *American Historical Review* 41 (1936): 652–81.

Girard, James W. "Practice of Forestry in Western Yellow Pine." *Forest Club Quarterly* 5, no. 2 (1926): 39–43.

Gose, John A. "Trust Deed Act in Washington." 1 *Washington Law Review* 94 (1926).

Hardesty, W. E. "Municipal Grain and Freight Port Terminal at Portland, Oregon." *Engineering News-Record* 84, no. 4 (Jan. 22, 1920): 179–82.

Harding, Bruce C. "Water from Pend Oreille: The Gravity Plan for the Columbia Basin." *Pacific Northwest Quarterly* 45, no. 2 (April 1954): 52–60.

Harris, R. K. "Life in Potlatch was Different." *Pacific Northwesterner* 20, no. 1 (Winter 1976): 1–16.

Hedges, James B. "Promotion of Immigration to the Pacific Northwest by the

Railroads." *Mississippi Valley Historical Review* 15, no. 2 (September 1928): 183–203.

Highways Green Book. 1st ed., 1920; 2d, 1921. Washington: American Automobile Assn., 1920 and 1921.

Hindley, Wilbur W. "His $20 Log Started a $12,000,000 Fortune." *Spokesman-Review,* May 26, 1929. Biographical article on Fred Herrick.

——. "Story of Grand Coulee Dam, 1890–1942." *Spokesman-Review,* Progress edition, pt. 1, pp. 3–23, January 25, 1942.

"History of Albers Brothers." *Carnation* 10, no. 1 (February 1930): 1–6.

Hodgson, Dr. Edward R. "Early Spokane's 150,000 Club." *Pacific Northwesterner* 21, no. 2 (Spring 1977): 17–22, 24–32.

Holli, Melvin G. "Varieties of Urban Reform." In Alexander B. Callow, Jr., ed., *American Urban History: An Interpretive Reader with Commentaries,* pp. 249–65. New York: Oxford University Press, 1973.

Holmes, Philip. "First Telephone System." *Okanogan County Heritage* 3, no. 1, (December 1964): 17–18.

Horowitz, Charles. "Riparian and Appropriation Rights to the Use of Water in Washington." 7 *Washington Law Review* 197 (1932).

Hutchison, S. Blair. "Century of Lumbering in Northern Idaho." *Timberman* 39, no. 10 (August 1938): 20–21, 26; no. 11 (September 1938): 14–15, 28; and no. 12 (October 1938): 34–39.

International Apple Association. *Statement Presented to the National Transportation Committee in Regard to Certain Problems Confronting Rail Carriers.* Seattle: Western Fruit Jobbers Association of America, 1933.

Johnson, D. Gale. "Credit Programs Supervised by the Farm Credit Administration." In George F. Break, et al., *Federal Credit Agencies,* pp. 259–318. Englewood Cliffs, N.J.: Prentice-Hall, Inc., 1960.

Johnson, Harry. *Washington Schools in the Good Old Days.* Olympia: Superintendent of Public Instruction, 1969.

Jones, David C. "Strategy of Railway Abandonment: The Great Northern in Washington and British Columbia." *Western Historical Quarterly* 11, no. 2 (April 1980): 151–58.

Kemmerer, E. W. "Agricultural Credit in the United States." *American Economic Review* 2, no. 4 (December 1912): 852–72.

Kensel, W. Hudson. "Early Spokane Lumber Industry, 1871–1910." *Idaho Yesterdays* 12, no. 1 (Spring 1968): 25–31.

Koch, Elers. "Region One in Pre-Regional Office Days." *Early Days in the Forest Service* 1:100–105.

——. "1903 and 1904 Boundary Examinations." *Early Days in the Forest Service* 1:106–8.

Koerselman, Gary H. "Secretary Hoover and National Farm Policy: Problems of Leadership." *Agricultural History* 51, no. 2 (April 1977): 378–95.

Langloe, Lawrence. *Synopsis of Report on the Horse Heaven Irrigation District.* Pasco: Horse Heaven Irrigation District, December 31, 1920.

Lewis, William S. *Story of Early Days in the Big Bend Country.* Spokane: W. D. Allen, 1926. Lewis's address to Lincoln and Adams county pioneer associations June 17, 1919.

Lovin, Hugh T. "Moses Alexander and the Lumber Strike of 1917: The Wartime Ordeal of a Progressive." *Pacific Northwest Quarterly* 66, no. 3 (July 1975): 115–22.

———. "Red Scare in Idaho." *Idaho Yesterdays* 17, no. 3 (Fall 1973): 2–13.

———. "World War Vigilantes in Idaho, 1917–1918," *Idaho Yesterdays* 18, no. 3 (Fall 1974): 2–11.

McDonald, Rita, and Robert G. Dunbar. "Initiation of the McNary-Haugen Movement in Montana and the Pacific Northwest." *Pacific Northwest Quarterly* 71, no. 2 (April 1980): 63–71.

Marple, Elliott. "Movement for Public Ownership of Power in Washington." *Journal of Land and Public Utility Economics* 7 (February 1931): 61–66.

Mead, Walter J. "Forest Products Economy of the Pacific Northwest." *Land Economics* 32, no. 2 (May 1956): 127–33.

———. "Seasonal Variation in Lumber Prices." *Journal of Forestry* 62 (February 1964): 89–95.

Mitchell, Bruce. "By River, Trail, and Rail." *Wenatchee Daily World,* Sept. 23, 1968.

———. "Flowing Wealth: The Story of Water Resource Development in North Central Washington." *Wenatchee Daily World,* March 6, 1967.

———. "Story of Rufus Woods and the Development of Central Washington." *Wenatchee Daily World,* June 28, 1965.

Moore, Marvin. "Palouse Hills Farmstead Architecture, 1890–1915." *Oregon Historical Quarterly* 85, no. 2 (Summer 1984): 181–93.

Morgan, George T., Jr. "Conflagration as Catalyst: Western Lumbermen and American Forest Policy." *Pacific Historical Review* 47, no. 2 (May 1978): 167–88.

Mosk, Sanford A. "Land Policy and Stock Raising in the Western United States." *Agricultural History* 17, no. 1 (January 1943): 14–30.

Murphy, John C. *Facts Concerning the Government Palouse Project.* Pasco (?): Franklin County Development League, August 18, 1912.

Nash, Gerald D. "Rural Society in the Far West: A Comment on the Problem of Values." *Agricultural History* 41, no. 1 (January 1975): 51–55.

Nesbit, Robert C., and Charles M. Gates. "Agriculture in Eastern Washington." *Pacific Northwest Quarterly* 37, no. 4 (October 1946): 279–302.

Newell, F. H. "Reclamation of the West." *Annual Report 1904,* Smithsonian Institution. H. Doc. 748, 58th Cong., 2d sess. (serial 4620), pp. 827–42.

Oliphant, J. Orin. "Cattle Trade from the Far Northwest to Montana." *Agricultural History* 6 (1932): 69–83.

Osgood, Ernest S. "Cattleman in the Agricultural History of the Northwest." *Agricultural History* 3 (1929): 117–30.

Overholser, E. L. "History of Fruit Storage in the United States." *Better Fruit* 29 (August 1934): 8–9.

Pacific Northwest: A Guide for Settlers and Travelers. New York: Northern Pacific Railroad Co., 1882.

Paxson, Frederick K. "Highway Movement, 1916–1930." *American Historical Review* 51, no. 2 (January 1946): 236–53.

Peterson, Arthur G. "Government Policy Relating to Farm Machinery in World War I." *Agricultural History* 17, no. 1 (January 1943): 31–40.

Pollard, Lancaster. "Pacific Northwest." In Merrill Jensen, ed., *Regionalism in America.* Madison: University of Wisconsin Press, 1952: 187–212.

Pollard, W. L. "Outline of the Law of Zoning in the United States." *Annals of the American Academy of Political and Social Science* 155, pt. 2 (May 1931): 15–33.

Preston, Howard H. "Trust Business in Washington." *Pacific Northwest Quarterly* 43, no. 1 (January 1952): 3–26.

Proposed Public Belt Line: Information for Voters. Port of Seattle *Bulletin* 7, March 7, 1916.

Putnam, H. N. "Spread and Development of White Pine Blister Rust in the Inland Empire." *Northwest Science* 5, no. 3 (September 1931): 53–57.

Reuss, Carl F. "Farm Labor Problem in Washington, 1917–18." *Pacific Northwest Quarterly* 34, no. 4 (October 1943): 339–52.

———. "Pioneers of Lincoln County, Washington, a Study in Migration." *Pacific Northwest Quarterly* 30 (1939): 51–65.

Ridgeway, Gordon B. "Populism in Washington." *Pacific Northwest Quarterly* 39, no. 4 (October 1948): 284–311.

Rockie, W. A. "Man's Effects on the Palouse." *Geographical Review* 29 (January 1939): 39–45.

———. "Some Important Effects of the Summer Fallow System on Farming and Soil Erosion in the Pacific Northwest." *Northwest Science* 6, no. 1 (March 1933): 19–22.

Rosine, John. "Cattle Cycles—Past and Present." *Ninth District Quarterly,* Federal Reserve Bank of Minneapolis, 1, no. 4 (November 1974): 13–20.

Scheuerman, Richard D. "From Wagon Trails to Iron Rails: Russian German Immigration to the Pacific Northwest." *Journal of the American Historical Society of Germans from Russia* 2, no. 2 (Fall 1979): 37–50.

Schlomer, Harm. "Harders of the Big Bend." *Pacific Northwesterner* 11, no. 4 (Fall 1967): 49–62.

Schmitz, Henry. "State Lines vs. a Common Interest—What We Owe to Idaho." *Forest Club Quarterly* 2, no. 3 (November 1923): 5–10.

Schwantes, Carlos A. "Making the World Unsafe for Democracy." *Montana Magazine of History* 31, no. 1 (January 1981): 18–29.

Scott, Roy V. "American Railroads and Agricultural Extension, 1900–1914: A Study in Railway Developmental Techniques." *Business History Review* 34, no. 1 (1965): 74–98.

———. "American Railroads and the Promotion of Forestry." *Journal of Forest History* 23 (April 1979): 72–81.

Second National Apple Show, Spokane, November 15–20, 1909. St. Paul:

Great Northern Railway, 1909.

Shackleford, Charlotte. "Donation Land Claims." In *Building a State*. Olympia: Washington State Historical Society Publications, vol. 3 (1939): 403–52.

Shepherd, James F. "Development of Wheat Production in the Pacific Northwest." *Agricultural History* 41, no. 1 (January 1975): 258–71.

———. "Development of New Wheat Varieties in the Pacific Northwest." *Agricultural History* 54, no. 1 (January 1980): 52–63.

Shideler, James H. "Herbert Hoover and the Federal Farm Board Project, 1921–1925." *Mississippi Valley Historical Review* 42 (1955): 710–29.

Siegert, Wilmer H. "Wheat Harvest Primitive in 1928." *Pacific Northwesterner* 20, no. 3 (Summer 1976): 43–48.

Simpson, Peter K. "Social Side of the Cattle Industry." *Agricultural History* 41, no. 1 (January 1975): 39–50.

Sims, Robert C. "Idaho's Criminal Syndicalism Act: One State's Response to Radical Labor." *Labor History* 15, no. 4 (Fall 1974): 511–27.

Smart, Douglas O. "Spokane's Battle for Freight Rates." *Pacific Northwest Quarterly* 45, no. 1 (January 1954): 19–27.

"Sperry: 115 Years of Service." *Modern Millwheel* (General Mills employee magazine) 31, no. 5 (May 1967): 7.

Stark, Lawrence R. "Lewiston-Clarkston Improvement Company: City Planner in Southeastern Washington." *Record 1975*, Friends of the Library, Washington State University, 36 (1975): 59–70.

Stecker, Karl. "Review of the Commercial Carrier Motor Law." 6 *Washington Law Review* 1 (1930).

Story of the North Pacific Grain Growers, Inc., 1930–1962. Portland: North Pacific Grain Growers, Inc., 1962.

Strong, Helen M. "Export Wheat Producing Regions." *Economic Geography* 8 (1932): 161–90.

Teed, Ryle. "Reminiscences of Early Days in the Forest Service." *Early Days in the Forest Service* 2:50–65.

Tiffany, R. K. "State Reclamation in Washington." *Proceedings,* American Society of Civil Engineers, 53 (1927): 913–23.

Thompson, Allen E. "Forest Resources of Washington," *Forestry Club Quarterly* 3, no. 1 (1924): 19–32.

Tousley, Rayburn D., and Hoyt Lemons, "Washington Apple Industry: Economic Considerations." *Economic Geography* 21 (1945): 252–68.

Turner, Lela K. "Patches of History." *Okanogan County Heritage* 2, no. 2 (September 1964): 13–22.

Veiller, Lawrence. "Housing as a Factor in Health Progress in the Past Fifty Years." In Mazyck P. Ravenel, ed., *A Half Century of Public Health*, pp. 321–34. New York: American Public Health Assn., 1921.

Victor, Arthur E. "Fred Herrick and Bill Grotte." *Pacific Northwesterner* 16, no. 3 (Summer 1972): 33–48.

Washington for the Farmer. St. Paul: Chicago, Burlington and Quincy, Great

Northern, and Northern Pacific, 1923.

Washington Mutual Savings Bank. "The Housing Situation in Seattle." Seattle, November 1926.

Webb, C. S. "Some Incidents Occurring during My Employment with the U.S. Forest Service, 1913–1949." *Early Days in the Forest Service* 2:66–80.

Weigle, W. G. "Pulp Woods in the State of Washington." *Forest Club Quarterly* 2, no. 4 (January 1924): 5–22.

"What Happened to the Western Apple." *Sunset* 34 (January 1915): 49–50.

Wilcox, W. B. "Early History of Granby." *Northwest Mining Truth* 5, no. 1 (Feb. 16, 1920): 19–20.

Wilson, Bruce A. "Cow Country, a History of the Okanogan's Livestock Industry." *Okanogan County Heritage* 1, no. 1 (June 1963): 26–33.

Wilson, Joan Hoff. "Hoover's Agricultural Policies, 1921–28." *Agricultural History* 51, no. 2 (April 1977): 335–61.

Winser, Henry J. "Walla Walla and the Palouse Country." *Pacific Northwest Quarterly* 37 (July 1946): 176–85. Publication of a report to Henry Villard in 1879.

Woehlke, Walter V. "What Ails the Big Red Apple?" *Sunset* 35 (November 1915): 916–25.

Wooddy, Carroll H. "Populism in Washington: A Study of the Legislature of 1897." *Washington Historical Quarterly* 21, no. 2 (1930): 103–19.

Yakima Valley, Washington. Yakima: Commercial Club of North Yakima, 1905.

Yoder, Fred R. "Are the Brightest Young Men and Women Leaving the Farm?" *Northwest Science* 4, no. 2 (June 1930): 38–43.

———. "Farmers' Alliance in Washington—Prelude to Populism." Washington State University *Research Studies* 16, nos. 3–4 (September–December 1948): 124–78.

EXTENSION BULLETINS, GOVERNMENT PUBLICATIONS, PROCEEDINGS, LEGAL DOCUMENTS, AND MISCELLANEOUS

(Publications of book length appear under "Books." The Washington Agricultural Extension Service is abbreviated as WAES in the following list.)

Agricultural Crisis and Its Causes. House Report 408, 4 parts, 67th Cong., first sess. (1921–22).

Barbee, O. E. "A Comparison of Wheat Yields in Eastern Washington." WAES *Bulletin 289,* October 1933.

Brief on Behalf of the Oregon Public Service Commission. Walla Walla County Farm Bureau v. Northern Pacific Railroad et al., ICC Docket 15739, Aug. 4, 1924.

Bryan, Enoch A. "Summary of Experiment Station Work." WAES *Popular Bulletin 20,* July 15, 1909.

Buchanan, Mark T. "Washington Apples on the New York and Chicago Fruit Auctions." WAES *Bulletin 401*, June 1941.

Christ, J. H. "Cut-over Lands of Northern Idaho." Idaho AES *Bulletin 158*, May 1928.

Clark, J. Allen, and Karl S. Quisenberry. "Varieties of Hard Red Winter Wheat." USDA *Farmers Bulletin 1585*, June 1929.

Columbia Basin Survey Commission. *Columbia Basin Irrigation Project*. Olympia: Columbia Basin Survey Commission, 1920.

Columbia River and Minor Tributaries. 2 vols. H. Doc. 103, 73rd Cong., 1st sess., 1933 (serial 9757).

Cotton, J. S. "Report on the Range Conditions of Central Washington." WAES *Bulletin 60*, 1904.

Davidson, R. D. "Federal and State Rural Lands, 1950." USDA *Circular 909*, May 1952.

Dummeier, E. F. "Financing Cooperative Marketing of Farm Products in Washington." WAES *Bulletin 322*, October 1935.

Elsworth, R. H. "Statistics of Farmers' Cooperative Business Organizations, 1920–1935," Farm Credit Administration, Cooperative Division, *Bulletin 6*, 1936.

Establishment and Modification of National Forest Boundaries: A Chronological Record, 1891–1973. USDA Forest Service, Division of Engineering, October 1973.

Farmers Cooperatives in the United States. USDA Farmer Cooperative Service, *Bulletin 1*, December 1958.

Finding of Facts by the Railroad Commission of Washington Relative to the Valuation of Railroads in the State of Washington. Olympia: State Railroad Commission, 1909.

Findings of Facts by the Railroad Commission of Washington Relative to the Valuation of the Oregon Railroad & Navigation Company. Olympia: State Railroad Commission, 1909.

"Forest Products Industries: Spokane County." Spokane Chamber of Commerce, Industrial Development Bureau, April 1958, mimeographed.

Fortier, Samuel, and Arthur A. Young. "Irrigation Requirements of the Arid and Semiarid Lands of the Columbia River Basin." USDA *Technical Bulletin 200*, October 1930.

Gaines, E. F., and E. G. Schafer. "Wheat Varieties in Washington in 1939." WAES *Bulletin 398*, April 1941.

Hampson, Chester C. "Trends in the Apple Industry." WAES *Bulletin 277*, February 1933.

———. "Apple Prices Received by Washington Growers." WAES *Bulletin 326*, 1936.

———. "Indexes of Prices Received by Washington Farmers." WAES *Bulletin 328*, July 1936.

Heald, F. D., and G. D. Ruehle. "Rots of Washington Apples in Cold Storage." WAES *Bulletin 253*, May 1931.

Hunter, Byron, George Severance, and R. N. Miller. "Review of the Agriculture of the Big Bend Country." WAES *Bulletin 192*, September 1925.

Hutchins, Wells A. "Mutual Irrigation Companies." USDA *Technical Bulletin 82*, January 1929.

———. "Commercial Irrigation Companies." USDA *Technical Bulletin 177*, March 1930.

———. "Irrigation Districts, Their Organization, Operation, and Financing." USDA *Technical Bulletin 254*, June 1931.

Johnson, Neil W. "Economic Aspects of Apple Production in Washington." WAES *Bulletin 239*, April 1930.

Johnson, Neil W., and Rex E. Willard. "Trends in Agriculture in Washington, 1900 to 1930." WAES *Bulletin 300*, June 1934.

———. "Present Land Uses—Washington." WAES *Bulletin 288*, October 1933.

———. "Nature and Distribution of Farming in Washington." WAES *Bulletin 301*, July 1934.

Jones, J. S., and C. W. Colver. "Soils of the Cut and Burned-over Areas of North Idaho." Idaho AES *Bulletin 81*, January 1915.

Kass, Henry D. "Spokane Community Leadership and Public Policy." Eastern Washington University, Community Services Institute background paper, 1969, duplicated.

———. "Leadership in Spokane: Division of Labor and 'Style.'" Eastern Washington University, Community Service Institute background paper, 1969, duplicated.

Klemgard, J. G., and G. F. Cadisch. "Cost of Wheat Production by Power Methods of Farming, 1919–1929." WAES *Bulletin 255*, June 1931.

Kocher, A. E. *Soil Survey of the Wenatchee Area, Washington*. Washington: USDA, 1922.

Kocher, A. E., and A. T. Strahorn. *Soil Survey of Benton County, Washington*. Washington: USDA, 1919.

Landis, Paul H. "Fifty Years of Population Growth in Washington." WAES *Bulletin 419*, September 1942.

———. "Washington Farm Trade Centers, 1900–1935." WAES *Bulletin 360*, July 1938.

Little, C. N. "Trap Rocks of the Palouse Region as Road Material." University of Idaho, Civil Engineering Department *Bulletin 1*, July 1904. Also published as Idaho AES *Bulletin 45*, July 1904.

Mangum, A. W., Cornelius Van Duyne, and H. L. Westover. *Soil Survey of the Quincy Area, Washington*. Washington: USDA, 1913.

"Master Plan for Forestry in Washington." Washington State Planning Council *Research Publication 4*, December 1936, mimeographed.

Melander, A. L. "The Wormy Apple." WAES *Bulletin 68*, 1905.

Melander, A. L., and M. A. Yothers. "Coulee Cricket." WAES *Bulletin 137*, January 1917.

Metzger, Hutzel. "Cooperative Marketing of Fluid Milk." USDA *Technical Bulletin 179*, May 1930.

Morris, O. M. "Fertilizers and Cover Crops on Soils in the Irrigated Orchards of Washington." WAES *Bulletin 217,* August 1927.

Northern Pacific Railway et al. Interstate Commerce Commission Valuation Docket 959, in *Valuation Reports* 25 (February-May 1929): 397–868.

Overholser, Earle L. "Production and Marketing Problems of Apples in the States of Washington and New York Contrasted." *Proceedings, 32*nd Annual Meeting of the Washington State Horticultural Association, December 7–9, 1936.

Overly, F. L., J. L. St. John, E. L. Overholser, and Kermit Groves. "Lead and Arsenic Spray Residue Removal from Apples." WAES *Bulletin 286,* 1933.

Paulthorp, R. P., and J. W. Park. "Extent and Causes of Rejections of Boxed Apples from the State of Washington, Seasons 1922 to 1925." USDA *Circular 413,* April 1927.

Prince, George E., and L. B. Gerry. "Pacific Northwest Boxed Apple Deal, Season of 1925–26." USDA Bureau of Agricultural Economics, September 1926, mimeographed.

Proceedings, Second Annual Conference of Washington State, County, and City Health Officers, April 8–9, 1921.

"Proceedings of State Forestry Conference." *Forest Club Quarterly* 1, no. 4 (January 1923): 11–57.

Pubols, Ben H., and Carl P. Heisig. "Historical and Geographical Aspects of Wheat Yields in Washington." WAES *Bulletin 355,* 1937.

Regulation of Stock Ownership in Railroads. Pt. 3, H. Rep. 2789, 71st Cong., 3d sess., Feb. 21, 1931 (serial 9330).

Report of First Annual Conference. State, County, and City Health Officers, State of Washington, December 1910. Olympia: E. L. Boardman, public printer, 1912.

Report of Third Annual Conference. State, County, and City Health Officers, State of Washington, April 1913. Olympia: Frank M. Lamborn, public printer, 1913.

Report on Some Legal Aspects of Farm Tenancy in Oregon and Washington. Portland: Northwest Regional Council, November 1939.

Severance, George, Byron Hunter, and Paul Eke. "Farming Systems for Eastern Washington and Northern Idaho." WAES *Bulletin 244,* July 1930.

Severance, George, and Neil W. Johnson. "Production and Marketing of Spokane Valley Farm Products." WAES *Bulletin 221,* December 1927.

Smick, A. A., and F. R. Yoder. "Study of Farm Migration in Selected Communities in the State of Washington." WAES *Bulletin 233,* June 1929.

Stephens, David E., H. M. Wanser, and Aaron F. Bracken. "Experiments in Wheat Production on the Dry Lands of Oregon, Washington, and Utah." USDA *Technical Bulletin 329,* November 1932.

Taylor, E. A., and F. R. Yoder. "Rural Social Organization in Whitman County." WAES *Bulletin 203,* June 1926.

Tax Commission of the State of Washington. *Fourth Biennial Report.* Olympia: Tax Commission, 1932.

Transcript on Appeal. Idaho and Western Railway v. William Dollar. Boise: Supreme Court of Idaho, 1911 (bound copy in Gonzaga Law Library).

Transcript of Testimony. Washington Department of Public Service v. Pacific Power and Light Co., cause 6736 (September 1935) in Washington Water Power collection, Eastern Washington University, box 19. A rate proceeding.

United States v. Northern Pacific Railway et al. Equity case E-4389, U.S. District Court, Eastern District of Washington (Federal Records Center, Seattle, accession 57-A180, boxes 5033–35).

U.S. Congress. *Agricultural Crisis and Its Causes: Report of the Joint Commission of Agricultural Inquiry.* 4 parts. Washington: Government Printing Office, 1921. Report 408, 67th Cong., 1st sess.

U.S. Department of Commerce, Bureau of the Census. *Special Reports: Telephones: 1907.* Washington: Government Printing Office, 1910.

———. Eleventh (1890), Twelfth (1900), Thirteenth (1910), Fourteenth (1920), and Fifteenth (1930) Census of the United States.

———. *Special Reports: Religious Bodies.* Part 1 (1906).

———. Fifteenth Census: vol. 2, *Agriculture,* pt. 3, *Western States.* "Irrigation of Agricultural Lands."

U.S. Department of the Interior. *Federal Reclamation Laws Annotated.* Washington: Government Printing Office, 1943.

———. Bureau of Reclamation. *Reclamation Project Data.* Washington: Government Printing Office, 1948. Revised, 1961.

———. *Story of the Columbia Basin Project.* Washington: Government Printing Office, 1964.

U.S. Interstate Commerce Commission, Bureau of Statistics. *ICC Activities, 1887–1937.* Washington: Government Printing Office, 1937.

U.S. Senate Committee on Irrigation and Reclamation. *Columbia Basin Project, Washington.* Report of special commission, 1925. Report of engineers, 1924 and 1925. Gault report, 1924. Record of hearing, June 21, 1932.

Van Duyne, Cornelius, J. H. Agee, and Fred W. Ashton. *Soil Survey of Franklin County, Washington.* Washington: USDA, 1917.

Van Duyne, Cornelius, and Fred W. Ashton. *Soil Survey of Stevens County, Washington.* Washington: USDA, 1916.

Van Duyne, Cornelius, H. C. Mortlock, A. F. Heck, and E. D. Alvord. *Soil Survey of Spokane County, Washington.* Washington: USDA, 1921.

Wall, Norman J. "Agricultural Loans of Commercial Banks." USDA *Technical Bulletin 521,* July 1936.

Waller, O. L. "Report on Irrigation Conditions in the Yakima Valley, Washington." WAES *Bulletin 61,* 1904.

Washington Bureau of Statistics and Immigration. *Manufacturing Opportunities in the State of Washington.* Olympia: Department of State, 1918.

"Washington State Products." Olympia: Ernest N. Hutchinson, Secretary of State, 1934, mimeographed, extracted from Fifteenth Census.

Weidman, R. H. "Timber Growing and Logging Practice in Ponderosa Pine in the Northwest." USDA *Technical Bulletin 511,* June 1936.

"Wheat Supply and Distribution in the Pacific Northwest (Oregon, Washington, and Northern Idaho)." Oregon Wheat Commission and Washington Department of Agriculture, *Statistical Bulletin 1*, December 1956.

PERIODICALS

American City
Agricultural History
Better Fruit (Hood River and Portland, Oregon)
Carnation
Collier's
Engineering and Mining Journal
Engineering News-Record
Forest Club Quarterly (University of Washington)
Franklin Flyer (Franklin County, Washington, Historical Society)
Harper's Weekly
Idaho Yesterdays
Irrigation Age
Literary Digest
Pacific Northwest Quarterly
Pacific Northwesterner
North West
Northwest Mining Truth (Spokane)
Northwest Science
Spokane
Spokane Affairs (Spokane Chamber of Commerce)
Spokane Woman
Sunset
Timberman
USDA *Yearbooks*
West Shore

NEWSPAPERS

Cheney Free Press
Coeur d'Alene Press (Coeur d'Alene, Idaho)
Colfax Commoner
Colfax Gazette
Daily Idaho Press (Wallace, Idaho)
Daily World (Wenatchee)
East Washingtonian (Pomeroy, Washington)
Grange News
Grant County Journal
Idaho Daily Statesman (Boise)

Kettle Falls Pioneer (Kettle Falls, Wash.)
Missoulian
New York Times
Oakesdale Tribune
Odessa Record
Oregonian (Portland)
Oregon Journal (Portland)
Palouse Gazette (Colfax)
Pasco Herald
Portland Telegram
Post-Intelligencer (Seattle)
Press-Times (Wallace, Idaho)
Seattle Times
Spokane Daily Chronicle
Spokesman-Review (Spokane)
Walla Walla Statesman
Walla Walla Union
Weekly Capital (Olympia)
Winston's Weekly (Spokane)
Yakima Herald
Yakima Morning Herald
Yakima Sunday Herald

Index

Adams, J. B., 114
Adams County, 13, 20, 39, 46, 49, 68, 74, 75, 78, 81, 142
Advertising. *See* Promotion; *see also specific towns and products*
Agents, county, 81–82
Albers Brothers Milling Co., 51
Alliance, Farmers, 76–77
American Smelting and Refining Co., 173, 181–83, 185
Ankeny, Levi, 28, 91, 129, 130
Apples: national apple show, 110; selling, 111–15, 124; grading and packing, 112; glut of, 113, 115; advertising of, 114, 125, 126; cooperatives, 116–17, 125, 126; volume of, 117, 124, 125; commercial districts for, 117–18; refrigeration of, 118–19; freight rates, 119–20; storage of, 121–22, 245n38; pests, 122–23; cull, 123–24; canneries for, 123–24; varieties of, 124; brands, 125–26; boxes, 126
Arcadia Orchards Co., 103
Asotin County, 144
Automobile, 152–57 passim

Baker, Dorsey S., 22–23, 49, 130
Balfour, Guthrie & Co., 50–51
Banks, 23; in Spokane, 127–30, reserve city for, 129; pioneer, 130–31; state chartered, 131, 137–38; and farmers, 131–35, 138–43 passim; war loans, 135; failures of, 138, 141–42
Barge, Benjamin F., 99

Bassett, J. D., 128
Benson, E. F., 20
Benton County, 39, 68, 81, 98
Big Bend, 12–13, 20; drought, 67–68; irrigation, 92, 104–9. *See also* Columbia Basin
Blackwell, F. A., 194–97, 198. *See also* Idaho & Washington Northern Railroad
Blaine, Elbert F., 89, 106
Bloomer, Edward M., 216
Bone, Homer T., 169
Bouck, William, 77, 78–79
Boyer, John F., 23
Bradley, Joseph W., 85, 143
Brown, James, 206
Browne, John J., 215
Bryan, Enoch A., 81, 84
Bunker Hill & Sullivan Co., 173, 184–85
Bureau of Reclamation (and Reclamation Service), 90, 96; and Washington surveys, 91; and Washington projects, 94–95
Burke, Thomas, 5, 19, 96

Campbell, Amasa B., 130, 176, 179, 180, 182, 183
Canneries, 123–24
Cannon, Anthony M., 31–33, 179, 215, 216
Cashmere, Wash., 124, 126, 148, 168
Cattle: crowded from range, 7; herds, 13; Spokane stockyards, 222–23
Centennial Mills Co., 51–52

Goss, Albert A., 78–79, 80, 108, 146
Grand Coulee Dam, 109
Grange. *See* Patrons of Husbandry
Granger, Walter N., 87–89
Grant County, 13, 46, 49, 68, 154, 167
Graves, Jay P., 180, 187
Great Northern Railway, 36–37, 44,
    149, 151; and feeders, 46; and Wen-
    atchee irrigation, 96; and apple busi-
    ness, 118–19, 245*n*38
Guilbert, Frank, 85
Gunn, Arthur, 96–97
Gwin, W. F., 112–13

Harder, Max and Hans, 7, 104
Hartley, Gov. Roland, 68, 144, 157
Hay, Gov. Marion, 73, 99, 134
Hays, W. J. and L. G., 123
Health. *See* Sanitation
Hedlund Lumber Co., 200
Hegnauer, Leonard, 81–82
Herrick, Fred, 188, 198, 202–3, 206,
    211–12, 260*n*79
Hill, James J., 19, 36–37, 97, 189. *See
    also* Great Northern Railway
Hill, Samuel, 151–52
Holden, Perry G., 84–85
Hoover, Herbert C., 104, 108, 146
Houser, Max, 65–66
Humbird, John, 199
Humbird, Thomas, 129, 206
Humbird Lumber Co., 190, 198, 210
Hunt, George W., 31, 34
Huntington, David Lynde, 163. *See also*
    Washington Water Power Co.
Huntley, William, 104, 129–30
Hutton, Levi W., 183, 218, 221

Idaho & Washington Northern Railroad,
    195, 257*n*25 and *n*26
Idaho National Harvester Co., 61–62
Immigrants. *See* Settlers and settlement
Industrial Workers of the World: in agri-
    culture, 64–65; in lumber, 199, 203–4
Inland Automobile Association, 157
Insinger, Robbert, 85
Irrigation, 39; Schanno brothers and, 13;
    Shotwells and, 19, 96; at Yakima, 87–
    89, 90–95; in Washington, 91–95;
    and the Bureau of Reclamation, 91–
    95, 96; under Newlands plan, 92–93,
    96; under Carey Act, 93; federal proj-
    ects at Wenatchee, 96–97; and water
    rights, 98–100, 242*n*29; under Palouse
    project, 103–4; under Columbia Basin

project, 104–9; assessments for,
    243*n*43

Jewett, George C. (wheat man), 58, 59,
    140
Jewett, George F. (lumberman), 206, 211
Johnson, F. F., 130
Jones, Arthur D., 219
Jones, Wesley L., 90–94, 108

Kegley, Carey B., 76–77
Kelso brothers, 18
Kennewick, Wash., 72
Kerr, Harry, 96
Kerr-Gifford & Co., 50–51
Kettenbach, F. W., 130
Kittitas County, 98, 143, 209–10
Kizer, Benjamin H., 224
Klickitat County, 75
Kuhn, Aaron, 50, 130

Lancaster, Samuel C., 151
Land: laws regarding, 6; frauds in, 6–7;
    investors and speculators in, 15, 28;
    and railroads, 25–27; and title, 26–27
Lane, Thaddeus S., 161, 162
Lawrence, John C., 28, 43, 153
Lincoln County, 13, 20, 39, 46, 49, 68,
    71, 78, 154
Lind, Wash., 71, 81
Lilly Co., Charles H., 52
Lister, Gov. Ernest, 104, 156
Living conditions: for settlers, 9–11, 15,
    18–19; urbanizing, 42; styles, 66,
    226–27; on farm, 72
Long, George S., 204
Loyal Legion of Loggers and Lumber-
    men, 204
Lumber: pioneer mills, 188–89; freight
    volume and rates of, 189, 200–1, 206;
    stumpage sales and purchases, 190–
    92, 197; fraud in, 191–92; mills, 193,
    194, 201, 207, 211–12; transportation
    of, 193, 198, 199, 206; forest esti-
    mates, 193–94; paradigm of, 194; cut-
    ting of, 197–98, 200, 209, 211; work-
    ers in, 198–99, 203–4; markets for,
    201, 206–7, 209; fires in, 201–2, 204;
    cooperation in, 204–5; taxes on, 209–
    10, 259*n*70; and business collapse,
    213. *See also individuals and compa-
    nies*

McBride, Gov. Henry, 71, 99
McClaine, A. Fielding, 130

McCormick, Cyrus, 62
McCornack, J. K., 85, 137
McCroskey family, 5, 130, 131, 189
McGoldrick, James P., 197, 198, 202, 206, 210
McGregors, 7
Machines: for wheat, 60–64, 68–69; dealers, 62; fires in, 64
McNary, Charles, 67, 145
McWhorter, Lucullus Virgil, 91–92
Mail: rural free delivery, 162–63
Malden, Wash., 42–43
Malott, Connor, 85
Mamer, Nick, 226
Martin, Gov. Clarence D., 145
Martin, F. M., & Co., 54
Mason, Allan C., 17
Match companies, 207; Diamond, 195, 197
Mead, Gov. Albert, 93, 94
Menasha Wooden Ware Co., 196
Metaline Falls, Wash., 195
Miller, Samuel C., 14
Mining: and smelting, 173–74; gold rush for, 174–75; Coeur d'Alene district, 175–78, 180–81, 182–87, in World War I, 185–86; Rossland-Trail district, 178–80; Boundary district, 180
Mortgages, 39–40, 68, 133. See also Debt
Moses Lake, Wash., 167, 168
Motor carriers, 158–59, 251n30
Mottet, F. D., 130
Moxee farm, 15

Newell, F. H., 91
Newspapers, 42
Norman, William S., 162
Northern Pacific Railroad (Railway), 13, 14, 16, 35, 176; land sales by, 19, 26–27, 191; construction of, 22, 29–30, 31; land grant, 25–26, 28–29; subsidiaries of, 31–33; colonist cars, 38; taxes on, 46; irrigation subsidy by, 87–89; and apple business, 118
Northwestern & Pacific Hypotheekbank, 133

Ohio Match Co., 198, 207
Okanogan County, 12, 39, 68, 81, 102; irrigation project, 95–96; apple business of, 111
Old National Bank, 127, 128–29, 142, 220
Oregon Railway & Navigation Co., 22, 30–31, 34–35, 46, 48, 81

Oregon Short Line, 34–35
O'Shea, D. G., 136
O'Sullivan, James, 108
Overly, Fred, 123

Pacific Northwest Fruit Distributors, 116–17
Pacific Power & Light Co., 163–67, 168
Pacific Telephone & Telegraph Co., 160–61, 162
Packwood, S. L., 123
Paine, James L., 219
Palouse, 3, 6–7, 9, 19, 27, 28, 33, 54, 61, 63, 164–65; "gate," 10; rainfall in, 231n47
Panama Canal, 45, 120
Panhandle Lumber Co., 195, 196, 198. See also Blackwell, F. A.
Pasco, Wash., 20
Paterson, Robert B., 217, 218, 219
Patrons of Husbandry, 76–79, 139
Paulhamus, W. H., 116
Paulsen, August, 183, 221, 227
Paulsen, Mrs. Clarence I., 226
Peavey, F. H., & Co., 51
Pend Oreille County, 200
Percival, D. F., 130
Perham, Ben A., 116
Perkins, James A., 5
Peyton, Isaac N., 179
Portland, Ore., 24, 29, 49, 52; in grain trade, 49, 52; port of, 53
Portland Flouring Mills, 50–51, 65–66
Potlatch Lumber Co., 192–93, 194, 206
Preston, Josephine Corliss, 73–75, 82
Promotion, 3, 20–21; by railroads, 24; by towns and states, 38; of irrigation, 88
Prosser, Wash., 81–82
Puget Sound, 30; in grain trade, 49

Quincy, Wash., 102, 165

Radio, 86, 225–26
Railroads, 34, 37; to Spokane, 31–33; state commission for, 43–45; freight, 44, 118–19; rates, 45, 119–20; taxes on, 46; truck competition, 120, 158–59; electric, 149, 195. See also individual railroad companies
Rankin, George S., 90
Reardan, Wash., 12, 129
Reclamation. See Bureau of Reclamation
Religious affiliation, 12
Richards, Henry, 130
Richards, J. P. M., 130, 219

Wait, Samuel, 49
Waitsburg, Wash., 164, 165
Wakefield, W. J. C., 219, 220
Wales, Ernest F., 206
Walla Walla (city and county), 4, 12, 24, 39, 42, 46, 49, 68, 74, 76, 78, 81, 86, 102, 164, 168, 170
Waller, O. L., 81, 93
War Finance Corp., 140–41
Washington Irrigation Co., 89–90, 91, 94, 99, 240n5
Washington State University (and predecessors), 80–81
Washington Water Power Co., 149, 163–67; territory of, 164, 165; advertising by, 166; rural service of, 166–67; mining service of, 183
Washington Wheat Growers Association, 57, 58
Washtucna, Wash., 72
Wasmer, Louis A., 228
Water rights, 98–100, 242n29
Waterville, Wash., 68
Wells, A. Z., 112
Wenatchee, 19; irrigation near, 96–97; apple business of, 111
Wenatchee District Cooperative Association, 125, 126
Weyerhaeuser interests, 189, 190–91, 211–12; Lewiston mill of, 211–12
Wheat, 5, 233n41; in 1890–96, 16–19; yields and production, 39, 49, 56, 59–60, 65, 67–69; export of, 48–49, 55–56; farmers and farming, 53–54, 59–60, 68–69; varieties, 54–55; prices of, 55, 65, 235n22; diseases of, 55; harvest methods of, 56, by machines, 60–64; sacks for, 56–57; selling pools for, 57–60; in diet, 66. *See also* Flour; *associations and milling companies*
White, Aubrey Lee, 180, 214, 217
White Pine Sash Co., 200
Whitman County, 19, 25, 39, 49, 64, 68, 73, 74, 78, 83, 111, 142
Wilbur, Wash., 168
Wilcox, Theodore B., 50, 65
Wilmer, F. J., 140, 144
Wilson, Sam J., 227
Wilson Creek, Wash., 107, 165
Winston, Patrick Henry, 70, 71
Winter, C. W., 130
Winton Lumber Co., 198
Witherspoon, Archibald W., 219
Wobblies. *See* Industrial Workers of the World
Women, 10; as schoolteachers, 71; in war jobs, 223; denied franchise, 216
Woods, Rufus, 106, 118

Yakima (city and county), 14, 17–18, 20, 42, 46, 72, 86, 95, 164, 170, 230n31; land in, 13; population of, 39; irrigation near, 87–89, 98; apple business of, 111
Yakima Fruit Growers Association, 115, 125, 126
Yakima Horticultural Union, 114, 125
Yakima Indian reservation, 91–92

Zillah, Wash., 88, 124